THE MODERNISATION OF EC ANTITRUST LAW

Studies in European Law and Integration

General Editors
Professor Francis Snyder
Professor Miguel Maduro

Advisory Editors
Professor Christian Joerges (EUI, Florence)
Professor Jo Shaw (Leeds)
Professor Joseph Weiler (Harvard)
Professor Stephen Weatherill (Oxford)

Titles in this Series
Rein Wesseling: The Modernisation of EC Antitrust Law
Candido Garcia Molyneux: The Unfair Trade Instruments of the EU and USA
Francis Snyder (ed.): The Europeanisation of Law: The Legal Effects of
European Integration

The Modernisation of EC Antitrust Law

REIN WESSELING

·HART·
PUBLISHING
OXFORD – PORTLAND OREGON
2000

Hart Publishing
Oxford and Portland, Oregon

Published in North America (US and Canada) by
Hart Publishing c/o
International Specialized Book Services
5804 NE Hassalo Street
Portland, Oregon
97213-3644
USA

Distributed in the Netherlands, Belgium and Luxembourg by
Intersentia, Churchillaan 108
B2900 Schoten
Antwerpen
Belgium

Hart Publishing Ltd is a specialist legal publisher based in Oxford, England.
To order further copies of this book or to request a list of other
publications please write to:

Hart Publishing Ltd, Salter's Boatyard, Oxford OX1 4LB
Telephone: +44 (0)1865 245533 or Fax: +44 (0)1865 794882
e-mail: mail@hartpub.co.uk
Website http://www.hartpub.co.uk

British Library Cataloguing in Publication Data
Data Available
ISBN 1 84113–121–0 (cloth)

Typeset by Hope Services (Abingdon) Ltd.
Printed in Great Britain on acid-free paper
by Biddles Ltd, Guildford and King's Lynn.

To M.

Preface

This book is a revised and updated version of a PhD thesis, defended on 1 March 1999. The research for that thesis was conducted at the European University Institute (Florence, Italy). The thesis was revised and turned into this book during a leave of absence from practising law at De Brauw Blackstone Westbroek/Linklaters & Alliance.

I would like to thank the European University Institute, which provided funding, for the opportunity to write the thesis. I am also grateful for the financial support of NUFFIC and of the European Commission. While at the European University Institute I profited from the insights provided by Professors Giuliano Amato, Claus-Dieter Ehlermann, Christian Joerges and Francis Snyder. I thank them for their input.

The thesis was defended before a committee consisting of Professors Daniel Goyder, Piet-Jan Slot, Christian Joerges and Francis Snyder. I thank the committee members for their comments. In particular I would like to express gratitude to Christian Joerges and Daniel Goyder for their support after the defence, which stimulated me to write this book. It would not have been possible to do so without the support of De Brauw Blackstone Westbroek/Linklaters & Alliance.

In all stages my parents supported me in innumerable ways. I remain grateful for their continued generosity. No less am I indebted to Marieke Smithuis. Her incessant love and inspiration (and, admittedly, her capacity to do very well without me) enabled me to write this book.

R.W.

Amsterdam, 1 April 2000

Table of Contents

Abbreviations

AG	Advocate-General
AJCL	American Journal of Comparative Law
ALJ	Antitrust Law Journal
CDE	Cahiers de Droit Européen
CJEL	Columbia Journal of European Law
CMLR	Common Market Law Reports
CMLRev.	Common Market Law Review
DG	Directorate General
EBLR	European Business Law Review
ECLR	European Competition Law Review
ECR	European Court Reports
ECSC	European Coal and Steel Community
EC	European Community
EEC	European Economic Community
ELJ	European Law Journal
ELR	European Law Review
ELR/CC	European Law Review Competition Checklist
EuR	Europarecht
Euratom	European Atomic Energy Community
EuZW	Europäisches Zeitschrift für Wirtschaftsrecht
FILJ	Fordham International Law Journal
ICLQ	International and Comparative Law Quarterly
JCMS	Journal of Common Market Studies
JO	Journal officiel des Communautés Européennes
JTDE	Journal des tribunaux Droit Européen
JZ	Juristen Zeitung
LIEI	Legal Issues of European Integration
MLR	Modern Law Review
nyr	not yet reported (judgments)
OJ	Official Journal of the European Communities
RIW	Recht der Internationalen Wirtschaft
RTDE	Revue trimestrielle de droit européen
SEW	Sociaal Economische Wetgeving
TEU	Treaty on European Union
WTO	World Trade Organisation
WuW	Wirtschaft und Wettbewerb
YEL	Yearbook of European Law
ZHR	Zeitschrift für das gesamte Handelsrecht und Wirtschaftsrecht

Table of Cases

Introduction

In 1999 the Commission of the European Communities (the "Commission") issued its White Paper on Modernisation of the Rules Implementing Articles 81 and 82 of the EC Treaty (the "White Paper").[1] On the basis of the White Paper the Commission intended to confront the all-embracing critique of the EC antitrust law regime.[2] By the end of the 1990s the system was generally considered to be unworkable.[3] In its White Paper the Commission acknowledged that Community competition policy is now applied in a world which is very different from that known by the framers of the original system. On the basis of the reforms proposed in the White Paper the Commission therefore aimed to modernise the system which was developed in the early 1960s and to bring Community antitrust policy up to date with the Community realities in the late 1990s.

Naturally, a policy document like the White Paper cannot discuss comprehensively the origins of Community antitrust policy, its development between the establishment of the European Economic Community in 1958 and the European Union of 1999, and the current operation of the system. Practical considerations alone rule out such a comprehensive approach in the context of a white paper. Moreover, the Commission discussion document logically aims to indicate the direction which the reforms should take. A White Paper must be clear and unequivocal about the policy consequences which the findings in the document should have. This book adopts a broader approach. It aims to study current issues in Community antitrust law with explicit reference to the development of EC antitrust law, and to contrast this development with more general developments in Community law and policy.

The main hypothesis underlying this study is that the nature and objectives of European Community antitrust law have altered fundamentally, if gradually, between the Rome and Maastricht Treaties, but that the constitutional

---

[1] [1999] OJ C132/1. The new numbering of the Treaty Arts. after the coming into force of the Amstersdam Treaty was the only amendment in a revised version of the White Paper of 12 May 1999; COM(1999)101 final/2.

[2] This book uses the terms antitrust law and competition law alternatively. However, the term "antitrust law" refers exclusively to Arts. 81 and 82 EC and the Merger Control Reg. When the term "competition law" is used this generally refers to a broader concept, covering Arts. 81–9 EC and the Merger Control Reg. As the book's title suggests, the focus is on EC "antitrust law".

[3] See B. Hawk, "System Failure: Vertical Restraints and EC Competition Law" (1995) 32 *CMLRev*. 973–89; S. Wilks, "Options for Reform in European Competition Policy", in A. van Mourik (ed.), *Developments in European Competition Policy* (Maastricht, EIPA, 1996) 153–76; and R. Van den Bergh, "Modern Industrial Organisation versus Old-fashioned European Competition Law" (1996) 17 *ECLR* 75–87.

implications and the consequences for the antitrust law system on the substantive, procedural and institutional level remain under-emphasised.

The book starts from the observation that the objectives of Community competition policy have changed fundamentally in the more than 40 years of European integration. In 1960 the Commissioner responsible for competition affairs stated that the objectives of Community competition policy were "to prevent *trade between the Member States and the exchange of services in the widest sense being hampered* either by distortions of competition i.e. by differences in national regulations or administrative practices, or restricted by price agreements or the taking of improper advantage of economic power".[4] In 1997, the competition Commissioner summarised the objectives of EC competition policy as ensuring "that markets acquire or maintain the flexibility they need to allow scope for initiative and innovation and *to allow an effective and dynamic allocation of society's resources*".[5] The remarkable divergence in these two depictions of its objectives characterises the transformation which Community antitrust law has undergone. Between 1958 and today the objectives of antitrust law changed significantly as they were adapted to the changing background against which they were applied. Most importantly, separate national markets were gradually integrated into one common European market. Partly as a consequence, the nature of European integration changed. As market integration was gradually achieved, broader European integration aspirations materialised. The continuation of European integration beyond economic integration, enshrined in the substitution of the European Economic Community Treaty by the European Community Treaty, forms only the most evident illustration of this process.

Acknowledgement of the dynamic way in which antitrust jurisprudence and case law developed indicates that the original basis for the European Economic Community antitrust law regime has become obsolete. Likewise, the institutional and procedural frameworks which were designed for the original system cannot provide adequate solutions to dilemmas in EC antitrust law which arise in today's altered context. Solutions to the range of problems which arose in the area of EC antitrust law over the last decade can therefore be found only with reference to the systemic changes in Community antitrust law. In recognition, this book aims to place the debate on the modernisation of EC antitrust law in a broader context.

The structure of the book is as follows. Part I recounts the transformation of European law in general and that of Community antitrust law in particular. Chapter 1 describes the development of Community antitrust law in isolation.[6]

---

[4] See H. von der Groeben, "A European Policy on Competition" [1960] *Bulletin of the European Economic Community* (No. 3), 5ff.

[5] Commission of the European Communities, *XXVIth Annual Report on Competition Policy 1996*, 17. Cf., in the same sense, the Commission's Draft Policy Paper on Vertical Restraints, issued by DG IV (now "DG Competition") on 31 July 1998, at 2: "[t]he protection of competition is the primary objective of EC competition policy as this *enhances consumer welfare and creates an efficient allocation of resources*; market integration, in the light of enlargement, remains a second important objective when assessing competition issues" (emphasis added).

Although the separate elements in the history of EC antitrust law are well known, they are seldom presented chronologically. Chapter 2 examines the way in which the European integration process changed over that same period. It contrasts the general development of the Community and of Community law with the specific course which EC antitrust law has taken. The differences which are then revealed between the general development of Community law and that of Community antitrust law are central to the detailed analysis of the modernisation of Community antitrust law in Part II.[7]

Chapters 3 and 4 of Part II address substantive law issues. Chapter 3 argues that EC antitrust law—in particular Article 81 EC—can be enforced in such a way as to allow for a distinction between the assessment of competition concerns in a first phase (under Article 81(1) EC) and consideration of non-competition policy concerns in a second phase of procedures (under Article 81(3) EC). Chapter 4 argues that the traditional criterion on the basis of which the Community has antitrust law jurisdiction ("effect on trade between Member States") is less useful in the current context within which EC antitrust law is applied. Instead, Community antitrust law jurisdiction should be limited to what is of Community interest. If (potentially) anti-competitive behaviour is too insignificant to be of concern at the Community level, there should not be Community jurisdiction. Chapters 5 and 6 of Part II focus on institutional developments. Chapter 5 takes up the longstanding question whether enforcement of EC antitrust law should be left to an independent European cartel office. With reference to general institutional developments in the European Community it is concluded that such an independent office should not be established. Current problems in Community antitrust law enforcement at the central level stem from lack of transparency in its institutional and procedural structure rather than from the lack of independence of the Commission. Chapter 6 turns to decentralised Community antitrust law enforcement. While the Commission's desire to decentralise part of EC antitrust law enforcement to national courts

---

[6] The book's focus is on European Community (EC), formerly European Economic Community (EEC), antitrust law. It does not generally address the situation of the other European Communities; the European Community for Coal and Steel (ECSC) and Euratom. Neither does it deal specifically with the European Economic Area (EEA). Furthermore, within the field of EC antitrust law only the general context is discussed. Exceptions to the general Community antitrust rules, as in force in, for example, the agricultural and transport sectors are highlighted only in so far as the general discussion requires these cross-references.

[7] Obviously, it is not unproblematic to discuss EC antitrust law in such general terms. There are huge differences between the various types of cases. EC antitrust law cases vary from mergers between multinational firms operating in globalised sectors of the economy to distribution agreements between small- or mediumsized enterprises operating in a region of a Member State only. Different cases pose different procedural, institutional and substantive problems. Institutions and procedures which are pertinent for big mergers may not fit well in cases which review co-operation agreements between smaller undertakings. Nevertheless, it is considered useful in the context of this book to portray the development of EC antitrust law in general terms. Part II of the book, which reviews specific issues of EC antitrust law, recognises that solutions to the substantive, institutional and procedural problems which are addressed are not uniform but should instead vary along with the type of antitrust law case which is treated.

and national antitrust authorities is supported, the discussion in Chapter 6 reveals various objections to the way in which the Commission promotes decentralisation of EC antitrust law enforcement in its White Paper on Modernisation.

METHODOLOGY

The considerations about its objectives have informed both the methodology used for the research and the way in which the results are presented. Interpretations of Community substantive law generally, and of EC antitrust law in particular, are interrelated with and dependent upon institutional, procedural, political and economic aspects of the system. This book therefore recognises explicitly the systemic context in which antitrust law is developed and applied. The interdisciplinary perspective adopted in this book is based on the "law in context" approach, which studies legal principles and processes with reference to their social, political and institutional settings.[8] Such an approach is especially beneficial to the study of EC law in view of the characteristics of the European Community, being so manifestly a combination of legal, political, social and economic processes.[9] EC antitrust law in particular, as an area of substantive law, is a combination of economics, politics and law. It has been succinctly described as "part jurisprudence, part political realism".[10]

In recognition of the relevance of antitrust law's evolving political and economic contexts, this study makes use of political science, historic and economic literature. Part I, which focuses on the transformation of European integration in general and of Community antitrust law in particular, draws on studies of the history of EC integration. The historical perspective supplements the perception of today's reality in a number of ways. It reveals alternatives that might have been chosen and the ensuing divergent status antitrust law would have in the EC today. A historic viewpoint also renders it possible to identify and analyse more carefully the factors which have affected, and which may still affect, the decisions made within the system.[11] In the study of Community law a sense of evolution which reveals "the dynamics of the system" is particularly apt.[12] The

---

[8] See F. Snyder, *New Directions in European Community Law* (London, Weidenfeld & Nicholson, 1990).

[9] See, in explicit recognition, U. Everling, *Das Europäische Gemeinschaftsrecht im Spannungsfeld von Politik und Wirtschaft: Ausgewählte Aufsätze, 1964–1984* (Baden-Baden, Nomos, 1985).

[10] G. Ross, *Jacques Delors and European Integration* (Oxford, Polity Press, 1995), 129–31.

[11] Cf. J. Weiler, "The Transformation of Europe" (1991) 100 *The Yale Law Journal* 2403–83 at 2403–10. For the importance of historic perspectives supplementing static views, see Snyder, above, n. 8, at 100.

[12] D. Gerber, "European Law: Thinking about It and Teaching it" (1995) 1 *CJEL* 379–95, at 390. The importance of adding a historical dimension to the study of EC law is stressed in P. VerLoren van Themaat, "Einige Betrachtungen über die Zukunft der Europäischen Union aus der Sicht eines weltoffenen Nachbarlands", in O. Due, M. Lubber, J. Schwarze (eds.), *Festschrift für Ulrich Everling* (Baden-Baden, Nomos, 1995), 1543–60.

Community, both substantively and in the internal principles of its operation, is a process as much as it is a state of being. Although any polity is both process and state, the changing constellation is more easily perceived in the European Community.[13] Moreover, in this book the insights into the development of the Community's antitrust system, gained from the historical investigation, are instrumental to Part II which examines current issues of Community antitrust law with reference to the systemic changes described in Part I.[14]

Part II makes ample use of economic and political science literature. Chapter 3 reconsiders the objectives of Community antitrust law in view of the formal realisation of the internal market by the end of 1992. The imminent loss of the integration paradigm has generated broad support for an enhanced role for economics in the application of the Community's antitrust rules. The other three chapters of Part II focus on constitutional and institutional aspects of Community antitrust law enforcement. In particular, the balance of powers between the Community and its Member States and the role of politics in antitrust law practice are discussed. With the help of concepts which were developed in other areas of Community policy, Part II aims to shed new light on the issues discussed.

Nevertheless this book is a study of antitrust law and its focus is on law.[15] Accordingly, the main sources for this study are the Treaty's substantive provisions, secondary legislation and Commission decisions and Court of Justice case law. Law and legal rules have generally been central to EC integration, and no less to EC competition policy.[16] Focusing on law and legal processes is pertinent in the context of Community antitrust law because the role of law has been so notable. The legalist context in which antitrust was developed can be appreciated only by concentrating on the development of that law. In the first 30-odd years most of EC competition—and especially antitrust—policy was simply seen and applied as an inevitable, ancillary tool in the market integration

---

[13] S. Bulmer, "Institutions and Policy Change: The Case of Merger Control" (1994) 72 *Public Administration* 423–44 at 425: "[e]very political system is in constant evolution but the EC is extreme in this sense". In the same sense, see J. Weiler, "The Community System: The Dual Character of Supranationalism" (1981) 1 *YEL* 267–306 and S. Weatherill, *Law and Integration in the European Union* (Oxford, Clarendon Press, 1995).

[14] Weiler, above, n. 11, at 2408. The relevance of historical insights into the study of antitrust has recently been reiterated: J. May, "Historical Analysis in Antitrust Law" (1990) 35 *New York Law School Law Review* 857–79. Moreover, Bork's *Antitrust Law's Paradox—A Policy at War with Itself*, arguably the most influential book of recent decades on United States antitrust law, was to a large extent based on his distinctive reading of the legislative history of the US antitrust acts and the way the case law had evolved from there: R. Bork, *The Antitrust Paradox. A Policy at War with Itself* (New York, The Free Press, 1993).

[15] Cf. F. Snyder, "Soft Law and Institutional Practice in the European Community", S. Martin (ed.), *The Construction of Europe—Essays in Honour of Emile Noel* (Dordrecht, Kluwer, 1994), 179–225 at 180.

[16] Cf. W. Hallstein, cited in C. Joerges, *States Without a Market? Markets Without a State?*, EUI Working Paper Law 96/2 (Florence, EUI, 1996), at 1: "[t]he European Community is a phenomenon of law in three respects: It is a creation of law, it is a source of law, and it is a legal order." See also R. Dehousse and J. Weiler, "The legal dimension", in W. Wallace (ed.), *The Dynamics of European Integration* (London, Pinter, 1983), 242–60 at 243.

process. There was a general perception of Community competition law enforcement as a non-partisan and a-political process. Hence institutional battles were absent. The exclusive control over competition policy was firmly held by the Commission.[17] Therefore, it is argued that, even if it is useful to stress the social, political and economic implications of competition policy, it is necessary to approach those years, or that phase of the development of EEC competition law from a legal perspective.

Finally, some organisational notes. The book refers to Article numbers of the treaties after the renumbering on the basis of the Amsterdam Treaty. The first time the new Article number is mentioned in each chapter the old number is given in brackets ("ex Article x"). The old numbers are retained in citations and references, with a reference to the new number ("now Article x") in brackets.

The cut-off date for the research is 1 January 2000.

---

[17] *Cf.* Bulmer, above, n. 13.

Part I

The Development of the Current System of EC Antitrust Law Enforcement

1

The Transformation of Community Antitrust Law Enforcement

INTRODUCTION

THIS CHAPTER aims to illustrate the development of Community antitrust law from a set of relatively ill-defined rules on competition enshrined in the EEC Treaty in 1958 to the present comprehensive system of substantive provisions, procedural rules and case law. The intention is not to discuss systematically the whole corpus of EC antitrust law. Rather it is to demonstrate how the system of Community antitrust law has evolved from its inception to what it is today. It will, necessarily, do so in broad lines. A meticulous depiction of all cases, or for that matter even of all those cases with a particular relevance to antitrust jurisprudence, is not sought. The purpose is rather to present the dynamics in the development of the system. Hence, the emphasis is on variation and on change, not on similarity or continuity.

The chapter contains five sections. The first sketches the general background. It presents the substantive Treaty provisions as well as the institutional and procedural framework developed in the initial period of the Community's existence. Although the basic elements of the system are well-known, a review of its genesis is indispensable to the purpose of this study. The subsequent sections depict the transformation of Community antitrust practice, each coinciding with important events or developments in the history of EC antitrust law.

Three phases are identified. In the first, roughly encompassing the early 1960s and 1970s, Community antitrust jurisprudence was established through the first Commission decisions and Court of Justice judgments. This case law forms the basis of all subsequent E(E)C antitrust law enforcement. The third section reviews the essential developments in the second phase, which roughly covers the end of the 1970s and the first half of the 1980s. The significance of the events following the Single European Act, notably adoption of the Community's Merger Control Regulation, are central to the fourth section.[1] The concluding section provides a summary of the findings in this chapter.

---

[1] This chapter's periodisation is based on two earlier "transformation" accounts, that of Joseph Weiler ("The Transformation of Europe") and that of Daniel Gerber ("The Transformation of European Community Competition Law"). Their periodisation recognises three phases: (1) the foundational period in which much progress in integration was made (1958–73); (2) the period of "Eurosclerosis" in which further steps towards integration could not be made for various political reasons (1973–85); (3) completion of the internal market on the basis of the SEA and TEU (1985 and

The initial legal framework is set out in the following order. The first sub-section reviews the early origins of Community antitrust rules in the negotiation process which led to the adoption of the Rome Treaty. The initial practice which, absent secondary law, was based exclusively on the Treaty rules is then discussed before the fourth and final section reports on the pivotal procedural provision, Regulation 17. It is useful in the context of this study to recall that context since the purpose of the chapter is to perceive the development of Community antitrust law. Next, the relevant substantive provisions are set out. If adopted, the plans set out in the Commission White Paper on Modernisation will alter important elements of the system which was established in this early period of EC integration.

1.1.1 The Origins of the Antitrust Rules in the Process of Negotiating the EEC Treaty

"Resolved to ensure the economic and social progress of their countries by com-mon action to eliminate barriers which divide Europe", the heads of state of six European countries decided in 1957 to establish among themselves the European Economic Community.[2] Although the same states had already estab-lished the European Coal and Steel Community six years before, their signing of the EEC Treaty implied more than just an extension of the scope of that Community. The core of the European Economic Community was to be a com-mon market encompassing all sectors of industry. In terms of population the size of that market would be comparable to that of the United States, which the economies of the Member States at the time lagged far behind. The belief was that the ensuing potential for enhanced economies of scale would boost European firms' competitive position, thus reducing the existing gap between the American and European economies.[3] That the European *Economic* Community had the furthering of Member States' economies as its central object is therefore implied not only in its name but also in what was envisaged as its central component, a common market. The common market among Member States would enable European firms to compete transnationally under equal conditions. The resulting elevated level of competition was in turn con-

beyond): J. Weiler, "The Transformation of Europe" (1991) 100 *The Yale Law Journal* 2403–83 and D. Gerber, "The Transformation of European Community Competition Law?" (1994) 35 *Harvard International Law Journal* 97–147.

   [2] A. Milward, *The Reconstruction of Europe, 1945–1951* (London, Methuen, 1984); R. Mayne, *The Recovery of Europe: 1945–1973* (New York, Harper Row, 1970); and H.-J. Küsters, *Fondements de la Communauté Économique Européenne* (Luxembourg, Office des Publications Officielles des Communautés Européennes, 1990).

   [3] Küsters, above, n. 2, at 130ff.

sidered essential to the general effort of increasing Europe's competitiveness and, ultimately, its economic prosperity. The central role which was envisaged for market integration in the EEC Treaty logically ascertained the significance of the rules on competition in that Treaty.[4]

The negotiations between future Member States in the preparatory phase of the EEC Treaty shed additional light on the role which was originally envisaged for the Treaty's competition rules. The principal preparatory base for the negotiations was the Spaak Report.[5] Its drafters argued that the enduring division of Europe was detrimental to the capacity of the separate states to advance and regulate their economies.[6] In the view of the Spaak Committee the incapacity of individual states to strengthen their economies could be overcome by pooling efforts at a higher, supranational level. A common market would return, if in a collective form, part of the economic regulative power to its Member States. In addition, the vast scope of a common market covering the territory of the six Member States would provide increased opportunities for European business. Enterprises would be able to profit from increased specialisation, modes of mass production and the ensuing economies of scale. Enhanced international competition would, moreover, boost European business' competitiveness.[7] The principal advantage of the common market was therefore considered to be the reconciliation of mass production with the absence of monopolies.[8]

The perceived advantages of the common market would, however, materialise only if market conditions were equal for all actors in the European-wide market. Obstacles to intra-Community trade, repartitioning the newly established common market, would be fatal to the whole project. In order to ensure the correct functioning of the market mechanism it was essential that competition would not be hampered by private or public impediments to free trade. It was in this light that the members of the Spaak Committee contemplated the

---

[4] The different objectives of the ECSC and EC Treaties continue to be reflected in diverging interpretations of the respective antitrust rules, despite the similar wording of the Treaty provisions on antitrust law. ECSC antitrust law jurisdiction, for instance, is exclusive, whereas that of the EC is concurrent with those of the Member States. Most significantly, the ECJ ruled that the ECSC competition rules, contrary to those of the EC, do not have direct effect: Case C–128/92 *H. J. Banks & Co. Ltd.* v. *British Coal* [1994] ECR I–1268. In view of the fact that the ECSC and the EC now both form part of the European Union, the judgment has been criticised for its negative conceptual and practical effects on the unity and uniformity of the Union's legal order. See P. Meunier, "La Cour de justice des Communautés européennes et l'applicabilité directe des règles de concurrence du Traité CECA" (1996) 32 *RTDE* 243–58. For an analysis of the divergences between early ECSC and EEC antitrust law, see D. Gerber, "Law and the Abuse of Economic Power in Europe" (1987) 62 *Tulane Law Review* 57–107 at 86ff.

[5] The Spaak Report, or "Rapport des Chefs de Délégation aux Ministres des Affaires Etrangères", was prepared by the Comité Intergouvernemental Créé par la conference de Messine and presented on 21 April 1956 in Brussels. It has adequately been described as the "non-categoric imperative" for the subsequent Treaty negotiations: Küsters, above, n. 2, at 354.

[6] Comité Intergouvernemental Créé par la conference de Messine, above, n. 5, at 9.

[7] P. Kapteyn, "Outgrowing the Treaty of Rome: From Market Integration to Policy Integration", in *Mélanges Fernand Dehousse* (Paris, Fernand Nathan, 1979), ii, 45–55.

[8] R. Griffiths, "The European Integration Experience" in K. Middlemas, *Orchestrating Europe* (London, Fontana Press, 1995), 1–70 at 58–9.

need for Treaty provisions directed at preventing private undertakings from obstructing the realisation of the common market.

Consequently, the Spaak Report, in addition to its support for provisions which would guarantee the free movement of production factors, explicitly promoted adoption of competition rules directed to enterprises.[9] They were considered fundamental to the successful operation of the common market. The rules on competition were to guarantee fair competition on the common market. They were to preclude the division of national markets through public measures, which the Treaty would disqualify, being substituted by market foreclosure on the basis of private agreements.[10]

Yet the role of competition policy in the Community was not limited to ensuring that competition on the common market, once established, would not be distorted. The provisions on competition were also included with a view to their potential function in the integration process itself. Economic integration in the framework of the EEC would basically imply reallocation of the means of production. From the economic order on the basis of national schemes the separate economic processes were to merge into one. New potential for specialisation on a larger scale and on a European-wide basis was envisaged to direct production to those locations with comparative advantages in the respective sectors. Elevated economies of scale could then be generated. The most efficient way to organise the ensuing reallocation of production factors was, in the eyes of the Spaak group, by way of the functioning of the market mechanism.[11]

The dual role for the rules on competition envisaged in the Spaak Report defines their "normative-functional" character. Free competition was functional in view of its envisaged role in generating one common market on the basis of a prohibition on discrimination along national lines. At the same time the com-

---

[9] Agreement on the principle need for introduction of competition rules was reached relatively soon. Nevertheless there was initial disagreement on the textual formulation of the principle. Three texts circulated in the Spaak group. One focused on the prohibition of different pricing. Another wanted to prohibit all discriminatory practices. A third declared that discriminatory agreements could be prohibited. The final Article 81(1) EC (ex Art. 85(1)) assimilates the second proposal the most. The concerns of the framers of the third proposal were considered by introducing the exemption possibility in para (3) of the Art. and the prohibition to discriminate on nationality was promoted to a principle in Art. 12 EC (ex Article 6). See S. Neri and H. Sperl, *Traité instituant la Communauté Economique Européenne, Travaux préparatoires* (Luxembourg, Cour de Justice des Communités Européennes, 1960), 210–12.

[10] Spaak Report, above, n. 5, at 16: "Le premier fait dont il convient de tenir compte, c'est la dimension atteinte par les entreprises, ou l'usage des ententes entre entreprises et, par suite, les pratiques de monopole, les facultés de discrimination, les possibilités de répartition du marché. *Des règles de concurrence qui s'imposent aux entreprises sont donc nécessaires pour éviter que des doubles prix aient le même effet que des droits de douane, qu"un dumping mette en danger des productions économiquement saines, que la répartition des marchés se substitue à leur cloissonement.*"

[11] Indeed, a centrally planned reallocation of production factors on the basis of a common industrial policy would have required such a degree of *dirigisme* that it could hardly be envisaged. There was therefore no realistic alternative to integration on the basis of the functioning of the market mechanism: B. Van der Esch, "E.E.C. Competition Rules: Basic Principles and Policy Aims" (1980) 7 *LIEI* II–75–85, and similarly, W. von Simson, "The Concept of Competition in the European Community" in J. Schwarze and H. Schermers (eds.), *Structure and Dimensions of European Community Policy* (Baden-Baden, Nomos Verlagsgesellschaft, 1988), 139–46 at 140.

petition rules portended a normative socio-political choice for competition, and not regulation, as a means of integrating the economies as well as governing economic processes in the common market once it was established.[12] It is unlikely that the representatives of all Member States realised the far-reaching political implications which the latter would have.

The conviction of the members of the Spaak group that a market economy on the basis of free and undistorted competition would form the appropriate economic principle for establishing, as well as governing, the common market was picked up in the next phase of preparation for the Treaty; the negotiations between the future Member States. The German delegation in particular was inclined to promote free competition as the regulating economic tool for the common market. On the one hand German insistence on the introduction of competition provisions into the EEC Treaty was due to American influence on Germany's post-Second World War economy. The United States identified the big industrial cartels as fundamental parts of Germany's war machine. Therefore it insisted on the decartellisation of German industry after the Second World War, of which the US inspired split-up of IG Farben is probably the most well-known example. On the other hand, American desire for decartellisation happened to find fruitful ground in mainstream German economic thinking. The idea of a social market economy in which an "economic constitution" would govern the relationship between the state and private enterprise in the economy had won ground under German economists in the period after the 1920s. The consensus among political elites on the value of competition ensured swift acceptance of a German Competition Act, the *Gesetz gegen Wettbewerbs-beschränkungen*. The existence of that Act in turn provided an important impetus to the German delegation's insistence on adoption of similar principles in the EEC Treaty.[13]

The French reaction to the suggested rules on competition was less receptive. Its delegation was disinclined to participate in establishing a common market which would mainly be governed by the market mechanism. Two motives for

[12] Kapteyn, above, n. 7, at 49. *Cf.* Lagrange AG's Opinion in the first antitrust case before the ECJ, Case 13/61 *De Geus* v. *Bosch* [1962] ECR 45 at 64: "[t]he application of Articles 85 to 90 [now: Arts. 81 to 86 EC] is not only a necessary factor, but one of the most important ones, in the gradual establishment of the Common Market, rather than merely one of the ways in which it functions". Nevertheless, the normative limb was by no means absolute. Treaty provisions denying the principle of free trade and competition for certain sectors, like those on the Common Agricultural Policy (Articles 32–8 EC) (ex Articles 38–47), Common Transport Policy (Articles 70–80 EC) (ex Articles 74–84), and the provided in Article 295 EC (ex Article 222), are typical in this respect: Van der Esch, above, n. 11, and D. Goyder, *EC Competition Law*, at 14.

[13] H. von der Groeben, *Die Europäische Gemeinschaft und die Herausforderungen unserer Zeit*; *Aufsätze und Reden 1967–1987* (Baden-Baden, Nomos Verlagsgesellschaft, 1987). Although the German Constitutional Court later ruled that the concept of an "economic constitution" does not exist in Germany, the German delegation played an important role in creating a liberal economic order for the EEC. The link between German belief in free competition and the substance of the EEC Treaty is extensively analysed in D. Gerber, "Constitutionalizing the Economy: German Neo-liberalism, Competition Law and the 'New' Europe" (1994) 42 *AJCL* 25–84.

opposing the establishment of a common market on the basis of free competition have been advanced. First, the French delegation is considered to have feared the loss of industrial policy power, which acceptance of the Spaak Report as the basis of a common market implied. Secondly, there was little confidence that French firms would be able to compete succesfully with German firms and products in view of the the supposed superiority of German products. The French delegation was not at all keen on opening up the French market to German business by reducing restrictions on trade.[14]

The remaining delegations were less outspoken on the issue, although a tendency on the Benelux side to accept the German position and somewhat more understanding for French fears in the Italian delegation have been identified.[15]

The positions of the two central actors in the negotiation process provided a logical opportunity for what would become a typical feature of European Community integration; the package deal. The German desire for Treaty rules guaranteeing freedom to compete throughout the common market under equal market circumstances was rewarded. The French were compensated through the exception of the agricultural sector from the competition rules and the adoption of a common agricultural policy.[16]

With the notable exception of the agricultural and transport sectors, the competition rules were therefore accepted, in accordance with the intentions of the Spaak Report, as guiding principles of the Common Market. Yet, it was one thing for the Member States to agree on the value of free competition in principle; it was quite another to give substance to the legal provisions. Accepting free competition as the principal economic regulatory tool implied a fundamental shift away from the dominant form of industrial organisation in most Member States. State interventions and redistributive policies tended to distort the market mechanism on most of the national markets.[17] Though the Member States had recently demonstrated that they were capable of displacing state intervention in favour of free international competition for the limited but important economic sectors of coal and steel, it was not as simple to eliminate the room for national industrial policies for the entire economy. Moreover, in spite of their aspiration to co-determine the Treaty's competition rules, the Member States

[14] R. Griffiths, "Agricultural Pressure Groups and the Origins of the Common Agricultural Policy" (1995) 3 *European Review* 233–42, at 238.

[15] See, comprehensively, on the respective positions held by the national delegations in particular regarding competition law, Küsters, above, n. 2.

[16] It should be noted that the form, and even the very existence, of this package deal is contested. Griffiths, for instance, holds that the "CAP was not linked to the introduction of competition rules as such. Rather the existence of a regulated agricultural market was a prerequisite for French participation in the Common Market in general". Griffiths, above, n. 14. Rieger argues that the exception for agriculture was mainly due to its relative importance for the national economies at the time. Talk of a Franco-German package deal is in his view no more than a legend; E. Rieger, "Agrarpolitik: Integration durch Gemeinschaftspolitik?" in M. Jachtenfuchs and B. Kohler-Koch (eds.), *Europäische Integration* (Opladen, Leske + Budrich, 1996), 401–28 at 407.

[17] Goyder, above, n. 12, at 19.

lacked expertise in the field of competition law. Only Germany could claim some experience with the principles of an economy structured on free competition between companies—and even that experience was mainly theoretical.[18] The competition rules were formulated broadly and vaguely and the contracting states agreed on the inclusion of competition rules in the Treaty without necessarily being of the same mind as to the exact status of the provisions beyond their role in the market integration process. Perhaps the Member States' delegations were comforted by the decisive role they reserved for the Council of Ministers in the implementation and further development of EEC competition law and policy.[19]

1.1.2 The EEC Treaty's Antitrust Law Provisions

Article 2 of the EEC Treaty provided that the Community would have as its task, by establishing the common market and by progressively approximating the economic policies of the Member States, to promote harmonious development of economic activities in the Community. Article 3 defined the instruments which the Community had at its disposal for the succesful establishment of the common market. They included a number of common policies, most notably guaranteeing free movement of goods, persons, services and capital between Member States and exceptional provisions which established common policies in the agricultural and transport sectors. Establishing a system which would ensure undistorted and free competition was another instrument which Article 3 EEC Treaty provided.

Detailed provisions on the practical operation of the policies set out in general terms in Article 3 followed in the remainder of the Treaty. The competition rules were formulated in Articles 81 to 90 EC (ex Articles 85 to 94), which formed the first chapter of the "Common Rules".

The competition rules were partly directed to the Member States and partly to private enterprises. Article 91 EC (repealed by the Amsterdam Treaty) prohibited dumping practices, Articles 87 to 89 EC (ex Articles 92 to 94) declared state-aids favouring certain (national) undertakings, incompatible with the common market unless endorsed by the Treaty or in some other way approved

---

[18] The German Competition Act, the *Gesetz gegen Wettbewerbsbeschränkungen*, was adopted in 1958 and became operative only after the EEC Treaty had come into force. See, more extensively on the role of German competition law and competition lawyers in developing the EEC Treaty's competition law provisions, Gerber, above, n. 13.

[19] See, e.g., Art. 83 EC (ex Art. 87) which determined that the Council when adopting appropriate implementation measures to give effect to the principles of Arts. 81 and 82 EC (ex Arts. 85 and 86) would act unanimously. By insisting on the central role for the, intergovernmental, Council of Ministers in developing competition policy the Member States ignored the experience with the ECSC competition law regime which had revealed the need for more, not less, supranational powers in the establishment and enforcement of an active competition policy: E. Haas, *The Uniting of Europe, Political Social, and Economic Forces 1950–1957* (Stanford, Stanford University Press, 1958), 75ff.

by the EEC Commission. Articles 81 to 86 EC (ex Articles 85 to 90) contained the rules applicable to undertakings. Article 86 EC (ex Article 90) itself was a particular provision which aimed to ensure compliance of public undertakings and undertakings to which special rights were otherwise entrusted with the Treaty's competition rules. The others, Articles 81 to 85 EC (ex Articles 85 to 89), contained the provisions on antitrust law. Articles 81 and 82 EC (ex Articles 85 and 86) embodied the substantive antitrust rules, the other three, Articles 83–85 EC (ex Articles 87–89), the procedural principles.

Article 81(1) EC prohibited as incompatible with the common market all agreements between undertakings, decisions by associations of undertakings and concerted practices which might affect trade between Member States and which had as their object or effect the prevention, restriction or distortion of competition within the common market. A non-exhaustive list of examples followed this general statement. The second paragraph advised that all agreements and decisions prohibited pursuant to Article 81 EC would be automatically void. The third and last paragraph of the Article tempered the unequivocal nature of the preceding paragraphs by providing the possibility of declaring inapplicable the provision of Article 81(1) EC. Exemptions would be available for agreements contributing to the improvement of the production or distribution of goods or to the promotion of technical or economic progress, provided that three additional criteria were met. A fair share of the resulting benefit had to fall on consumers. The restrictions concerned would have to be indispensable to the attainment of the positive objectives. And it was to be ruled out that the relevant undertakings would be able to eliminate competition in respect of a substantial part of the products in question. The second substantive antitrust law provision, Article 82 EC, prohibited any abuse by one or more undertakings of a dominant position within the common market, or in a substantial part of it, in so far as it might affect trade between Member States. Like Article 81(1) EC, Article 82 EC listed a number of examples of which the abuse might consist.

The procedural provisions, Articles 83 to 85 EC, focused on the enforcement of the Treaty's antitrust rules in the period immediately after adoption of the EEC Treaty. It had been foreseen that it would take some time for the Council to adopt, in accordance with Article 83 EC, the appropriate regulations or directives which would give effect to the principles set out in Articles 81 and 82 EC. Thus, Article 84 EC charged Member States' authorities with the administration of the Treaty's antitrust rules in accordance with the laws of their countries until the entry into force of the provisions adopted in pursuance of Article 83 EC. All the same Article 85 EC provided that the Commission, as soon as it took up its duties, was to ensure the application of the principles laid down in Article 81 and 82 EC. In this the Commission, because of the lack of implementing powers, was to co-operate closely with the competent authorities in the Member States.

The most important task for the Commission in the initial period, however, consisted of preparing its proposals for the provisions which, pursuant to

Article 83 EC, were to give effect to the Treaty's antitrust principles. In particular, the framers of the Treaty envisaged that the appropriate regulations or directives could include provisions on fines and periodic penalty payments, rules for the most effective and efficient application of Article 81(3) EC, provisions defining the application of the antitrust rules to specific sectors, the respective functions of the Commission and the Court of Justice in the application of the antitrust provisions and the relationship between national and Community antitrust laws. Those were the issues the Commission concentrated on in the initial phase of antitrust policy.

1.1.3 Establishing the Principles: The Period between 1958 and 1962

When the EEC Treaty came into force on 1 January 1958 the antitrust rules therefore existed merely in skeleton form. It was for the institutions of the Community to garnish the structure with substantive interpretations and procedural rules in order for the system to become truly operative. The Commission administration, still very small at the time, concentrated on the fundamental problems of substance and procedure. Actual enforcement of Community antitrust law was left to the Member States. In accordance with Article 84 EC the authorities of the Member States had the power to rule on the admissibility of agreements, decisions and concerted practices in accordance with their national laws until the entry into force of enforcement provisions for Community antitrust rules. This power included application of the exemption provision. Due to inexperience with competition law in general and with EEC antitrust law in particular, Member States made little use of these competences. Nevertheless, some Member States' authorities, especially the German one, did grant various exemptions for agreements which were judged to fall within the scope of Article 81(1) EC. However, those judgments proved not to be relevant to the further development of the EEC antitrust system and will not be discussed further.[20]

Meanwhile, the Commission studied, discussed and tentatively decided on the desirable interpretation of the Treaty's antitrust provisions. Much of the

---

[20] Since the general enforcement regulation, Reg. 17, excluded from its scope certain economic sectors (e.g. transport) the competence for Member States to apply Arts. 81 and 82 EC, in the absence of enforcement provisions, continued to be of practical importance until all sectors of the economy fell within the scope of an enforcement reg. One of the last sectors of the industry to remain without specific enforcement regulation is air transport between the Community and third countries. Thus, the UK Office of Fair Trading was able to announce its intention to provide an exemption for a joint venture between British Airways and American Airlines on the basis of Art. 84 EC. (Three years after notification of the joint venture the Commission announced that it would not provide an exemption unless the mother companies gave up a number of "slots" (landing rights) on the basis of which the mother companies decided to end the joint venture.) In its "White Paper on the Modernisation of the Rules Implementing Articles 81 and 82 of the EC Treaty" the Commission announces that it wants to restore the capacity of national antitrust authorities to provide exemptions on the basis of Art. 81(3) EC. See further, below, Part II, *passim*.

effort and time was usurped by deliberation and meetings between the Commission and national delegations on these issues.[21] In 1960 the principal conclusions which the Commission drew from these meetings were presented by the Commissioner for competition matters. They would form the basis for the development of Community competition law over the next four decades.

Four basic characteristics were identified.[22] First, the rules on Community competition law needed to be read in conjunction with the other Treaty provisions. The objectives of EEC antitrust policy were strongly interrelated to the basic motivation behind the EEC Treaty, European economic integration. The antitrust provisions were to be interpreted in permanent recognition of their effect on the establishment of the common market. Relatedly, the second principle of antitrust law held that the conception of EEC competition provisions would be "political", which apparently implied that Community antitrust law was based on a concept different from traditional national competition laws.[23] The third principle of EEC competition law was institutional in character. To be able to take into account and to weigh the relative importance of the different and potentially conflicting interests, and in view of the broad political analysis which was required for adjudication of single cases, implementation of Community competition law required a supranational and centralised administration. Its central position and supranational character in the Community's institutional framework made the Commission the appropriate body to employ the discretion which was implicit in the application of EEC competition law.[24] The final principle stipulated that the wide margins for discretion in the application of the antitrust rules would be limited by legal constraints. Uniformity of market conditions and, hence, uniform interpretation of the competition rules were essential limits to the Commission's discretionary margins. Accordingly, interpretation of Community antitrust law and the very concept of competition was to be framed in legal terms.

While the basic principles of the system were thus developed, a range of immediate issues remained unresolved. It was not clear, for example, what exactly constituted an enterprise. Neither had it been determined whether the

---

[21] Commission of the European Economic Community, *Premier Rapport Général sur l'activité de la Communauté Économique Européenne* (Brussels, 1958), 62–3.

[22] H. von der Groeben, "A European Policy on Competition" [1960] *Bulletin of the European Economic Community*, no. 3, 5–9.

[23] Von der Groeben, above, n. 22, 9.

[24] The second general report on the activities of the EEC Commission formulates it as follows: "[s]'il devient ainsi nécessaire d'intervenir dans les mécanismes du marché, on devra prendre soin de sauvegarder, autant que possible, le mécanisme des prix et de ne pas mettre en danger l'existence d'une saine concurrence. Il convient, à cet effet, de rechercher la méthode appropriée; dans cette tâche on peut s'appuyer en particulier sur l'article 85, paragraphe 3 [now: Art. 81(3) EC], dont les provisions relatives à l'admissibilité des ententes contiennent des principes qui revêtent une importance considérable pour la politique de concurrence": Commission of the European Economic Community, *Deuxieme Rapport Général sur l'activité de la Communauté* (Brussel, 1958–1959), 83–4.

prohibition on agreements restrictive of trade encompassed the numerous "vertical" agreements between companies in various stages of the distribution chain. Most of these issues would be resolved by the first Council enforcement Regulation, the first Commission decisions and the initial judgments of the Court of Justice.

1.1.4 Regulation 17

Notwithstanding the relevance of the tentative debates on interpretation of the basic concepts of EEC antitrust law in the initial years, the most important development in the first decade of Community antitrust law was the adoption of the first enforcement regulation.[25] With the adoption of Regulation 17 the Commission could start applying the Treaty's antitrust provisions. Moreover, the procedural principles established continue to determine the interpretation of substantive as well as procedural aspects of Community antitrust law.

It took the Commission roughly three years of study before it submitted its first proposal to the Council. After that it would take another year and a half to adopt the Regulation. Amendments to and alterations of the Regulation have remained extremely limited.[26]

The Regulation defined three types of decisions which the Commission would be able to take. First, it could provide a negative clearance decision on those agreements which, according to the information available to the Commission, did not raise competition concerns for the Community. Secondly, a decision could be taken by which the Commission established infringement of Article 81 or 82 EC. The third alternative comprised the possibility for the Commission to exempt an agreement or practice from the prohibition contained in Article 81(1) EC on the basis of Article 81(3) EC. This exemption power was subject to a number of conditions. The exemption could be provided only if all four conditions enshrined in Article 81(3) EC were fulfilled and the exemption was to be provided only for a specific and limited period of time.

Though some degree of limitation of Commission discretion in providing exemptions was thus secured, its impact was limited. Interpretation of the four

---

[25] EEC Council Reg. 17 of 13 March 1962 [1962] JO 13/204 [1959–62] OJ Spec. Ed. 87.

[26] It is interesting to note that Reg. 17, at the time of its adoption, was perceived to be merely the first enforcement reg. which would be revised once sufficient knowledge had been extracted from experience with its application: P. VerLoren van Themaat, "Einige Betrachtungen über die Entwichlung der Wettbewerbspolitik vor und seit dem husbandekommen der Verordnung 17/62" in U. Everling, Noyes and Sedemund (Hrsg.) *Europarecht, konsellrecht, Wirtschaftsecht, Festschrift für Aired Deringer* (Baden-Baden, Noimos Verlagsgesellschaft, 1996), 398–415 at 403. Nevertheless, until 1999 the Commission was extremely reluctant to propose revisions of the Reg., despite fierce and comprehensive criticism of the Reg. The Commission feared that opening up the Reg. to reform would trigger an unstoppable series of challenges which would obstruct the system's operation: C.-D. Ehlermann, "Ist die Verordnung Nr. 17 noch zeitgemäß?" (1993) 43 *WuW* 997–1001. By issuing the "White Paper on the Modernisation of the Rules Implementing Articles 81 and 82 of the EC Treaty" in 1999, the Commission finally acknowlegded that Reg. 17 needed to be amended. See on this issue, Chs. 3 and 6 below.

criteria formulated in Article 81(3) EC implied abundant room for discretion, which was moreover subsequently interpreted expansively in the case law of the Court of Justice.[27]

The second important issue at the time, which is of particular relevance to the modernisation of EC antitrust law, was whether a duty to notify potentially anti-competitive agreements would be enshrined in Regulation 17. This issue concerned a balancing act between the need for effective enforcement and the need to ensure practicality of administration. The Commission was convinced that a duty to notify was called for because notifications would provide it with the necessary insights into European business practices. Opponents to notification stressed the burden for business which the notification duty would generate. In balancing the requirements of effective supervision on the one hand and simplified administration on the other, as required by Article 83(2)(b) EC, the balance tilted towards the effectiveness of the supervision. In order to qualify for exemption, agreements had to be notified.[28]

The third major—and related—issue in the debate which led to adoption of Regulation 17 was the application of the exemption provision. The question arose whether an official decision was needed to establish that a restrictive business agreement fulfilled the exemption criteria in order to be able to rely on the exemption. The French and German delegations differed in their views. The French believed that exemption was automatic without the requirement of a Commission decision if the criteria of Article 81(3) EC were fulfilled. The German delegation was opposed to that form of self-interpretation and regulation, mainly because of its desire to see strict application of Community antitrust law. The disagreement was solved with reference to the wording of Article 81(3) EC which left little room for the French view. It read, "the provision of paragraph 1 may be declared inapplicable". However, it was decided that all notified agreements which had been concluded before Regulation 17 entered into force remained valid without an individual exemption decision being required.[29]

---

[27] Not providing the possibility of eliminating competition in respect of a *substantial* part of the market, allowing consumers a *fair* share of the resulting benefits, contributing to improving the production or distribution of goods or to *promoting technical or economic progress*, and the requirement that restrictions be *indispensable* (to an undefined goal), all enshrined in Art. 81(3) EC, are vague enough to allow for a wide discretionary scope. The ECJ expanded the degree of Commission discretion in applying Art. 81(3) EC: see for an early example, Case 17/79 *Transocean Marine Paint Association* [1974] ECR 1063. See, more extensively below, Ch. 3.

[28] The French delegation in particular was against a duty to notify agreements. It favoured more self-determination by business whether to notify or not. Yet support from the German and Dutch delegations for the Commission position ensured that the desire for transparency of business agreements was satisfied and a notification duty adopted: Goyder, above, n. 12, at 36. The debate on the (scope of the) duty to notify is highly topical in the context of the Commission's "White Paper on the Modernisation of the Rules Implementing Arts. 81 and 82 EC". See further below, Ch. 3.

[29] Old agreements received the benefit of the doubt and remained provisionally valid. Only after they had been declared to run counter to Art. 81(1) EC did the nullity take effect. New anti-competitive agreements, concluded after the coming into force of Reg. 17 were to be considered null and void immediately in accordance with the determined in Art. 81(2) EC without confirmation by

Various other matters of more or less importance to the present operation of the antitrust law system were decided in the process of the adoption of Regulation 17. In the context of the present account of the transformation of Community antitrust law the Regulation's important long-term institutional and procedural features can be summarised in three keywords. The Regulation generated a *centralised* system through *administrative* procedures with extensive *supranational* powers for the European Commission. Of these features the most remarkable is perhaps the supranational character of the mode of implementation of Community antitrust law. The Regulation conferred on the Commission powers directly to apply and enforce the antitrust rules without significant involvement of Member State authorities. Furthermore, Member States lost control of the decision-making process because Regulation 17 excluded the Council from day-to-day application of the antitrust rules. The supranational, exclusive Commission powers in the area of competition were subsequently reinforced by more delegation from the Council when it adopted a regulation which conferred the right on the Commission to exempt certain specified groups of agreements from the application of Article 81.[30] The supranational powers of the Commission were further strengthened by the exclusive competence which Article 9(1) of Regulation 17 gave the Commission for exempting in accordance with Article 81(3) EC those agreements which were held to be prohibited by Article 81(1) EC. Regulation 17 thus "stripped" national authorities of the right to exempt agreements which they considered beneficial to competition despite the fact that these agreements limited competition in some way.[31]

Due to a number of reasons, the power of the Member States to influence Commission decision-making was not significantly enhanced through their role in the Advisory Committee on Restrictive Practices and Monopolies (the "Advisory Committee").[32] Moreover, Member States' competition authorities, in so far as they existed, lacked expertise in the field of antitrust law. The German authority may in this respect have have been an exception. Yet, the German authority did not constitute a strong counterforce to the Commission's autonomous powers because the Community competition law regime was

---

an administrative body being required: Case 48/72 *Brasserie de Haecht* v. *Wilkin-Janssens (No 2)* [1973] ECR 77. See, extensively on the merits of the French proposal for an "*exception légale*" with reference to the Commission White Paper on Modernisation, E.-J. Mestmäcker, "Versuch einer Kartellpolitischen Wende in der EU" (1999) 49 *WuW* 523–9.

[30] Reg. 19/65 of the Council of 2 March 1965 on the Application of Art. 85(3) of the Treaty to certain categories of Agreements and Concerted Practices; [1965] OJ 36/533 [1965–6] OJ Spec. Ed. 35.

[31] Kelleher, above, n. 21, at 1221. The European Parliament had suggested going still further by proposing that the Commission, in parallel to the High Authority under the ECSC Treaty, be exclusively competent to apply Arts. 81 and 82 EC altogether. *Cf.* the recent case *H. J. Banks Co. Ltd.* v. *British Coal*, above, n. 4, especially Van Gerven AG's Opinion.

[32] The Advisory Committee is a committee of respresentatives of the Member States which obtained the right to deliver opinions on draft Commission decisions. The opinion of the Committee is merely advisory. Neither the opinion nor the draft decision on which it is based is made public.

modelled after that of Germany. Therefore there was no direct need for the German authorities to intermingle with Community antitrust policy.[33]

To an extent the direct effect of the antitrust provisions, which enables private agents to enforce Community competition law before national courts, could have moderated the exclusive role of the Commission in competition procedures. However, the Commission's monopoly on the application of the exemption provision in combination with the indivisibility of paragraphs (1) and (3) of Article 81 EC reduced the significance of the direct effect which Article 81(1) and (2) EC has. Final decisions from institutions other than the Commission were hardly conceivable. In practice there has not been significant enforcement of the EC antitrust provisions by bodies other than the EC Commission in the present procedural framework.[34]

1.2   THE FIRST PHASE OF COMMUNITY ANTITRUST LAW ENFORCEMENT: ELIMINATING IMPEDIMENTS TO TRADE

Once the enforcement infrastructure was in place, Commission attention turned to its main responsibility in the antitrust law field, enforcing the Treaty's competition law rules. The duty conferred on European undertakings by Regulation 17 to notify all agreements for which they sought exemptions formed the starting point for the Commission's enforcement activities. The flood of notifications which entered the Commission offices when Regulation 17 came into force created an immense case load for its competition services. Managing the backlog of notified, but not yet assessed, agreements became a dominant element of Commission antitrust law administration.[35] Further, the Commission antitrust law decisions immediately prompted annulment actions before the Court of Justice. Thus, the first Commission decisions in combination with Court of Justice case law soon revealed the basic contours of EEC antitrust law.

[33] The role of Member States in Community antitrust law decision-making is further discussed below, Ch. 5. In the context of the Commission "White Paper on Modernisation of the Rules Implementing Articles 81 and 82 of the Treaty", which envisages more intimate co-operation between the Commission and national antitrust authorities in the application of EC antitrust law, it is interesting to note that in the process of negotiating Reg. 17 the French had strongly resisted the concentration of decision-making power in the Commission, the scant influence of the Advisory Committee and the resulting "disequilibrium" between the Community and Member States. The French delegation repeatedly stressed the need for joint decisions between the Commission and representatives of the Member States. Only after several Council meetings did the French acknowledge that they were isolated in their demand for a national veto on antitrust matters.

[34] *Cf.* G. Marenco, "The Uneasy Enforcement of Article 85 EEC as Between Community and National Levels" in B. Hawk (ed.), *Annual Proceedings of the Fordham Corporate Law Institute 1993, Antitrust in a Global Economy* (New York, Transnational Juris Publications, 1994), 605–27.

[35] In spite of a range of (quasi-)legislative measures adopted with a view to reducing the administrative burden arising from antitrust notifications, a backlog still persists today. By the end of 1998 there were 1,204 antitrust cases pending at DG IV: EC Commission, *Twenty-eighth Annual Report on Competition Policy 1998* (Brussels, 1999), at 51. The Commission now intends to tackle the problem on the basis of its "White Paper on the Modernisation of the Rules Implementing Articles 81 and 82 EC". See below Chs. 3 and 6.

1.2.1 Commission Antitrust Policy in the Early Period

Because of the huge number of notifications, the Commission was incapable of answering all of them with formal decisions. The relatively small size of the Commission's bureaucracy in general and that of the Directorate-General for competition matters (DG IV) in particular, and the resulting limited capacity for issuing decisions, necessitated alternative means of dealing with the thousands of notified agreements.[36] The Commission had two instruments on the basis of which it could provide simultaneous approval to specific categories of agreements, notices and "block-exemption" regulations.[37] At the outset the Commission made use of the former, more informal instrument. The notices certified that the Commission did not consider specific types of agreements restrictive of competition in the sense of Article 81(1) EC. Agreements falling within the scope of the notice therefore did not need to be notified in order to obtain an exemption. Notices merely restate the Commission's general opinion about the relevant agreements. They do not provide absolute legal certainty to the parties to the agreement. Other institutions, and even the Commission itself, may find in a particular case that an agreement does infringe Article 81(1) EC. Nevertheless, parties to agreements which fall within the scope of a "negative clearance" notice will normally not notify their agreements. The notices were therefore certainly useful as an instrument for reducing the number of agreements notified to the Commission.[38] It took some more time to adopt block-exemption regulations. However, block-exemption regulations gradually became a major Commission instrument in the development of Community antitrust policy. They continue to be highly relevant to current policy, in particular in the context of "vertical" agreements.

Alongside the notices, which were principally aimed at reducing the administrative backlog at the Commission offices, the Commission in this period issued

---

[36] Statistics give an impression of the problem's magnitude. By the end of 1963, 34,000 bilateral agreements had been lodged. To administrate this DG IV initially consisted of close to 20 officials, rising to 78 by April 1964: D. Goyder, above, n. 12, at p. xli. Even this small number of officials was not able to concentrate fully on competition, let alone antitrust, matters since they were at the same time responsible for taxation matters and the approximation of laws. By 1971, 30,000 exclusive dealing agreements alone had been notified to the Commission. The Commission issued 19 official decisions in that same year: Commission of the EEC, *First Annual Report on Competition Policy* (Brussels, 1972), 15 and 57.

[37] The power to adopt exemption decisions *en bloc* was not provided for in Reg. 17. Consequently, additional delegation of powers from the Council was needed to confer this power on the Commission. Council Reg. 19/65 enabled the Commission to adopt block exemption regs. for certain exclusive dealing agreements.

[38] Early "negative clearance" notices were provided for Exclusive Agency Contracts made with Commercial Agents [1962] OJ 139/2921; Cooperation Agreements between small and medium-sized enterprises [1968] OJ C75/3; and for Agreements of Minor Importance [1970] OJ C64/1. The last-mentioned notice, the "de minimis" notice, proved most important in practice. It was repeatedly updated, e.g. in [1977] OJ C313/3; [1986] OJ C231/2; [1994] OJ C368/20. The most recent update, [1977] OJ C372/13, produces a qualitative change to the substance of the notice, in that a market share test replaces the previously prevailing turnover threshold.

its first formal decisions. In doing so it stressed the fundamental role which the antitrust rules were designed to play in the process of European integration in general, and in establishing the common market in particular. In accordance with the intentions of the framers of the EEC Treaty, initial Commission antitrust law enforcement was focused on private obstacles to inter-state trade within the Community. The resulting emphasis in the assessment on guaranteeing undertakings' options for re-selling, including re-importing, became an important element of Commission antitrust jurisprudence which is clearly reflected in its decisions.[39] The tendency to apply the Treaties' antitrust rules with a view to promoting integration of the separate national economies is also evident from the Commission decisions with respect to agreements between small- and medium-sized enterprises (SMEs). Cross-border co-operation agreements between SMEs typically obtained individual exemptions provided that a degree of competition within the common market remained.[40]

Against this background the Commission handed down its decision in the landmark *Consten and Grundig* case. The Commission was called upon by an undertaking which wanted to import Grundig products from Germany into France but was prevented from selling the relevant products because of the exclusive right to the Grundig trade mark held by Consten.[41] The Commission found that the agreement between Consten and Grundig ran counter to the EEC Treaty's competition rules. In particular, the possibility of preventing parallel imports, inherent in the absolute territorial protection of the GINT (Grundig) trademark in France, was found to be incompatible with EEC antitrust law.[42]

The *Consten and Grundig* decision is notable because it heralded the dual character of early Community antitrust law. On the one hand EEC antitrust law aimed to promote integration by guaranteeing the proper functioning of the free

---

[39] Emphasis in enforcement action lay on market-sharing, quotas and price-fixing. See Commission of the EEC, above, n. 40, at 25ff. and Commission of the EEC, *Fifth Annual Report on Competition Policy* (Brussels, 1976), 8ff.

[40] An instructive example is provided in the Commission decision in *Transocean Marine Paint I* [1967] JO 163/10.Several European and non-European firms which manufactured marine paints had formed the Transocean Marine Paint Association. The Association had as its object the distribution and sale of special types of marine paint, next to the normal ones which were marketed by the member individually. In spite of a clause in the agreement which conferred territorial protection (normally *per se* prohibited under EC antitrust law), the Commission exempted it from the prohibition in Art. 81(1) EC because it permitted the members to rationalise and intensify production and marketing of the paint.

[41] Commission decision *Consten and Grundig* [1964] OJ 161/2545. Unsurprisingly given the frequent use of these contracts and their obvious effects on the unity of the common market, the decision concerned exclusive distribution. Grundig had concluded an agreement with Consten on the basis of which Consten would be the sole distributor of Grundig products in France. Grundig transferred its trade mark rights for the French territory to Consten, which in turn agreed not to sell Grundig products outside France. The territorial protection thus established on the basis of an exclusive distribution agreement prevented any form of parallel imports.

[42] The ECJ annulled the Commission decision but the judgment did not challenge the Commission's view that EEC antitrust law prohibits hindering parallel trade. Subsequently, the ECJ also ruled explicitly that agreements between undertakings may not, under the EC antitrust rules, restrict the free flow of goods. See, e.g., Case 22/71 *Béguelin* [1971] ECR 949.

market mechanism. On the other, freedom of competition did not include those business practices which were capable of dividing the market along national lines, even if such behaviour enhanced competition. The effect of these principles on practice is evident from the early Commission decisions regarding selective distribution systems.[43] An example is provided by the Commission decision with respect to the selective distribution agreements notified by Omega, a producer of luxury watches.[44] The Commission considered most criteria in the standard agreement which required certain qualitative standards to be upheld by the retailers not to be a restriction of competition in the sense of Article 81(1) EC. It provided a negative clearance for those clauses. The fact that Omega had limited the number of authorised sellers in proportion to the expected level of sales in the relevant area was, however, judged to restrict competition because it could lead to market division on a territorial basis. Contrary to the "qualitative" selection criteria, the territorial conditions were labelled "quantitative" restrictions on competition which were considered to fall within the scope of Article 81(1) EC. The Commission did not provide an exemption to the provisions on the basis of Article 81(3).[45]

The typical importance given to the effects of vertical agreements on integration can also be perceived in the Commission's approach towards horizontal agreements. The Commission's forthright condemnation of horizontal restraints on the economic freedom of parties was as much in line with orthodox antitrust jurisprudence as it assisted in eliminating impediments to cross-border trade.[46] But the distinctive nature of early Community antitrust law did come to the fore in the Commission's handling of horizontal restraints, for example in its policy with respect to joint ventures. In its examination of the compatibility of joint ventures with Article 81 EC the Commission tended to conclude at first instance that co-operation between potential competitors was likely to restrict competition. The Commission would thus hold joint ventures to infringe Article 81(1) EC because of the restriction they implied on the freedom of firms to deal with others. Not blind to the positive effects on competition, however, the Commission often exempted those anti-competitive

---

[43] Selective distribution is a distribution system in which only those distributors which fulfill certain criteria, usually regarding presentation, the outlet or expertise of the distributor, are permitted to sell a product.

[44] Commission decision of 28 October 1970, *Omega* [1970] OJ L242/22.

[45] Other early examples of the emphasis on free cross-border trade include *Miller International Schallplatten GmbH* [1976] OJ L357/40, where the Commission did not authorise export prohibitions in exclusive dealing agreements because it reckoned that the negative effect on the flow of trade between the Member States would jeopardise the attainment of the objectives of a single market. In *GERO-fabriek* [1977] OJ L16/8, the Commission repeated that clauses in wholesale and retail sales conditions which relate to export prohibitions constituted non-exemptable infringements of Art. 81(1) EC.

[46] Early examples of the Commission's clear condemnation of genuine cartels are *International Quinine Agreement* [1969] JO L192/5, which concerned price-fixing and territorial quotas and *Dyestuffs* [1969] JO L195/11. The first fines for antitrust law infringements were levied for naked restraints. See *European Sugar Industry* [1973] OJ L140/17 and *Vereniging van Cementhandelaren* [1972] OJ L13/34.

agreement on the basis of Article 81(3) EC where it considered that the joint venture could contribute to European integration.[47]

Before turning to the second substantive limb of EC antitrust law, enforcing Article 82 EC, it is useful to note a procedural consequence of the Commission's practice with respect to Article 81 EC. As has been seen, the Commission first considered whether agreements contained restrictions on the parties' freedom to trade across borders. If so, the agreement was automatically judged to restrict competition and to fall within the scope of Article 81(1) EC. That assertion then opened the way for a more comprehensive assessment of the actual effects of the agreement on competition. The Commission exempted those elements of the agreement which it considered not to be detrimental to the establishment of the common market and in which the supposed anticompetitive effects of the restraints on the freedom of one of the economic parties were balanced by other beneficial effects on competition. As a consequence of this approach, the Commission would regularly issue an exemption to the prohibition to restrict competition for agreements which the Commission itself considered not to reduce competition. Companies were therefore obliged to notify agreements with a positive or neutral effect on competition in order to obtain an exemption.[48]

Application of Article 82 EC was rare in the first period of Community antitrust law. Commentators at the time even feared that the provision might remain a "dead letter".[49] The relative low profile of Article 82 was probably due to two factors. First, time was needed to interpret the concept of abuse of a dominant position within the framework of the EEC Treaty.[50] Secondly, reticence may have been exercised for political reasons. Large companies, those most likely to hold dominant positions, were still very much identified with their

---

[47] Here the most instructive examples are *Henkel/Colgate* [1972] JO 14/14, in which joint research activities, although falling within Art. 81(1), because the research activities could also have been undertaken individually, received an exemption. See also *MAN-SAVIEM* [1972] JO L31/29 and *Transocean Marine Paint (No 1)* [1967] JO 163/10 (mentioned above). An exception to this line of practice was *SHV-Chevron* in which the Commission provided a negative clearance for a joint-venture: [1975] OJ L38/14.

[48] The Commission was however not completely consistent in its approach. In its *SABA* decision, e.g., it applied a comprehensive test of the overall competition effects when assessing whether the agreements fell within Art. 81(1) EC; *SABA* [1976] OJ L28/19, at 26. Although it acknowledged that the contractual prohibition on SABA wholesalers in Germany supplying goods covered by the agreement to private customers restricted their economic freedom, the Commission concluded that such a prohibition was "neither in its object nor in its effect a restriction of competition within the meaning of Article 85(1) [now Art. 81 EC]. This prohibition admittedly prevents SABA wholesalers from competing with SABA specialist retailers in Germany and SABA dealers from other countries of the Community however the restriction of the retailers economic freedom implies certain positive effects on competition". See further on the balancing of the economic effects when applying Art. 81(1) EC, below, Ch. 3.

[49] I. Samkalden and I. Druker, "Legal Problems Relating to Article 86 of the Rome Treaty" (1966) 3 CMLRev 158–83 at 162.

[50] The only experience in Europe with the abuse concept derived from the similar provision in the ECSC Treaty (Art. 66) and the German *Gesetz gegen Wettbewerbsbeschränkungen*, which themselves had only recently been established. See, extensively on the origins of the abuse concept in Europe, Gerber, above, n. 4.

home countries. The importance given to the notion of "national champions", present even in today's European Union, made it inopportune for the recently established new European bureaucracy to apply the prohibition of Article 82.[51]

The dormant state of Article 82 EC was brought to an end only in the early 1970s with the high profile *Continental Can* case.[52] The case concerned the acquisition by Continental Can, an American company, of controlling shares in a Dutch company.[53] The key question was whether the prohibition formulated in Article 82 of the Treaty covered mergers and acquisitions. The Commission's interpretation was in the affirmative. It concluded that an already dominant firm which expanded that dominance through an acquisition thus abused its dominant position. This reasoning was inventive. From the text of Article 82 EC it appeared that the provision would be activated only where a dominant undertaking actually abused its dominance. The appropriate test would then have been whether Continental Can would have been able to acquire the shares of the Dutch company had it not held a dominant position. Continental Can pleaded this test but the Commission turned it down. The Commission reasoned, consistently with its decisions in the area of Article 81 EC, that a reduction in the number of different products available, which the take-over would cause, restricted the free choice of consumers and, thus, restricted competition.[54]

The further development of the Commission's concept of abuse of dominant position was determined mainly by judgments of the Court of Justice. Article 82 EC is therefore less illustrative of the Commission conception of Community antitrust law. Still, it is clear even from this brief description that elements of the Commission's interpretation of Article 81 EC reappear in its Article 82 EC practice. First, free competition is interpreted in a way specific to the European Community. The main objective of the EEC, economic integration, played an important role in Commission enforcement of Community antitrust law. Secondly, the conception of free competition is derived from a belief in economic freedom of parties. Restricting the economic freedom of undertakings and consumers to chose between suppliers and products constitutes an infringement of Community antitrust law.

---

[51] Gerber, above, n. 1, at 113. It should be noted however that the absence of official Commission decisions does not mean that there was no enforcement of Art. 82 EC. Rather, the Commission used its powers in the realm of Art. 82 informally. It was often able to ensure protection of SMEs without having to reach final decisions. Commission threat of action where small firms suffered from boycotts was typically sufficient for restoring competition without its having to have recourse to formal decisions: W. Hallstein, *Die europäische Gemeinschaft* (Düsseldorf, Econ Verlag, 1973), 128.

[52] *Continental Can* [1972] JO L7/25. The first Commission finding of an abuse of dominant position, *GEMA (No 1)* [1971] JO L134/15, predated *Continental Can*.

[53] The abovementioned political objections to applying Art. 82 EC therefore did not arise. There was broad political concern among the Member States about take-overs of European companies by American ones. In addition anxiety had arisen more generally about the increasingly concentrated state of European industry: J. Bentil, "Control of the Abuse of Monopoly Power in EEC Business Law" (1975) 12 *CMLRev* 59–75 and Gerber, above, n. 4, at 89.

[54] *Continental Can*, above, n. 52.

1.2.2 Court of Justice Case Law in the Early Period

From the outset the Court of Justice took up a central position in the development of EC antitrust law. Even before Regulation 17 had come into force and the Commission became active in policing antitrust problems, the Court had handed down a judgment in a preliminary reference procedure dealing with Community antitrust law. The question to be answered in that procedure was whether the EC Treaty's antitrust provisions were directly effective. The Court ruled that although Articles 81 and 82 EC had in principle been applicable from the time of the entry into force of the Treaty they could not be relied upon before national courts in absence of an adequate enforcement framework. The procedural Articles in the Treaty, Articles 84 and 85 EC, were not of such a nature to ensure complete and consistent application of the Treaty's substantive antitrust provisions without the guidance provided by an enforcement regulation.[55] All subsequent Court of Justice judgments were delivered after Regulation 17 had come into force.[56] Although the Court of Justice's case law largely coincided with Commission practice, it diverged notably in some instances.

The area of Community antitrust law which the two institutions approached differently was the interpretation of Article 81 EC. The Court considered that, because Article 81 EC speaks of a prohibition for agreements which have as their "object or effect" the distortion of competition, there is a need to consider the precise purpose of the agreement in its economic context. Where the object of the agreement is not clearly and intentionally damaging competition, its market consequences should be examined before a conclusion on its anticompetitiveness can be drawn. In *STM* v. *Maschinenbau Ulm*, for instance, the Court ruled explicitly that the competition in question was to be understood in its economic context. Reference was made to the market situation as it would materialise in

---

[55] *De Geus* v. *Bosch*, above, n. 12. The significance of the Court's implicit judgment that, in principle, the EC Treaty did provide rights for individuals which could be relied upon before national courts is hardly underestimated. Roemer AG's Opinion in *Van Gend en Loos*, which is considered the landmark judgment in connection with the direct effect of Treaty provisions, relied heavily and explicitly on the precedent formulated in *De Geus* v. *Bosch*. In *Van Gend en Loos* Roemer AG concluded that "[a]nyone familiar with Community law knows that in fact it does not just consist of contractual relations between a number of States considered as subjects of the law of nations. The Community has its own institutions, independent of the Member States, endowed with the power to take administrative measures and to make rules of law which directly create rights in favour of and impose duties on Member States as well as their authorities and citizens. . . . The EC Treaty contains in addition provisions which are clearly intended to be incorporated in national law and to modify or supplement it. Examples of such provisions are Articles 85 and 86 [now Arts. 81 and 82 EC] relating to competition (prohibition of certain agreements, prohibition of the abuse of a dominant position in the Common Market), the application of the rules on competition by the authorities of Member States (article 88)[now Art. 84 EC]: Case 26/62 *Van Gend en Loos* v. *Nederlandse administratie der belastingen* [1963] ECR 1, Opinion of Roemer AG at 20.

[56] Direct effect for Arts. 81 and 82 EC was explicitly granted in Case 127/73 *BRT* v. *SABAM* [1974] ECR 51 at 62 and Case 155/73 *Sacchi* [1974] ECR 409, respectively. As has been said, Arts. 81 and 82 EC do not have direct effect in those economic sectors which are excluded from the scope of Reg. 17 as long as there is no specific reg. in force.

the absence of the relevant agreement or clauses.[57] Clauses in agreements which restricted the economic freedom of the parties to it but which were indispensable to the introduction of a product or service on the market did not, in the Court's view, necessarily restrict competition in the sense of Article 81(1) EC. In this respect the Court's conception of competition, which underlay the interpretation of the Treaty's antitrust law provisions, diverged from that of the Commission. While the Commission focused on the economic freedom of the competitor, the Court principally examined an agreement's effect on the degree of competition prevailing on the relevant market.

Yet the Court was not consistent in this approach. The seminal *Consten and Grundig* judgment, which was handed down in the same year as *STM* v. *Maschinenbau Ulm*, is illustrative.[58] First, the Court agreed with the Commission's view that Article 81 EC applied to a distribution ("vertical") agreement although the parties concerned operated at different levels of economic activity and were therefore unlikely to compete with each other in the first place. Departing from its market analysis, the Court held that an agreement between a producer and distributor could restore the division of the common market along national boundaries. Since such a development would frustrate a fundamental objective of European market integration, the Court, like the Commission, considered it intolerable under Community antitrust law: "[s]ince the agreement thus aims at isolating the French market for Grundig products and maintaining artificially . . . separate national markets within the Community, it is therefore such as to distort competition in the common market". Sheltered from all effective competition the distributor could charge arbitrary prices for Grundig products on the French market. In the face of these observations the Court held that "no further considerations of economic data" and "no possible favourable effects of the agreement in other respects" could in any way lead to a different solution under Article 81(1) EC.[59] The Court concurred with the Commission which equated a limitation of the freedom to trade a product across borders with a restriction of competition under Article 81(1)

---

[57] When considering an agreement's effect on competition the Court considered commercial features of the relevant market. In particular, the nature and quantity of the products covered by the agreement, the position on the market of the relevant companies, the isolated nature of the disputed agreement or its position in a series of agreements, the severity of the clauses and the opportunities allowed for other commercial competitors in the same products by way of parallel re-exportation and importation. See Case 56/65 *Société la Technique Minière* v. *Maschinenbau Ulm* [1966] ECR 234 and Case 23/67 *Brasserie de Haecht* v. *Wilkin (No. 1)* [1967] ECR 407.

[58] Joined cases 56 & 58/64 *Etablissements Consten Sàrl and Grundig-Verkaufs GmbH* v. *Commission* [1966] ECR 299.

[59] *Consten and Grundig* v. *Commission*, above, n. 58, at 343. Analogously, the Court held with respect to the alternative criterion which has to be fulfilled in order for Art. 81 EC to be applicable, effect on Member State trade, that it was "particularly important . . . whether the agreement is capable of constituting a threat, either direct or indirect, actual or potential, to *freedom of trade between Member States* in a manner which might harm the attainment of the objectives of a single market between states". See further on the effect on trade between Member States, Ch. 4.

EC.[60] Consequently, it ruled that the "absence in the contested decision of any analysis of the effects of the agreement on competition between similar products of different makes does not, in itself, constitute a defect in the decision". Thus, the Court in its application of Article 81 EC disregarded the economic context of the agreement which it considered in *STM* v. *Maschinenbau Ulm* essential to an assessment of an agreement's effects on competition.

The inconsistencies in the application of Article 81 EC to contractual restraints on the economic freedom of distributors persists in the Court's subsequent case law. Now it based its assessment of an agreement's compatibility with Article 81(1) EC on an analysis of market realities, following *STM* v. *Maschinenbau Ulm*.[61] Then it followed its *Consten and Grundig* judgment by limiting the analysis to an interpretation of the wording of the clauses of the agreement at issue. It ruled for instance that an agreement which contains *a clause that restricts* exports, by its very nature constituted a restriction of *competition* since the agreed purpose of the contracting parties is the endeavour to isolate parts of the market from the rest. These types of agreements distort competition because they may contribute to a more or less rigorous division of the markets. An analysis of the market circumstances was not considered necessary in this case.[62]

In sum, the Court's initial case law, despite the noted ambiguity, was clearly directed to market integration. Generally, the Court applied a more extensive test of the market circumstances and laid less emphasis than the Commission did on the wording of the clauses in an agreement. The Court's economic analysis became erratic when agreements sported territorial restrictions. Then the Court, like the Commission, typically equated unrestricted competition with unrestricted cross-border trade.

With respect to horizontal agreements the Court's case law followed Commission practice very closely. The Court endorsed the Commission's strict prohibition under Article 81 EC on fixing prices or dividing markets among potential competitors. Since these kinds of agreements have the restriction of

---

[60] Contrast Roemer AG and the intervening German government, who pleaded for an assessment of the economic consequences of agreements when applying Art. 81(1) EC. Roemer AG concluded that "[i]t seems to me wrong to have regard to such observation only for the application of paragraph (3) of Article 85 [now Art. 81 EC], because that paragraph requires an examination from other points of view which are special and different. But in particular (as is shown by *Société Technique Minière* v. *Maschinenbau Ulm GmbH*) it would be artificial to apply Article 85(1) [now Art. 81], on the basis of purely theoretical considerations, to situations which upon closer inspection would reveal no appreciable adverse effects on competition, in order then to grant exemption on the basis of Article 85(3) [now Art. 81 EC]". Properly understood therefore the application of Art. 81(1) EC (ex Art. 85) requires concrete examination of the real effects on competition of a given agreement. In this analysis Roemer AG relied explicitly on analogic provisions of the German Law against Restraints of Competition: Roemer AG's Opinion in *Consten and Grundig* v. *Commission*, above, n. 62, at 358–9.

[61] Case 5/69 *Völk* v. *Etablissements Vervaecke* [1969] ECR 295, at 302. See also Case 1/71 *Société Anonyme Cadillon* v. *Firma Höss Maschinenbau KG* [1971] ECR 351 and Case 26/76 *Metro-SB-Größmärkte GmbH* v. *Commission* [1977] ECR 1875 at 1904–8.

[62] Case 19/77 *Miller International Schalplatten GmbH* v. *Commission* [1978] ECR 131.

competition as their objective the question of their effect, on which Court and Commission could possibly disagree, was redundant.[63]

The same can be said for Article 82 EC. Like the Commission, the Court was less active in applying Article 82 EC. Apart from a small number of preliminary references, the Court presented its view on the Article only in 1973 in the appeal from the Commission's decision in *Continental Can*.[64] The Court confirmed the Commission interpretation of Article 82 EC. The EC Treaty's rules on competition should be understood in the light of the general objectives of the Treaty. The overriding question was not therefore whether in acquiring the relevant shares in the Dutch company Continental Can had used its dominant position, but rather what consequences the behaviour had on competition in the common market. That concept, competition in the common market, did not refer to an exclusively economic test of the effects. Instead the objectives of the Treaty are central to an interpretation of competition on the common market. A dominant enterprise which, by increasing its dominance, substantially alters the supply situation in the common market, thus reducing the range of consumer choice, may undermine the objectives of the Treaty and be contrary to Article 82 EC, the Court ruled.

The Court's concepts of "abuse" and of "dominant position" were subsequently refined within this framework. Abuse, it ruled, is "an objective concept relating to the behaviour of an undertaking in a dominant position which is such as to influence the structure of a market where, as a result of the very presence of the undertaking in question, the degree of competition is weakened and which, through recourse to methods different from those which condition normal competition in products or services on the basis of the transactions of commercial operators, has the effect of hindering the maintenance of the degree of competition still existing in the market or the growth of that competition".[65] The dominant position itself consists of "a position of economic strength enjoyed by an undertaking which enables it to hinder the maintenance of effective competition on the relevant market by allowing it to behave to an appreciable extent independently of its competitors and customers and ultimately of consumers".[66] By formulating these interpretations of the Treaty in this way the Court largely endorsed Commission practice with respect to Article 82 EC.

Despite the divergence with respect to the economic analysis required in the application of Article 81(1) EC then the Court and the Commission were of the

---

[63] Case 41/69 *ACF Chemiefarma NV* v. *Commission* [1970] ECR 661, at 695ff.

[64] Case 6/72 *Europemballage and Continental Can* v. *Commission* [1973] ECR 215. The case, it will be recalled from the discussion of the Commission decisions above, concerned the take-over of a Dutch firm by an American firm which itself was already dominant in the relevant market before the acquisition.

[65] See, e.g., Case 85/76 *Hoffmann-La Roche* v. *Commission* [1979] ECR 461 at 541. See also Case 27/76 *United Brands* v. *Commission* [1978] ECR 207; Case 322/82 *Michelin* v. *Commission* [1983] ECR 3461.

[66] See *United Brands* v. *Commission*, above, n. 65, *Michelin* v. *Commission* , above, n.65.

same mind in developing Community antitrust law through their interpretation of Articles 81 and 82 EC.

1.2.3 The Prime Objective of EC Antitrust Law: Integration

By adopting Regulation 17 the Council had conferred broad autonomy on the Commission, under exclusive control of the Court of Justice, to develop Community antitrust law. The exclusive powers of the Commission and Court of Justice in the antitrust law field ensured that the market integration objective played a dominant role in the interpretation of the broad Treaty provisions on competition. Relatively unhindered by political preferences in the Member States, the two Community institutions which have the closest affinity with the supranational limb of European integration shaped an antitrust law practice which was in the first instance functional to the process of market integration. The Court of Justice's noted preference for teleological interpretation of the EC Treaty played an important role in the construction of the system.[67] That the Court interpreted the Treaty's antitrust rules in this light emerges most clearly from its judgment in *Italy* v. *Council and Commission*. The Court asserted that the antitrust rules were to be read in the context of the Treaty's Preamble which clarifies the thrust of the rules on competition. Reference was particularly to be made to those provisions relating to elimination of barriers and to fair competition, both of which in the Court's opinion were necessary for bringing about a common market.[68] The Treaty's rules on trade and competition were directed to abolishing formal obstacles to trade between Member States which hindered the proper functioning of the market mechanism and, thus, the integration process. Articles 28–30 EC (ex Articles 30–36) and Articles 39–55 (ex Articles 48–66) guarantee free movement. These provisions directed to the Member States were incorporated in the Treaty to prevent states from obstructing the establishment of the common market. The EC Treaty's antitrust rules which are primarily addressed to private parties, equally support the principle of integration through the functioning of the common market. The result was that agreements which potentially facilitated the erection or continuation of impediments

---

[67] For instance in *De Geus* v. *Bosch*, above, n. 59. This was expressed particularly clearly in Lagrange AG's Opinion: "il faut se référer, . . . au contexte ou à l'esprit du texte". See also Judge Pescatore who reveals that in the area of antitrust the "spirit of the Treaty" served as the framework of reference for deciding "hard cases": P. Pescatore, "Les Objectifs de la Communauté Européenne comme Principes d'Interprétation dans la Jurisprudence de la Court de Justice" in *Miscellanea W.J. Ganshof van der Meersch* (Brussels, Émile Bruylant, 1972), ii, 325–63. An early recognition of the role of teleology as the main interpretative tool is provided in W. van Gerven, "Twelve Years EEC Competition Law (1962–1973) Revisited" (1974) 11 *CMLRev* 38–61, at 49; although the AG considers the decision well reasoned in law he recognises that "the Court could have motivated the opposite opinion as adequately". Cf. B. van der Esch, "The Principles of Interpretation Applied by the Court of Justice of the European Communities and their Relevance for the Scope of the EEC Competition Rules" (1991–2) 15 *FILJ* 366–97.

[68] Case 32/65 *Italy* v. *Council and Commission*, [1966] ECR 234 at 405

to inter-Member State trade were considered contrary to Community antitrust law, irrespective of their effect on competition. Moreover, where antitrust law was explicitly considered an element in the system, other Treaty provisions and aspects of the Community system could be used for the interpretation and application of Community antitrust policy.[69]

1.3 THE SECOND PHASE: CERTAIN POSITIVE MEASURES

The emphasis on integration elements in the analysis would continue to determine the direction of EC antitrust law well into the 1990s. However, whilst integration persisted as the principal motivation behind antitrust law enforcement, the type of reasoning gradually shifted during that period. From the early 1980s onwards the "second generation" of EC antitrust law decisions emerged. This next phase was characterised by a shift in focus away from establishing the common market towards regulating processes on that market. In antitrust law this coincided with a shift from the focus on potential private barriers to intra-Community trade towards a perception of antitrust law in which broader concerns of the Common Market's political economy played a role. Albeit with continued reference to the integration paradigm, the emphasis on the freedom of inter-state trade in the assessment of antitrust cases gradually made way for increased use of alternative economical and political considerations.

The development was mainly driven by the European Commission which, looking for tools to advance the Community's integration venture, discovered the broad potential for genuine supranational economic policy on the basis of the Treaty's competition rules. The relevance of the economic context in which competition took place, repeatedly enunciated in Court of Justice case law, indicated that the changing economic environment in the Community justified an adjusted Community competition policy.[70]

The factors at the origin of this development, which influenced the further evolution of the EC's antitrust system, are central to the discussion in this section. The section consists of two subsections.[71] The first addresses the prelude

---

[69] That this was not only the Court's view but also that of the Commission can be observed in the Commission's Annual Reports on Competition Policy. Antitrust law was commonly applied in conjunction with various other policy aims. In its Fourth Report, for example, the Commission declared that it had intensified antitrust law enforcement action in view of rising inflation in order to prevent additional price increases. Commission of the EC, *Fourth Annual Report on Competition Policy* (Brussels, 1975), 7.

[70] The "economic environment" had changed in two senses by the early 1980s. First, the common market was gradually being established, as a consequence of which concern for inter-state trade lost some of its prominence. Secondly, the economic circumstances in the Community's Member States had detoriated significantly as a result of the effects of the oil crises in the 1970s. Together these developments opened the route towards more positive Commission policy towards competition.

[71] In this second phase the scope of Community antitrust law expanded so rapidly that it is even less practicable to discuss all, or even most of, the individual decisions. The discussion is therefore even more overtly limited to identifying a general trend. The Commission and Court continued to share their basic understanding of the objectives of Community antitrust law. The analysis of their

to the shift in the central objectives of Community antitrust policy. The second illustrates how the new goals were accomodated in antitrust practice.

1.3.1 "Workable" Competition

The gradual change in emphasis in assessment of antitrust problems which took shape by the late 1970s was anticipated by a Court of Justice judgment in the previous stage of Community antitrust law development. The Court asserted that the Commission in its antitrust policy was authorised to consider objectives which went beyond those directly linked to eliminating barriers to intra-Community trade. In addition to promoting the swift establishment of a common market, the Court held that the Commission could validly consider arguments related to administering the operation of that market. Even if the primary object of the Treaty's antitrust provisions was to eliminate obstacles to free movement, these rules also enabled "the Community authorities to carry out *certain positive, though indirect, action with a view to promoting a harmonious development of economic activities within the whole Community, in accordance with Article 2 of the Treaty*".[72] Initially, as the previous section revealed, the Commission concentrated on the elimination of the obstacles to the free movement of goods and generally refrained from taking such "positive" action.[73] Towards the end of the 1970s, however, the secondary objective of Community competition policy, as pronounced by the Court, came to be used more prominently. Emphasis on the market-building objective in antitrust law decisions subsided to "certain positive action".[74]

The start of the application of the antitrust provisions beyond guaranteeing inter-state trade was provided in one of the landmark Court of Justice judgments. In *Metro I* the Court explored the type of standard by which the Commission was to test the competition effects of notified agreements.[75] In the relevant decision the Commission had exempted a selective distribution system

---

practice is therefore united. It is only in the early 1990s, after the establishment of the CFI, that a certain dichotomy between the two institutions—relevant to the thrust of this book—can be discerned.

[72] Case 14/68 *Walt Wilhelm* v. *Bundeskartellamt* [1969] ECR 1, at 13ff (emphasis added).

[73] J.-F. Verstrynge, "Current Antitrust Policy Issues in the EEC: Some Reflections on the Second Generation of EEC Competition Policy" in B. Hawk (ed.), *Annual Proceedings of the Fordham Corporate Law Institute 1984: Antitrust and Trade Policies in International Trade* (New York, Transjuris, 1985), 673–98. It should be noted that this generalisation is qualified by elements of "positive" antitrust law enforcement in the first phase. The preceding para. revealed that a number of joint ventures between firms from different Member States were assessed positively and granted an exemption under Art. 81(3) EC in spite of the restrictions on competition they entailed. Thus the Commission already "positively" promoted pan-European integration of firms in the first phase.

[74] Note that this is not to suggest that there was a clear-cut division between the first and second generation type of antitrust law cases. Both "generations" explicitly refer to the integration paradigm and the type of reasoning more closely associated with the first generation, directly aimed at guaranteeing intra-Community trade, remained an important element in "second generation" case law.

[75] *Metro-SB-Großmärkte* v. *Commission* ("*Metro I*"), above, n. 61.

in the electronic consumer goods sector. A wholesaler lodged an action for annulment of the exemption decision with the Court because it could not obtain access to the system. It held that competition was restricted through the selective distribution system. The Court upheld the Commission exemption. It clarified that the appropriate competition standard which the Commission should apply when examining whether it should grant an exemption was not necessarily that of "perfect competition". The Treaty's requirement that competition shall not be distorted, the Court explained, implies the existence of workable competition on the market. The degree of competition which is aspired to under the concept of "workable" competition is that degree of competition which is required for the attainment of the objectives of the Treaty, in particular the creation of a common market. The Court further ruled that the degree of competition required under Community antitrust law could vary in nature and intensity according to particular features of producs and markets.[76] In particular the powers conferred on the Commission under Article 81(3) EC showed, in the Court's opinion, that the requirements for the maintenance of workable competition could be reconciled with safeguarding other objectives. Restrictions of competition could therefore be permissible in some instances as long as they were essential to the attainment of the alternative objectives pursued. The concept of "workable competition", thus set out, revealed broad margins for discretion which the Commission had in its enforcement of Article 81(3) EC.[77]

Two elements of the Court's reasoning proved to be particularly important for the further development of Community antitrust policy by the Commission. First, the Court explicated once more that free competition does not form an absolute superior value under EC antitrust law. The pertinent degree of competition varies among different markets, depending on what is required for achieving the objectives of the European Community as defined in the Treaty. The degree of competition required by the Treaty could accomodate alternative Treaty objectives in antitrust law enforcement action. Secondly, the degree of competition could vary, in nature and intensity, depending on the economic structures of the markets at hand. It was in this context that the Court mentioned explicitly that the powers conferred on the Commission under Article

---

[76] *Ibid.*, at 1904.

[77] The basic concept of "workable competition" was derived from a study of competition policy by an American scholar: J. Clarck, *Competition as a Dynamic Process* (Washington, DC, Brookings Institution, 1961). As a competition standard "workable competition" has been susceptible to continued criticism. It is clear that "workable" is sufficiently vague to generate a vast area of administrative discretion in applying it to individual cases. Commentators argue that there should be no place under competition laws for balancing pure competition objectives with other policy objectives. See the critical appraisal of the "workable competition" notion as applied by the ECJ, in A. Väth, *Die Wettbewerbskonzeption des Europäischen Gerichtshof* (Bayreuth, P.C.O., 1987), at 162; "[h]ier offenbarte der Gerichtshof exakt jene wenig überzeugende Mischung aus Ansätzen der Wettbewerbsfreiheit und administrativen Dirigismen". Equally critical is W. Kerber, *Die Europäische Fusionskontrollpraxis und die Wettbewerbskonzeption der EG* (Bayreuth, P.C.O., 1994) at 185–8. More positive on the practicality of "workable competition" as a conceptual basis for Community antitrust laws R. Whish, *Competition Law*, 3rd ed. (London, Butterworths, 1993), 10–11.

81(3) EC allow for a degree of policy discretion. Thus, the Court in its *Metro I* judgment ruled that the Treaty's antitrust provisions may be implemented with a view to pursuing a mix of policy objectives.[78] On this basis the Commission reconciled its role in guaranteeing the maintenance of "workable competition" on the basis of the antitrust provisions with broader economic policy objectives which it pursued.

Indeed, the potential for Community economic policy on the basis of the antitrust rules was considerable if one read the Court decisions in *Walt Wilhelm* and *Metro I* together. The former entitled the Commission to carry out certain positive action to promote the harmonious development of economic activities within the Community. The latter explained that the Commission was free, within certain limits, to establish the degree of competition in the different markets according to the degree of competition the Commission considered desirable in each market, given its structure and the nature of the product concerned.

What happened was that the Commission based its antitrust policy on these two dicta, read together. Where economic circumstances in certain markets were such (*Metro I*) as to require it to carry out certain positive, though indirect, action under Article 81(3) EC with a view to promoting a harmonious development of economic activities within the whole Community (*Walt Wilhelm*) the Commission felt free to adjust the enforcement of antitrust law accordingly.

1.3.2 The Sectorial Approach

This formed the legal background against which the Community and its Member States felt the economic effects of the oil crises in the 1970s. Partly as a consequence of the economic malaise, a lull occurred in the process of European economic integration. Member States wanted to retain what little remained of the power to regulate their economies in order to moderate the effects of the crisis. Sentiments turned against economic integration and in favour of protection of national industries.[79]

The economic crisis and consequent problems for Community integration unhappily coincided with the exhaustion of the Community's integration tools. The EC integration means were tailored to the needs of market integration, as opposed to policy integration. The Rome Treaty provided powers to the Community institutions mainly with reference to their role in ensuring the free flow of goods between Member States.[80] Most measures towards establishing

---

[78] Verstrynge, above, n. 73, at 678.

[79] A depiction of the prevailing mood and the resulting obstacles to the furtherance of Community integration is provided by E. Stein, "The European Community in 1983: A Less Perfect Union?" (1983) 20 *CMLRev* 641–56. In the same sense, see T. Koopmans, "Europe and Its Lawyers in 1984" (1985) 22 *CMLRev* 9–18.

[80] Explanations for the predominance of negative integration type of measures in the Rome Treaty varies. It has been held that at the time the basic economic orders of the states concluding the Rome Treaty included only very limited policies beyond those that ensured the framework in which

the common market on this basis, so-called "negative" integration measures, had been taken.[81] Yet although the Community had thus "outgrown" the Treaty of Rome, the sentiments of "Eurosclerosis" precluded that the necessary next steps towards increased "positive" integration were taken. The types of measures which were required to take the next step either were absent in the EEC Treaty or their application met political objections.

In the specific area of competition and antitrust law the result of the crisis, in accordance with general trends, was a tendency to protect national industry from foreign competition. Generally the importance given to the competition law rules abated. The reduced belief in the benefits of free competition was natural and fertile ground for Member States' acceptance of the mitigated degree of competition, enshrined in the concept of "workable" competition. Strict application of the Community's competition rules was not feasible in these circumstances. The Commission accepted that "the persistence of conditions of crisis prompts questions as to the role that competition policy should play and as to the respective merits of rigidity and flexibility in its application".[82] Answering this question itself, the Commission concluded that the merit of "flexibility" had to prevail over "rigidity". In this period the Commission therefore refrained from enforcing the antitrust rules in politically sensitive areas.

Yet, the Commission was not empowered to conduct a genuine ("positive") industrial policy. This reduced the degree of flexibility that the Commission could apply in its antitrust policy. At the same time, the Community's Member States themselves had largely been deprived of the power to conduct industrial policies, precisely by the Treaty's competition rules. In the (industrial) policy vacuum, thus established, the Commission took recourse to "certain positive", though necessarily indirect, policy measures on the basis of the Treaty's antitrust law provisions. In particular the Commission relaxed its stance on competition issues in view of the crisis.[83] It started to vary the application of the antitrust rules, particularly the exemption provision in Article 81(3) EC, between the different economic sectors. The Commission's sectorially differentiated application

---

free competition could thrive. The need for positive policy integration perceived at the turn of the 1980s in such a vision derived from the gradual increase in redistributive policies in European states generally: Kapteyn, above, n. 7, at 48. Others hold that it would have been impossible to agree upon the principles and substance among all Member States which were needed to re-regulate policy-making at a supranational level. Therefore the integration measures enshrined in the EC Treaty were limited to market integration measures. See VerLoren van Themaat, above, n. 26.

[81] The distinction between positive and negative integration goes back to J. Tinbergen, *International Economic Integration* (Amsterdam, Elsevier, 1965). Negative integration is considered to comprise those measures which increase market integration by eliminating impediments to inter-state trade. Positive integration consists of common measures determining policies for the operation of the market. See more extensively on the relevance of the difference between positive and negative integration policies below, Ch. 2.

[82] Commission of the EC, *Ninth Annual Report on Competition Policy* (Brussels, 1980), 9.

[83] "In the current circumstances in particular, the Commission's competition policy not only has to sustain effective competition; it has to support an industrial policy which promotes the necessary restructuring": Commission of the EC, *Tenth Annual Report on Competition Policy* (Brussels, 1981), 9.

of the antitrust rules, derived from the flexible "workable competition" paradigm, started in the first half of the 1980s. Most strikingly it emerges from the Commission's response to the formation of "crisis cartels" in a number of economic sectors.[84]

Two specific industrial sectors profited most clearly from Community industrial policy on the basis of the antitrust rules, the synthetic fibres and steel production sectors. The crisis in those sectors led major companies to conclude common agreements on production cuts, specialisation and various other practices which restricted competition.[85] Although the "crisis cartels" took different forms and, accordingly, the restrictions of competition varied along the sectors, both "crisis cartels" constituted genuine cartels. They would be prohibited by Article 81(1) EC unless they were exempted on the basis of the third paragraph of the Article. However, under normal circumstances an exemption could not be provided. In addition to the fact that the Commission had not exempted similar agreements which had been notified a few years earlier, the agreements contained clauses which were generally considered *per se* violations of antitrust law. In particular the existence of agreed quotas for production divided among the participating firms goes against the principle of undistorted competition. The fact that the firms which participated in the crisis cartel agreements held market shares higher than two-thirds of the relevant market further suggested that an exemption could not be provided. For one of the prerequisites of an exemption under Article 81(3) EC is that competition is not eliminated in respect of a substantial part of the products in question. It was, moreover, unlikely that another requirement of the exemption provision—that consumers benefit from the restriction of competition—was fulfilled. Yet, the Commission did provide exemptions for a large number of the agreements which limited competition between firms in the crisis sectors.[86] In its own view, the Commission was constrained to let industrial policy consderations prevail over a strict interpretation of Community antitrust law because the "market mechanism had

---

[84] See, generally, above, Tenth Annual Report of Commission of the EC, n. 83, at 11: "[w]hen the economic and social effects of rationalizing an industry are particularly grave, the Commission introduces measures to deal with the specific circumstances involved, for instance those applied to the synthetic fibres, steel, shipbuilding and textiles industries to help them regain their competitive capacity".

[85] For example, agreements were adopted which guaranteed that 35% of the expected increase in demand resulting from the crisis cartel would be allocated to the participating companies; Commission decision of 4 July 1984 [1984] OJ L207/18. See also R. Bouterse, *Competition and Integration—What Goals Count?* (The Hague, Kluwer Law International, 1994), 87ff.

[86] See the following decisions: (i) for the synthetic fibre agreements; Commission Decision of 4 July 1984, above, n. 85; (ii) for petro-chemicals; Commission Decision of 19 July 1984, Case IV/30.863—*BPCL/ICI* [1984] OJ L212/1 (including the duty to reduce surplus capacity by implicit and reciprocal obligation not to compete (*cf* [1984] OJ L212/8); Commission Decision of 4 December 1986, Case IV/31.055—*ENI/Montedison* [1988] OJ L5/13 (including agreement to specialise in separate areas and mutually to transfer activities accordingly); and Commission Decision of 22 December 1987, Case IV/31.486—*Enichem/ICI* [1988] OJ L50/18 (including a joint-venture agreement and agreements to shut down or reduce capacities of certain plants).

failed to resolve the crisis".[87] Yet, as has been said, granting an exemption under Article 81(3) EC appeared irreconcilable with the wording of that provision. In order to overcome this problem the Commission interpreted the four preconditions for an exemption to the antitrust prohibition expansively. With respect to the required benefits for consumers, for instance, the Commission argued that the agreed production scheme guaranteed the continuation of supplies. If, conversely, producers had to close plants according to the market mechanism the developments would be less predictable. That insecurity of supplies, the Commission argued, would be harmful to consumers. Further the Commission argued that consumers would stand to gain from the improvement in production since the industrial structure which would eventually emerge would be healthier and more competitive, and therefore able to offer them better products thanks to greater specialisation. This reasoning goes directly against belief in competition as the main principle for economic organisation. If guaranteed and programmed production plans benefit consumers better than inter-firm rivalry than the whole concept of antitrust law which aims to protect free competition as a process of discovering consumer preferences and as a means of allocating production factors on a decentralised basis would be flawed. In this light it was particularly remarkable to hear these arguments being forwarded by the Commission, the Community's competition authority.[88]

The decisions were all the more remarkable in the light of earlier proposals to sanction crisis cartels as a matter of industrial policy on the basis of the antitrust law provisions, notably Article 81(3) EC or alternatively 83(2)(c) EC, which provides that appropriate regulations and directives may be adopted which could be designed, *inter alia*, "to define, if need be, in the various branches of the economy, the scope of the provisions of Articles 81 and 82". The Commission itself considered this option unauthorised. Nevertheless, it used the exemption provision as a tool for industrial policy in individual cases.

The sectorial approach, characterised by increased use of the discretion for positive policy measures on the basis of the application of Article 81(3) EC, was not limited to sectors which suffered from economic crisis. Similar, though less dramatic, exemptions were provided for a number of agreements in other sectors, for instance the banking sector. There the "positive" policy element pursued on the basis of antitrust policy was the establishment of European-wide services. A series of decisions under Article 81(3) EC declared the antitrust rules inapplicable to a number of, mainly national, agreements between banks. The agreements between the banks contained clauses which restricted competition

---

[87] Commission of the EC, *Thirteenth Annual Report on Competition Policy* (Brussels, 1983), para. 39.

[88] In this respect it is interesting to note that two subsidiaries of US firms did not sign the cartel crisis agreement for fear of (extra-territorial) sanctions on the basis of US antitrust laws. The legality of the Commission decisions also remains uncertain within the EC sphere because they were not appealed against. The only third party that complained and lodged an appeal with the ECJ subsequently withdrew it: Whish, above, n. 77, 229.

between themselves but those restrictions allegedly made it possible for the parties to offer services which otherwise would not have been offered.[89] The exemption granted to the *Eurocheque* agreement reveals most clearly the Commission's motivation for its policy. That agreement between a large number of banks fixed the payment of certain charges in connection with a European-wide cheque-cashing service. The Commission exempted the agreement, including the clauses which fixed prices, from the antitrust law prohibtion because it considered those restrictions indispensable to the emergence of a European-wide service.[90] The pan-European services themselves were considered desirable since they would facilitate integration of the separate economies of the Member States. The Commission's motivation for the exemption was therefore based on the importance of transnational economic integration. By exempting restrictions of competition which furthered integration, the Commission pursued positive antitrust policy in addition to the negative policy on the basis of which it prohibited agreements which separated markets along national lines.[91]

The positive sectorial policy with respect to individual agreements was extended to the Commission's exemption policy on the basis of block exemptions. Following the differentiated approach along economic sectors in individual cases, the Commission issued block-exemption regulations which were valid in specific sectors only. Exclusive distribution agreements in the motor vehicle industry, for example, obtained a block exemption even though they separated markets along national lines. Thus, competition and even economic integration concerns were sacrificed in favour of alternative (industrial) policy considerations.[92]

By way of its innovative application of the competence to declare the competition rules inapplicable to certain agreements, the Commission conducted "positive" economic policy on the basis of Community antitrust law. On top of its antitrust policy directed toward negative integration, the Commission pursued policy objectives which went beyond market building. In its own words the Commission started to issue decisions which reflected "a desire to *encourage* industrial restructuring, to improve the competitiveness of European industry,

[89] E.g. Commission Decision of 12 December 1986, Case IV/31.356—*ABI* [1987] OJ L43/51 (exemption for part of agreement in the context of the Italian Association of Banks which also contains negative clearance for some elements) and Commission Decision of 11 December 1986, Case IV/261–1–*BVB* [1987] OJ L7/27 (exemption for agreement between Belgian banks).

[90] [1985] OJ L35/43, pra. 37–9.

[91] Alternative policy goals pursued by the Commission on the basis of its discretion to provide an exemption for the antitrust rules under Art. 81(3) EC include cultural and monetary policy. See extensively Bouterse, above, n. 85.

[92] Reg. 123/85 on the Application of Art. 81(3) of the Treaty to Certain Categories of Motor Vehicle Distribution and Servicing Agreements [1985] OJ L15/16. The industrial policy arguments in favour of the group exemption are discussed in F. Lukoff, "European Competition Law and Distribution in the Motor Vehicle Industry: Commission Regulation 123/85 of 12 December 1984" (1986) 23 *CMLRev* 841–66. Other sectors that profited from the Commission's industrial policy under Art. 81(3) were the beer and petroleum (distribution) sectors; Titles II and III of Commission Reg. 1984/83 of 22 June 1983 [1983] OJ L173/5.

to *promote* research and development and innovation, and to *accelerate* the progress towards a single Community market".[93] Thus, the Commission was able to answer the needs, which increased as the internal market was gradually established, for a common industrial policy at the European level.

1.4. COMPLETING THE INTERNAL MARKET: THE SINGLE EUROPEAN ACT AND MERGER CONTROL REGULATION

The next period commenced when the Member States endorsed a Commission initiative to finalise the internal market project by 1992.[94] Enhanced legislative effectiveness by reason of the return to majority voting in some areas and the expansion of the catalogue of Community competences provided an important impetus to the realisation of the "Internal Market" project.[95] Antitrust policy itself was not an immediate issue in the debates related to the Single European Act (the "SEA"). It did not need to be because competences and tools which the Community generally lacked in other policy areas were well established in the area of antitrust law. Indeed, the previous section of this study illustrated that the Commission in the antitrust policy area had already been able to take the step from establishing the internal market toward regulating that market. Nevertheless, the events surrounding acceptance of the SEA provoked a general change in the environment and mission of the Community which indirectly affected antitrust policy. The SEA generated reinforced interest in the role of competition as a tool for regulating the Internal Market to be established.[96]

The SEA consisted primarily of a comprehensive deregulatory programme of national regulatory schemes which still obstructed the emergence of the Internal Market.[97] In this process the role of competition policy was to ensure that deregulation of markets and economic sectors brought about the expected macro-economic advantages. Deregulation expanded the scope of free competition and, thus, it enhanced the significance of Community competition policy.[98] Establishment of Community competences for environmental and industrial policy in the Single European Act had a further indirect effect on Community competition law. The expansion of Community competences in those fields

---

[93] Commission of the EC, above, n. 87, 11. Emphasis added.

[94] Leading to the Single European Act of 17 February 1986 [1987] OJ L169/7, following the Commission White Paper, "Completing the Internal Market", COM(85)310 final, of June 1985.

[95] See further, below, Ch. 2.

[96] P. Müller-Graf, "Die Freistellung vom Kartellverbot" (1992) 27 *EuR* 1–40 at 14.

[97] C.-D. Ehlermann, "The Contribution of EC Competition Policy to the Single Market" (1992) 29 *CMLRev* 257–82. The characterisation of the SEA as exclusively "deregulatory" is incomplete. Deregulation at the national level was accompanied by a considerable degree of common re-regulation at the Community level. The ability to come to re-regulation was a fundamental element of the success of the SEA and the 1992-programme. See G. Majone, *Deregulation or Re-Regulation? Policymaking in the European Community Since the Single Act*. EUI Working Paper SPS No. 93/2 (Florence, EUI, 1993).

[98] Ehlermann, above, n. 97, at 260.

discharged competition policy from these extra-competition concerns. The ensuing focus on the competition element in antitrust law facilitated the Commission's turn to confronting anti-competitive state regulation. The development of EC competition policy was finally affected in another indirect manner. The SEA had an effect on the attitude of the European business community. Trust that the internal market would be realised provoked a wave of mergers, acquisitions and joint ventures on a European scale.[99]

The principal effect of these developments on the operation of the Community's antitrust law system was twofold. First, in the quest to complete the Internal Market programme the Commission in its antitrust law enforcement actions turned increasingly to national public measures which were capable of restricting, distorting or preventing competition. Secondly, the wave of mergers on a European basis enhanced the relevance of supranational antitrust policy. That led to the officialisation of the Community's competence in merger control by way of adoption of the Community Merger Control Regulation in 1989.

The next two sections address these two developments in EC antitrust law following adoption of the Single European Act.

1.4.1. Antitrust Policy and State Measures

Until the SEA the Commission had in accordance with their wording applied the Treaty's antitrust rules exclusively to private undertakings.[100] Yet when the SEA was adopted the Commission profited from the momentum, favourable to deregulation and competition, by interpreting the scope of the Community antitrust rules broadly.[101] It started to enforce the Treaty's antitrust rules in what were traditionally public sectors of the economy.[102] Community antitrust law's "public turn" took three forms.[103] First, the Commission—and the Court of Justice—extended the interpretation of the Treaty antitrust rules' *effet utile*. The reach of Community antitrust law was expanded so as to include a ban on any Member State regulation which supported, enabled or compelled anti-competitive behaviour. In particular the Treaty's commitment to establishing a system which

---

[99] Thus diverging from previously prevailing national mergers. For an account of the economic processes following the Single European Act see L. Tsoukalis, *The New European Economy—The Politics and Economics of Integration* (Oxford, Oxford University Press, 1993), 102–17 and Gerber, above, n. 1, at 124ff.

[100] P. Pescatore, "Public and Private Aspects of European Community Competition Law" (1987) 10 *FILJ* 373–419.

[101] S. Wilks, "The Metamorphosis of European Competition Law" in F. Snyder (ed.), *European Community Law* (Aldershot, Dartmouth, 1993), i, 270–93 at 276.

[102] The link between the completion of the Common Market programme and the Commission's move to attacking anti-competitive regulation in force in the Member States is explicitly made in the Commission's *20th Annual Report on Competition Policy*: "[a]t the present stage of economic integration in the Community the barriers are greatest in markets currently subject to state regulation". Commission of the European Communities, *20th Annual Report on Competition Policy* (Brussels, 1990), 50.

[103] Gerber, above, n. 1, at 137–9.

ensures that competition in the internal market is not distorted, Article 3(g) EC, in combination with the Member States' duty to abstain from any measure which could jeopardise the attainment of the objectives of the Treaty, Article 10 EC (ex Article 5), encouraged the interpretation that state measures which facilitated behaviour contrary to the Treaty's antitrust rules themselves fell into the scope of the Treaty's prohibition on distorting competition. Secondly, Article 86 EC (ex Article 90) which had scarcely been applied before the Single European Act was actively implemented. A restrictive interpretation of the public policy exception enshrined in Article 86 EC, which allowed a derogation from antitrust rules for public undertakings in so far as this was required by the performance of the particular tasks assigned to them, effectively led to the liberalisation of various traditional state monopolies.[104] Finally, the state-aid rules which had until the 1980s been laxly applied were applied more vigorously following the adoption of the SEA.[105] While the latter two limbs to the public turn are no less important to the general development of Community competition law, they fall outside the antitrust law area, as defined in this book.[106] The discussion is therefore limited to the first line of development.

The foundation of the multi-staged and indirect application of the antitrust rules to Member States' regulative schemes had been laid in the 1970s. The Court ruled that the *effet utile* of the Treaty's antitrust rules would be compromised if Member States were allowed to develop regulation which forced undertakings into behaviour which was prohibited by Articles 81 and 82 EC. States were therefore not allowed to adopt or to maintain in force any measure which could deprive the antitrust Articles of their effectiveness.[107] Although the principle was established a decade in advance of the SEA it did not recur in the Court's case law until the mid-1980s. The noted general trend towards more active surveillance of the competitive effects of Member State regulation in the wake of the 1992 programme led the Commission actively to monitor those effects. The first step was to clarify, and expand, the interpretation of the concept of an undertaking in the sense of Articles 81 and 82 EC. The Commission proposed that public and quasi-public bodies could constitute undertakings for EC antitrust law purposes. This broad interpretation was endorsed by the Court of Justice.[108] Simultaneously, the Commission's antitrust law enforcement

---

[104] See Case 41/83 *Italy* v. *Commission* (*"British Telecom"*) [1985] ECR 873 and Case 311/84 *Télé-Marketing* [1985] ECR 3261. It would go beyond the scope of this ch.—sketching in broad lines the general development of EC antitrust law—to go into the complex development of related case law. See further on the application of Art. 86 EC (ex Art. 90): M. Edward and D. Hoskins, "Article 90: Deregulation and EC Law: Reflections arising from the XVI FIDE Conference" (1995) 32 *CMLRev* 157–86 and C.-D. Ehlermann, "Managing Monopolies: The Role of the State in Controlling Market Dominance in the European Community" (1993) 14 *ECLR* 61–9.

[105] On increased Commission action towards state aids, see Ehlermann, above, n. 104, at 274–7.

[106] See, above, Introduction, n. 2.

[107] Case 13/77 *GB-INNO-BM* v. *ATAB* [1977] ECR 2115.

[108] Thus the exercise of certain regulatory functions by British Telecom did not deprive that company of its nature as an undertaking in the exercise of those powers: *Italy* v. *Commission* (*"BritishTelecom"*), above, n. 104. Similarly the fact that the German public employment office was

action turned to anti-competitive corporate behaviour which was backed by public regulation. The Commission employed two dominant methods of action. The first was directed to state measures which defined a legal framework in which private undertakings were positively required to break the antitrust rules or where national regulation facilitated anticompetitive behaviour or reinforced its effects. The other category of Commission action challenged schemes by which Member States delegated power to groups of undertakings for producing economic regulation, which contravened Article 81 EC.

Under the first strand of analysis national legislation which required travel agents not to depart from official tariffs and not to share commission with customers by reducing fares was held incompatible with Article 81 EC read in combination with Articles 3(g) and 10 EC.[109] State regulation which forced undertakings into price-fixing was likewise prohibited.[110] The second strand stemmed from the problem of economic regulative power delegated to groups of undertakings. The Court ruled that it is incompatible with the *effet utile* of the Treaty's antitrust rules to deprive national legislation of its official character by delegating to private traders responsibility for taking decisions affecting the economic sphere.[111]

Hence the combination of widespread support for establishing a fair system of competition, reflected in the predominantly deregulative nature of the SEA, and the need to establish a genuine level playing field for business as a fundamental element of the Internal Market enabled the Community institutions to expand the reach of the Treaty's antitrust rules.[112] The far-reaching political implications of the broad application of the antitrust rules and of their deregulatory effects on national policies were subordinate to the swift completion of the internal market.

1.4.2. The Merger Control Regulation

In the same period, immediately predating formal establishment of the internal market, the Council adopted the most important legislative act in the antitrust

engaged in what could be considered an economic activity implied that it was an undertaking regardless of its legal status and the way it was financed: Case C–41/90 *Höfner and Elsner* v. *Macrotron* [1991] ECR I–1979. The Court's case law disregards the legal satus of an entity. Even a (part of) a ministry may be considered an undertaking: Case C–92/91 *Ministère Public* v. *Taillandier* [1993] ECR I–5383.

[109] Case 311/85 *Vlaamse Reisbureaus* [1987] ECR 3801. See also Joined Cases 209–13/84 *Ministère Public* v. *Asjes and others* ("*Nouvelles Frontieres*") [1986] ECR 1425.

[110] Case 66/86 *Ahmed Saeed* [1989] ECR 803. A ministerial order which endorses a minimum price system run by a trade organisation is also incompatible with the antitrust provisions because it strengthens the impact of the prior private price-fixing agreements. Case 136/86 *BNIC* v. *Aubert* [1987] ECR 4789.

[111] Case 267/86 *Van Eycke* v. *ASPA*, [1988] ECR 4769. Nevertheless, in the case at hand laws that rectrict tax advantages for certain savings were not considered incompatible with Arts. 3, 10 and 81 EC. See also the earlier Case 231/83 *Cullet* v. *Leclerc* [1985] ECR 305.

[112] Thus, A. Gardner, "The Velvet Revolution: Article 90 and the Triumph of the Free Market in Europe's Regulated Sectors" (1995) 16 *ECLR* 78-86, and Gerber, above, n. 1, at 130–1 and 145.

law area since Regulation 17. In 1989, it approved a regulation which provided the Community with the competence to control corporate mergers and acquisitions ("concentrations") of a "Community dimension".[113] The Merger Regulation formalised and completed the Commission's competence to control—as an element of its competition policy—the processes by which undertakings merge, wholly or in part.

Sixteen years of negotiations had preluded adoption of the Regulation in 1989.[114] A combination of events, in which the drive to complete the Internal Market was crucial, ensured that the regulation was ultimately adopted. First, there was the "exogenous" business dynamic prompted by the finalisation of the Internal Market programme. As has been said, the certainty that the internal market would be accomplished by the end of 1992 led to a dramatic increase in the number of concentrations. An extensive corporate restructuring programme occurred in which the whole of the European market increasingly formed the relevant framework of reference.[115] Secondly, these concentrations on a European scale logically required control at the supranational, European level. The territorial reach of national merger control laws proved insufficient for administering the European-wide processes. This development enhanced the force of the outstanding Commission claim on competence in this area of antitrust.[116] Thirdly, legal developments in the Community furthered the Commission's cause. In 1987 the Court of Justice handed down a judgment which added an element to the already existing Commission competence to pro-hibit, on the basis of Article 82 EC, mergers which engendered an increase of the market share of an undertaking which was itself already in a dominant position before the merger.[117] In *Philip Morris* the Court ruled that other types of merg-ers could fall within the prohibition of Article 81 EC.[118] Together, these events rendered adoption of the Community Merger Control Regulation possible.[119]

In addition to a qualitative expansion of the scope of EC antitrust law, the Regulation included a move from the Commission's competence to control

[113] Council Reg. 4064/89 of 21 December 1989 on the control of concentrations between under-takings [1989] OJ L395/1 (the "Merger Reg.").

[114] See the detailed discussions in E. Schwartz, "Politics as Usual: The History of European Community Merger Control" (1993) 18 *Yale Journal of International Law* 607–62 and Goyder, above, n. 12, at 386–94.

[115] Tsoukalis, above, n. 99.

[116] See, e.g., Commission of the European Communities, *19th Annual Report on Competition Policy* (Brussels, 1990): "[t]he progress made towards completing the internal and the new political environment provided a key impetus towards approval of the merger control regulation. The logic of the single market prompted Member States to agree unanimously on a system of merger control at Community level for Community-scale mergers".

[117] *Europemballage and Continental Can* v. *Commission* above, n.64.

[118] Cases 142 & 156/84 *BAT and R.J. Reynolds* v. *Commission* [1987] ECR 4487.

[119] See, more extensively, G. Majone, "The European Commission as Regulator" in G. Majone, *Regulating Europe* (London, Routledge, 1996), 61–79 at 75 and R. Dehousse and G. Majone, "The Institutional Dynamics of European Integration: From the Single Act to the Maastricht Treaty" in S. Martin (ed.), *The Construction of Europe* (Dordrecht, Kluwer, 1994), 91–112.

competitive *behaviour* towards the control of the internal market competition *structure*. The potential to influence the Community's industrial structure on the basis of administration of the Merger Control Regulation implied a broad scope for pursuing broader economic and industrial goals through antitrust policy. The Merger Control Regulation can therefore be perceived as a further embodiment of the shift which gradually took shape within Community antitrust from the legal conception of competiton, focused on the freedom to trade across borders and therefore on integration, to a broader conception of competition policy, on the basis of which the Commission was able to conduct economic policy.[120] This trend was confirmed by the actual implementation of the Merger Regulation.

The nature of the test which the Commission should apply when assessing whether a particular merger was compatible with the Common Market had been a crucial issue in the negotiations which led to the adoption of the Merger Regulation. The German representatives in Council in particular had insisted that a "pure competition" test be applied. A "pure competition" test rules out the Commission being able on the basis of the Merger Regulation to prohibit a merger for extra-competition policy reasons, e.g. because it would reduce the number of jobs. In other words the Commission should be competent to pro-hibit mergers falling within the scope of ther Merger Regulation only if these mergers would raise objections from a competition policy point of view. The German delegation made its approval of the Merger Regultion conditional on acceptance of a "pure competition" test. Accordingly, Article 2 of the Regulation stipulates that the Commission in its assessment is only to determine whether or not the concentration *creates or strengthens a dominant position* as a result of which *effective competition* in the common market or in a substan-tial part of it will be significantly impeded. A two-tiered competition test there-fore applies. First, the Commission has to determine whether the concentration creates or strengthens a dominant position. Secondly, if the answer to the first question is affirmative, the Commission will have to determine whether that dominant position impedes effective competition significantly. If the answer to this second question is also positive then the merger is incompatible with the common market. Conversely, if the answer to one of the questions is negative then a merger is *per se* compatible with the common market.[121]

---

[120] J. Davidow, "Competition Policy, Merger Control and the European Community's 1992 Program" (1991) 29 *Columbia Journal for Transnational Law* 11–40.

[121] But see the Commission's Interpretative Notes on some of the Reg.'s provision (published in *EC Bulletin*, Supplement 2/90 Community Merger Control Law). Reference to cohesion policy con-sideration is frank in the first point *re* Art. 2. It states that among the factors to be taken into con-sideration account will particularly be taken of the competitiveness of undertakings located in regions which are greatly in need of restructuring owing *inter alia* to slow development. The mar-gins for extra-competition policy considerations are also implicit in the final point *re* Art. 2 of the Notes where the Commission considers "that the concept of technical and economic progress [in Art. 2 of the Merger Reg.] must be understood in the light of the principles enshrined in Article 85(3) EC [now Article 81], as interpreted in the case law of the Court of Justice". As will be argued more extensively below (in Ch. 3) the case law of the ECJ allows for non-competition criteria to be taken into account in applying Art. 81(3) EC.

While Commission decisions generally appear to be faithful to an assessment on the basis of the pure competition criteria in their application of the Merger Regulation,[122] other policy considerations have apparently played a crucial role in the assessment of the compatibility with the common market of a number of mergers. The clearest example is the Commission decision with respect to the merger between Mannesmann, Vallourec and Ilva.[123] The Commission acknowledged that the merger, which established a duopoly with a combined market share of 65 per cent of the relevant market, would reduce competition significantly. It considered it unlikely that significant competition would result between these two firms. Yet the Commission ruled that the takeover was compatible with the common market in view of the enhanced effiency—and therefore supposedly the competitiveness—of the new entity.[124] In so far as they have been tested hitherto, the Commission's decisions which take up extra-competition policy considerations in its assessment of the compatibility of a merger with the common market have been endorsed by the European courts. The Court of First Instance has explicitly ruled that, although the Merger Regulation is primarily concerned with establishment and maintenance of a system which ensures that competition is not distorted, the Commission may nevertheless take into consideration other effects of a concentration if objectives of Article 2 EC are likely to be adversely affected.[125] Under Community antitrust law application the broad margins afforded to considerations which go beyond those narrowly linked to free competition are thus particularly apparent from Community merger control practice.

The Merger Regulation can therefore be considered a substantiation of the altered nature of Community antitrust policy. It represents a shift of influence from the juridical components of the Commission's activity to its political

---

[122] See, thus, T. Downes and D. MacDougall, "Significantly Impeding Effective Competition" (1994) 19 *ELR* 286–303; M. Siragusa and M. Subiotto, "The EEC Merger Control Regulation: The Commission's Evolving Case Law" (1991) 28 *CMLRev* 877–99; and R. Snelders, "Developments in E.C. Merger Control in 1995" (1996) 21 *ELR/CC* 66–88.

[123] Case IV/M.315 [1994] OJ L102/12.

[124] In Mannesmann/Vallourec/Ilva the suspicion of political motives is particularly strong because DG IV's "Merger Task Force", which had proposed not to approve of the merger in view of the negative effect on competition, had drafted the decision accordingly. As a consequence the motivation provided in the Commission decision for endorsing the concentration held clear inconsistencies which last-minute redrafting could not repair. See P.-E. Noël, "Efficiency Considerations in the Assessment of Horizontal Mergers under European and U.S. Antitrust Law" (1997) 18 ECLR 498–519 at 514. Other cases in point are Kali+Salz/MdK/Treuhand, Case IV/M.308 [1994] OJ L186/38, in which a merger which created a 90% marketshare in one of the relevant markets was nevertheless approved; and Boeing/McDonnel Douglas, Case IV/M.877 [1997] OJ L336/16, in which the Commission required Boeing to end its long-term exclusivity contracts with various airlines. The decisions have been subject to much criticism. See, e.g., F. Heistermann, "Praxis der EG-Kommission und des Bundeskartellamtes zur Fusionskontrolle", 51–70 at at 60–70, in *Schwerpunkte des Kartellrechts 1993/94—Referate des Zweiundzwanzigsten FIW-Seminars 1994* (Köln, Carl Heymanns, 1995) and A. van Mourik, "Five Years of Community Merger Control", 19–52 at 27–34, in (ed.) *Developments in European Competition Policy* (Maastricht, European Institute of Public Administration, 1996).

[125] Case T-12/93 *Comité central d'enterprise de la S.A. Vittel v. Commission* [1995] ECR II–1247.

elements. Equally, it represents the turn from market building to market regulation, or from negative to positive integration, on the basis of antitrust law
implementation. The possible effects of mergers on cross-border flows of
intra-Community trade, originally the basis for the Community's antitrust
rules, are no longer the most significant factor in Community antitrust
law. Therefore, both events of the 1980s—antitrust's "public turn" and adoption of the Merger Regulation—reveal the shifting nature of EC antitrust
policy.

CONCLUSION

This chapter identified three phases in the development of EC antitrust law.
Initially, the antitrust law provisions were inserted into the Treaty in view of
their role in the process of market integration. The antitrust rules were no more
than the private counterpart to the rules, enshrined in Articles 28–30 EC which
guaranteed freedom to trade across borders without hindrance from the
Community's Member States. The framers of the Treaty wanted to preclude
private undertakings replacing the prohibited public obstacles to inter-state
trade. The first period of Community antitrust policy saw the Commission
enforcing the rules with constant reference to ensuring the free flow of goods,
thus promoting market integration.

Subsequently, in the second period, antitrust policy was employed to establish a broader Community industrial policy. Exemptions for the antitrust rules
were granted to forms of (trans-national) co-operation between undertakings
which the Commission considered desirable, to promote either integration
(*Eurocheque*) or broader Community policy aims (for example employment in
crisis sectors). Thus, a Community industrial policy was gradually developed on
the basis of the Treaty's antitrust rules.

The momentum generated by the Commission's "1992 programme" then provided the occasion for expanding the scope of Community antitrust policy even
further. With continued reference to the needs of market integration, the
Commission acquired powers under the Merger Regulation to regulate the
structure of markets. Furthermore it extended the enforcement of the antitrust
rules to the public sectors of the various Member States. While reference was
still made to the underpinning of Community antitrust law in economic integration, the socio-political implications of integration by competition (law)
became ever more apparent. In this respect the control of corporate mergers and
the gradual liberalisation of public economic sectors, both highly political exer-
cises, which commenced by the end of the 1980s, symbolise the altered character of Community antitrust law enforcement.

Although the system was originally devised for promoting market integration, antitrust policy is now also—and mainly—directed at promoting the various other objectives of the Community enshrined in Article 2 EC. Absent a clear

hierarchy between those objectives, priorities are selected on a case by case basis. Agreements between undertakings have been exempted from the prohibition in Article 81(1) EC when their negative effect on the intensity of competition on the relevant market was outweighed by positive consequences for European industry's competitiveness, or for social and economic cohesion. Likewise, mergers are sometimes held compatible with the common market, in spite of the significant reduction in the degree of competition they engender, when the Commission considers that they may contribute to one or more of the objectives laid down in Article 2 of the Treaty. While it is not submitted that the majority of antitrust issues is settled on the basis of extra-competition elements, it is evident from the Commission decisions, endorsed by the European Courts, that the Commission is able to pursue "flanking" policies on the basis of its enforcement of the antitrust rules.

Because there was Community-wide consensus on the market integration objective as the underpinning of EC antitrust policy, the Member States delegated unprecedented powers to the supranational Community institutions, mainly the Commission, in the field of antitrust policy. The Commission, under the judicial control of the Court of Justice, was primarily responsible for furthering the common market project. In view of the intimate link between antitrust law enforcement and market integration it was logical for the Commission to be provided with strong autonomous powers in the field. These extensive and exclusive powers remained in force as market integration considerations gradually gave way to alternative policy concerns. After formal realisation of the internal market it is apparent that there are various policy choices implicit in antitrust law enforcement. And while the Member States did agree on the primacy of the original objective of EC antitrust law, market integration, this is not necessarily the case with respect to the new policy priorities, set by the Commission in its decisions.[126]

Thus the basis of the Commission's strong and autonomous powers may be affected. The realisation of the internal market, at least formally, in 1992 underscored that market integration had—or would—become obsolete as the main objective of Community antitrust policy. This book argues that a fundamental reassessment of the Community antitrust law system is warranted. The qualitative changes in EC antitrust policy which have gradually taken shape since 1958 necessarily affect the substantive, insitutional and procedural cornerstones of EC antitrust policy.[127] By summarising the general development of EC law and contrasting that with the transformation of EC antitrust law, the next chapter

---

[126] This is explicitly recognised by Gerber: "[c]ompetition law was politically acceptable precisely because it was a necessary tool of economic integration. . . . the integration imperative both defined the competition law system and provided it with legitimacy": D. Gerber, *Law and the Protection of Competition* (Oxford University Press, 1998).

[127] For more extensive discussion see T. Frazer, "Competition Policy after 1992: The Next Step" (1990) 53 *MLR* 609–23 and R. Wesseling, "Subsidiarity in Community Antitrust Law; Setting the Right Agenda" (1997) 22 *ELR* 35–54.

aims to define the direction which the required substantive, institutional and procedural adjustments should take. On the basis of that analysis, the second part of the book will address four specific aspects of the modernisation of EC antitrust law.

2

The Transformation of the
Community's Constitution

THE PREVIOUS CHAPTER provided an account of the transformation of
Community antitrust policy in isolation from other developments in EC
law. But that transformation did not occur in isolation. The changes in
antitrust policy unfolded parallel to analogous and correlated broader developments within the European Community and its Member States. Just as the gradual evolution of antitrust policy influenced and furthered European integration
in general, so was that process itself informed by developments taking place in
related legal, political and economic Community fields. Today, Community
antitrust policy operates in a framework which scarcely resembles the original
context in which the EEC Treaty rules were drawn up, the procedural framework was defined and in which the first interpretations of the Treaty's antitrust
law provisions were conceived.

In this respect numerous changes which affect the way Community antitrust
policy is enforced spring to mind. First, the character of Western European
economies has changed significantly since the 1950s. In short, from economies
in which the agricultural and industrial sectors dominated, Western European
economies turned toward a focus on the services sectors. The increasing business potential of information technology plays a major role in this development.
Information technology and the resulting improved forms of communication
also influenced the pattern of industrial organisation itself. Simply put, it has
enabled the shift in mass production from a supply-driven ("push") to a
demand-driven ("pull") process. Obviously, the changing forms of industrial
organisation are of direct relevance to antitrust policy. Although agreements
between companies which restrict competition are prohibited by antitrust law
rules, close links between firms at different levels of the production and distribution chain ("vertical" relations) are indispensable to "customised" or "just-in-
time" management. The development in industrial organisation thus challenged
the cornerstone of antitrust law doctrine, particularly within the European
Community where the focus on integration had generated a strong stance
against "vertical" agreements.[1] Secondly, gradual liberalisation of global trade

---

[1] In-depth discussion of the background to these developments and its effects on antitrust policy
are provided in D. Deacon, "Vertical Restraints under EU Competition Law: New Directions", in
B. Hawk (ed.), *Annual Proceedings of the Fordham Corporate Law Institute 1995* (London, Sweet
& Maxwell, 1996), 307–24. See also R. van den Bergh, "Modern Industrial Organisation versus
Old-fashioned European Competition Law" (1996) 17 *ECLR* 75–87. For an overview of the

and innovation in (communication) technologies have furthered economic interdependence between national economies. Growing interdependence of national economies affects antitrust policy since restrictions of competition at the national level can be rendered insignificant by competition from outside those countries. Thirdly, at a more specific level, political support in the European Community's Member States for the market economy, characterised by free and fair inter-firm rivalry, increased since the foundation of the EEC. The steady growth of competition law systems at the national level provides merely the most conspicuous evidence of this development. Fourthly, the nature of European integration itself changed significantly between the outset of the European Economic Community in 1958 and today's European Union. It is "broader" and "deeper". The Union is broader because the Community's territorial scope has increased. Instead of the original six the Community now comprises 15 Member States. Moreover, the Union is committed to further expansion in the near future. The Union is deeper than the EEC because the degree of integration evolved as the originally separated and compartmented markets of the national economies gradually blended into a common market which formally acquired the status of an internal market by the end of 1992. Thus, the Communities, originally set up as an international organisation, developed into a *sui generis* form of inter- and supranational co-operation, with ever wider policy competences.

Evidently, all four types of contextual developments mentioned above have affected Community antitrust policy. This chapter focuses on the changes in one specific context only. It contrasts the transformation of Community antitrust law with the general development of the Community's legal order, a process described as the "constitutionalisation" of the Treaty.[2] The constitutionalisation process is well documented.[3] For present purposes it suffices therefore to recapitulate the hallmarks of that process with continuous reference to the transformation of Community antitrust law, presented in Chapter 1.

There are good reasons for selecting the Treaty context when examining the developing contexts within which EC antitrust policy is implemented. Not only

developments in US antitrust policy, which predate those in Europe, see E. Gellhorn, "Climbing the Antitrust Law Staircase" (1986) 30 *The Antitrust Bulletin* 341–57. See further below Ch. 3.

[2] Basically, the term "constitutionalisation" denotes the process which lay between the coming into force of the Treaty of Rome in 1958 and the ECJ's pronouncement that the Treaty constitutes the "constitutional charter of a Community based on the rule of law" in 1992. *Opinion 1/91 Opinion delivered pursuant to the second subparagraph of Article 228(1) of the Treaty* [1991] ECR 6079 at para. 21. See also the earlier reference to the Treaty as a constitution in Case 294/83 *Parti Ecologiste "Les Verts" v. European Parliament* [1986] ECR 1339.

[3] See, e.g., E. Stein, "Lawyers, Judges, and the Making of a Transnational Constitution" (1981) 75 *The American Journal of International Law* 1–27; K. Lenaerts, "Constitutionalism and the Many Faces of Federalism" (1990) 38 AJCL 205–63 at 208–13; and T. Hartley, "Federalism, Courts and Legal Systems; The Emerging Constitution of the European Community" (1986) 34 *AJCL* 229–47. Weiler has noted the "constitutionalising" effect of these studies themselves. By adopting the constitutional discourse these contributions, irrespective of their contents, have reinforced the constitutional idea: J. Weiler, "The Reformation of European Constitutionalism" (1997) 35 *JCMS* 97–131.

are the antitrust rules formulated in the Treaty, the European Court of Justice has consistently emphasised the preeminence of the Treaty as the primary framework of reference for application of those rules. The Court holds that the antitrust provisions "should be read in the context of the provisions of the Preamble to the Treaty which clarify it and reference should particularly be made to those relating to 'the elimination of barriers' and to 'fair competition' both of which are necessary for bringing about a single market".[4]

Although objections can be made to the comparison which is made in this chapter,[5] presenting the development of EC integration and that of Community antitrust policy in parallel is useful for the limited purpose of this chapter, that is highlighting the similarities and differences which exist in the development of the legitimacy for Community antitrust policy and the general debate on the legitimacy of EC law and its constitutional principles. Moreover, the comparison of the "whole" ("constitutionalisation") with a "part" (antitrust policy) facilitates a re-emphasis of the legitimacy which EC antitrust policy finds in the EC Treaty. The independent way in which EC antitrust policy developed fostered an isolated approach to the study of this field of Community policy. By re-emphasising that the legitimacy of EC antitrust policy derives from the EC Treaty, this chapter aims to demonstrate that the general development of EC law has direct implications for the way in which EC antitrust law is implemented. EC antitrust law's basis in the EC Treaty and its interrelation with general developments in EC law are, however, often disregarded. In particular the pertinent course for the modernisation of EC antitrust policy cannot be identified in isolation. Any modernisation of EC antitrust policy should start from EC antitrust policy's basis in the EC Treaty, which itself operates within the framework set by the Treaty on European Union. This book, in particular Part II, therefore addresses the substantive, procedural and institutional modernisation of EC antitrust policy with explicit reference to the altered context, sketched in this chapter, within which EC antitrust law is enforced.

The chapter consists of three section. As in the previous chapter, each represents a stage in European integration, which roughly coincides with phases in the constitutionalisation process. The first paragraph covers the initial stage of the European Economic Community. The second centres on the 1970s and 1980s. The TEU and what followed is discussed in the third paragraph.

---

[4] Case 32/65 *Italy* v. *Council and Commission* [1966] ECR 389, at 405. *Cf.* B. van der Esch, "The Principles of Interpretation Applied by the Court of Justice of the European Communities and their Relevance for the Scope of the EEC Competition Rules" (1991–2) 15 *FILJ* 366–97.

[5] A first objection pertains to the level of comparison. One may question the value of a comparison of the process of European integration in general with the development of one particular policy field which forms part of the general process. Secondly, the processes are mutually related. The general development of EC law—or the process of constitutionalisation—itself was influenced by developments in an important field of Community law, antitrust law. Conversely, as mentioned in the previous section, the implementation of Community antitrust law was influenced by the constitutionalisation process.

2.1 FROM INTERNATIONAL TREATY TO CONSTITUTIONAL CHARTER

As has been said, the general development of European Community law can be characterised by the constitutionalisation of the EC Treaties. The European Court of Justice laid the basis for the substantive course of the constitutionalisation process when it interpreted the EEC Treaty as the articulation of an ambition to constitute a new sort of international legal order among the Member States. The Court found that the degree and form of international co-operation sought within the EEC was unlike any other international organisation. In the words of the Court in the *Van Gend & Loos* judgment, "[t]he objective of the EEC Treaty, which is to establish a Common Market, the functioning of which is of direct concern to interested parties in the Community, *implies that this Treaty is more than* agreement which merely creates mutual obligations between the contracting states". The major ("constitutional") consequences of the Court's initial interpretation of the wording and spirit of the EEC Treaty were enhanced by the judgment in *Costa* v. *Enel* in which the Court held "[b]y *contrast with ordinary international treaties*, the EEC Treaty has created its own legal system . . . By creating a Community of unlimited duration, having its own institutions, its own personality, its own legal capacity of representation on the international plane and, more particularly, real powers stemming from a limitation of sovereignty or a transfer of powers from the States to the Community, the Member States have limited their sovereign rights, albeit in limited fields, and have thus created a body of law which binds both their nationals and themselves".[6]

The perception that the Member States intended to create a genuine Community and consequently a unique international organisation formed the basis for subsequent interpretations of the EEC Treaty. It defined two essential aspects of the constitutionalisation process. First, it implied that Treaty provisions were interpreted in view of the implicit objective of the Member States to constitute among themselves a new legal order, binding the participating states as well as the subjects of those states.[7] Secondly, within the newly established international society, the legitimacy of the law derived from the effective protection of rights conferred by the EEC Treaty which the law guaranteed. These two constitutional principles—limitation of Member State sovereign rights and

---

[6] Case 26/62 *Van Gend en Loos* v. *Nederlandse Administratie der Belastingen* [1963] ECR 1 at 12 and Case 6/64 *Costa* v. *ENEL* [1964] ECR 585 at 593.

[7] In this process teleology acquired a natural role as the main interpretative tool to reveal the implied Treaty objectives: *Costa* v. *ENEL*, above, n. 6, at 593. See also K. Lenaerts, "Some Thoughts About the Interaction Between Judges and Politicians" [1992] *The University of Chicago Legal Forum* 93–133, at 133; "the ECJ based its whole jurisprudence, in the final analysis, on the object and purpose of the Treaty itself". *Cf.* Judge Pescatore on the use of teleological, dynamic interpretation in order to promote the "unexpressed" goals of the EEC Treaty: P. Pescatore, "Les Objectifs de la Communauté Euopéenne comme Principes d'Interprétation dans la Jurisprudence de la Court de Justice" in *Miscellanea W.J. Ganshof van der Meersch* (Brussels, Emile Bruylant, 1972), ii, 325–63.

effective protection of individual rights—were particularly prominent during the first phase of the Community's development.[8]

One of the main constitutional principles which the Court of Justice discerned in this early period sprang from the proposition that by signing the EEC Treaty the Member States intended to create a new legal order. It followed that within the area covered by that new order a prime (constitutional) principle read that provisions of the Treaty should be interpreted in such a manner as to enable the Community to operate effectively. This observation formed the basis for the legitimacy of the Court's "*effet utile*" jurisprudence. The Court's reasoning in *Van Gend en Loos* is again instructive: "[a] restriction of the guarantees . . . would remove all direct legal protection of the individual rights of their nationals. There is the risk that recourse to the procedure under these Articles would be *ineffective* if it were to occur after the implementation of a national decision taken contrary to the provisions of the Treaty. . . . It follows from the foregoing considerations that, according to the spirit, the general scheme and the wording of the Treaty, Article 12 [repealed by the Amsterdam Treaty] must be interpreted as producing direct effects and creating individual rights with national courts must protect".[9]

The "useful effect"—or "effectiveness"—of the new order designed by the EEC Treaty was reinforced through a number of powers which, although not specifically mentioned, were nevertheless essential for the new legal order to operate adequately within the policy areas designed for it. The constitutional principle of the Community's "implied powers" found its basis in the search for the effective operation of the substantive rules set out in the Treaty; "[t]o determine in a particular case the Community's authority to enter into international agreements, regard must be had to the whole scheme of the Treaty no less than to its substantive provisions. *Such authority arises not only from an express conferment* by the Treaty . . . but may equally flow from other provisions of the

---

[8] Snyder distinguishes three main aspects of the EU constitution: constitutional principles, constitutionalising processes and constitutional culture: F. Snyder, "General Course on Constitutional Law of the European Union" in Academy of European Law (ed.), *Collected Courses of the Academy of European Law 1996, Volume VI, Book 1* (Dordrecht, Kluwer, 1997). Though Snyder himself does not employ such a crude correlation, the present examination of constitutionalisation treats the interrelation between these constituents as if constitutional principles induced constitutionalising processes and as if those constitutionalising processes, in turn, informed the Community's constitutional culture. *Cf.* Snyder, at 135: "[t]hese constitutionalizing processes not only help to generate constitutional principles. They also apply, refine and transform them together with EU constitutional culture."

[9] See *Van Gend en Loos*, above, n. 6, at 13. "*Effet utile*" continues to be of utmost relevance for the development of EC jurisprudence. See, for examples in case law, Case C–213/89 *Factortame I* [1990] ECR I–2433 at para. 21: "[i]t must be added that the full effectiveness of Community law would be just as much impaired if a rule of national law could prevent a court seised of a dispute governed by Community law from granting interim relief in order to ensure the full effectiveness of the judgement"; Joined Cases C–6 & 9/90 *Francovich* [1991] ECR 5357 at 5414: "[t]he full effectiveness of Community rules would be impaired and the protection of the rights which they grant would be weakened if individuals were unable to obtain redress when their rights are infringed by a breach of Community law for which a Member State can be held responsible".

Treaty and from measures adopted, within the framework of those provisions, by the Community institutions".[10]

Interestingly, direct effect—which the Court had granted to some of the Treaty's provisions—enabled the effective protection of the rights conferred by the Treaty but it also endangered the effectiveness of the Treaty. The capacity for individuals of the Member States to rely on Community law before national courts created the danger of diverging interpretations of Community law in the various jurisdictions. Furthermore, the obligations undertaken under the Treaty establishing the Community would in the Court's opnion be merely contingent if they could be called into question by subsequent legislative acts of the signatories. The ensuing danger for divergent interpretations of Community law formed the basis for establishing the primacy of Community law over the separate and diverging laws of the Member States in those areas where the new order was active. It still establishes the legitimacy for the broadly interpreted "supremacy" of EC law over national laws.[11] However, certain areas of the Community's regulatory competence required an even higher degree of homogeneity than the supremacy of EC law over diverging national laws could generate. Within the policy fields within which a degree of divergency would potentially hamper the effectiveness of the Community's policies, the Community wished to be competent to the exclusion of Member States' power to regulate that area. These considerations formed the basis for the Court's ruling that the Community's constitution pre-empts the application of national law in some policy areas.[12]

The Court judgments which pronounced the constitutional principles concerning the protection of Community rights and the relationship between Community law and national law dominated the development of the Community's legal order in the first stage of its existence. The main consequence of the Court's teleological reasoning was twofold. First, the Community acquired autonomous powers *vis-à-vis* its Member States. The Court perceived

---

[10] Case 22/70 *Commission* v. *Council ("ERTA")* [1971] ECR 263 at paras. 15–16.

[11] *Costa* v. *ENEL*, above, n. 6, at 593–4. Case 106/77 *Simmenthal* [1978] ECR 629, at para. 16, further amplified the scope of Community law's supremacy: "[f]urthermore, in accordance with the principle of precedence of Community law, the relationship between provisions of the Treaty and directly applicable measures of the institutions on the one hand and the national law of the Member States on the other is such that those provisions and measures not only by their entry into force render automatically inapplicable any conflicting provision of current national law but—in so far as they are an integral part of, and take precedence in, the legal order applicable in the territory of each of the Member States—also preclude the valid adoption of new national legislative measures to the extent to which they would be incompatible with Community provisions".

[12] *Opinion 1/75 Opinion delivered pursuant to the second subparagraph of Article 228(1) of the Treaty* [1975] ECR 1355: "distortions can be eliminated only by means of a strict uniformity . . . It cannot therefore be accepted that, in a field such as that governed by export policy and more generally by the common commercial policy, the Member States should exercise a power concurrent to that of the Community, in the Community sphere and in the national sphere". Subsequently, the basis for pre-emption was enlarged when the ECJ concluded that expiration of a deadline for agreeing a common policy takes the power to act out of the hands of the individual Member States even absent any Council action at that time: Case 801/79 *Commission* v. *United Kingdom* [1981] ECR 1045.

the EEC as a legal area, carved out of the "political process", in which the Member States were administered by the legal order of the Community which they had themselves established.[13] The constitutional principles mentioned above have in common that they consider the Community as a new independent entity, immune from direct interference by one or more of the Member States. The Community's supranational institutions, the Court of Justice together with the European Commission—and to a lesser extent, the European Parliament— operated as autonomous actors with respect to the issues which were most directly linked to market integration.[14] Judicial conflicts with respect to the core area of the EEC were solved on the basis of the Treaty. Although the dichotomy between the national and Community spheres was not interpreted rigidly,[15] the legal principles pronounced by the Court generated the "dual character" of the Community's legal order.[16]

This observation leads to the second implication of the jurisprudence on which the Court based its constitutional judgments. Since the Community's powers were directly linked to the common market, the boundary between the Community and the Member States coincided with what was required for the purposes of market integration. The EEC was established in order to replace the separate national markets by a common European market. There was a clear basis for the Community's constitutional principles within the, mainly economic, policy areas which affected the process of market integration. But there was no legitimate basis for these principles outside that area. The Member States retained their sovereignty in remaining policy areas.

Because the Court of Justice judgements legitimated the far-going Community claims to dictate the relationship between the Community and its Member States these judgments helped to form the Community's constitutional principles.[17] The relatively rigid borders between the sphere of competence of the Community and that of the Member States, for instance, has had important consequences. On the one hand, a strong and autonomous legal order emerged with respect to the Community's market integration project. In the area which the Court had identified as the core of the Community, European integration could thus thrive on the basis of legal processes. On the other hand, the scope of

---

[13] Lenaerts, above, n. 7, at 132–3.

[14] *Ibid.*, at 100: "[n]ot willing to wait for the political process to respond to that appeal, the ECJ crossed the line of separation between the Community and national legal orders".

[15] E.g. the ECJ emphasised that Community law formed part of the national law systems of the Member States and, conversely, that Member States courts had become part of the Community's judiciary: S. Weatherill, *Law and Integration in the European Union* (Oxford, OUP, 1995) at 99.

[16] *Cf.* Weiler on the distinction within the Community sphere between a supranational and an intergovernmental limb: J. Weiler, "The Community System: The Dual Character of Supra-nationalism" (1981) 1 *YEL* 267–306.

[17] P. Eleftheriadis, "Begging the Constitutional Question" (1998) 36 *JCMS* 255–72 at 259. See also Lenaerts, above, n. 7. Treating the EEC Treaty—and the ECJ judgments based on it—as "functional equivalents" of a constitution is not unproblematic. See W. Sauter, "The Economic Constitution of the European Union" (1998) 4 *CJEL* 27–68, at 67–8. Nevertheless, the principles pronounced by the ECJ had such evident constitutional elements that they can at least be seen to have induced constitutionalising processes: Snyder, above, n. 8.

that legal order was limited. The legitimacy of the Community's claim to supremacy was explicitly confined to the economic processes linked to market integration.

The first phase of the Community's general legal development is therefore very much in line with the essential developments in the specific area of Community antitrust policy. Chapter 1 illustrated that Community antitrust policy was applied in connection with its functional role in market integration. The Community's competence to conduct antitrust policy was grounded in the contribution to market integration. Antitrust policy belonged to the core competences of the Community and its development profited considerably from the strong and autonomous Community powers that the Court had assigned, on the basis of its interpretation of the Treaty, to the Community in those fields.

Indeed one of the core constitutional principles was first pronounced in Court judgments relating to antitrust law. It was in a preliminary reference dealing with a question relating to Article 81 EC that the Court established its doctrine of direct effect. In *De Geus* v. *Bosch*, a judgment which preceded *Van Gend en Loos*, the Court considered it possible to grant direct effect to certain, specifically clear, Treaty provisions but declined to give direct effect to Article 81 EC at the time. The Court considered Articles 81 and 82 EC not sufficiently clear to be able to have direct effect until the envisaged implementing provisions had been adopted.[18] More important than the outcome of that specific case, however, was the reference which the Court made to the useful effect (*effet utile*) of the Treaty. For, as seen above, the *effet utile* reasoning formed the basis of many of the constitutional principles which the Court uncovered.

Similarly, the Court described the constitutional principle of supremacy of Community law over national laws in the realm of antitrust law, as it had formulated it in a general context in *Costa* v. *ENEL*. In the landmark antitrust law judgment in *Walt Wilhelm*, the Court held that the ultimate aim of the Treaty, a common market, could be achieved only if Community competition law would take precedence over the various national competition laws in case of conflict.[19]

These two judgments illustrate that the initial development of antitrust law coincided with the general legal development of the Community in those first years. On the basis of its interpretation of the Treaty, the Court of Justice granted the Community strong autonomous powers. The legitimacy for these powers was based in their role in market integration.

[18] After the general implementing provision, Reg. 17, came into force Arts. 81 and 82 were granted direct effect in Case 127/73 *BRT* v. *SABAM* [1974] ECR 51 and Case 155/73 *Sacchi* [1974] ECR 409 respectively.

[19] Case 14/68 *Walt Wilhelm* v. *Bundeskartellamt* [1969] ECR 1 at 14.

2.2 FROM NEGATIVE TO POSITIVE INTEGRATION

In the second phase the course of the Community's general development and that of Community antitrust policy started to diverge. Antitrust policy steadily developed into a genuine European, supranational policy field. Most other EC policy fields suffered from political obstacles to furthering European integration. This division emerges clearly when the general course of European integration in the second phase is again contrasted with the development of antitrust law implementation.

The Court's early case law, and the ensuing constitutional principles, contributed significantly to the European economic integration process. The legitimacy of that contribution was, as seen, limited to one specific limb of European integration, that of "negative" integration. The term negative integration refers to the measures which advance market integration by eliminating potential barriers to intra-Community trade. Crucial to the important role which negative integration played in European integration was its basis in the text of the Treaty. Since negative integration operated within the domain of the provisions of the EEC Treaty, the legitimacy for European policy was evident. The EEC Treaty had charged the Community institutions with applying the Treaty provisions in such a manner as to enable a common market to take shape. No additional ("positive") action was required from the Member States in order to enable the Community to further the market integration process. The realm of negative integration therefore was the area which the Member States, by legally committing themselves to promoting market integration, had removed from their autonomous powers. Building the common market on the basis of the Treaty provisions could therefore be considered a matter of applying the Treaty provisions in light of "legal and economic techniques and common sense".[20]

Considerable progress in establishing the common market was made on the basis of negative integration measures. The significantly broad interpretation given by the Court of Justice to the four economic freedoms enshrined in the Treaty—the freedom of movement of goods, labour, capital and the freedom of establishment—provides an important example. The Court ruled that the free movement of goods which the Treaty pronounced implied that "all trading rules enacted by Member States which are capable of hindering, directly or indirectly, actually or potentially, intra-Community trade" were prohibited by EC law.[21] On this basis the Court declared a large number of national rules, *potentially* capable of hindering import and export, incompatible with the Treaty. The broad formulation of the Court's interpretation of the prohibition to obstruct free movement rendered the actual purpose of the national legislation in question irrelevant. Even rules which were not designed to restrict cross-border

---

[20] P. Kapteyn, "Outgrowing the Treaty of Rome: From Market Integration to Policy Integration" in *Mélanges Fernand Dehousse* (Paris, Fernand Nathan, 1979), 45–54.
[21] Case 8/74 *Procureur du Roi* v. *Dassonville* [1974] ECR 837.

transactions were thus considered to be capable of hampering the free movement of goods. Accordingly, the Court judged that they were incompatible with
the Treaty and it declared those rules void.[22] Market integration thrived.

Implicitly, however, a dichotomy grew within the process of European integration. On one side, that of negative integration, supranational institutions—
the Commission and the Court of Justice—struck down impediments to
cross-border trade on the basis of the interpretation of the Treaty provisions.
On the other, there was the form of integration which required positive, regulatory action by the Member States. In this last area the supranational
Community institutions lacked autonomous powers. Progress in integration
was essentially dependent on Member State action. Consequently, positive integration withered whenever the political will lacked.[23]

While the distinction between negative and positive integration, thus
sketched, is too crude to provide an accurate picture of the integration process,
it does serve to illustrate the way in which the Court of Justice's constitutional
principles, and the constitutional culture which emerged on that basis, held
inherent limits to the legitimacy for European law and policy beyond market
integration.[24]

The limits to common market integration on the basis of negative integration
became apparent following the first phase European integration. While national
regulations which hindered inter-state trade were abolished on the basis of the
EEC Treaty and the common market was gradually established, the need for
regulation of processes on that market emerged. As a result of the Court's broad
interpretation of the prohibition on hindering intra-Community trade, Member
States' regulatory capacity was considerably restrained.[25] Deregulation at the
national level on the basis of negative integration reinforced the need for (re-
)regulation at the Community level.[26] But development of a "second generation" of Community policies which, even if their direction may have been
derived from broad indications defined in the Rome Treaty, were not explicitly
set out therein proved to be a "much more delicate and politically sensitive task"
than the pursuit of negative integration had been.[27]

---

[22] Case 120/78 *Rewe-Zentral* v. *Bundesmonopolverwaltung für Branntwein* ("*Cassis de Dijon*")
[1979] ECR 649. See the discussion in R. Dehousse, "Integration v. Regulation? On the Dynamics of
Regulation in the Community" (1992) 30 *JCMS* 383–402.

[23] On the parallel between the intergovernmental–supranational distinction, on the one hand,
and the distinction between negative and positive integration, on the other see F. Scharpf, "Negative
and Positive Integration in the Political Economy of European Welfare States" in G. Marks et al.,
Governance in the European Union (London, Sage, 1995), 15–39.

[24] See Weiler, above, n. 16 and Weatherill, above, n. 15.

[25] Dehousse, above, n. 22, at 386.

[26] G. Majone, "Deregulation or Re-regulation? Policymaking in the European Community Since
the Single Act", *EUI Working Paper SPS No. 93/9* (Florence, EUI, 1993). In this respect the
Community gradually "outgrew" that Treaty as integration proceeded: Kapteyn, above, n. 20, at
50ff.

[27] Weiler, above, n. 16, at 290

This was most apparent in the 1970s when, for various reasons, Member State support for European integration subsided.[28] One of the effects of the developments was the return to the requirement of unanimity in Council voting procedures, which rendered adoption of Community legislation more difficult.[29] Absent the political consensus among the Member States with respect to the required regulatory measures, European integration faltered in this period. The Community's autonomous powers in the sphere of market integration no longer sufficed for making substantial progress beyond negative integration.

The situation changed in the 1980s when the Commission rebooted the internal market project. Most importantly, it led to the adoption of the Single European Act (SEA). The SEA provided the framework within which Member States, in co-operation with the Commission, reached consensus on packages of positive integration measures.[30] It entailed a return to majority voting in areas of legislation directly related to establishment of the common market. Furthermore, attempts to harmonise national regulation completely were departed from in favour of a new approach to level the Community's economic playing field based on mutual recognition of Member State regulatory schemes.[31] The Delors package following the SEA, the "1992" programme, facilitated further adoption of positive integration measures where they were required for the completion of the common market. In sum, the Single European Act finally provided the impetus which had been lacking to realise the common market.

In the meantime, the development of Community antitrust policy had taken a different course. This was mainly due to the perceived objective of EEC antitrust policy. As was argued at length in the previous chapter, EEC antitrust policy was enforced with a view to striking down private barriers to unhindered trade between Member States. The dominant perception of Community antitrust law at the time underscored its legal, functional and politically neutral character. The direct link between antitrust policy and the common market project emphasised the negative integration elements of EEC antitrust policy enforcement. Antitrust policy's incorporation into the area of negative integration, then, ensured the autonomous role it played in the process of further integration. In view of the uncontested legitimacy of the Community's powers to

---

[28] See above, Ch. 1.3.

[29] Weiler has related the success of negative integration, and the ensuing constitutionalisation process, to these processes, by which the Member States took firm control over (positive) integration measures. Thus the Member States, in Weiler's view, minimised the threatening features of the autonomous negative integration and constitutionalisation processes: J. Weiler, "The Transformation of Europe" (1991) 100 *The Yale Law Journal* 2403–83 at 2429.

[30] The SEA was only the first comprehensive revision of the EEC Treaty: G. Bermann, "The Single European Act: A New Constitution for the Community?" (1989) 27 *Columbia Journal for Transnational Law* 529–87.

[31] The SEA was explicitly geared up to completion of the internal market programme on the basis of provisions of the EEC Treaty, supplemented by the *acquis communautaire* which was mainly derived from the ECJ's constitutional judgments which had expanded the Community's competences. See Weiler, above, n. 29, at 2453ff.

develop and enforce an antitrust policy in order to promote economic integration, the development of EEC antitust policy continued without the need for additional positive, regulatory measures by the Council. As the previous chapter demonstrated the implicit classification of Community antitrust policy as a negative integration policy was reflected in the institutional framework. The close connection between antitrust policy and the Common Market project ensured that the supranational institutions of the Community were almost exclusively competent within the area of antitrust law enforcement. This enabled the Community institutions to apply the Treaty antitrust rules, akin to the way in which they had enforced the free movement rules, as autonomous actors in a genuine supranational manner. The significance of the institutional framework is apparent in the statement by a former Commissioner, then responsible for competition policy: "[t]he Commission has its own powers here and is consequently not dependent on the reluctance or inability of the Council of Ministers to reach decisions . . .. The Commission itself takes a number of decisions in the competition area virtually every week".[32]

The development of EEC antitrust policy was consequently characterised by a close alliance between the Commission and Court. Together they ensured the furthering of the process of integration by interpreting the scope of competition policy increasingly broadly.[33] While the Commission's role focused on vigorous observance of the freedom to trade across borders, the Court's role was to support the Commission by providing "windows of opportunity" to expand the scope of the Treaty's competition law provisions. The significant role of the Court of Justice itself in the development of antitrust jurisprudence enhanced the already noted legal concept of Community antitrust policy.

Because the Court set broad margins within which Community antitrust law was applicable, the Commission was able to pursue certain elements of positive integration policy by way of its antitrust law enforcement action. Chapter 1 emphasised the importance of the Court's *Walt Wilhelm* judgment, in which it ruled that Community antitrust policy had a "transitory character". The Court explained that EEC antitrust policy contained a "negative integration" limb as well as a "positive integration" limb. Although the Commission continued, after *Walt Wilhelm*, to base its individual antitrust decisions primarily on the requirements of the common market, the measures gradually moved beyond guaranteeing the free movement of goods. Thus, the Commission moved away from a "negative" concept of competition and increasingly used its competence to carry out positive, though indirect, action on the basis of the competition rules.

---

[32] F. Andriessen, "The Role of Anti-trust in the Face of Economic Recession; State Aids in the EEC" (1983) 4 *ECLR* 286–96 at 288.

[33] The key role of the Commission in developing new concepts is confirmed by Hallstein's appraisal of the relationship between the two institutions: "the European Court of Justice, which plays a key role in this whole process, had adopted the concepts of the Commission practically in their entirety, a trend that is clearly reflected in its decisions, which are couched in modern yet impressively authoritative language": W. Hallstein, *Europe in the Making* (London, George Allen & Unwin, 1976) at 116–17.

It is not evident why there was no opposition from the Member States to the increasing supranational features of Community antitrust policy, a policy which was potentially very significant. Chapter 1 demonstrated that the Member States, through the Council, even enhanced the autonomy of the Commission in competition policy through the implementing Regulation 17, which conferred strong autonomous, supranational powers on the Commission, and through Regulation 19/65, which delegated the power to adopt block-exemption regulations to the Commission. Two explanations have been proposed though. First, the parties to which antitrust policy was addressed were not Member States themselves but private parties which perhaps were less powerful, or at least less well organised and institutionally represented. Secondly, most Member States did not have or did not enforce national competition laws. No substantial transfer of competences from the Member States was required. The normal counterweight to expansion of Community powers into the supranational area was therefore lacking. Indeed, only Germany, which had—as has been seen—a national antitrust policy and national antitrust institutions tried successfully to influence Community antitrust policy. However, since the German delegation had influenced the substance and the institutional structure of the Community antitrust law system from the outset there was not much need to demonstrate that influence expressly. The clearest manifestation of Germany's intellectual dominance in Community antitrust law implementation emerges from the long-established tradition of having a German national as director-general of the Commission competition directorate-general.[34]

In sum, the development of Community antitrust policy in this second period diverged significantly from the general course of European policy. Community antitrust policy, perceived as negative integration policy and institutionally framed within the area of "normative supranationalism", did not suffer from the lack of positive integration measures which characterised the general development of EC integration over this period. The Commission was able to employ this autonomy in policy-making in order to further market integration. Since the familiar distinction between negative and positive integration measures was irrelevant within the area of antitrust policy the implications of this development in Community antitrust policy have gone largely unnoticed. Although the legitimacy of EC antitrust policy remained based on its role in "negative" (market) integration, the policy substantively moved on to the kind of policy which would typically be categorised as "positive" policy. The Member States had transferred powers to the Community in the competition policy field to enable the Community institutions to act against obstacles to inter-state trade. Yet by the 1980s the Commission pursued various alternative policy goals on the basis

---

[34] D. Allen, "Managing the Common Market: The Community's Competition Policy" in H. Wallace *et al.* (eds.), *Policy-Making in the European Community* (London, Wiley & Sons, 1983), 209–36 at 230. On German dominance in the development of EC competition policy see P. Oberender and S. Okruch, "Gegenwärtige Probleme und zukünftige Perspektiven der europäischen Wettbewerbspolitik" (1994) 44 *WuW* 507–20.

of its competence in the competition policy field. This process of "qualitative" expansion of Community antitrust policy created a legitimacy gap between its basis in the Treaty and the way it was enforced in practice.

In addition to the "qualitative" extension, the scope of Community antitrust policy also expanded in a "quantitative" manner. The successive enlargements of the Community formed the most conspicuous element in this development. In addition the Commission and the Court of Justice extended the reach of Community antitrust law by their interpretation of the main jurisdictional criterion, the effect on inter-state trade. The Community institutions consistently interpreted the geographical scope of Article 81 EC broadly, relying on integrationalist goals for justification. The very broad interpretation of the inter-state trade effect criterion ultimately rendered it functionless as a criterion for separating the spheres of applicability of national and EC antitrust law, for which it was originally included in Articles 81 and 82 EC.[35]

The extended "qualitative" and "quantitative" scope for EC antitrust policy has far-reaching implications for the Community–Member State balance in view of the absolute supremacy which the Court had granted to EC antitrust law in *Walt Wilhelm*. Member States played an extremely minor role in the next stage of the development of antitrust policy. This has been particularly relevant since the internal market was formally established by the end of 1992. Logically, the legitimate objectives of Community antitrust policy, beyond the market integration objective, need to be defined in the context of the modernisation of EC antitrust policy. The determination of the policy objectives behind Community antitrust policy implies clear political choices. Yet, contrary to the market integration objective, the Member States clearly did not—and do not— agree on the objectives of Community antitrust policy beyond that objective. However, since the Member States do not play a decisive role in the implementation of antitrust policy, the problematic debate among the Member States on the objectives to be pursued on the basis of Community antitrust policy could be avoided. Instead, the Commission is capable of determining the future objectives of EC antitrust policy independently.

2.3 BEYOND THE INTERNAL MARKET

In accordance with the timetable set out in the Single European Act the Internal Market was formally established by the end of 1992. Formal establishment formed a major accomplishment for the European Community because the primary objective of the EEC Treaty was thus fulfilled. At the same time, however, it marked the loss of the natural basis for the determination of the course of— and the limits to—the European integration process. Until the formal realisation of a common European market the market integration objective had

---

[35] D. Goyder, *EC Competition Law* 3rd edn. (Oxford, Clarendon Press, 1998), 107–27.

operated as a yardstick along which the desirability and legitimacy of the Community's law and policy measures were tested. Therefore the formal realisation of the Internal Market confronted the Community and its Member States with the fundamental question whether, and, if so, to what extent, the European integration process should proceed.

The Maastricht Treaty (TEU) and the Amsterdam Treaty have answered this question only in part. The Community's Member States decided that European integration was to continue beyond the narrow objective of market integration. That is reflected in the TEU's dual character. On the one hand, it embodied the accomplishments of the preceding European Economic Community, the *acquis communautaire*. On the other, it revealed the incompleteness of the thus established degree of integration. It emphasised the on-going nature of the European integration process by providing for new Community competences. The extension of economic integration in combination with other forms of European integration emerges clearly from the preamble to the TEU in which the Member States underscore their determination to "implement policies ensuring that advances in economic integration are accompanied by parallel progress in other fields". By explicitly envisaging integration of Member States' policies beyond the economic sphere, the TEU marked the expanded scope and degree of integration which is now sought among the Member States. The Community competences in new policy fields, like economic and monetary union and industrial policy, have a high political profile. The TEU thus underscored the political prominence which European integration acquired.[36]

The TEU, however, did not exclusively entend the scope and depth of European integration. Though the Treaty clearly enlarged the number of policy fields in which the Community is active, it also curbed the extent to which the Community sphere of competence interferes with that of the Member States. In other words, the Member States curbed the ever expanding catalogue of Community competences by re-emphasising the limited character of the powers which they transfered to the Community. The Member States made clear that there would be limitations to the constitutionalisation process.[37] Yet the TEU did not present a blueprint for the form and degree of future European integration. Whereas before 1993 the Community could find a natural hallmark in the requirements of market integration, there is no such hallmark within the process of European integration beyond the common market. Within the framework of the TEU the boundaries of European integration, both in scope and in depth, are no longer evident. The Treaty of Amsterdam, which mainly clarified aspects of political co-operation between the Member States outside the area of the EC Treaty, brought few substantive changes to the EC Treaty itself.

[36] F. Snyder, "EMU—Metaphor for European Union? Institutions, Rules and Types of Regulation" in R. Dehousse (ed.), *Europe After Maastricht—An Ever Closer Union?* (Munich, Beck, 1994), 63–99.
[37] A. Dashwood, "The Limits of European Community Powers" (1996) 21 *ELR* 113–28.

In parallel to these developments important elements of the Community's constitution have come under scrutiny since the internal market was formally established and since the TEU was adopted by the end of 1992. In the framework of European integration beyond market integration, the value of traditional Community constitutional principles, like supremacy, pre-emption and uniformity, is uncertain.[38] Accordingly, the legal and political debates on European Community integration are now concerned with finding an appropriate normative underpinning for European policies, on the basis of which its interface with Member State policies may be defined. Manifestations of the ensuing search for adapted (constitutional) principles can be noticed at the political, the judicial and the academic level.

First, on the political level, the Treaty on European Union itself is the most evident manifestation of a break with traditional values of European constitutionalism. While the new policy fields in which the Community is competent may be considered in line with the continuous expansion of Community powers, the TEU breaks with the gradual but immutable expansion of the Community's constitution, for instance by secluding various fields of European Union policies from the European Community ("constitutional") domain. The Treaty on European Union's three "pillars" structure emphasises the limited scope of the Community's constitution.[39] The Court of Justice's jurisprudence remains applicable with respect to the area covered by the European Community Treaty (the "first pillar"), but novel elements of European integration, like foreign and security policy and co-operation in the area of justice and home affairs (the second and third "pillars"), are explicitly excluded from the jurisdiction of the Court of Justice, and hence (partly) from the Community's constitution.[40]

Likewise, the political process curbed the operation of traditional constitutional principles which stretched, on the basis of the requirements of market integration, the depth of Community powers to an unanticipated level. The TEU re-emphasised the limited nature of the powers conferred upon the Community.[41] Adoption of the subsidiarity principle in the TEU is the most evident manifestation of this development. Subsidiarity underscores that, outside

---

[38] See J. Weiler, "The Reformation of European Constitutionalism" (1997) 35 *JCMS* 97–131 and *The Constitution of Europe* (Cambridge, Cambridge University Press, 1999), 96–101.

[39] The pillar structure of the TEU has led to criticism, particularly with respect to its effect on the constitutional structure of the Community treaties. See, for instance, D. Curtin, "The Constitutional Structure of the Union: A Europe of Bits and Pieces" (1993) 30 *CMLRev* 17–69 and V. Constantinesco, "La structure du Traité instituant l'Union Européenne" (1993) 29 *CDE* 251–84, at 266ff.

[40] Art. 46 TEU (ex Art. L) which basically restricts the jurisdiction of the ECJ to the first pillar, seems to confirm Weiler's earlier analysis of the dynamics of European integration. Enhanced powers in the supranational area are in some way accompanied by reinforcement of Member State control over integration policy in other areas by their preference for intergovernmental forms of policy-making, without strong powers for the Community's supranational institutions. Weiler, above, n. 16, at 267; *cf.* K. Mortelmans, "Community Law: More Than A Functional Area of Law, Less Than A Legal System" (1996) *LIEI* 1–23, at 28.

[41] Dashwood, above, n. 37.

the competences which have been allocated to the Community on an exclusive basis, the Community should decline to take legislative or regulatory action when the policy objectives can be achieved by the Member States themselves. Following adoption of the TEU, politicians have regularly referred to the subsidiarity test as the appropriate conceptual basis for a further determination of the division of competences between the Community and its Member States.[42] Still, the subsidiarity concept is too vague to serve as a substitute for the market integration criterion, as the basis for the division of competences between the Community and the Member States. Moreover, subsidiarity does not address the division of competences but rather the exercise of those competences. As a consequence the question of the respective limits to Community and Member States powers remained unanswered in the TEU.

Underlying this problem are the diverging visions among the Member States on the future of European integration. Diverging perceptions of the future course of European integration are for instance manifest in debates on the desirability of a multi-speed Europe, a Europe *à la carte*, opt-outs in a core Europe and other discussions of forms of "variable geometry" which intensified after adoption of the TEU. Again the Treaty of Amsterdam provides only partial answers to the questions on the future direction of European—and in particular EC—integration.[43] While the fundamental questions on the future of European integration have not been answered on the political level, it is evident that the loss of the market integration paradigm has generated a debate on the structure of the Community's constitution within the framework of the TEU and EC Treaty.

Secondly, establishment of the internal market and the coming into force of the TEU affected the attitude of the European judiciary. First, there are challenges to classic Community "constitutional" doctrines from the national judiciary. Most notably, the German constitutional court examined the compatibility of the TEU with the German Constitution. In its "*Maastricht*" judgment, the Bundesverfassungsgericht reformulated limits to the supremacy of European law, while preserving for itself the competence to determine these limits ("*Kompetenz-Kompetenz*").[44] Although that judgment of the German constitutional court is undoubtedly the most prominent manifestation of challenges

---

[42] In the context of the Amsterdam Treaty a Protocol was adopted which amplified the operation of the principle: Protocol (No. 30) on the application of the principles of subsidiarity and proportionality.

[43] On "variable geometry" see the overview in A. Stubb, "The 1996 Intergovernmental Conference and the Management of Flexible Integration" (1997) 4 *Journal of European Public Policy* 37–55. On the implications of the Amsterdam Treaty, see J. Shaw, "The Treaty of Amsterdam: Challenges of Flexibility and Legitimacy" (1998) 4 *ELJ* 63–86 and T. Heukels, N. Blokker and M. Brus (eds.), *The European Union after Amsterdam—A Legal Analysis* (The Hague, Kluwer Law International, 1998).

[44] Bundesverfassungsgericht 89, 155, English text in [1994] 31 CMLR 251. On the background to and consequences of this judgment see C. Joerges, "The Market without the State? States without a Market?", *EUI WP Law 96/2* (Florence, EUI, 1996) and J. Weiler, "The State 'über alles'. Demos, Telos and the German Maastricht Decision" (1995) 1 *ELJ* 219–58.

to the Community constitution, similar challenges to the Court of Justice's read-ing of the Community constitution emerged in relation to conflicting values of Community and national economic law.[45] So far national courts have declined to attack directly the Community's constitutional principles but "open conflict" may be unavoidable in the future.[46]

Even the key actor in the constitutionalisation process, the European Court of Justice, has signalled the limits to the prevailing legal constitutionalism fol-lowing the realisation of the internal market.[47] It has retreated from its renowned judicial activism. Apparently the Court is not prepared to continue "substituting" the judicial for the political process and is willing to accept the limits to the Community competences in policy-making on the basis of the free-dom to trade across borders within the Community.[48]

Moreover, the Court has begun to reconsider elements of its constitutional jurisprudence which were based on the *effet utile* of the common market. Following the formal establishment of the internal market, the Court reinter-preted the demarcation of Community powers, even where they have tradition-ally been intimately linked to the Community's core competences. The scope of the prohibition on Member States hampering the free movement of goods was, for instance, redefined in such a way as to leave more room for Member States' public policy concerns. The most notable example of this jurisprudence is found in the *Keck* judgement in which the Court interpreted the prohibition on national regulation restricting free movement of goods in such a way as to exclude, contrary to what it had previously held, national measures regulating the circumstances in which products may legally be sold.[49] The fact that the Court mentioned explicitly that the contents of its judgment was "contrary to what has previously been decided" has emphasised the constitutional impor-tance of the *Keck* judgment. It was only the second time that the Court explic-itly overruled its own case law.[50] The decision can be perceived as an exponent of a more general trend in the Court's case law towards policing more inten-

---

[45] Case C–280/93 *Germany* v. *Council* [1994] ECR I–4973. See also the 1995 "television judg-ments" which, in respect of the dominant power of the *Länder* to regulate broadcasting, limit the capacity of the German federal government to act in Council, discussed in U. Everling, "The *Maastricht* Judgment of the German Federal Constitutional Court and its Significance for the Development of the European Union" (1994) 14 *YEL* 1–19.

[46] U. Everling, "Will Europe Slip on Bananas? The Bananas Judgement of the Court of Justice and National Courts" (1996) 33 *CMLRev* 401–37, esp. at 401–3.

[47] Weiler rightly underscores that the ECJ should not be perceived as a homogeneous actor: Weiler (1999), above, n. 38, at 100–1. The most evident example of divergence of views is the Court's continued rejection of "horizontal" direct effect of directives, contrary to the Opinions of AG Van Gerven (in Case C–271/91 *Marshall II* [1993] ECR I–4381), Lenz AG (in Case C–91/92 *Faccini Dori* v. *Recreb Srl* [1994] ECR I–3338), and Jacobs AG (in Case C–316/93 *Vaneetveld et al.* v. *Le Foyer SA et al.* [1994] ECR I–763).

[48] T. Koopmans, "The Role of Law in the Next Stage of European Integration" (1986) 35 *ICLQ* 925–31; G. Mancini and F. Keeling, "Language, Culture and Politics in the Life of the European Court of Justice" (1995) 1 *CJEL* 397–413; and Lenaerts, above, n. 3.

[49] Joined Cases C–267 & 268/91 *Bernard Keck and Daniel Mithouard* [1993] ECR I–6097.

[50] A. Arnull, "Owning Up to Fallibility: Precedent and the Court of Justice" (1993) 30 *CMLRev* 247–75 at 265.

sively the divide between the Community and Member State jurisdictions, in order to regain legitimacy as an institution.[51] Likewise it can be interpreted as a token of the Court's reluctance to determine the jurisdictional divide, in the absence of measures from the legislature, and as a general signal that the old "certainties" of EC constitutionalism are in peril within the context of the post-1992 European Community.[52] While *Keck* is the most famous and explicit recognition of the challenges to the traditional understanding of the EC constitution, the jurisdictional divide between Community and Member State has been reassessed in various cases since 1992.[53]

Thirdly, and finally, challenges to traditional constitutional principles have also resulted from intensified academic inquiries into the character of the Community's legal and political order.[54] In the context of the TEU, traditional perceptions of the constitutional relationship between the Community and the Member States, including the limits to the Community's regulatory competencies, are re-examined.[55] Further, and akin to the developments within the judicial sphere, scholarly reviews of the Community's constitutional principles centre on the supremacy of EC law over national law. The functional "effectiveness" basis is considered to constitute a narrow basis for the unconditional supremacy of EC law—even over national constitutional norms. Limits to Community law's pre-eminence are increasingly explored.[56] The case law of *Keck* and following cases is seen to reflect the altered realities of the European Community in the context of the TEU. The Court's new case law reveals that the Community level is not *a priori* superior and hence that normative claims on supremacy at both levels, Community and state, require justification. A justification for Community law's supremacy over national law can no longer be

---

[51] T. Friedbacher, "Motive Unmasked: The European Court of Justice, the Free Movement of Goods, and the Search for Legitimacy" (1996) 2 *ELJ* 226–50.

[52] J. Weiler, "The Constitution of the Common Market Place: Text and Context in the Evolution of the Free Movement of Goods" in P. Craig and G. de Búrca, *The Evolution of EU Law* (Oxford, Oxford University Press, 1999), 349–76. See also J. Shaw, "European Legal Studies in Crisis? Towards a New Dynamic?" (1996) 16 *Oxford Journal of Legal Studies* 231–53 at 239 and S. Weatherill, "Beyond Pre-emption? Shared Competence and Constitutional Change in the European Community" in D. O"Keeffe and P. Twomey (eds.), *Legal Issues of the Maastricht Treaty* (Chichester, Wiley Chancery, 1994), 13–33.

[53] E.g. Case C–292/92 *Hünermund* [1993] ECR I–6800; Joined Cases C–69 & 258/93 *Punta Casa* [1994] ECR I–2355 and Case C–412/93 *Leclerc-Siplec* [1995] ECR I–179 and, in the area of competition law, Case C–2/91 *Meng* [1993] ECR I–5751; Case C–245/91 *Ohra* [1993] ECR I–5851; Case C–185/91 *Reiff* [1993] I–5801. Ch. 4 examines the jurisdictional divide between Community and Member State antitrust law in view of the Court's shifting case law.

[54] J. Weiler, "European Neo-constitutionalism: In Search of Foundations for the European Constitutional Order" (1996) 44 *Political Studies* 517–33 at 518. Following the establishment of the internal market and coming into force of the TEU a shift can be noted in academic studies of the law and politics of European Community integration: Shaw, above, n. 52; Weatherill, above, n. 15; Joerges, above, n. 44.

[55] See in addition to the literature cited above, in n. 54, Dashwood, above, n. 37 and R. Dehousse, "Community Competences: Are there Limits to Growth?", in R. Dehousse (ed.), *Europe after Maastricht—An Ever Closer Union* (Munich, Beck, 1994), 103–25.

[56] Weatherill, above, n. 15, at 105 and Joerges, above, n. 44. In the same sense, see T. Koopmans, "Het post-Maastrichtse Europa" (1996) 71 *Nederlands Juristenblad* 305–15 at 311.

exclusively sought in the requirements of market integration. Further, "neo-constitutional" commentaries are starting to examine the extent to which diversity can be accomodated within the Community's legal order without compromising its integrity and the *acquis communautaire*.[57]

Thus, the terms of the constitutional debate after 1992 move away from the absolute pre-eminence of Community legal norms towards a constitutional principle which accomodates the compatibility of the national and the Community legal order.[58] Moreover, although viewpoints and areas of emphasis diverge, the writings are united in claiming an increased role for political processes as opposed to the perceived dominant role which law and legal processes have played in the earlier development of European integration.

The search for an innovative normative underpinning of the Community itself has generated new investigations into the European Community's institutional framework. For, while the institutional and constitutional frameworks are still primarily based on the previous phase of European integration, the degree of integration sought and the geographical scope of the present European Union differ fundamentally from what was originally envisaged under the Rome Treaty. It is questionnable whether the legal, economic and political processes which were pertinent for the latter are suitable in the context of the former.[59] Hence, a conception of the EC legal order is sought which adequately reflects the sophistication of the present Community system and which goes "beyond the old simplicities of the unified legal order".[60] The debate now increasingly confronts the "constitutional dimension" of the Europeanisation of national economies and laws, as well as its ever more relevant counterpart; the nationalisation, decentralisation and "intergovernmentalisation" of Community law.[61]

What unites these "neo-constitutional" conceptualisations of European integration is that they implictly move beyond the functional legitimacy of the EC constitutional principles which dominated pre-TEU discourse. The three models of European integration which have traditionally dominated the understanding of the European Community are rejected as a basis for future European integration. Thus, first, the concept of the European Community as an international entity developed in order to pursue a number of objectives on the basis of the rule of law cannot provide an adequate depiction of the economic and political union as incorporated in the TEU.[62] Similarly, the notion of the

---

[57] Most comprehensively, see Weatherill, above, n. 15.

[58] Joerges, above, n. 44.

[59] Cf. Curtin, above, n. 39 and T. Hartley, "Constitutional and Institutional Aspects of the Maastricht Agreement" (1993) 42 *ICLQ* 213–37.

[60] Shaw, above, n. 52.

[61] E.g. A. Dashwood, "States in The European Union" (1998) 23 *ELR* 201–16. Dashwood balances "conservatory" elements (which preserve Member State regulatory powers) and "constitutionalising" elements (which enhance the effectiveness of Community policies) of the Union's constitutional order.

[62] This does not imply that the European Union is not governed on the basis of the rule of law. Moreover, numerous commentators still place law and legal processes at the heart of integration within the European Union: J. Usher, "Variable Geometry or Concentric Circles: Patterns for the

European Community as a neo-liberal economic constitution shared by the Member States is held untenable in view of the numerous Court judgments which proclaim that the Treaty is mixed with respect to the nature of the economic policies which may be pursued on its basis.[63] The third traditional model for the Community, that of a federation, is also refuted. The main reason these three conceptualisations of the Community's constitution are rejected lies in their adherence to the conception of the Community as a unitary entity. The "neo-constitutionalist" approaches all originate in the observation that the Community framework is a mixture of various hybrid forms of co-operation. The question is no longer whether European integration will "overtake the nation-state" but the analysis focuses on functional differentiation, co-operation and other forms of interaction between the various levels of governance. In this perspective the emphasis in the analysis of the relationship between the Community and other levels shifts from hierarchy to polycentred, infranational, horizontal forms of co-operative governance.[64] The altered constitutional perception of the Community engenders various novel institutional concepts for policy-making and enforcement in the European Union.[65]

Suffice it to note in the present context that there is much more to the shift from "Community" to "Union" than first meets the eye.[66] From the political, judicial and academic levels fundamental challenges have been made to the values and principles of the Community's traditional constitution. The development of the Community, and of Community law, is affected by the realisation of the internal market. Following the establishment of the internal market a "crisis in European constitutionalism" appears to emerge. The crisis in the Community's traditional constitutionalism is allegedly based on the incapacity of conceptions of European law "of coping with the dynamics of the integration process which on the one hand erodes the competences of the constitutional states and which, on the other hand, has not yet generated a European polity".[67]

European Union" (1997) 46 *ICLQ* 243–73 at 273: "the rule of law remains at the heart of the European Community"; and Everling, above, n. 45, at 19: "the Community is only able to exist as a Community of law".

[63] "The neo-liberal agenda is neither a realistic nor a normatively attractive programme for the europeanisation of economic law": C. Joerges, "European Economic Law, the Nation-State and the Maastricht Treaty" in R. Dehousse (ed.), *The European Union Treaty* (Munich, Beck, 1994), 29–62.

[64] M. Jachtenfuchs, "Theoretical Perspectives on European Governance" (1995) 1 *ELJ* 115–33 and Weiler, above, n. 38, 96–101.

[65] While they are united by their invalidation of traditional constitutionalist views, which were based on unity and a clear hierarchy and division of powers, neo-constitutionalist conceptualisations of European integration diverge considerably *inter se*; Jachtenfuchs, above, n. 64. See also G. Majone, *Regulating Europe* (London, Routledge, 1997) and K.-H. Ladeur, "Towards a Theory of Supranationality—The Viability of the Network Concept" (1997) 3 *ELJ* 33–54.

[66] See Shaw, above, n. 52.

[67] Joerges, above, n. 44. See, similarly, on the consequences of this intermission for social policies, F. Scharpf, "Economic Integration, Democracy and the Welfare State" (1997) 4 *Journal of European Public Policy* 18–36.

So far the modernisation of Community antitrust law has ignored these general developments in Community law. The constitutional questions which arose in the context of the TEU are not addressed in the area of Community antitrust law. This is remarkable when it is taken into consideration that the legitimacy of the Community's antitrust policy too resided in its role in market integration. Shorn of its role in achieving economic integration the objectives of Community antitrust policy need to be redefined.[68] The same can be said for various other topical substantive, institutional and procedural issues in Community antitrust law. Arguably these issues should not be considered as single or isolated issues of substance or procedure. Rather the modernisation programme provides an opportunity to approach these concerns comprehensively. The modernisation process should start from acknowledgement of the fundamental shift in Community antitrust policy objectives between 1958 and the formal establishment of the internal market.

The previous section argued that the remarkable disparity in general development of EC law and that of EC antitrust law stems from the autonomous course which Community antitrust policy has followed since the early 1970s. Unlike most other fields of Community policy, antitrust policy did not suffer from the defects of European integration, which emerged most notably in times of economic stagnation. The relative autonomy which antitrust policy acquired on the basis of its status as a negative integration policy appears to extend its immunity to the current challenges to Community constitutionalism. But in view of the ("positive") political salience which Community antitrust law has gradually acquired, particularly after the adoption of the EC Merger Regulation, there is no apparent justification for the continued *status aparte* of Community antitrust policy.

CONCLUSION

The comparison between antitrust law's transformation and the general process of EC integration, characterised by the process of constitutionalisation and what followed, revealed important differences. Generally, it was the second generation of policies, that is the step from negative to positive integration, which "brought the democracy deficit to the fore" and, thus, revealed the limits to European integration on the basis of the constitutional principles defined by the Court. In contrast, the competition rules—parallel to the free movement provisions, and in accordance with their role as originally perceived—were considered to form an a-political, technical set of rules which could be enforced in order to promote realisation of the common market. Because Community antitrust policy was so firmly established as a negative integration policy, its positive or political elements—which already occurred in the market integra-

---

[68] D. Gerber, "The Transformation of European Community Competition Law?" (1994) 35 *Harvard International Law Journal* 97–147, at 143.

tion era—remained concealed until the internal market was formally established. The strong supranational powers allocated to the European Commission thus ensured a relatively autonomous course for competition policy. The autonomy, in turn, advanced competition policy's role in the general process of European integration.

In the same line, formal establishment of the internal market by the end of 1992 and the events which followed have challenged the traditional elements in the Community's constitution. The "politicised" context of the new Community competences, introduced in the TEU, for instance rendered the traditional perception of the relationship between Community law and national law questionnable. Again, Community antitrust law appears immune from these developments. Yet, there is no evident reason why Community antitrust law should continue to diverge from the general development of Community law. Following the formal establishment of the internal market the market integration objective of Community antitrust policy needs to be substituted. In this respect it can be seen to have "normalised" as an area of Community policy which is reflected in the fact that issues which are central in the general debate on the future of EC integration—the objectives beyond integration, the division of competences between the Community and its Member States, and diversity versus uniformity—as is apparent from the neo-constitutionalism debate, are equally central to the field of antitrust policy. But whereas new and more appropriate models for European integration, and European constitutionalism, are generally sought, this dynamic cannot be observed within the field of EC antitrust policy.

The three main proponents of general neo-constitutionalism (Member States, Courts, the Academy) are silent in the area of antitrust. The Court of Justice generally repeats the formula it established in the first period of antitrust enforcement.[69] At the political level the Community's powers are not balanced by those of the Member States because the latter are practically excluded from day-to-day Community antitrust policy which is firmly set in a supranational context. Academic commentaries tend to perceive antitrust policy isolated from its Community context and thus address the issues on the basis of a singular approach.[70]

The thesis underlying this book is that the course which the modernisation of Community antitrust policy should take has to acknowledge the general developments in Community law following establishment of the internal market and adoption of the TEU. The remainder of the book will therefore address current

---

[69] For instance the differentiation between the objectives of Community and Member State antitrust laws, on which the Court ruled in 1969 in the context of *Walt Wilhelm*, above, n. 19, has remained unchanged. In 1992, in the "Spanish Banks" case (Case C–67/91 *Dirección General de Defensa de la Competencia* v. *Asociación Española de Banca Privada* [1992] ECR I–4785) the Court simply repeated that Community antitrust law is enforced in view of the potential obstacles to interstate trade which may result from agreements, whereas Member State antitrust laws consider business behaviour from a different angle.

[70] Van der Esch, above, n. 4.

EC antitrust law issues with reference to the political, judicial and academic challenges to traditional Community constitutional principles which generally emerged after the formal establishment of the internal market within the framework of the TEU.

Part II

The Modernisation of EC Antitrust Law in Light of the General Development of EC Law

3

Objectives of EC Antitrust Law

INTRODUCTION

P ART I OF this study aimed to demonstrate that, parallel to the objectives of the Community as a whole, the character of Community antitrust policy altered. From a very clear emphasis on its role in market integration, the focus in antitrust policy shifted towards a common industrial policy, in the broadest sense of that term, which aims to strengthen European competitiveness and to maintain a single market characterised by a high degree of internal competition. It was further argued that any modernisation of EC antitrust policy has to take into account the constitutional framework provided by the TEU. The constitutional direction set out in the TEU is ambiguous. On the one hand the Community acquires ever wider competences in new policy fields. On the other, the degree or depth of Community interference with national policies is more explicitly limited than before. Thus, the inevitability of ever more Community competences is accepted by the Member States but the limited nature of those competences is re-emphasised.

Part II of this book examines the modernisation of Community antitrust law in the light of the constitutional framework provided by the EC Treaty. The issues addressed can be categorised under four headings, which correspond with the four chapters of this part. The first two chapters deal with substantive issues, the other two with institutional issues. The present chapter, Chapter 3, addresses the issue of the objectives of EC antitrust law. The next chapter examines the relationship between Community and Member State antitrust law jurisdiction. Chapter 5 discusses institutional issues at the Community level. Chapter 6 examines the relation between Community and Member State institutions.[1]

The thesis underlying Part II is that these issues are intimately correlated in several ways, most notably by their link with broader Community developments and their setting in the framework of the Treaty on European Union.[2]

---

[1] Thus, the divide between substantive (Chs. 3 and 4) and institutional issues (Chs. 5 and 6) can be supplemented with the alternative divide between constitutional developments at the central (Chs. 3 and 5) and the decentral (Chs. 4 and 6) level.

[2] On the strong ties between substance, procedure and institutions, specifically in Community antitrust law, see A. Pappalardo, "Les relations entre le droit Communautaire et les droits nationaux de la concurrence" (1995) 9 *Revue Internationale de Droit Economique* 123–60 and B. Rodger, "Decentralisation, the Public Interest and the 'Pursuit of Certainty' " (1995) 16 *ECLR* 395–9.

Chapter 3, then, comes back to the issue of the objectives of European Community antitrust policy. While Part I of this study provided an overview of the way in which the objectives of Community antitrust law evolved, this chapter examines the current objectives of Community antitrust law with reference to the Treaty on European Union. To avoid repetition, this chapter uses a more specific perspective than that adopted in Part I. Here the focus is on one aspect of Community antitrust law: Article 81 EC (ex Article 85). Article 81 prohibits restricting competition by way of inter-firm agreements. The objective of antitrust law is to avoid restrictions of competition. Determining the objectives of antitrust law is therefore intimately connected to answering the question of what constitutes a "restriction of competition" in the sense of Article 81 of the Treaty. This chapter's examination of the objectives of EC antitrust law will therefore focus on the interpretation of the concept of a restriction of competition.

Another motivation for focusing on the interpretation of a restriction of competition when discussing the objectives of EC antitrust law is the recent substantive modernisation of Community antitrust law on the basis of the Commission's revised stance towards so-called "vertical agreements".

Vertical agreements are agreements concluded between operators at different stages of the production and marketing chains of one and the same product or service.[3] These agreements typically include provisions on the rights and obligations of the supplier and distributor. The restrictive element is found in clauses, typically adopted in distribution agreements, which limit the modes of re-selling and the type of customers or retailers. These restraints may promote competition and market integration but they are also capable of restricting these processes.

Positive effects on competition derive from new and specialised forms of distribution which can be involved. Producers do not always have the skills or knowledge to be competitive in, for example, retailing. In addition, specialised distributors do not only have superior knowledge but they may also gain economies of scale by specialising in distribution. Thirdly—as will be demonstrated in more detail below—contractual restrictions on the behaviour of supplier and distributor may be required to guarantee that parties which make subtantial efforts in connection with distributing the goods involved are rewarded for their efforts. This relates to the potential positive effects of vertical restraints on the integration process, which is likely to follow from increased potential to penetrate new (cross-border) markets. A stable and possibly exclusive business relationship between a foreign producer and local distributor with specialist knowledge of the regional market may reduce the producer's perceived risks, while at the same time it may increase the chance of a succesful launch of the product on that market.

---

[3] R. Whish, *Competition Law* (London, Butterworths, 1993), 45.

Potential effects of vertical restraints on competition and on integration are not unequivocally positive. First, the effects on competition may be negative. Where several producers employ exclusive distributors to sell their products, it is possible that the collected bundles of exclusive distribution agreements effectively encompass all outlets. Foreclosure may be the result since it would be difficult to find distributors for the products where the distributors are all engaged in exclusive relations with another producer. Likewise the effect on integration can be negative. The organisation of a distribution system with exclusive distributors appointed on a Member State basis for example is likely to facilitate continued partitioning of the single market along those borders.

The ambiguous effects of vertical restraints on the process of competition and on the market integration process have assured that the regulation of this type of business relation was central to the development of the notion of a restriction of competition in Community context.[4] The tension between antitrust policy's role in promoting integration and the role it plays—outside the Community—in promoting allocative and productive efficiency is crucial to the problems encountered in Community policy towards vertical restraints.[5] It is in this area that Commission antitrust law enforcement practice was criticised most fervently during the 1990s.[6]

When confronted with the expiration of several block-exemption regulations in this area, the Commission therefore decided to call for a debate on the future course of EC antitrust policy *vis-à-vis* vertical restraints. Instead of mechanically renewing the various block-exemption regulations it issued a Green Paper which set out a number of options for future Community antitrust policy towards contractual restrictions of parties' economic freedom. The Green Paper led to a follow-up document in which the intended changes to the Commission's policy were set out. The Council endorsed the Commission plans which led to a new general block exemption for categories of vertical agreements.[7] Given its

---

[4] It is interesting to note that it was initially contested that vertical agreements fell with the scope of Art. 81(1) EC at all. The ECJ endorsed the Commission's and the Council's (contested) opinion that vertical agreements are capable of restricting competition in the sense of Art. 81(1): Case C–32/65 *Italy* v. *Council and Commission* [1966] ECR 389 and Joined Cases 56 & 58/64 *Consten and Grundig* v. *Commission* [1966] ECR 299.

[5] Allocative efficiency is improved where free competition ensures that the relation between consumer prices and demand is optimal. In the United States it is one of the main driving forces in current antitrust enforcement objectives. Promotion of allocative efficiency is equal to increasing consumer welfare. Thus, promoting consumer welfare has become the basic tenet of US antitrust policy. Productive efficiency seeks to promote the processes of production within firms. It aims to promote generally the "competitiveness" of the industries of the relevant jurisdiction. See, for an elaboration, the depiction of current objectives of US antitrust law in Hovenkamp's contribution to the 1997 Robert Schuman Centre Workshop on Competition Law: H. Hovenkamp, in L. Laudati and C.-D. Ehlermann (eds.), *Robert Schuman Centre Annual on Competition Law—1997* (Oxford, Hart, 1998).

[6] B. Hawk, "System Failure: Vertical Restraints and EC Competition Law" (1995) 32 *CMLRev* 973–89. See also D. Deacon, "Vertical Restraints under EU Competition Law: New Directions" in B. Hawk (ed.), *Annual Proceedings of the Fordham Corporate Law Institute 1995* (Irvington-on-Hudson, International Transjuris Publications, 1996), 307–24 at 307: "[v]ertical restraints seem to arouse more passion and cause more ink to be spilt thant any other area of antitrust".

prominent place in the modernisation of Community antitrust policy, the notion of restriction of competition in the area of vertical agreements provides an adequate basis for this chapter's examination of the pertinent objectives of EC antitrust law in light of the EC Treaty.

The chapter proceeds with a description of the three main lines of criticism on the Community's traditional antitrust policy toward vertical restraints (3.1). The subsequent section examines whether that critique was based on authentical perceptions of antitrust law practice (3.2). On the basis of that examination the three strands of criticism as well as the vertical restraints policy laid down in the general block-exemption regulation are held against the Court of Justice interpretation of the objectives of Community antitrust policy in view of Article 81 EC (3.3).

3.1 CRITIQUE OF EC ANTITRUST LAW OBJECTIVES

Since the internal market was formally established and the EC Treaty entered into force, the objectives of Community antitrust policy, especially as pursued in the area of vertical restraints, have been subject to three different—though strongly related—strands of criticism. The common element to the critique is that the Community institutions—the Commission and, to a lesser extent, the Community Courts—have adopted a flawed concept of what constitutes a restriction of competition. As a consequence, it is argued, Community antitrust law is sometimes enforced in such a way as to hamper competition. Of the three main categories of objections to current practice, two are directed to the interpretation of Article 81(1) of the Treaty, the other concerns the application of Article 81(3).

3.1.1. EC Antitrust Policy Promotes Integration—not Competition

The interpretation of the first paragraph of Article 81 has been criticised often and for various reasons but two dominant lines of analysis can be distinguished.

Proponents of the first line of criticism proceed from the observation that in EC antitrust law integration has been elevated to a goal in itself and that, consequently, that objective has supplanted the protection of competition as the main objective pursued by enforcing Article 81 EC. The absolute prohibition under EC antitrust law on concluding agreements which contain territorial

---

[7] Commission Reg. (EC) No 2790/1999 of 22 December 1999 on the application of Art. 81(3) of the Treaty to categories of vertical agreements and concerted practices; OJ [1999] L336/21. The Council Reg. enabling the Commission to adopt the general block exemption Reg. is Reg 1215/1999 of 10 June 1999 [1999] OJ L148/1 and that withdrawing the requirement of notification prior to exemption in Council Reg. 1216/1999 of 10 June 1999 [1999] OJ L148/5.

restrictions is challenged. Competition policy, critics argue, should aim to enhance competition, not integration and parallel trade.[8]

The critics assert that the notion of competition which is employed by the Community institutions overlooks the fact that competition can take various forms. They argue, for example, that the emphasis on the protection of parallel trade disregards the difference between two forms of competition: *inter*-brand and *intra*-brand competition. The former denotes competition between products of a different make; the latter describes competition between retailers of products of the same make. While a producer who imposes restrictions on his distributors in order to ensure that they market his products in the most effective way may entail a reduction of competition between those distributors in his own goods (intra-brand competition), these reductions and the marketing scheme thus developed may enhance the competitive edge of these products *vis-à-vis* products of a different make. Consequently, the contractual restrictions on the freedom to trade (across borders) may enhance competition between these products (inter-brand competition).[9] In markets where intensive interbrand competition exists, there is no obvious objection from a competition policy perspective to restrictions on the freedom to trade in a particular brand. To do otherwise and declare contractual restrictions on parallel trade invariably prohibited by EC antitrust law may in fact reduce competition. To provide an example, the prohibition under Community antitrust law on establishing a distribution system in which parallel exports are banned renders it problematical to protect investments made by one of the parties, for example, in relation to promotional efforts. Particularly where a producer seeks to enter a new market through an independent distributor, building up the market may be costly and risky for that distributor. The distributor is likely to demand guarantees that the fruits of his efforts to market the product will actually fall into his hands. Clauses in distribution agreements which protect the distributor from competition by importers may enable the distributor to protect himself from "free riders".[10] As a consequence of the lack of protection from free riders, firms are deterred from "joining the chain" because it will be impossible for them to ensure that they will themselves reap the full fruits of the required investments. Competition may actually be reduced because of the requirements of free parallel trade under EC antitrust law.[11]

---

[8] Korah for instance has continuously opposed the lack of economic reasoning in Commission decisions and ECJ case law with respect to agreements which contain restrictions to free cross-border trade. See especially, V. Korah, "EEC Competition Policy—Legal Form or Economic Efficiency" (1986) 39 *Current Legal Problems* 85–109 at 91ff and below.

[9] Whish, above, n. 3, at 8.

[10] Free riders are those distributors which will try to enter the market once the pioneering distributor has established it. Free riders come into the distributor's territory and undercut him with the same brand of products obtained from other sources. The typical business answer to this form of competition from free riders is to provide protection to the distributor by granting him an exclusive right to market the relevant brand in an allocated area. Such a right is supported by a prohibition for other distributors to market imported goods.

[11] See the Court's recognition of this mechanism in Case 161/84 *Pronuptia* [1986] ECR 353 at p. 384.

Accordingly, the criticism of Community antitrust law enforcement was particularly fierce when the Commission condemned a distribution agreement containing a surcharge clause for goods exported from the United Kingdom to be marketed on the continent. The surcharge on the exported goods was levied in order to compensate for the additional promotional efforts required for marketing the (whiskey) brand on the continent. The Commission considered that the differential pricing scheme hindered free trade between Member States and thus distorted competition in the sense of Article 81 of the Treaty.[12]

3.1.2. EC Antitrust Policy Protects Economic Freedom—not Competition

The second strand of criticism is strongly related to the first. It is nevertheless essential to distinguish between the two. Whereas the first line of criticism, identified above, contrasts the equation of a restriction of competition with a restriction of *trade between Member States*, the second challenges the more general conflation of a restriction of competition with any restriction of *the economic freedom* of parties to an agreement.

Commentators argue that Commission practice and, to a lesser extent, Court of Justice case law tend to balance the ultimate competitive effects of an agreement which contains one or more clauses which restrict the economic freedom of one of the parties when considering whether an *exemption* for the prohibition laid down in Article 81(1) can be granted. Hence, the principal test which the Commission applies when considering whether vertical agreements restrict, distort or prevent competition in the sense of Article 81(1) is whether the economic freedom of parties to the agreement is restricted. If this is the case, the agreement is held to restrict competition for the purposes of Article 81(1) and the agreement is null and void under Article 81(2), unless the agreement can benefit from an exemption of the antitrust prohibition on the basis of Article 81(3). Exemptions are granted to agreements which generate overall pro-competitive effects.

Supporters of the second strand of criticism argue that this procedure is flawed. They claim that the Commission and the Court should weigh the anticompetitive and pro-competitive effects of (distribution) agreements when they consider whether an agreement entails a restriction of competition in the sense of Article 81(1). In their view there is no legitimate rationale behind *exempting* agreements from the prohibition to restrict competition if their ultimate effect is not a restriction but, on the contrary, enhancement of competition. The objective of Community antitrust law, they argue, is to guarantee not the economic freedom of private parties but to protect competition. Again the free rider con-

---

[12] *"Irish Distillers"*, decision of 20 December 1977 [1978] OJ L50/16. I. van Bael, "Heretical Reflections on the Basic Dogma: Single Market Integration" (1980) 10 *Revue Suisse du droit international de la concurrence* 39–56; V. Korah, "Goodbye, Red Label; Condemnation of Dual Pricing by Distillers" (1978) 2 *ELR* 62–71, at 71, but see, more positively, T. Sharpe, "The Distillers Decision" (1978) 15 *CMLRev* 447–64, at 459.

cept is relevant. Restraints on the freedom of parties to an agreement to market the product in whichever way they like should not be deemed to restrict competition in the sense of Article 81(1) of the Treaty if they are ancillary to an otherwise pro-competitive agreement or if they are included in agreements between parties without market power.

In support of their contention that it would be wise to bring economic analysis into the application of Article 81(1) these critics point to the procedural problems and costs for European business generated by the current Commission interpretation of that provision, which consist of extensive notification duties, the standard need for exemptions and the problems which it generates in competition law enforcement before institutions other than the EC Commission. Also they point to the problems which the broad interpretation of the prohibition defined in Article 81(1) creates in view of the rigid structure of Article 81(3). Exemptions to the prohibition formulated in Article 81(1) may be provided only if all four conditions which are defined in Article 81(3) are fulfilled. If one of the conditions is not met an exemption *cannot* be provided. As a consequence, agreements which contain a restriction of the economic freedom of parties but which promote competition have to be null and void if, for instance, they do not advance economic progress. Thus, critics argue, the broad interpretation of Article 81(1)'s prohibition hampers competition within the common market.[13]

Within the second line of criticism there are those who stress that the Commission's interpretation of Article 81(1) of the Treaty is incompatible with the Court of Justice's case law. The Court's case law reveals that agreements need to be considered in their economic context before it can be judged whether they restrict competition in the sense of Article 81(1) of the Treaty. The critics argue that these Court judgments do not leave room for the broad and legalistic interpretation of the prohibition to restrict competition, favoured by the Commission.[14]

3.1.3. EC Antitrust Policy Provides Exemptions to Anti-competitive Agreements

Contrary to the first two strands of critique which disapprove of the interpretation given to Article 81(1), the third line of criticism is directed towards the interpretation and application of Article 81(3) of the Treaty. The criticism relates to the nature of the objectives which the Commission takes into account under that provision. Broad discretion in the hands of the Commission in the application of Article 81(3) has allowed exemptions to be granted on the basis of concerns derived from fields of policy other than competition policy.

---

[13] See for instance, C. Bright, "EU Competition Policy: Rules, Objectives and Deregulation" (1996) 16 *Oxford Journal of Legal Studies* 535–59, at 545.

[14] Hawk, above, n. 6 and R. van den Bergh, "Modern Industrial Organisation versus Old-Fashioned European Competition Law" (1996) 17 *ECLR* 75–87.

In exempting anti-competitive agreements from the prohibition of Article 81(1) the Commission has demonstrated concern for a wide range of policy issues. Critics argue that this practice is undesirable, particularly in view of the non-transparent and unaccountable manner in which the extra-competition objectives are pursued under Article 81(3).[15]

In spite of the differences in perspectives there are direct links between the three forms of critique of EC antitrust policy. Broad application of the prohibition to restrict competition automatically generates pressure on the exemption prohibition. The need for numerous exemptions under the broad interpretation of Article 81(1)'s ambit in turn generated problematic procedures. In the absence of a significant number of formal individual exemptions, alternatives have been invented, but various objections arise in connection with the dominant tools in this respect, "comfort letters" and block exemptions. Comfort letters are administrative letters from the Director General of DG IV which declare that the Commission sees no reason to take action. Although a form of solace may be found in such letters, their practical value is limited. They cannot, for example, be relied upon before national courts even if they *may* be taken into account by the national judge. Moreover, the effects of comfort letters can be repealed at any moment by the Commission. Block-exemption regulations, being regulations which apply Article 81(3) of the Treaty, do not lay down any mandatory provisions directly affecting the validity or the content of contractual provisions or oblige the contracting parties to adapt the content of their agreement. Their effect is in principle limited to providing economic agents, potentially falling into the categories mentioned in the block exemptions, with the possibility of removing their agreements from the scope of the prohibition contained in Article 81(1) of the Treaty, in spite of the inclusion of certain types of potentially restrictive clauses.[16] Nevertheless block-exemption regulations have been objected to as well. They are considered to operate as straitjackets, encouraging parties to adapt their contracts to fit the prescription of the relevant exemption regulation. Block-exemption regulations thus compel undertakings to follow closely the contents of the relevant clauses if they want to profit from them. Block-exemption regulations therefore thwart an important element of the competition process, for example relating to the terms and conditions of the contracts concerned.[17]

---

[15] For instance, see G. Amato, *Antitrust and the Bounds of Power* (Hart, Oxford, 1997), 58–62, and, more generally, on the Commission's balancing of competition and extra-competition objectives under Art. 81(3) of the Treaty: R. Bouterse, *Competition and Integration—What Goals Count?* (The Hague, Kluwer Law International, 1995).

[16] Case C–226/94 *Grand Garage Alibigeois* v. *Grand Garage de la Gare* [1996] ECR I–651 and Case C–309/94 *Nissan* v. *Dupasquier* [1996] ECR I–677.

[17] T. Groger and T. Janicki, "Weiterentwicklung des europäischen Wettbewerbsrechts" (1992) 42 *WuW* 991–1005 at 992; and V. Korah and M. Horspool, "Competition" (1992) 37 *Antitrust Bulletin* 337–85 at 356–7.

3.2 ANALYSIS OF THE CRITICISM OF EC ANTITRUST POLICY OBJECTIVES

This section examines to what extent the various forms of criticism to Commission and Court of Justice antitrust law jurisprudence and case law, presented in the previous section, reflect reality. It successively addresses the three main streams of critique.

3.2.1. Does EC Antitrust Policy Promote Integration instead of Competition?

It appears that in the enforcement of Community antitrust law great interest has been taken in guaranteeing free inter-state trade. Integration formed the focal point of EC antitrust law enforcement.[18] It has been consistent practice to condemn all agreements or concerted practices which potentially hinder intra-Community trade, and thus integration, on the basis of Article 81(1) of the Treaty. Clauses in agreements which restrict trade between Member States do not qualify for exemption under Article 81(3).

It will be recalled that the Court's decision in the *Consten & Grundig* case laid the basis for the interpretation of Article 81 EC as a means to protect the free flow of products. The judgment linked the concept of competition in Community antitrust law directly to the process of common market integration by holding that an agreement which aims artificially to maintain separate national markets for particular products, thus restraining free flow of goods, constitutes a restriction of *competition*. This was considered to be the case irrespective of the actual effects on competition of the specific agreement. For an agreement between a producer and distributor which restores national divisions in trade between Member States is likely to frustrate the most fundamental objective of the Community, market integration. The EC Treaty, which aims to abolish barriers between states, does not allow undertakings to reconstruct such barriers. Article 81(1) of the Treaty was interpreted in this light. The Court reasoned that the antitrust provisions were not to be interpreted narrowly, i.e. exclusively and immediately directed towards the promotion of competition. Instead, the Court ruled, the Treaty's antitrust rules are designed to contribute to the overall aim of the Community, European integration.[19]

The unequivocal Court of Justice statement with respect to the objective of the Treaty's antitrust provisions in *Consten & Grundig* formed the basis of the Commission's antitrust law decisional practice. Following the Court's reasoning, the Commission interpreted the competition rules as a tool in its policy towards market integration. This is most evident from the Commission's statement that "[t]he first fundamental objective is to keep the common market open

---

[18] See above, Ch. 1 passim.
[19] *Consten and Grundig* v. *Commission*, above, n. 4, at 340. See also Ch. 1.

and unified. . . . There is accordingly a continuing need—and this is the primary task of the Community's competition policy—to forestall and suppress restrictive or abusive practices of firms attempting to divide up the market again so as to apply artificial price differences or impose unfair terms on their customers".[20] Accordingly, the Commission generally found that agreements which contained export bans restrict competition under Article 81(1) EC.[21] The same emphasis on guaranteeing free movement of goods on the basis of the antitrust rules is observed in the positive limb to the Commission's antitrust practice under Article 81(3) of the Treaty. A precondition for qualifying for an exemption for the prohibition on restricting competition has invariably been that inter-state trade is not hampered by the agreement. Analagously, the Commission has enshrined safeguards on parallel trade in the block-exemption regulations which it issued for vertical agreements.

The Court of Justice has been equally uncompromising in its observance of possible restrictions on inter-state trade, notably export bans, when applying Community antitrust law. As with the Commission practice set out above, the Court has generally held Article 81(1) of the Treaty to be infringed by those agreements which contain clauses capable of hindering or obstructing parallel trade.[22] Hindering parallel trade through indirect measures which have similar effects, for instance denying benefits of guarantees to imported goods has also consistently been held to be contrary to Article 81(1) EC.[23] Conversely, agreements which provide for free parallel trade are less likely to fall within Article 81(1).[24]

The unity of the common market continues to form an important element in the Court's antitrust case law. Neither the gradual establishment of the internal market nor its formal conclusion by the end of 1992 has led the Court to alter its case law in this respect. In 1994, when the internal market had been operative for more than a year—and intra-Community trade was supposedly borderless—the Court repeated that "by its very nature, a clause *prohibiting exports* constitutes a restriction of *competition*" because its objective is to isolate a part of the market.[25] In a parallel case the Court ruled that stipulations in a distrib-

---

[20] Commission of the EEC, *Ninth Annual Report on Competition Policy* (Brussels, 1979).

[21] See, for instance, *Teacher* ([1978] OJ L235/20), *Bell* ([1978] OJ L235/15), *Kawasaki* ([1979] OJ L16/9) and, more recently, *Viho/Toshiba* ([1991] OJ L287/39), *Dunlop* ([1992] OJ L131/32) and *Viho/Parker Pen* ([1992] OJ L233/27). Today, undertakings which still attempt to isolate markets can count on huge fines: see *BASF Lacke+Farbe/Accinauto* ([1995] OJ L272/16), *ADALAT* ([1996] OJ L201/1) and *Volkswagen* ([1998] OJ L124/60).

[22] See e.g. Case 19/77 *Miller International Schallplatten GmbH* v. *Commission* [1978] ECR 131 at 148: "*by its* very *nature,* a clause *prohibiting exports* constitutes a *restriction* of *competition*"; and Case 32 & 36–82/78 *BMW and BMW Belgian Dealers* v. *Commission* [1979] ECR 2435.

[23] Case 31/85 *ETA Fabriques d"Ebauches* v. *DK Investments* [1985] ECR 3933.

[24] Case 1/71 *S.A. Cadillon* v. *Fa. Höss* [1971] ECR 351 at 356: an agreement which is not likely to hinder the attainment of the objectives of a single market is *even more* unlikely to fall within the prohibition laid down in Art. 81 EC "when such an agreement does not prohibit third parties from effecting *parallel imports* into the territory covered by the agreement or the licensee from re-exporting the products covered by the agreement".

[25] Case T–66/92 *Herlitz* v. *Commission* [1994] ECR II–531 and Case T–77/92 *Parker Pen* v. *Commission* [1994] ECR II–549.

ution system which prohibit resale of the relevant goods, "the effect of which is to partition national markets and in so doing thwart the objective of achieving a common market, are *inherently* contrary to Article 85(1) [now Article 81] of the Treaty".[26] That EC antitrust law continues to consider agreements mainly with an eye to their effects on inter-state trade was underscored explicitly by the Court in the *Spanish Banks* case, where it held that "Community law and national law consider cartels from a different point of view. Whereas Article 85 [now Article 81] regards them in the light of the obstacles which may result for trade between Member States, each body of national legislation proceeds on the basis of the considerations peculiar to it and considers cartels only in that context".[27] It is evident that the prohibition on hindering the free flow of goods within the Community certainly is a dominant element in the Court's antitrust law jurisprudence.[28]

Hence, both Commission decisions and Court of Justice case law reveal that promotion of integration is an important element of Community antitrust policy. The viewpoint may be confirmed that Article 81 has been interpreted in such a way as to equate a restriction on the free movement of goods with a restriction of competition. Indeed the Commission "obliged the businessman reluctantly to participate in creating the Common Market by forcing him to ignore governmental barriers to trade and discrepancies in the market conditions between the different Member States".[29]

As has been said, critics of current practice have argued that the emphasis on integration, and the ensuing requirement that there remain room for parallel trade, hampers competition. Contrary to the previous examination whether parallel trade is valued under EC antitrust law, it is difficult to test what the effect of this practice has been on competition. Comparing the effects of two policies, one of which has not been pursued, necessarily implies a degree of speculation. Yet there is a clear case in support of the view that territorial exclusivity—irrespective of the ensuing restraints on parallel trade—is likely to enhance competition.[30] As a consequence the practice described above in which the freedom of parallel trade prevails over this type of restrictions may well have reduced the level of competition in the Community.

---

[26] Case T–43/92 *Dunlop Slazenger International* v. *Commission* [1994] ECR II–441 at 467.

[27] Case C–67/91 *Dirección General de Defensa de la Competencia* v. *Asociación Española de Banca Privada* (*"Spanish Banks"*) [1992] ECR I–4785 at 4825.

[28] Although the discussion in this ch. focuses on vertical agreements, it may be noted that restrictions on cross-border trade are generally considered *per se* restrictions of competition. Irrespective of the actual effects on competition—which may be positive—agreements containing clauses which restrict intra-Community trade are considered to be anti-competitive under EC antitrust law. For examples outside the "vertical" sphere see Cases 29 & 30/83 *Compagnie royale Asturienne des Mines and Rheinzink* v. *Commission* [1984] ECR 1679 at 1704 and Cases 96–102, 104, 105, 108, 110/82 *IAZ International Belgium* v. *Commission* [1983] ECR 3369 at 3412.

[29] I. Forrester, "The Current Goals of EC Competition Policy" in C.-D. Ehlermann and L. Laudati (eds.), *Robert Schuman Centre Annual on Competition Law—1997* (Oxford, Hart, 1998).

[30] See Whish, above, n. 3, at 8.

The effects of the focus on free cross-border trade were however limited by an unique antitrust law concept, that of "passive" sales, which the Commission developed in order to reduce the negative effects on competition of the policy to promote integration. Essentially, passive sales are sales by distributors to customers which come from outside the territory which has been allocated to them exclusively. It constitutes an infraction of the exclusivity of the dealer's allocated area. The Commission acknowledges that exclusivity in vertical agreements can have positive effects and accepts such restrictions, provided that the parties to the agreements are not confined to satisfying the demand for contract goods within their contract territories but are also able to meet unsolicited demand from persons and undertakings from other areas of the common market.[31]

Nevertheless, criticism that the prohibition on limiting parallel trade as currently kept in force on the basis of EC antitrust law is likely to reduce competition seems to be in point. Whether the reduction of competition generated by current practice implies that Community antitrust doctrine is misguided and that is should be altered in the context of the TEU is a question which will be addressed in the next section.

3.2.2. Does EC Antitrust Policy Protect Economic Freedom instead of Competition?

The second line of criticism identified above posits—irrespective of the question whether unrestricted competition requires unrestricted parallel trade—that under EC antitrust law a restriction of the economic freedom of the parties to an agreement is, wrongly, put at par with a restriction of competition. The result is that the prohibition in Article 81(1) of the Treaty encompasses numerous agreements which do not constitute a restriction of competition in practice. In order to remain valid under EC antitrust law these agreements require an exemption, individually or *en bloc*, from the Commission. As seen above, critics oppose the unjustified burden which results for business and the inconsistency, thus created, of "exempting" agreements which are not anti-competitive from the prohibition on restricting competition enshrined in Article 81(1) EC.

To examine whether the above description of EC antitrust practice is adequate, it is again useful to return to *Consten and Grundig*. Under the specific circumstances of the case, the restriction on economic freedom of the parties to an exclusive distribution agreement corresponded to a restriction on the freedom

---

[31] See the motor vehicle distribution block exemption; Commission Reg. 1475/95 on the application of Art. 81(3) of the Treaty to certain categories of motor vehicle distribution and servicing agreements [1995] OJ L145/25, in particular recitals 7, 9, 16, 26 and Art. 3(9). Similarly with respect to franchising agreements the Commission, following an explicit Court judgment, has issued a block-exemption reg. for that type of agreement even where a degree of territorial protection is included; Reg. 408/88 [1988] OJ L359/46.

of cross-border trade. The Court considered that the exclusivity clause in the agreement, which naturally restricted the potential for parallel trade, constituted a restriction of competition prohibited by Article 81(1) EC. It is useful to repeat in the present context the crucial elaboration which the Court provided with respect to the concept of competition underlying the Treaty's competition rules in general and that of Article 81(1) in particular. The Court ruled that:

> the principle of freedom of competition concerns the various stages and manifestations of competition. Although competition between producers is generally more noticeable than that between distributors of products of the same make, it does not thereby follow that an agreement tending to restrict the latter kind of competition should escape the prohibition of Article 85(1) [now Article 81] merely because it might increase the former. Besides, for the purposes of applying Article 85(1) [now Article 81], there is no need to take account of the concrete effects of an agreement once it appears that it has as its object the prevention, restriction or distortion of competition. Therefore the absence in the contested decision of any analysis of the effects of the agreement on competition between similar products of different makes does not, of itself, constitute a defect in the decision.[32]

The Commission followed the Court's conception of a restriction of competition carefully. In accordance with what is submitted by critics of its practice, the Commission has preserved the interpretation of a restriction on parties' economic freedom equaling a restriction of competition under Article 81(1) of the Treaty.

One of the clearest Commission decisions in this respect is that addressed to INRA and Eisele (trading as Nungesser). The Commission considered Article 81(1) to be infringed by the grant by INRA to Nungesser of exclusive rights to produce and sell its seeds in Germany because INRA thereby deprived itself of the ability to license other undertakings in Germany or to trade itself.[33] The same reasoning underlies the Commission's holding that a patent licence agreement potentially restricts competition where licensees are prevented from manufacturing products other than that of the licensor.[34] Indeed examination of Commission decisional practice reveals too many examples of equating contractual (non-territorial) restrictions on parties' economic freedom to restrictions of competition to warrant a presentation of the complete set here.

Although it is not of direct relevance to the examination of the claim that the Commission interprets Article 81(1) of the Treaty too broadly, it should nevertheless be noted here that the fact that the Commission generally considers agreements containing clauses which restrict the economic freedom of parties to fall within Article 81(1) does not imply that it overlooks the potentially pro-competitive effects of these agreements. The Commission tends to assess the ultimate effects on competition of agreements which contain restraints on the parties' commercial freedom in its application of Article 81(3) of the Treaty. It

[32] *Consten and Grundig* v. *Commission*, above, n. 4, at 342.
[33] [1978] OJ L286/23.
[34] [1978] OJ L47/42 ("Philips VCRs").

normally exempts from the prohibition of Article 81(1) those clauses which it considers to be both pro-competitive and pro-integration.[35] Moreover, there are now various exceptions to the practice of considering any contractual restriction of the economic freedom of parties as a restriction of competition under Article 81(1). When dealing with selective distribution agreements, commercial agency agreements and certain co-operative joint-venture agreements, the Commission tends to balance the pro- and anti-competitive effects under Article 81(1).[36]

The second limb to the critique that the Commission interprets the antitrust prohibition too expansively was seen to be that this interpretation diverges from the Court of Justice case law on Article 81(1). An examination of the Court's case law on Article 81(1) should start in 1966 with, on the one hand, the *Consten & Grundig* judgment, and, on the other, the *STM* v. *Maschinenbau Ulm* judgment. In the latter judgment the Court ruled that in order to assess whether an agreement is prohibited by Article 81(1), in the absence of evidence that it was concluded with the objective of impeding competition, the agreement's effects on competition need to be assessed. The Court held that the competition in question is to be understood "within the actual context in which it would occur in the absence of the agreement in dispute. In particular it may be doubted whether there is an interference with competition if the said agreement seems really necessary for the penetration of a new area by an undertaking".[37] The nature of the appropriate test was elaborated upon in a subsequent case in which the Court clarified that agreements fall outside the Article 81(1) prohibition when there is only an insignificant effect on the markets, taking into account the weak position which the parties concerned have on the market for the product in question. An exclusive dealing agreement even one with absolute territorial protection, may escape the prohibition laid down in Article 81(1).[38]

---

[35] A good example is provided by the "German Ice-cream" decisions (*Schöller* and *Langnese-Iglo* [1993] OJ L183/1 and 183/19 respectively). Although the agreements were held to be contrary to Art. 81(1), that judgment was reached on the basis of extensive economic analysis of the market conditions and the effects of the relevant agreements on the market, thus going beyond a test limited to the wording of the clauses.

[36] For selective distribution see, recently, *Grundig* [1994] OJ L20/15; for commercial agency agreements see the Commission Notice of 24 December 1962 (JO 139/62), the "Preliminary draft Commission Notice on Commercial Agency Agreements of 1990" and the *World Cup Football* decision ([1992] OJ L326/31); for joint-venture agreements see *Odin Metal Box* ([1990] OJ L209/15), *BT/MCI* ([1994] OJ L223/36)in which obvious restrictions of the economic freedom of the parties were declared not to infringe Art. 81(1), although the joint venture itself was provided with an exemption). See also the Commission Notice on Ancillary Retrictions to Concentrations ([1990] OJ C203/5). Finally, see the ninth recital of Commission Reg. 240/96 of 31 January 1996 on the application of Art. 81(3) of the Treaty to certain categories of technology transfer agreements ([1996] OJ L31/2): "[e]xclusive agreements . . . *may not be in themselves incompatible with Article 81(1)* where they are concerned with the introduction and protection of a new technology in the licensed territory, by reason of the scale of the research which has been undertaken, of the increase in the level of competition, *in particular inter-brand competition*, and of the competitiveness of the undertakings concerned resulting from the dissemination of innovation within the Community".

[37] Case 56/65 *Societé la Technique Minière* v. *Maschinenbau Ulm GmbH* [1966] ECR 235 at 250.

[38] Case 5/69 *Franz Völk* v. *Etablissements Vervaecke* [1969] ECR 295.

This line of reasoning, which clearly departs from the equation of "freedom to act" and "free competition" was followed in numerous subsequent Court judgments. Particularly in its judgments relating to vertical agreements the Court repeated that in assessing the terms of the prohibition contained in Article 81(1) regard must be had to the effects of clauses on competition in the economic and legal contexts in which they occur. It reasoned that, in order to examine whether an agreement restricts competition it cannot be examined in isolation from the factual or legal circumstances causing it to prevent, restrict or distort competition.[39] The doctrine has also been followed with respect to various forms of exclusivity clauses in licensing agreements. In contrast to the Commission's assessment, the Court of Justice held for instance that the exclusive patent licence for Nungesser to produce and market the maize seeds developed by INRA did not fall within the prohibition of Article 81(1).[40] On the basis of the same rationale the Court judges that various other licensing agreements fall outside the scope of Article 81.[41]

Although the case law has not been entirely consistent,[42] the Court of Justice appears to have opted for a genuine "economic" reading of Article 81(1) and adhered to it, at least since its judgment in *Delimitis*.[43] In that case the Court confirmed that vertical restraints restrict competition only if examination of the economic and legal contexts of the agreement, in particular of the conditions on the relevant market, reveals that it is difficult to obtain access to the market and that the pertinent agreement contributes significantly to the existing barriers to entry. In other words, if there is sufficient inter-brand competion on a relevant market contractual restraints on the economic freedom of parties will not in itself restrict competition in the sense of Article 81(1) EC.

The same focus on the economic context in which business agreements are implemented is visible in the Court's case law concerning "ancillary restraints". The picture that emerges is that reasonable clauses, even if they entail restrictions on the economic freedom of parties, in an agreement which is in itself

---

[39] See, *inter alia*, Case 23/67 *Brasserie de Haecht* v. *Wilkin-Janssen* ("*Brasserie de Haecht I*") [1967] ECR 525; Case 99/79 *Lancôme* v. *Etos* [1980] ECR 2511; Case 107/82R *AEG Telefunken* v. *Commission* [1983] ECR 3151.

[40] Case 258/78 *Nungesser* v. *Commission* ("*Maize Seeds*") [1982] ECR 2015.

[41] For instance, *Pronuptia* v. *Schillgalis*, above, n. 4 (exclusive supply and non-competition clause deemed necessary for enabling franchising to fulfill its typical pro-competitive function and therefore not to be prohibited by Art. 81); Case 262/81 *Coditel* v. *Ciné Vog Films (No. 2)* ("*Coditel II*") [1982] ECR 3381 (exclusivity in licensing of copyrights is not prohibited by Art. 81); and Case 65/86 *Bayer-Süllhofer* [1988] ECR 5249, at 5249 (no-challenge clause in patent licence agreement not contrary to Art. 81).

[42] The two most noted cases are *Hasselblad* and *Ciments*. In the first judgment the ECJ ruled in relation to an exclusive distribution network run by Hasselblad that a prohibition of sales between authorised dealers "constitutes a restriction of their economic freedom and, *consequently*, a restriction of competition": Case 86/82 *Hasselblad* [1984] ECR 883, at 908–10. In *Ciments*, it declared an obligation imposed on the buyer of products to use these goods himself and not to resell them, a restriction of his economic freedom and thus a clause which has as its object the restriction of competition: Case 319/82 *Société de vente de ciments et bétons de l'Est* v. *Kerpen & Kerpen* [1983] ECR 4173 at 4182.

[43] Case 234/89 *Delimitis* v. *Henninger Bräu* [1991] ECR I–935, at 986–7.

regarded as pro-competitive, do not infringe Article 81(1). Restrictions are generally considered to be reasonable when they are necessary to make the operation of the pro-competitive agreement possible and, moreover, as long as they are proportionate to the competitive benefits envisaged. Consequently, only those restrictions which are indispensable for attaining the legitimate objectives pursued by the agreement as a whole are not prohibited by Article 81.[44]

The case law of the Court of First Instance is in line with that of the Court of Justice. This emerges clearly from the *German Ice Cream* cases, where the CFI ruled with respect to vertical restraints that:

> it is appropriate . . . to consider whether, taken together, all the similar agreements entered into in the relevant market and the other features of the *economic and legal context* of the agreements at issue show that those agreements *cummulatively* have the effect of *denying access to that market* for new domestic and foreign competitors. If, on examination, that is found not to be the case, the individual agreements making up the bundle of agreements as a whole cannot undermine competition within the meaning of Article 85(1) [now Article 81(1)], of the Treaty. If, on the other hand, such examination reveals that it is difficult to gain access to the market, *it is necessary to assess the extent to which the contested agreements contribute to the cummulative effect produced*, on the basis that only agreements which make a significant contribution to any partitioning of the market are prohibited". . . .
>
> However, . . . the extent of tying-in is only one factor among others pertaining to the economic and legal context in which the network of agreements must be assessed. *It is also necessary to analyse the conditions prevailing on the market and, in particular, real and specific possibilities of new competitors to penetrate the market despite the existence of a network* of exclusive purchasing agreements.[45]

Similarly, the Court of First Instance judges that restraints on the economic freedom of parties which are part of what is on balance a pro-competitive agreement do not fall within Article 81(1).[46] In fact the Court of First Instance has been most explicit in stressing that the pro- and anti-competitive effects of agreements must be weighed in order to determine whether the agreement restricts competition is the sense of Article 81(1). In the *European Night Services* judgment the Court reasoned that in assessing an agreement under Article 81(1) of the Treaty, "account should be taken of the actual conditions in which it functions, in particular the economic context in which the undertakings operate, the products or the services covered by the agreement and the actual structure of the market concerned, unless it is an agreement containing obvious restrictions of competition such as price-fixing, market-sharing or the control of outlets".[47]

---

[44] Case C–250/92 *Gottrup-Klim* v. *Dansk Landsbrugs Grovvareselskab* [1994] ECR I–5641 and Case C–399/93 *Oude Luttikhuis* v. *Coberco* [1995] ECR I–4515. See the Opinion of Lenz AG in Case C–415/93 *Bosman* v. *UEFA* [1995] ECR I–4921.

[45] Case T–7/93 *Langnese-Iglo* v. *Commission* [1995] ECR II–1533 at paras. 99 and 106 (emphases added). *Cf.* Case T–9/93 *Schöller* v. *Commission* [1995] ECR II–1611. The appeal has been dismissed: Case C–279/95 P, *Langnese-Iglo* v. *Commission* [1998] ECR I–5609.

[46] Case T–61/89 *Dansk Pelsdyravlerforening* v. *Commission* [1992] ECR II–1931.

[47] Joined Cases T–374, 375, 384 & 388/94 *European Night Services* v. *Commission* [1998] ECR II–3141.

It is evident that the European Courts do not adopt a narrow concept of a restriction of competition in which any restraint on the economic freedom of one of the parties is by itself an infringement of Article 81(1), provided that there are no direct impediments to inter-state trade. Instead, the Courts' analysis originates in the prevailing conditions on the market. The examination of the case law of the Court of Justice and that of the Court of First Instance therefore supports the claim that the Commission's interpretation of Article 81(1) of the Treaty diverges from that of the Court. More than the Commission has done, the Court of Justice has cast the assessment of what constitutes a restriction of competition in the sense of Article 81(1) in economic terms.

However, the noted discrepancy between the Commission's practice of considering the ultimate competition effects under Article 81(3) and that of the Court of applying a comprehensive test under Article 81(1) is subject to two qualifications. It concerns an apparent trend in the Commission's approach and inconsistencies in the Court's case law. First, the Commission, contrary to the practice set out above, increasingly employs economic analysis before concluding that a specific agreement falls within the prohibition of Article 81. Similarly, recent group-exemption regulations have demonstrated the Commission's increased concern with market circumstances.[48] Secondly, the divergence between the Commission's and Court's approach is mitigated by inconsistencies in the case law of the Court. The Court's judgment in *Consten and Grundig*, upon which the Commission apparently based its practice, is not unique in equating a restriction of parties' economic freedom to a restriction of competition in the sense of Article 81(1). The underlying jurisprudence has subsequently been repeated in a number of judgments, also outside the field of territorial restrictions. Although it appears that the European Courts, subsequent to the decision in *Delimitis*, have been consistent in applying an economic test of the prevailing market conditions, a number of post-*Delimitis* Court judgments have led to challenges to the vision that the Court is now commited to a market-based economic approach in its interpretation of Article 81(1).[49]

---

[48] This trend may have come to an end because the Commission itself considers that more systematic use of Art. 81(1) for analysing the pro- and anti-competitive aspects of agreements would cast aside Art. 81(3). Commission White Paper on Modernisation of the Rules Implementing Arts. 81 and 82 of the EC Treaty, para. 57.

[49] Schröter, for example, points to the *German Car Leasing* cases as evidence for continued ECJ support for interpreting Art. 81(1) as a prohibition on reducing parties' economic freedom: H. Schröter, "Vertical Restrictions under Article 85 EC: Towards a Moderate Reform of Current Competition Policy", in L. Gormley (ed.), *Current and Future Perspectives on EC Competition Law* (London, Kluwer Law International, 1997), 15–30 at 26. But his interpretation of the *German Car Leasing* cases appears disputable. Although it should be acknowledged that the Court does, unhelpfully, refer to the reduction of the freedom of commercial action for parties to the relevant distribution agreements in its assessment of whether they infringe Art. 81(1), the real motives for the Court to hold the relevant agreements anti-competitive under that provision is arguably based on its analysis of the economic conditions on the relevant market. This is certainly so in one of the two cases: Case C–266/93 *Bundeskartellamt v. Volkswagen AG and VAG Leasing* [1995] ECR I–3477. In that judgment the ECJ considers the foreclosure effects of the agreements and refers in this respect explicitly to their effects on access to the market (para. 23) and on the leading positions of the

3.2.3. Does EC Antitrust Provide Exemptions to Anti-competitive Agreements?

The third line of concern with the objectives pursued on the basis of Community antitrust policy concerns the way in which the third paragraph of Article 81 is interpreted and applied. Before examining, in the next section, whether it is inappropriate to take into consideration extra-competition objectives in the application of the exemption provision, it is first tested whether the Commission in its application of Article 81(3) allows considerations from policies other than that of competition to play a role.[50]

The clearest recognition that the Commission does occasionally take into account non-competition concerns when deciding whether or not to provide an exemption can be found in relation to industrial policy concerns. Historically this is evident in the exemptions which the Commission provided in the 1980s for the synthetic fibre "crisis cartels".[51] The position that antitrust law exemptions may form an element of a Community industrial policy has not been abandoned. The Commission views competition policy as an element of overall Community industrial policy.[52] One of the main elements in industrial policy as pursued by the Commission on the basis of its antitrust law exemption practice is the protection of small- and medium-sized enterprises (SMEs). The motor vehicle distribution and servicing agreements block-exemption regulation, for example, includes provisions clearly designed to protect the interests of the less powerful parties to those agreements, the dealers. Article 5(2)(2) of the regulation dictates that in order to profit from the exemption *en bloc* the period of notice for termination of the distribution or servicing agreement between manufacturer and dealer must be at least two years.[53] The Commission *de minimis* notices are also explicitly aimed at reducing the burdens on SMEs.[54]

Of the various elements of what can be called social policy concerns, employment has been the most manifest issue taken into account by the Commission in its exemption practice. The Commission interprets stabilisation of employment as an improvement of the general conditions of production within the

companies involved in the relevant markets (para. 25). The second case is *Bayerische Motorenwerke* v. *ALD Auto-Leasing D*, above, n. 23. In that judgment the relevant agreements are revealed to contain absolute territorial protection in combination with an export ban. As was demonstrated above, it is consistent Court practice to consider *that* type of restriction on the economic freedom incompatible with Art. 81(1).

[50] The ECJ is less directly involved in the application of Art. 81(3). Its case law is therefore not discussed in this section but comprehensively in section 3.3.

[51] See Ch. 1.

[52] See e.g. the Commission communication "Industrial Policy in an open and competitive environment", COM(90)556.

[53] Commission Reg. 1475/95 [1995] OJ L145/25.

[54] S. Rating, "Die Kommission schlägt eine neue Bagatelbekanntmachung vor" (1997) 3 *Competition Policy Newsletter* 8–10 at 9–10.

Community.[55] Thus, the effects of an agreement on employment are a factor which the Commission has taken into account when deciding whether or not to grant an exemption.[56] The Commission exempted an agreement restricting competition in the Dutch brick industry because it contributed to promoting economic progress by permitting the necessary restructuring of that sector of the economy under "acceptable social conditions".[57]

Another non-competition concern which is increasingly considered by the Commission in its exemption practice is environmental policy. Akin to employment concerns the protection of the environment is judged by the Commission to contribute to improving conditions of production as well as to promoting economic or technical progress.[58] In recognition of this principle the Commission exempted an agreement which restricted competition but which also led to reduction of pollution and energy use.[59]

A final category of extra-competition concerns which can be seen to have played a role on various exemption cases are those of cultural policy. Cultural policy considerations played an explicit role in the Dutch/Flemish book distribution cases. Although the Commission declined to provide an exemption for the anti-competitive agreements on the basis of cultural policy arguments in that particular instance, it did recognise that cultural policy concerns may affect a decision whether or not to exempt an agreement from the prohibition in Article 81(1) of the Treaty.[60] Another example of cultural concerns in the application of the exemption provision is provided by the Commission decision addressed to United International Pictures ("UIP"). The Commission exempted the relevant agreements under the obligation for UIP to invest in production of European films.[61] A final recent decision in which cultural policy considerations played a role was the Commission's exemption for the agreement between numerous public broadcasting companies ("Eurovision"). Although that Commission decision was subsequently annulled by the Court of First Instance on other grounds, the Commission based its positive assessment of the agreement between the large number of public broadcasters on the fact that it enabled

---

[55] This interpretation that a stabilisation of employment constitutes an improvement in production in the sense of Art. 81(3) of the Treaty was explicitly endorsed by the ECJ in Case 42/84 *Remia and others* v. *Commission* [1985] ECR 2545, at para. 42.

[56] Case 26/76 *Metro* v. *Commission* [1977] ECR 1875.

[57] *Stichting Baksteen* [1994] OJ L131/15.

[58] See Commission of the European Communities, *Twenty-Fifth Annual Report on Competition Policy* (Brussels, 1995), para. 85.

[59] See the Commission Decision in *Philips/Osram* [1994] OJ L378/37.

[60] Commission decision in *VBVB/VBBB* [1982] OJ L54/36. The decision was challenged but upheld by the ECJ in Joined Cases 43 & 63/82 *VBVB and VBBB* v. *Commission* [1984] ECR 19. See on this issue Lenz AG's Opinion in Case C–360/92 P *Publishers Association and others* v. *Commission* ("*Net Book Agreements*") [1995] ECR I–25. The Commission ultimately closed its file on the Dutch/Flemish book distribution agreements in view of the absence of an effect on trade between Member States.

[61] [1989] OJ L226/25. The Commission intends to extend the duration of the exemption on the basis of the same preconditions [1999] OJ C205/6

notably the smaller parties to the agreement to show minority sports and sports programmes with an educational, cultural or humanitarian content.[62]

It must therefore be acknowledged that the Commission has regularly taken into account non-competition policy considerations as an element of its assessment whether or not to provide an exemption for an agreement which would otherwise be counter to Article 81 of the Treaty.

3.3. MODERNISATION OF EC ANTITRUST POLICY OBJECTIVES

The preceding section revealed that the three main strands of criticism directed at Community antitrust law practice are based on adequate perceptions of Commission and Court of Justice decisions in this area of EC law. This section turns to the question how the modernisation of EC antitrust policy may address the various strands of criticism.

3.3.1. Parallel Trade and Integration

It is evident from the survey in the previous section that Community antitrust policy is characterised by a fundamental ambivalence. On the one hand it is beyond doubt that certain contractual restraints on parties' commercial freedom may enhance competition. On the other, restraints on the free, unrestricted flow of goods are considered incompatible with the concept of the single market. In particular, territorial restraints in vertical agreements which produce market compartementalisation are likely to run counter to market integration concerns. Agreements can therefore be beneficial to competition but detrimental to the internal market. It is this conflict which lies at the basis of the criticism that Community antitrust law is not applied in a proper way.

As discussed above, the market integration objective has indeed been promoted on the basis of Community antitrust policy. By condemning territorial restrictions in distribution agreements as restrictions of *competition* the Commission and the Court have ensured the potential for parallel trade (free movement) at the expense of specific competition considerations. A "pure" competition analysis may lead to the conclusion that restrictions on the free movement of products are pro-competitive in view of the positive effects that they generate for (interbrand) competition. The negative appraisal of territorial restraints on the economic freedom of parties is also evident from the fact that the highest fines for competition law infractions have been levied for behaviour

---

[62] *EBU/Eurovision System* [1993] OJ L179/23. The exemption decision was annulled by the CFI because the criteria for membership of EBU were too vague and imprecise to have enabled the Commission to assess whether they were all indispensable to the improvements in distribution which the agreement was considered to generate: Cases T–528, 542, 543 & 546/93 *Métropole and others* v. *Commission* [1996] ECR II–649.

which restricted the free movement of goods. They are exemptable only in exceptional circumstances and always under the condition that "passive sales" are guaranteed.

"Cross-border trading" therefore continues to be "a hugely favoured economic activity in the Community".[63] It is likely to remain so in the near future in view of the continued need for policies which further integration. Establishment of the Internal Market in 1992 provides no more than a formal hallmark of the integration process under which important market disparities remain. Moreover, Community antitrust policy is used by the Commission to preserve the degree of integration reached so far. Finally, future enlargements of the Community, to which it is now clearly committed, will revitalise the need for active integration policy.

The interpretation of the Treaty's competition rules objectives as primarily functional to integration seems justified in view of the intentions of the drafters of the competition provisions. The correlation between the free movement of goods and the Community rules on fair competition between undertakings was clearly perceived by the drafters of the EEC Treaty. In particular it appears that the Treaty's provisions on antitrust were initially adopted in order to preclude private undertakings from re-establishing impediments to free intra-Community trade where public rules with a similar effect were prohibited.[64] Community antitrust law was considered to constitute the private limb of the general provisions on free movement. Articles 81 and 82 EC are therefore best perceived as "private" equivalents of Article 28 EC (ex Article 30), which guarantees free movement of products.[65] Even though it may rightly be argued that for competition purposes it does not make a difference whether goods cross borders or not, the criticism that promoting integration is not a valid objective

---

[63] Forrester, above, n. 29, at 22. In his view "[i]t would be splendid if one day the Commission were frankly to state that an arrangement was acceptable even though in certain respects it made cross-border trade more difficult". It is interesting to note that, conversely, agreements with an anti-competitive effect have obtained exemptions and even negative clearances in view of the agreements' positive effects on integration. *Cf.* I. Forrester, "Competition Structures for the 21st Century" in B. Hawk (ed.), *Annual Proceedings of the Fordham Corporate Law Institute 1994—International Antitrust Law & Policy* (New York, Kluwer, 1995), 445–503.

[64] *Cf.* M. Waelbroeck, "Competition, Integration and Economic Efficiency in the EEC from the Point of View of the Private Firm" in Michigan Law Review Association (ed.), *The Art of Governance. Festschrift zu Ehren von Eric Stein* (Ann Arbor, Michigan).

[65] H. Schröter, "Antitrust Analysis Under Article 85(1) and (3)" in B. Hawk (ed.), *Annual Proceedings of the Fordham Corporate Law Institute 1987*. See also the Opinion of Lenz AG in *Bosman*, above, n. 44, at para. 278 where he holds that although it is "theoretically conceivable" that the Commission would grant on the basis of Art. 81(3) an exemption to an agreement which falls within Art. 81(1) and additionally runs counter to Art. 39 EC (ex Art. 48), this is not likely to happen. Instead, in the opinion of Lenz AG, a uniform result in the application of Art. 81 EC (antitrust law) and Art. 39 EC (free movement) should be aimed at. Similarly, the Commission based its claim on exclusive competence in the area of competition law on it being ancillary to the four freedoms. Together free movement and competition, in the view of the Commission, form the block of the Community's exclusive powers: Commission of the European Communities, "The Principle of Subsidiarity, Communication of the Commission to the Council and the European Parliament", SEC(92)1990, Annex (October 1992), 7.

of Community antitrust policy is therefore not sustained. In so far as the Commission considers it necessary to enforce Community antitrust law in order to protect the level of integration reached so far or to continue to promote integration after future enlargements of the Community's internal market, neither the formal establishment of the Internal Market by the end of 1992 nor the adoption of the TEU changes that assessment.[66]

It should be emphasised however that the above does not regard the *effectiveness* of employing antitrust policy as integration policy. That is a completely different question. The fact that the interpretation of EC antitrust law as a tool for furthering market integration is justified from a Treaty perspective and that it is likely to continue to be employed as an integration tool within the context of the TEU does not imply that it necessarily forms the most effective interpretation of the antitrust provisions for integration purposes. In the past the prohibition to restrict the freedom of parties to an agreement to trade across border has led to withdrawal of products from markets. Consequently, it may be questioned whether the current absolute prohibition on restricting parallel trade does indeed serve the integration objective. Particularly in the *Irish Distillers* case it emerged that it may be counter-productive to the integration objective to require firms to treat the market as integrated where this is not the case.[67] As long as different regulatory regimes and differences in consumer preferences prevail in the common market, dual pricing systems, or other types of differentiation between Member States markets may constitute appropriate business behaviour which may have pro-competitive as well as pro-integration effects. If EC antitrust policy continues to prohibit this type of behaviour this may result in certain products not being marketed throughout the Community or only at uniform, but higher, prices.[68] Indeed the apparent conflation of uniform markets with uniform prices seems dubious as a basis for the integrated internal market, for two reasons. First, because the efforts are unsuccessful. The various Commission efforts to generate uniform prices on the basis of antitrust policy have not eliminated price differences. The motor vehicle market is a good example. Secondly, because uniform markets do not necessarily mean uniform prices. The United States provides evidence of markets with a central competition law regime—as well as diverging state competition law regimes—where prices continue to vary within different regions of that market.[69]

---

[66] *Cf.* Commission of the European Communities, *Twenty-Fourth Annual Report on Competition* (Brussels, 1995) and *Twenty-Fifth Annual Report on Competition Policy* (Brussels, 1996).

[67] Korah, above, n. 12, and Waelbroeck, above, n. 64, who refers to instances in which differences of market conditions have led to acceptance of a lack of uniformity in market regimes (e.g. agriculture).

[68] See the Commission comfort letter for Sony in connection with its Pan-European Dealer Agreement (European Commission Press Release IP/95/736). The Commission imposed an obligation on Sony to maintain the wholesale level in order to facilitate parallel trade. This may just as well lead to *higher* as to *uniform* end prices. Thus, see J.-Y. Art and D. van Liedekerke, "Developments in EC Competition Law in 1995: An Overview" (1996) 33 *CMLRev* 719–75 at 732–3.

[69] See, e.g., Deacon, above, n. 6.

In order to assess the role that antitrust policy can play in promoting integration it would first have to be established which business behaviour does indeed promote integration. That has been done rarely and understanding of the actual effects remains vague. The perceived conflict under Community antitrust law between competition and market integration may therefore be non-existent.[70] Unfortunately, the Commission's programme for modernising Community antitrust policy, expressed in the block-exemption regulation for vertical restraints (following the Green Paper) and in the White Paper on Modernisation of the Rules implementing Articles 81 and 82 of the EC Treaty (the "White Paper on Modernisation"),[71] do not consider the interrelationship between antitrust policy and the promotion of integration. It may therefore be expected that the Commission—and the Court—will continue to apply the Treaty's antitrust law in the current manner. The effects of this policy on integration will remain unclear.[72]

3.3.2. Restriction of Competition

The situation is different with respect to contractual restrictions of the economic freedom of parties where no territorial restrictions on trade are involved. It has emerged from the previous section that the manner in which non-territorial restraints are treated under EC law is not entirely consistent. The Commission generally considers that agreements which contain a restriction of the economic freedom of one or more of the parties restrict competition and therefore are prohibited by Article 81(1) EC. In order to be valid such agreements require an exemption. The Commission normally provides an exemption if the agreement's overall effect is pro-competitive. In contrast, the Court of Justice and the Court of First Instance examine the overall effects of agreements, including those which contain restrictions on the economic freedom of parties, when applying Article 81(1).

Critics consider that the Commission thus interprets Article 81(1) too broadly. The overbroad interpretation of the prohibition enshrined in Article 81(1) restricts innovation—and competition—by limiting the freedom of undertakings to formulate their contracts in the way they consider appropriate from a business perspective. Moreover, looked at systematically by critics, it appears that the Commission tends to exempt agreements which, upon inspection, are seen not to restrict competition from the prohibition on restricting competition. This practice is illogical. The scarce and mostly unofficial exemptions which the Commission provides for agreements which promote competition are

---

[70] Van den Bergh, above, n. 14, at 77.

[71] [1999] OJ C132/1.

[72] It may be argued that integration which has not been established by 40 years of competition law enforcement will not be promoted by more enforcement of the same type: T. Koopmans, "De plaats van het kartelrecht in het EG mededingingsrecht" (1987) 35 *SEW* 421–31.

considered unsatisfactory solutions from a practical as well as from a systematic point of view.

On the basis of the discussion of Commission practice in the previous section it was concluded that these critics are right. The Commission generally interprets Article 81(1) in an overbroad and legalistic manner. However, the Commission's modernisation plans will affect the interpretation of Article 81. The question is whether the expected changes will answer the noted criticism concerning the interpretation of Article 81(1).

Vertical Restraints

For some time it seemed that the Commission planned to bring its interpretation of Article 81(1) into line with that of the Court of Justice. In the wake of the Commission's 1997 Green Paper on vertical restraints various DG IV officials announced, in a personal capacity, that a reduced scope for Article 81(1) on the basis of greater economic analysis of the effects of agreements on competition was warranted.[73] Yet the Commission's Green Paper on vertical restraints, which formed the basis for the modernisation of the interpretation of Article 81(1), revealed that the Commission was not seeking a total realignment of its interpretation of Article 81(1) with the case law of the Court. Although the Green Paper heralded increased use of economic analysis in the application of Community antitrust rules, it proposed to block-*exempt* vertical agreements containing restrictions of the economic freedom of parties from Article 81(1) in view of the prevailing pro-competitive effects of such restraints.

Indeed the Commission decided to adopt a block-exemption regulation for vertical restraints. Mirroring the considerations which led to the Green Paper, the block-exemption regulation acknowledges that assessment of an agreement's impact on competition should concentrate on the economic circumstances in the relevant product market rather than on the form of the agreement. The compatibility of vertical restraints with EC antitrust law should therefore commence with an assessment of the market structure. In the absence of substantial market power vertical restraints are considered not to harm competition. Therefore the block-exemption regulation declares that Article 81(1) shall not apply to all vertical agreements containing restrictions of competition provided that the market share held by the supplier on the relevant market does not exceed 30 per cent of the relevant market. Agreements between parties which do exceed that market share threshold are not exempted by the regulation, but the Commission underscores that these agreements may also contain vertical restraints which will be subject to an economic analysis of their effects on competition. Regulation 17 was amended in such a way as to allow for exempting

---

[73] Deacon, above, n. 6, and E Paulis, "Decentralisation of Enforcement of Community Law—Panel Discussion" in C.-D. Ehlermann and L. Laudati (eds.), *Robert Schuman Centre Annual on European Commpetition Law 1996* (London, Kluwer Law International, 1997), 98–100.

agreements irrespective of the date on which the vertical agreement was notified with a view to obtaining an exemption.

Thus, the Commission departs from its traditional legalistic approach on the basis of the block-exemption regulation for vertical agreements. Contrary to prior block exemptions, which were based on clauses in agreements which had earlier been notified to the Commission, the regulation is based on an economic assessment of the potential effects of vertical restraints on competition. Hence the regulation does not list which clauses are acceptable under EC antitrust law. The new regulation provides a broad safe haven for vertical agreements, irrespective of the wording of the restraints, on the basis of the general observation that vertical restraints are unlikely to restrict competition in the absence of significant market power of the parties to these agreements.

While the block-exemption regulation for vertical agreements therefore answers the criticism that Commission practice in applying Article 81 is legalistic and that it is not based on an economic assessment of the effects on competition, the vertical restraints exemption regulation is still an *exemption* regulation. This gives rise to at least two principal objections. First, the Commission will not therefore make the assessment of the effects on competition when applying Article 81(1). It continues to assume that agreements containing vertical restraints restrict competition and that they therefore need an exemption (in view of the fact that they turn out *not* to restrict competition).[74] Commission practice will thus continue to diverge from the case law of the European Courts. Secondly, although the exact wording of agreements is no longer a relevant factor for falling within the terms of the block-exemption regulation, the regulation continues to have a straightjacket effect. After all only some of the feasible contractual provisions are allowed under the regulation. Others are not. As before, undertakings are likely to draft their agreemens in order for them to fall within the terms of the exemption regulation. Thus, the margins for competition remain confined in this respect by the block-exemption regulation.[75]

The White Paper on Modernisation[76]

In the White Paper on Modernisation the Commission sets out the general direction which modernisation of EC antitrust policy should take. With respect to the interpretation of Article 81 EC the Commission departs from the assertion that

---

[74] V. Korah, "The Future of Vertical Agreements under E.C. Competition Law" (1998) 19 *ECLR* 506–12. See also J. Venit, "Economic Analysis, 'Quick Looks' and Article 85: A Way Forward?" in L. Laudati and C.-D. Ehlermann (eds.), *Robert Schuman Centre Annual on Competition Law 1997* (Oxford, Hart, 1998). Formally the Reg. applies exclusively to agreements which fall within Art. 81(1); see Art. 2(1) Reg.No 2790/1999.

[75] Cf. I. S. Forrester, "Modernisation of EC Competition Law" in B. Hawk (ed.), *Annual Proceedings of the Fordham Corporate Law Institute 1999* (forthcoming, 2000).

[76] The following section draws on R. Wesseling, "The Commission White Paper on Modernisation of E.C. Antitrust Law: Unspoken Consequences and Incomplete Treatment of Alternative Options" (1999) 20 *ECLR* 420–433.

"the current division between paragraphs 1 and 3 in implementing Article 81 is artificial and runs counter to the integral nature of Article 81, which requires economic analysis of the overall impact of restrictive practices".[77] In a passage entirely devoted to the interpretation of Article 81 the Commission notes the following:

> 56. One option that is sometimes put forward is to change the interpretation of Article 81 so as to include analysis of the harmful and beneficial effects of an agreement in the assessment under Article 81(1). Application of the exemption provided for in Article 81(3) would then be restricted to those cases in which the need to ensure consistency between competition policy and other Community policies took precedence over the results of the competition analysis. *It would in a way mean interpreting Article 81(1) as incorporating a "rule of reason"*. Such a system would ease the notification constraints imposed on undertakings, since they would not be required to notify agreements in order to obtain negative clearance.
>
> 57. The Commission has already adopted this approach to a limited extent and has carried out an assessment of the pro- and anti-competitive aspects of some restrictive practices under Article 81(1). *This approach has been endorsed by the Court of Justice*. However, the structure of Article 81 is such as to prevent greater use being made of this approach: *if more systematic use were made under Article 81(1) of an analysis of the pro- and anti-competitive aspects of a restrictive agreement, Article 81(3) would be cast aside, whereas any such change could be made only through revision of the Treaty. It would at the very least be paradoxical to cast aside Article 81(3) when that provision in fact contains all the elements of a "rule of reason"*. It would moreover be dangerous if modernisation of the competition rules were to be based on developments in decision-making practice, subject to such developments being upheld by the Community Courts. Any such approach would mean that modernisation was contingent upon the cases submitted to the Commission and could take many years. Lastly, *this option would run the risk of diverting Article 81(3) from its purpose, which is to provide a legal framework for the economic assessment of restrictive practices and not to allow application of the competition rules to be set aside because of political considerations*."[78]

In the context of the current discussion of the future interpretation of Article 81(1) there are two crucial assertions in the cited passage. The first is that adoption of a rule of reason would "cast aside" Article 81(3). The second is that the purpose of Article 81(3) is to provide a framework for the economic assessment of the effects of an agreement on competition. Both statements are dubious in view of the case law of the European Courts—and indeed in view of Commission practice in the first 40 years of Community antitrust law enforcement.

In order to see whether adopting a rule of reason would cast aside Article 81(3) it is inevitable to discuss briefly what is meant by the "rule of reason". The term "rule of reason" comes from US antitrust law, in particular the Sherman Act which diverges considerably from EC antitrust law. When read literally, the

---

[77] White Paper, para. 49.
[78] *Ibid.*, paras. 56 and 57 (emphases added).

prohibition in the Sherman Act on restraining trade is absolute. The prohibition is not subject to exemptions. Because certain contractual restraints on trade may well promote competition, it was soon established that a reasonable interpretation of the Sherman Act's prohibition should prevail. In particular, the overall effects on competition are assessed in order to judge whether agreements which contain clauses which restrain trade are prohibited by the Sherman Act. In other words, a reasonable interpretation of the Sherman Act implies that only those agreements which, on balance, restrict competition are prohibited by it.

Nevertheless, some (clauses in) agreements are prohibited irrespective of the effects on competition. These are the so-called "*per se*" infringements. They are not subject to the "rule of reason". The exception to the rule of reason has a procedural background. On the basis of experience there is very little doubt that the "*per se*" infringements restrict competition in the sense of the Sherman Act. In this light it is considered inefficient if plaintiffs have to demonstrate in every single case under the rule of reason that such a "*per se*" infringement on balance restricts competition.[79]

Article 81 EC is formulated differently. The first paragraph of Article 81 prohibits all agreements which restrict competition but the third paragraph of the Article provides for the possibility of issuing exemptions to the prohibition. There are no "*per se*" prohibitions under Article 81 EC because all agreements are theoretically susceptible to exemption. Each and every agreement, and all clauses therein, has to be examined in order to asses whether it is compatible with Article 81 EC.[80] In this sense the White Paper on Modernisation correctly asserts that a "rule of reason" is present in Article 81(3) EC. Arguably, however, adopting a rule of reason under Article 81(1) would not necessarily "cast aside" Article 81(3).

To understand this, it is essential to note that supporters of a revised interpretation of Article 81—supporters of a "rule of reason"—argue for balancing the pro- and anti-competitive effects of an entire agreement when applying Article 81(1). Those agreements which do not, on balance, restrict competition are in their view compatible with Article 81(1). Thus, these commentators argue for an "*economic* rule of reason" under Article 81(1), in line with the case law of the European Courts.

Assessing the overall effects on competition under the first paragraph of Article 81 would therefore not "cast aside" the third paragraph of that Article, as the White Paper on Modernisation suggests. On the contrary, the structure of Article 81 EC is such as to make it possible that agreements which on balance restrict competition—and which therefore are prohibited by Article 81(1)—are

---

[79] See O. Black, "Per Se Rules and Rules of Reason: What Are They?" (1997) 18 *ECLR* 145–61 and Bright, above, n. 13, at 555–6.

[80] Case T–17/93 *Matra Hachette* v. *Commission* [1994] ECR II–595. See also R. Wesseling, "Subsidiarity in Communtiy Antitrust Law: Setting the Right Agenda" (1997) 22 *ELR* 35–54 at 50–1. Admittedly, this is somewhat theoretical because there are various clauses which will never be exempted. Restraints on cross-border intra-Community trade may be considered "*per se*" prohibited on the basis of EC antitrust law.

exempted from that prohibition on the basis of Article 81(3). Even though competition is restricted, agreements may be considered valid under EC antitrust law.[81] As the previous section demonstrated, the application of Article 81(3) which implies answering the question whether the objectives pursued by companies on the basis of the agreements at hand qualify as improvements of production or distribution of goods or promotion of technical or economic progress. There are various Community policy concerns, in principle unrelated to the protection of competition, which have been taken into account by the Commission when applying Article 81(3) EC. If agreements contribute to these policy objectives of the Community they are eligible for an exemption, in spite of the restriction of competition which they entail—provided that the restriction of competition is as minimal as possible.

This balancing of policy interests may be called a "rule of reason", as the Commission does in the White Paper on Modernisation, but it is evident that this is a completely different "rule of reason" from the "*economic* rule of reason" under Article 81(1) which is promoted by critics of the way in which the Commission interprets Article 81(1). The White Paper's assertion that a revised interpretation of Article 81(1) on the basis of the "economic rule of reason" is not feasible because this would cast aside Article 81(3) of the Treaty, which would require revision of the Treaty, therefore seems unjustified.[82]

The second doubtful assertion in the White Paper is that the purpose of Article 81(3) is "to provide a legal framework for the economic assessment of restrictive practices and not to allow the application of the competition rules to be set aside because of political considerations". It is true that the competition rules may not be set aside because of political considerations. But it is also true that, notably, the Commission has demonstrated in its decisional practice that it is possible to take into account political considerations in the application of Article 81(3), provided that a degree of competition is guaranteed. As will be discussed in more detail below (in section 3.3.3.) the Court of Justice has repeatedly endorsed Commission decisions which took into account non-competition concerns when determining whether an agreement fulfilled all four preconditions of Article 81(3). It may therefore be said that the Commission's practice of assessing an agreement's overall impact on competition under Article 81(3) runs counter to the purpose of that Article, which is to provide a legal framework within which the bodies competent to apply it may pursue certain non-competition policy objectives provided that competition is restricted as little as

[81]   Most explicitly Lenz AG argued in the *Bosman* case that "[i]f a rule, which at first sight appears to contain a restriction of competition, is necessary in order to make that competition possible in the first place, it must indeed be assumed that such a rule does not infringe Article 85(1) [now Art. 81(1)]. It would be unconvincing to reject that argument on the ground that paragraph 3 of Article 85 [now Art. 81] in any event provides the possibility of exemption from the prohibition in paragraph 1"; *Bosman*, above, n. 44, at para. 265.

[82]   It is also incompatible with the Commission's stated aim to "adopt a more economic approach to the application of Article 81(1), which will limit the scope of its application to undertakings with a certain degree of market power". See White Paper on Modernisation, at para. 78.

possible. To do otherwise and to restrict the application of Article 81(3) to applying an economic rule of reason implies that social considerations (e.g. of environmental, cultural, and employment policies) cannot be taken into account under Article 81(3). That is clearly in contrast with standing Commission practice in the application of Article 81(3), as endorsed by the European Courts.[83]

The Commission's assertion that applying Article 81(3) is a pure economic test which does not allow for administrative discretion is at odds with the case law of the European Courts. Moreover, the general development of the Community indicates that the Community institutions should consider an increasing number of policies.[84] If the application of the Community antitrust rules, in particular Article 81(3) EC, would be reduced to a "pure" competition test this would go against this trend. The Commission might ultimately not be able to consider, for example, environmental policy concerns under Article 81(3) which would be contrary to Article 6 EC.[85]

It is therefore submitted that the modernisation of Community antitrust policy should be based on a revised Commission interpretation of Article 81(1) to bring it into line with that of the Court. Article 81(3) would then allow for public policy considerations where other Community policy concerns can be considered, provided that competition is not eliminated completely and provided that the restriction of competition does not go further than is required to achieve the policy objectives pursued by the Community. There is practical experience which demonstrates that it is feasible to divide the application of Article 81 in such a manner.[86]

3.3.3. Political Exemptions

The most notable consequence of the general unwillingness of the Commission to assess the overall effects of agreements on competition under the first paragraph of Article 81 is that the Commission is obliged to exempt agreements from the prohibition on reducing competition if their overall effect on competition is positive. The question of the degree of economic analysis required in the

---

[83] See (then) Commissioner Van Miert's written answer to a question from a MEP of 28 April 1998: "[t]he Commission can within the scope of its policy discretion under Article 85(3) [now Art. 81(3)] and in relevant cases take account of cultural arguments' [1999] 4 CMLR 394–5.

[84] See above, Ch. 2.

[85] Cf. Art. 2 TEU and Arts. 174 ff. EC.

[86] Practical support for the feasibility of separating the "economic" test, which indicates whether a distortion of competition occurs on the one hand, and the "political" potential to exempt an agreement which contains such a restriction from the prohibition is provided by the French and Italian experience with their systems analoguous to that of the Community. See *Survey of the Member State National Laws Governing Vertical Distribution Agreements*, above, n. 10, at 5–10 esp., and M. Siragusa, "Rethinking Article 85: Problems and Challenges in the Design and Enforcement of the EC Competition Rules" in B. Hawk (ed.), *Annual Proceedings of the Fordham Corporate Law Institute 1997* (New York, Juris Publishing, 1998), 271–95.

application of Article 81(1) is therefore directly connected to the application of the exemption provision in Article 81(3). At present a distinction must be made between two types of exemptions. First, the Commission exempts a category of agreements from the prohibition on restricting competition on the basis of Article 81(3) because these agreements, on further investigation, do not restrict competition. Secondly, the Commission exempts a category of agreements which restrict competition but, in the Commission's opinion, merit immunity from the prohibition on restricting competition, for reasons unrelated to competition policy.

When examining the criticism which has been vented of the Commission's exemption practice it is useful to keep in mind this analytical distinction between the two types of "exemptions" which the Commission provides. For questions concerning the first type of exemption are more related to the debate on the interpretation of Article 81(1) than to that on Article 81(3) of the Treaty.

The problem with exempting agreements which have no negative effects on competition from the prohibition on restricting competition emerges when the limits to the Commission's discretion in exempting agreements on the basis of Article 81(3) are recalled. Article 81(3) confines the types of agreements for which an exemption may be granted to those which fulfill four conditions. Agreements which restrict competition in the sense of Article 81(1) can be exempted only if they (a) contribute to improving the production or distribution of goods or to promoting technical or economic progress, while (b) allowing the consumers a fair share of the resulting benefit, and then only if the agreement (c) does not impose on the parties to it restrictions which are dispensable to the attainment of these objectives, and (d) does not afford them the possibility of eliminating competition in respect of a substantial part of the market for the products in question. In spite of the fact that many agreements which under a full economic analysis are not considered anti-competitive are likely to fulfil the conditions prescribed in Article 81(3), it does not necessarily follow that all these agreements fulfil all conditions throughout the entire agreement. Therefore it is not "paradoxical to cast aside Article 81(3) when that provision in fact contains all the elements of a rule of reason". It was illustrated above that there is an important analytical difference between the "economic rule of reason" and the possibility of applying a "rule of reason" under Article 81(3). If the Commission continues to interpret Article 81(1) in an over-broad manner, by holding that a restriction on the economic freedom of parties constitutes a restriction of competition in the sense of Article 81(1), this will thwart the application of Article 81(3). Agreements which contain restrictions on the economic freedom of parties but which have on balance a pro-competitive effect do not necessarily fulfil all four preconditions enshrined in Article 81(3). This implies that either a pro-competitive agreement is prohibited on the basis of EC competition law or the interpretation of one or more of the four preconditions in Article 81(3) is forged. In this respect the criticism of Commission practice in so far as it applies the prohibition of Article 81(1) too broadly seems even more appropriate than what was already concluded in the previous section.

Further, the broad interpretation of Article 81(1) and the ensuing need for parties to request an exemption even for pro-competitive agreements has led to what commentators describe as "industrial engineering". Within the procedure leading to an individual exemption or, alternatively, on the basis of the conditions for complying with a block-exemption regulation, the Commission may direct companies to adjustments of the terms of their agreements.[87] Contrary to what is thought to be its proper role in supervising the competitive process, the Commission thus reduces the number of business-options for firms.

The second category of exemptions has a different character. With respect to the agreements thus exempted the question is no longer whether or not there is a restriction of competition. That there is such a restriction is taken for granted. The question is, first, what are the policy concerns on the basis of which the Commission may legitimately exempt agreements from the prohibition formulated in Article 81(1) and, secondly, what the limits to the Commission's discretion are in so far as those concerns are based on extra-competition policies. As has been said, criticism is twofold. First, there are commentators who claim that the Commission illegitimately takes into consideration extra-competition policy concerns when providing exemptions. Secondly, commentators, who have argued conversely that it is appropriate for the Commission to base its competition law exemptions on extra-competition policy considerations, criticise the intransparent and unaccountable manner in which these concerns have been taken into account.

As to the first line of criticism, the survey of the exemptions which the Commission has provided under Article 81(3) demonstrated clearly that concerns related to policies other than that of competition are taken into account. The objectives of Community antitrust policy are pursued with respect to various other policy concerns set out in the Treaty. In the practical application of the Community antitrust law provisions the Commission has thus taken into account industrial and agricultural policy, research policy, transport policy, environmental policy, and consumer protection policy. Exemptions have been granted, more or less openly, for agreements which restrict competition but which also generate positive effects in those other Community policy fields. To examine the validity of the critique the question is therefore whether it was legitimate for the Commission to consider these other policy objectives when applying Article 81(3) of the Treaty.

In this respect it should first be recalled that the Court of Justice has ruled that the notion of competition to which Community antitrust law adheres is that of "workable competition". In *Metro I* the Court reasoned that workable competition is the degree of competition necessary to ensure the observance of the

---

[87] Groger and Janicki, above, n. 17, at 992. See also Whish, above, n. 3, at 235, where he argues that any individual exemption "is to some extent the expression of a negotiated compromise".

basic requirements and the attainment of the objectives of the Treaty.[88] The Court ruled that it is possible to allow a reduction in the degree of competition where this is necessary for pursuing non-competition policies, because Community antitrust law does not aspire to perfect competition. The concept of "workable competition" allows for considerations which go beyond a narrow competition analysis. In accordance with this concept the nature and intensity of competition may vary. This is reflected in the text of Article 81(3). The wording of that provision demonstrates that "the requirements for the maintenance of workable competition may be reconciled with the safeguarding of objectives of a different nature and that to this end certain restrictions of competition are permissible".[89]

The possibility for a limitation of the intensity of competition had already been implicitly acknowledged by the Court in *Walt Wilhelm*. As demonstrated earlier, the Court ruled in that case that the Treaty's antitrust rules do not merely entitle the Community authorities to eliminate the obstacles to the free movement of goods. Article 81 also permits the Community authorities to carry out certain positive, though indirect, action with a view to promoting a harmonious development of economic activities within the whole Community. At the same time the judgment contained a hint of the limits of that kind of positive action where the Court indicated that it should be undertaken *in accordance with Article 2 of the Treaty*.[90] Subsequently, in *Continental Can* the Court extended the list of policy concerns which could justify a restraint on competition to Articles 2 *and* 3. The Court suggested that this list of policy concerns which can be taken into account when considering whether a restraint of trade is justified for reasons related to other policies was exhaustive. It explicitly held that "the restraints on competition which the Treaty allows under certain conditions because of the need to harmonise the various objectives of the Treaty, are limited by the requirements of Article 2 and 3".[91] More recently, however, the Court of First Instance has departed from the notion that the policy basis for providing an exemption is limited to the objective defined in Articles 2 and 3 of the Treaty. In *Matra Hachette* it declared that in principle the Commission has the power to exempt any anti-competitive practice as long as the conditions of Article 81(3) are fulfilled.[92]

---

[88]   *Metro* v. *Commission* (*"Metro I"*), above, n. 56.

[89]   *Ibid.*, at para. 21. That is, provided that they are essential to the attainment of those objectives and that they do not result in the elimination of competition for a substantial part of the common market.

[90]   Case 14/68 *Walt Wilhelm* v. *Bundeskartellamt* [1969] ECR 1 at 14 (emphasis added).

[91]   Case 6/72 *Europemballage and Continental Can* v. *Commission* [1973] ECR 215 at para. 24.

[92]   *Matra Hachette* v. *Commission*, above, n. 80, para. 85: "[i]n other words . . . such reasoning presumes that there are infringements which are inherently incapable of qualifying for exemption—but Community competition law, the applicability of which is subject to the existence of a practice which is anti-competitive in intent or has an anti-competitive effect on a given market, certainly does not embody that principle. On the contrary, the Court considers that, in principle, no anti-competitive practice can exist which, whatever the extent of its effects on a given market, cannot be exempted, provided that all the conditions laid down in Article 85(3) [now Art. 81] of the Treaty are satisfied and the practice in question has been properly notified to the Commission".

The Commission practice of taking into consideration extra-competition policy concerns when contemplating whether or not to provide an exemption is therefore justified on the basis of Court of Justice case law.[93] Criticism that the Commission is not allowed under Community law to base an exemption on, for example, industrial policy motivations is not supported. The changes which adoption of the TEU and the formal establishment of the internal market generated cannot qualify that judgment, first, because the text of Article 81(3) remained unchanged and the Court's interpretation therefore remains valid. Secondly, in so far as the TEU and the Treaty of Amsterdam changed the policy concerns which the Commission may take into account when considering whether or not to provide an exemption, the range of policy issues has only expanded. The TEU widened the scope of Community competences and the objectives of the European Community, formulated in Article 2 of the Treaty, were also extended.[94] The Treaty of Amsterdam inserted into the Treaty Article 6 (ex Article 3c) which provides that environmental protection requirements must be integrated into the implementation of all Community policies referred to in Article 3. Competition law is one of those policies. Therefore the only limits to Commission discretion under Article 81(3) are the four conditions in that provision which need to be fulfilled. The wording of these conditions is ambiguous. Their vague formulation adds to the broad margins of discretion for the Commission in applying Article 81(3).

This last observation relates to the second objection to present exemption practice, which mainly concerns the unclear manner in which competition and non-competition concerns are balanced by the Commission in its application of Article 81(3). In this respect the broad margins of discretion allowed to the Commission by the Court of Justice have to be acknowledged. The Court rules that the political and administrative nature of the assessment whether the four conditions are fulfilled, and hence whether an exemption should be granted, is largely beyond judicial control.[95] Accordingly, in its judicial examination of Commission exemption decisions the Court tends not to judge on the substantive merits of the case. It explicitly declines to substitute its own assessment for that of the Commission.[96] This is in line with its general position in competition cases where complex economic facts are involved. The Court has limited

---

[93] The case law of the ECJ reveals that—in some instances—the competition rules may not apply to (collective) agreements which promote alternative Treaty objectives (e.g. social policy objectives): Case C–219/97 *Maatschappij Drijvende Bokken* v. *Stichting Pensioenfonds voor de vervoer-en havenbedrijven* [1999] ECR I–0000 (judgement of 21 September 1999); Case C–67/96 *Albany International* v. *Stichting Bedrijfspensioenfonds textielindustrie* [1999] ECR I–0000; Joined Cases C–115, 116, 117/97 *Brentjens' Handelsonderneming* v. *Stichting Bedrijfspensioenfonds voor de handel in bouwmaterialen* [1999] ECR I–0000.

[94] See new competences on industrial, cultural, education, environmental policy in the TEU (in so far as not already adopted in the SEA) and Art. 2 of the EC Treaty.

[95] *Consten and Grundig* v. *Commission*, above, n. 4; Case 71/74 *Frubo* v. *Commission* [1975] ECR 563 and *Matra Hachette* v. *Commission*, above, n. 80, at para. 104.

[96] Cases T–79 and 80/95 *SNCF and British Railways* v. *Commission* ("*Channel Tunnel Agreement*") [1996] ECR II–1491.

judicial control of the legal characterisation of the facts in those cases to the possibility of the Commission having committed a manifest error of assessment.[97] In *SPO* v. *Commission* the Court defined its own role in reviewing the Commission's application of the discretion conferred on it by Article 81(3) as "limited to ascertaining whether the procedural rules have been complied with, whether proper reasons have been provided, whether the facts have been accurately stated and whether there has been any manifest error of appraisal or misuse of powers".[98]

The wide discretion thus conferred on the Commission in the application of Article 81(3) has created an unclear decisional practice. The procedures through which exemptions are granted or refused are relatively limited and the different stages in the assessment remain intransparent. For outside observers the only official information on the reasons for granting or denying the right to an exemption is the ultimate Commission decision as published in the Official Journal. These decisions have been criticised for their sparse reasoning and their apparent tendency to argue towards conclusions which have been reached beforehand. Absent substantive judicial control, the intransparent procedures are considered to lead to decisions motivated by ambiguous and unstated objectives for which institutional accountability is lacking.[99]

One of the explanations for the ambiguous exemption practice is the rigid structure and wording of Article 81(3). It was mentioned above that all four conditions listed in 81(3) need to be fulfilled. The problem noted earlier that a pro-competitive agreement does not fulfil all four preconditions for exemption occurs in enhanced form where the Commission contemplates exempting agreements which are restrictive of competition but which it considers beneficial for other policy purposes. The wording of Article 81(3) makes it exceptionally difficult to provide an exemption for those agreements. Article 81(3) enables the Commission to exempt agreements from the cartel prohibition but only, the wording of the provision suggests, where the agreements do not restrict competition. For agreements can be exempted from the prohibition of Article 81(1) only if they contribute to improving the production or distribution of goods or if they contribute to promoting technical or economic progress. Even then, these agreements will be exempted only in so far as they do not eliminate competition in respect of a substantial part of the products in question; in other words, if the agreements enhance competition. The wording of these conditions appears to require balancing the competition effects of the agreements rather than that they overrule competition policy considerations. The wording of Article 81(3) makes it problematic to provide an exemption for agreements which, although restrictive of competition, further alternative policy objectives.[100] In order to overcome

[97] *Remia* v. *Commission*, above, n. 55.

[98] Case 137/95 *SPO and others* v. *Commission* [1996] ECR I–1611, at para. 288.

[99] Bouterse and Amato, above, n. 14.

[100] In fact the wording of Art. 81(3) forms clear support for the view that the competition rules were originally inserted into the Treaty as a ban on private restrictions on the free movement of

this obstacle to granting exemptions on extra-competition policy grounds, the Commission, within the wide margins of discretion which the Court has allowed it, has stretched the interpretation of the four conditions enshrined in Article 81(3). At some instances the exemptions provided by the Commission, for instance, claim that certain agreements contribute to promoting technical or economic progress though there is no such contribution.[101] This has indeed generated a flawed system. The broad interpretation of the prohibition in Article 81(1) has constrained the Commission to provide exemptions for agreements which are pro-competitive even if these agreements do not fulfil all four requirements of Article 81(3). In those cases the Commission's reasoning is sometimes unclear.

It appears therefore that the critique on the intransparent nature of the Commission's exemption practice is in point. The Commission has wide margins for discretion in balancing competition policy and other policy concerns but its reasoning is not always apparent.[102] Since the Commission may clearly take into account non-competition policies when deciding whether or not to grant an exemption in respect of the cartel prohibition it is desirable that the relationship of those policy concerns to the rules of competition be clarified.[103] The limited judicial control of the Commission's exemption practice cannot cover the discretion of the balancing act which the Commission currently performs when applying Article 81(3) of the Treaty. In order for it to become more transparent that political element of the Commission's competition policy should therefore be subject to a form of accountability. But these problems are more closely connected to the institutional structure of EC antitrust law than that they are issues of substance. They will therefore be taken up below, in Chapter 5.

goods, parallel to the public one in Arts. 28–30 of the Treaty. It is only under such an understanding that it would make sense to exempt agreements which promote competition in traditional antitrust terms (that is, improving production or distribution of goods, promoting technical or economic progress and allowing consumers a fair share of the resulting benefit) from the absolute prohibition on restraining trade between Member States.

[101] Amato, above, n. 14, at 58–64.

[102] It should be noted however that the Court has become increasingly strict on procedural aspects of Commission exemption decisions. Possibly to compensate for the relatively intransparent way in which the Commission is able to decide on the merits of individual exemptions the Court has underscored the narrow margins of "procedural" discretion. In *Métropole* the Court quashed an exemption decision because the Commission had made a manifest error of appraisal by concluding that certain anti-competitive clauses were indispensable to the progress which the agreement was thought to bring about. The Court found the rules laid down in the agreements so vague and discretionary as not to allow the Commission to make a proper assessment of their indispensability. According to the Court the Commission should have refuses to grant the exemption because it was not in a position to consider whether all the clauses were indeed indispensable within the meaning of Art. 81(3): Joined Cases T–528, 542, 543 & 546/93 *Métropole Télévision SA and RTI v. Commission* (*"European Broadcasting Union"*) [1996] ECR II–649. See also *VBBB and VBVB v. Commission*, above, n. 60 and *SNCF and British Railways v. Commission* (*"Channel Tunnel Agreement"*), above, n. 96.

[103] The debate on the (constitutional) ranking of the various Community policy concerns is unfortunately limited to Germany. See for instance M. Dreher, "Der Rang des Wettbewerbs im europäischen Gemeinschaftsrecht" (1998) 48 *WuW* 656–66 and A. Schmidt, "Die europäische Wettbewerbspolitik nach dem Vertrag von Amsterdam" (1999) 49 *WuW* 133–40.

It is uncertain how the Commission's 1999 White Paper will affect the process of providing exemptions. The main consequence of the White Paper will be that the Commission will lose its monopoly on the application of Article 81(3). In the Commission's view national courts and national authorities are able to apply the exemption provision on the basis of the case law of the Court, the decisional practice of the Commission and on the basis of guidelines which the Commission intends to issue. The background to the dissemination of the power to grant exemptions is the Commission's assertion that the purpose of Article 81(3) is to "provide a legal framework for the economic assessment of restrictive practices and not to allow the application of the competition rules to be set aside because of political considerations". This statement may indicate that the Commission considers that non-competition concerns may not play a role at all in the application of Article 81(3). That would be very surprising in view of its consistent practice of doing so.

It is difficult to see how national antitrust authorities and, in particular, national courts will apply the policy discretion which exists under Article 81(3). The European Courts have ruled that there is a considerable degree of discretion and they have also stated that this discretion can be applied by the Commission only in view of balancing which is required between complex economic facts and non-competition Community policy concerns. The case law of the Court will therefore not be of much help. It is also unlikely that the Commission's decisions and guidelines will be able to provide sufficient insights for national courts to weigh the various policy concerns in individual cases.

In view of the problems which may be expected in decentralised application of the policy discretion implicit in applying Article 81(3) and in view of the case law of the European Courts it is therefore advisable to maintain the Commission monopoly on providing exemptions to the Treaty's competition rules. The practical problem of the heavy case load—which formed the main drive for the Commission to dispense with the monopoly in providing exemptions—can be solved in different ways. One of those ways is reducing the scope for Article 81(1), for instance by judging that only those agreements which on balance restrict competition fall within the prohibition provision.[104]

CONCLUSION

Taking Article 81 of the Treaty as a model, this chapter explored the current objectives of EC antitrust law[105] and the case law of the Court was compared

---

[104] Another element in restricting the scope of Art. 81(1) is addressed in the next ch. For a fuller discussion see Wesseling, above, n. 80.

[105] Although the examination was necessarily limited to a restricted field of EC antitrust policy, it can form a basis for generalisation of the findings. Even a quick look at developments in the other areas of EC antitrust policy, Art. 82 and the Merger Control Reg., reveals that the main problem is not one of objectives but rather one of transparency and accountability. Community antitrust law arguably suffers from a general transparency deficit. Akin to the application of Art. 81 there is a

with the principles set out in the TEU. The literature perceives three major problems with respect to the substance of European Community antitrust law.

First, commentators hold that Community antitrust law erroneously promotes integration instead of competition. The analysis in this chapter demonstrated that Community antitrust law does indeed primarily promote integration, sometimes to the detriment of competition. In the context of the European Community, where the main objective is to create an ever closer union between the Member States, integration is a valid object. This has not changed in the context of the TEU and the Treaty of Amsterdam. The Treaty's commitment to European integration remains central to all its provisions even after the formal establishment of the internal market.

The second strand of criticism argues that the Commission's overbroad interpretation of the prohibition enshrined in Article 81(1) of the Treaty is flawed. While formal establishment of the internal market and the TEU cannot be considered to affect current practice, the examination in this chapter revealed that this criticism is pertinent. Commission practice is out of line with the case law of the Court of Justice. The Commission's modernisation plans are based on a continued overbroad scope of Article 81(1). This chapter argued that it is feasible to interpret Article 81(1) in such a way that only agreements which on balance restrict competition are prohibited by it. On the basis of Article 81(3) the Commission could then consider for those agreements whether there are reasons to issue an exemption to EC antitrust law in spite of the reduction of competition which the agreement entails.

Thirdly, the Commission is criticised for taking into account extra-competition objectives when considering whether or not to provide an exemption for the prohibition on restricting competition. This chapter argued that the Commission may validly take into account other objectives. In so far as the Court's case law has changed under influence of the TEU, it appears that the expansion of the Community's competences in that Treaty has taken away the constraints on the policy objectives which the Commission may take into account in its application of Article 81(3). The problem with respect to the Commission's practice in the area of Article 81(3) which was identified in this chapter stems from the fact that the Commission exempts two different types of agreements. It exempts agreements which it considers in the first instance to fall within Article 81(1) but whose effect it then decides is pro-competitive. The Commission also exempts agreements from the prohibition restricting competition because of the positive effects of those agreements on other Community policy objectives. If the Commission were to adapt its practice to Court of Justice case law this problem would largely disappear. The problem which remains is the intransparent way in which the Commission provides exemptions. This is primarily an institutional and procedural problem which will therefore be discussed further in Chapter 5.

considerable lack of transparency in the application of Art. 82 and, notably, the Merger Control Reg. See, for instance, D. Neven, R. Nuttall and P. Seabright, *Merger in Daylight*. For fuller discussion see Ch. 5.

4

The Division of Jurisdiction between EC and Member State Antitrust Laws

INTRODUCTION

THE EC TREATY stipulates that Articles 81 and 82 apply to business behaviour which affects trade between Member States. The Court of Justice interpreted that criterion extensively. The scope for EC antitrust law is therefore very broad. The Treaty does not determine the interrelationship between Community and Member State antitrust laws in the case of concurrent claims to jurisdiction. It has therefore been up to the Court of Justice to establish rules on the interrelationship between these sets of laws. The main rule laid down by the Court of Justice is based on the principle of supremacy of EC law over national laws.

Chapter 2 illustrated that both the broad scope of EC law—in particular the rules on free movement—and the unqualified supremacy of Community law over national law have been challenged by various actors (courts, Member States, commentators) since the formal establishment of the Internal Market and the entry into force of the Treaty on European Union (TEU). This book argues that the modernisation of Community antitrust law should take account of this general debate on the constitutional values of the future European Community. Hitherto the process of modernising antitrust law has ignored the broader developments in EC constitutional law. In those instances where the debate on antitrust policy did take account of novel constitutional principles, these principles were set within the existing context. For instance, introduction of the principle of subsidiarity into the EC Treaty did not generate a debate on the meaning of that principle in the area of antitrust law. Rather, the principle was embraced as a sign that the *decentralisation* of enforcement of European Community antitrust law was to be furthered. The division of jurisdiction between Community and Member State laws was, however, not confronted. In the area of merger conrol the subsidiarity principle was employed in a similar practical manner. The Commission referred to subsidiarity when proposing to extend Community jurisdiction to mergers which would otherwise have to be notified in several Member States. Yet there is more to subsidiarity—and to the broader constitutional development following the formal establishment of the Internal Market—than a reduction of the administrative backlog of the Commission offices through intensified decentralised enforcement, on the one hand, and easing the burdens for business by enlarging the scope for a one-stop-administrative-shop on the other. The modernisation of Community antitrust law provides an occasion for reconsidering the pertinence of the current scope of EC antitrust law and the traditional interrelationship between Community and national antitrust laws, in the light of the developments which have taken place between 1958 and today. This chapter therefore aims to re-examine the scope for EC antitrust law as well as its interrelationship with Member State antitrust laws in view of the desire to modernise EC antitrust law.

In view of the significant divergences in scope for Community law and in the interrelation between Community and national law, the discussion in this chapter distinguishes between merger control law, on the one hand, and "traditional" Community antitrust laws, Articles 81 and 82 EC, on the other. The first two sections of this chapter therefore discuss the jurisdictional scope of Community antitrust law and the interrelationship between EC and national law in respect of both areas of antitrust law. The third section reviews the current interrelationship between the EC and national antitrust laws in view of the modernisation process.

4.1 THE RELATIONSHIP BETWEEN ARTICLES 81 AND 82 EC AND NATIONAL ANTITRUST LAW

4.1.1. The Scope for Articles 81 and 82 EC

The Treaty's antitrust rules—but not the Merger Regulation—apply to all agreements, decisions, concerted practices and abuses of dominant position which *may affect trade between Member States*. Article 81 EC therefore does not cover agreements that either do not restrict competition or, if they do restrict competition, that do not affect trade between Member States. In practice it is not always apparent whether agreements are considered to fall outside Article 81(1) because there is no restriction of competition or because the restriction of competition does not affect trade between Member States. One of the underlying reasons is that it is problematic to consider the two criteria in isolation from each other.[1] This renders it difficult in practice to apply the test whether trade between Member States is affected as the only criterion for establishing jurisdiction in Articles 81 and 82 EC.

Nevertheless the Court of Justice considers that the only jurisdictional criterion in EC antitrust law is the inter-state trade effect.[2] The basis for the interpretation of the effect on inter-state trade criterion was formulated in the *Consten and Grundig* judgment. The Court of Justice held that:

---

[1] See for instance Van Gerven AG at para. 17 of his Opinion in Case 234/89 *Delimitis* v. *Henninger Bräu* [1991] ECR I–952 and Case 5/69 *Völk* v. *Vervaecke* [1969] ECR 295.

[2] Cases 6 & 7/73 *Commercial Solvents* v. *Commission* [1974] ECR 223.

The concept of an agreement "which may affect trade between member States" is intended to define, in the law governing cartels, the boundary between areas respectively covered by Community law and national law. It is only to the extent to which the agreement may affect trade between Member States that the deterioration in competition caused by the agreement falls under the prohibition of Community law contained in Article 85 [now Article 81]; otherwise it escapes the prohibition.

In this connection, what is particularly important is whether the agreement is *capable of constituting a threat*, either direct or indirect, actual or potential, to freedom of trade between Member States in a manner which might *harm the attainment of the objectives of a single market* between States. Thus the fact than an agreement encourages an increase, even a large one, in the volume of trade between states is not sufficient to exclude the possibility that the agreement may "affect" such trade in the abovementioned manner.[3]

That interpretation was further refined in a subsequent judgment in which the Court ruled that the effect on trade between Member States provision should be read together with the introductory words of Article 81. Those words refer to agreements which are "incompatible with the Common Market". The inter-state trade criterion is therefore:

directed to determining the field of application of the prohibition by laying down the condition that it may be assumed that there is a possibility that the realization of a single market between Member States might be impeded. . . . For this requirement to be fulfilled it must be possible to foresee with a sufficient degree of probability on the basis of objective factors of law or of fact that the agreement in question may have an influence, direct or indirect, actual or potential, on the pattern of trade between Member States.[4]

Thus, the effect on trade between Member State criterion is interpreted in the light of the requirements of the common market. Along with the expansion of the objectives pursued by Community antitrust law as the common market was gradually established,[5] the Court expanded the interpretation of the inter-state trade effect criterion. A second reading of the clause was added to the original which focused exclusively on trade flows between Member States. In recognition of the fact that antitrust law objectives had partly shifted from market integration towards market governance and in view of the fact that Community antitrust law enforcement was increasingly employed as a means of pursuing a Community economic policy, the Court ruled that it does not matter whether inter-state trade is actually or potentially affected when it is obvious that restrictive practices shall have "repercussions on the competitive structure within the Common Market".[6] Similarly where agreements between undertakings or their behaviour affect "patterns of competition", they are now held to fall within the scope of the Community's antitrust law.[7] The shifting and gradually increasing

---

[3] Cases 56 & 58/64 *Consten and Grundig* v. *Commission* [1966] ECR 341 (emphasis added).
[4] Case 56/65 *Société La Technique Minière* v. *Maschinenbau Ulm* [1966] ECR 235.
[5] Above, Ch. 1.
[6] *Commercial Solvents* v. *Commission*, above, n. 2.
[7] Case 26/76 *United Brands* v. *Commission* [1978] ECR 207.

interpretation of Community jurisdiction in antitrust law was codified in *Hugin* where the Court merged the two criteria:

> Community antitrust law covers any agreement or any practice which is capable of constituting a threat to freedom of trade between Member States in a manner which might harm the attainment of the objectives of a single market between the Member States, in particular by partitioning the national markets or by affecting the structure of competition within the Common Market.[8]

This combined interpretation established a broad territorial scope for Community antitrust law, in spite of the fact that the Court had ruled that in order to come within the prohibitions of EC antitrust law agreements must affect trade between Member States "to an appreciable extent".[9] In order to fall within EC antitrust law it is, for instance, not necessary that each individual clause in an agreement affect intra-Community trade. Therefore if there is no doubt that the agreement as a whole is capable of appreciably affecting trade between Member States there is no need to examine whether each clause restricting competition, taken in isolation, also affects intra-Community trade.[10] Furthermore, cartels which are confined to one Member State are not outwith Community antitrust law. On the contrary, especially where they are nation-wide, such agreements will fall within EC antitrust law's jurisdiction because they tend "by their very nature" to affect the natural flow of goods.[11] Further, an agreement need not necessarily appreciably affect trade between Member States. It is sufficient that it is *capable* of having that effect.[12] Finally, even agreements which are incapable of restricting, potentially, trade between Member States individually can nevertheless fall within Community antitrust law jurisdiction. An agreeement, however minor it is itself, is still held to affect trade between Member States if it forms part of a network of agreements which, by its cumulative effect, is likely to prevent penetration by competitors from other Member States, and thus holding up economic interpenetration which the Treaty is designed to bring about. A good number of distribution agreements have been considered to have an effect on trade between Member States in spite

---

[8] Case 22/78 *Hugin* v. *Commission* [1979] ECR 1869.

[9] Case 22/71 *Béguelin* v. *GL Import Export* [1971] ECR 949. See also *Völk* v. *Vervaecke*, above, n. 1.

[10] Case 193/83 *Windsurfing* v. *Commission* [1986] ECR 611.

[11] See, for nation-wide agreements falling within Art. 81 EC; Case 8/72 *Vereniging van cementhandelaren* [1972] ECR 977; Case 22/79 *Greenwich Films* [1979] ECR 3275; Case 61/80 *Coop. Stremsel en Kleurfabriek* [1981] ECR 851; Case 246/86 *Belasco* v. *Commission* [1989] ECR 2117; Case 42/84 *Remia and Others* v. *Commission* [1985] ECR 2545 para. 22. Recently confirmed in the German car leasing cases Case C–266/93 *Bundeskartellamt* v. *Volkswagen* [1995] ECR I–3477; Case C–70/93 *Bayerische Motorenwerke* v. *ALD Autoleasing D* [1995] ECR I–3439. The same principle applies with respect to Art. 82 EC: Case 322/81 *Bandengroothandel Frieschebrug and Nederlandse Bandenindustrie Michelin* v. *Commission* ("*Michelin*") [1983] ECR 3461. Nevertheless, agreements which do not cover an entire state but are confined to a small part of it may fall outwith the Community's jurisdiction: *Hugin* v. *Commission*, above, n. 8.

[12] Case 19/77 *Miller International Schallplatten* v. *Commission* [1978] ECR 131.

of the fact that individually they are unlikely to be of direct relevance to the common market.[13]

Only in those instances in which an agreements is of purely local significance, does not form part of a bundle of similar agreements and where there is no genuine potential for the companies concerned to trade the relevant product across borders is there no Community jurisdiction. Community antitrust law jurisdiction therefore covers all behaviour within the territory of the Community but for purely local and insulated cartels or abuses of dominant position.[14]

4.1.2. The Interrelationship between Community and National Law

An immediate consequence of the broad scope of Community antitrust law is that there is a large degree of overlap with Member State antitrust laws.[15] In the absence of legislative provisions regulating the interface between EC and national antitrust law, the potential for conflicts is high.

The case law of the Court of Justice aims to reduce the likelihood of conflicting decisions being taken. The Court of Justice acknowledges that in principle Community and Member State antitrust laws operate concurrently.[16] The application of two—or more—sets of antitrust laws in parallel is justified by the divergent objectives of Community and national antitrust law respectively. The Court considers that Community antitrust law is enforced in view of

---

[13] Case T–7/93 *Langnese-Iglo* v. *Commission* [1995] ECR II–1539; and Case 23/67 *Brasserie de Haecht* v. *Wilkin-Janssen* [1967] ECR 407 at 415–16. But see Van Gerven AG in *Delimitis* v. *Henninger Bräu*, above, n. 1, at para. 24. He argues that an effect on trade between Member States may exist where a network of supply agreements covers the whole territory of a Member State but not by a single agreement concerning only one public house. "If it is found that, by virtue of the terms and effects . . . the agreement in question does not in itself affect trade between Member States, one cannot in my view conclude that that condition is met in the case of that individual agreement just because of the existence of a network. The agreement itself adds no element of restriction of trade between Member States to the network under consideration, and the negative effects of the latter may not therefore be attributed to the individual agreement". Van Gerven AG therefore concluded that the fact that an agreement forms part of a network of similar agreements is not *in itself* sufficient to support the conclusion that an individual agreement affects trade between Member States.

[14] D. Goyder, *EC Competition Law*, 3rd edn. (Oxford, OUP, 1998), 503.

[15] It may therefore be noted that the passage of the Court's *Consten & Grundig* judgment, cited above, in which it held that the interstate trade effect criterion "defines the boundary between the areas *respectively* covered by Community law and national law" is not entirely adequate. The criterion does after all not define the area covered by the antitrust laws of the Member States. Rather it defines the boundary of Community law jurisdiction and, thus, the area in which jurisdiction is shared. Beyond the boundary of Community law's applicability national antitrust law jurisdiction is exclusive. The scope of national law is defined by national law. This specification has become relevant now that a number of Member States have adopted antitrust laws, the scope of which is explicitly restricted to the area not covered by EC antitrust law. Only under those laws does the effect on trade between Member States criterion define the boundary respectively covered by national and Community law. See, e.g., on the Italian antitrust law which features such a provision, M. Siragusa and G. Scassellati-Sforzolini, "Italian and EC Competition Law: A New Relationship—Reciprocal Exclusivity and Common Principles" (1992) 29 *CMLRev* 93–131.

[16] Case 14/68 *Walt Wilhelm* v. *Bundeskartellamt* [1969] ECR 13.

potential obstacles which may result for trade between Member States. Member State antitrust laws, conversely, "proceed on the basis of the considerations peculiar to it and consider cartels only in that context".[17] In order for agreements between undertakings to be valid within the Community they therefore have to satisfy the concerns of Community as well as national antitrust law. This constitutes a so-called "double-barrier" antitrust law regime.

Yet, the Court of Justice made the concurrent applicability of Community and Member State law, the double-barrier test, subject to a qualification. With reference to the case law on the *effet utile* of Community law, it held that the application of national law, concurring with the application of Community antitrust law, may take effect only in so far as this does not prejudice the general aims of the Treaty.[18] In particular, the full and uniform application of Community competition rules, or the full effect of the measures adopted in the implementation of those rules, may not be effectively impeded in the process of the enforcement of national antitrust laws. Within the area of concurrent jurisdiction Community antitrust law therefore reigns supreme, wherever the parallel procedures would lead to conflicting outcomes. As a consequence of this procedural precedence the "double barrier" is reduced to a "single barrier" where commercial behaviour is exempted from the application of Community antitrust law. In order to distinguish it from a genuine "double barrier" regime the term "mitigated" or "qualified double barrier" has been invented for the Community system.

The preeminence of Community law in the case of a normative conflict is therefore clearly established under the Court's case law but the operation of this form of procedural supremacy is much less straightforward. The circumstances under which parallel application of national antitrust law undermines the uniform application of the Community competition rules remain unclear.[19] An overview of the potential conflicts in the concurrent application of national and Community antitrust law reveals the problems which occur.

No Conflict

Clearly, there is no conflict when Community and national antitrust laws either both ban an agreement on the basis of antitrust law or, conversely, both permit it.[20] The two alternative situations are theoretically more problematic since

---

[17] *Ibid.* Recently reconfirmed in Case C–67/91 *Dirección General de Defensa de la Competencia* v. *Asociación Española de Banca Privada* ("*Spanish Banks*") [1992] ECR I–4785 at para. 11.

[18] *Walt Wilhelm* v. *Bundeskartellamt*, above, n. 16.

[19] See Jacobs AG's Opinion in Case C–7/97 *Oscar Bronner* v. *Mediaprint* [1998] ECR I–7791 and C. Kerse, *E.C. Antitrust Procedure* (London, Sweet and Maxwell, 1998), 450ff.

[20] In the case of a double prohibition there is a potential problem with respect to the double imposition of fines. The ECJ clarified that under the Community's system which is based on a sharing of jurisdiction there is no objection to dual sanctions although general requirements of natural justice demand that any previous punitive decision must be taken into account in determining any sanction which is to be imposed: *Walt Wilhelm* v. *Bundeskartellamt*, above, n. 16, at para. 11.

application of national law might then imperil the uniform application of Community law or the full effect of measures which have been taken to implement those rules.

Where EC Antitrust Law is Stricter than National Antitrust Law

A first potentially problematic situation is where Community antitrust law prohibits business conduct which is allowed under national law. A conflict of laws occurs. Yet this conflict is clearly solved on the basis of the "mitigated double-barrier" system laid down by the Court of Justice in *Walt Wilhelm*;[21] where Community law prohibits conduct, more lenient national law cannot take effect. To decide otherwise necessarily implies that, contrary to the supremacy doctrine, the full and uniform effect of Community antitrust would be thwarted. Accordingly the Commission broke up a series of cartels on the basis of EC antitrust law even though they benefited from exemptions on the basis of national antitrust law.[22]

Where National Antitrust Law is Stricter than EC Antitrust Law

The situation which is problematic arises in the fourth type of conflict, i.e. where Community law does not prohibit a type of conduct which *is* prohibited by national law. The potential for conflict exists with respect to Article 81 as well as Article 82 EC but in practice conflicts between the latter and national law have not caused substantial problems. It is undisputed that behaviour can be considered to be unlawful under national law even though the conduct is not prohibited by Article 82 EC.[23] In practice the most difficult situation therefore occurs where agreements are prohibited by national (antitrust) law but allowed under Article 81 EC.

In order to appreciate the conflicts that may occur in this context, it is necessary to recall the substantive concerns of Article 81 EC and to relate them to the Court's supremacy doctrine. There are two conceptually different ways in which agreements between undertakings which may restrict competition and which may affect trade between Member States escape the nullity provided for in Article 81(2) EC. First, agreements remain valid if they do not restrict, distort or prevent competition or if they do not affect trade between Member States. Such agreements fall outside the prohibition defined in Article 81(1) EC altogether. They may obtain a declaration to that effect, a so-called "negative

---

[21] *Ibid.*

[22] The same result would be achieved in a genuine "double-barrier" regime where the strictest law would always apply. Cf. Trabucchi AG's considerations in his Opinion in Case 73/74 *Papier Peints de Belgique* v. *Commission* [1975] ECR 1491 at 1516ff. The EC antitrust law prohibition even prevails if anti-competitive behaviour is based on an obligation under national law: e.g. Case 311/85 *Vereniging van Vlaamse Reisbureaus* v. *Sociale Dienst* [1987] ECR 3801.

[23] See e.g. Commission of the European Communities, *Tenth Annual Report on Competition Policy* (Brussels, 1980), at 155.

clearance". Secondly, agreements between undertakings can remain valid in spite of falling into the antitrust prohibition where the Commission has declared the provisions of Article 81(1) EC inapplicable pursuant to Article 81(3) EC, the exemption provision. This can be either on the basis of an individual assessment or on the basis of a block-exemption regulation. The interrelationship between Community antitrust law and national law depends to some extent on the manner in which agreements are considered to be compatible with Article 81 EC.

Agreements Which do Not Fall within Article 81(1) EC

The Court of Justice considered the interrelationship between negative clearances on the basis of Article 81(1) EC and national antitrust law in the *Perfume* cases.[24] It ruled that agreements which do not fall within Article 81(1) EC and which are therefore acceptable under EC antitrust law may still be prohibited on the basis of national antitrust law. The Court of Justice judged that in these cases there is no potential for conflicts because Community antitrust law is not concerned with the agreements at issue at all. Therefore stricter national antitrust law may take effect.

The preliminary conclusion is therefore that agreements which do not fall within Article 81(1) may be prohibited on the basis of stricter national antitrust law. Nevertheless, a caveat is in order. The "*Perfume*" agreements were considered to fall outside the scope of Article 81(1) EC because there was no effect on trade between Member States—not because there was no restriction of competition. The question therefore remains how the principle of procedural supremacy operates if an agreement is considered to affect trade between Member States but at the same time is not considered appreciably to restrict competition in the sense of Article 81(1).

On the one hand, it can be argued that the uniform effect on EC antitrust law would be harmed if an agreement which affected trade between Member States but which was not considered to restrict competition under EC law could be prohibited on the basis of national antitrust law. Such an approach would lead to divergent market conditions among the Member States which would go against the concept of a common market. This suggests that the procedural supremacy rule precludes the application of national antitrust laws where this would lead to a prohibition on those agreements.[25] On the other hand, however, the Court specified in *Walt Wilhelm* that EC and national antitrust laws consider agreements from different points of view. The distinctive objectives of Community and national antitrust laws formed the basis for continued concurrent applicability of the two sets of law.[26] The force of the arguments in favour of continued applicability of national law in these types of conflicts is enhanced by the very broad interpretation of the effect on trade between Member States

[24] Case 253/78 *Procureur de la République* v. *Giry and Guérlain* [1980] ECR 2327.
[25] In this sense see Tesauro AG in Case C–266/93 *Bundeskartellamt* v. *Volkswagen and VAG*, above, n. 11.
[26] *Walt Wilhelm*, above, n. 16, at para. 3.

criterion. If all agreements which affect trade between Member States but which do not restrict competition under EC antitrust law could not be held contrary to national antitrust law this would in effect result in exclusive Community jurisdiction for all antitrust law cases with any commercial significance. While there may be good grounds for establishing a system of exclusive Community jurisdiction in cases of genuine Community importance (see below), that is not the case in the present system which is based on concurrent applicability of both sets of antitrust laws. In view of the concurrent applicability of national and Community antitrust laws the conclusion should therefore be that agreements which do not fall within Article 81(1) EC, either because there is no effect on trade between Member States or because there is no restriction of competition for EC law purposes involved, may be prohibited on the basis of stricter national antitrust law.[27]

Agreements Which are Exempted on the Basis of Article 81(3) EC

Secondly, there is the situation in which an agreement falling within Article 81(1) EC is exempted on the basis of Article 81(3) EC. What happens if such an agreement, compatible with EC antitrust law, is prohibited under national antitrust law? In order to address this situation it is useful to turn to the Court's formulation of the procedural supremacy rule in *Walt Wilhelm*. With respect to Article 81 EC the Court ruled:

> While the Treaty's primary object is to eliminate by this means the obstacles to the free movement of goods within the common market to confirm and safeguard the unity of that market, it also permits the Community authorities to carry out certain *positive*, though indirect, action with a view to promoting a harmonious development of economic activities within the whole Community in accordance with Article 2 of the Treaty. . . . The binding force of the Treaty and of measures taken in application of it must not differ from one State to another as a result of internal measures, lest the functioning of the Community system should be impeded and the achievement of the aims of the Treaty placed in peril. Consequently, conflicts between the rules of the Community and national rules in the matter of law on cartels must be resolved by applying the principle that Community law takes precedence. . . . Consequently, and so long as a regulation adopted pursuant to Article 87(2)(e) of the Treaty [now Article 83(2)(e) EC] has not provided otherwise, national authorities may take action against an agreement in accordance with their national law, even when an examination of an agreement from the point of view of its compatibility with Community law is pending before the Commission, subject however to the condition that the application of national law may not prejudice the full and uniform application of Community law or the effects of measures taken or to be taken to implement it.[28]

The ambivalence in this judgment with respect to exemption decisions is apparent. The Court seems to refer to exemptions where it declares that the Community institutions can take *positive* action on the basis of the antitrust

---

[27] See Kerse, above, n. 19, 451–2 and Goyder, above, n. 14, 504ff.
[28] *Walt Wilhelm*, above, n. 16.

provisions. Its assertion that conflicts between national and Community antitrust law should be resolved by applying the principle that Community law takes precedence therefore seems to apply to exemptions too. Yet the Court also underscores that EC and national antitrust laws apply concurrently as long as there is no Community regulation which provides for separate jurisdictions. Although the Court seems to suggest that agreements which benefit from an exemption on the basis of Article 81(3) EC may not be held contrary to national antitrust law, it is unclear whether this is indeed what the Court meant. Because of this ambivalence in the Court's case law opinions on the operation of the principle of procedural supremacy in connection with exemptions vary considerably.

First there is support for the view that agreements which benefit from a Commission exemption, in whatever form, are immune to the application of stricter national antitrust law. The Commission itself is the most notable proponent of this viewpoint. In the *Perfume* cases it argued that the full effectiveness and uniformity of the measures implementing Community antitrust law would be impeded if the type of positive action implied in the Commission granting an exemption could be overridden on the basis of national antitrust law.[29] It has been joined in this contention by a large number of commentators.[30] The underlying argument is that exemptions aim to promote the harmonious development of economic activities throughout the Community as per Article 2 EC. To allow a Member State to prohibit on the basis of national antitrust law an agreement which was exempted by the Commission for its overall benefits to economic progress in the Community would thwart a principal Treaty objective, all the more so because the positive assessment was formed *in spite of* the restriction of competition. Support is found in the recent Court judgment in relation to the ECSC Treaty in the *Banks* case.[31] There the Court ruled that Commission decisions taken pursuant to Articles 65 and 66(7) of the ECSC Treaty are binding in their entirety in view of the Commission's exclusive competence to take those decisions.[32] Analogously it is then argued that exemptions granted by the Commission on the basis of Article 81(3) EC in view of the exclusive competence of the Commission to take such decisions are also binding in their entirety and leave no room for the application of different national law.[33]

---

[29] *Procureur de la République* v. *Giry and Guérlain*, above, n. 24. See also the Commission's arguments in *Bundeskartellamt* v. *Volkswagen and VAG*, above, n. 11.

[30] J.-F. Verstrynge, "The Relationship Between National and Community Antitrust Law: An Overview after the Perfume Cases" (1981) 3 *Northwestern Journal of International Law and Business* 358–83; S. Klaue, "Einige Bemerkungen über die Zukunft des Zweischrankentheorie" in J. Bauer *et al.* (eds.), *Festschrift für Ernst Steindorf*; O. Lieberknecht, "Das Verhältnis der EWG-Gruppenfreistellungsverordnungen zum deutschen Kartellrecht" in O. von Gamm *et al.*, *Strafrecht, Unternehmensrecht, Anwaltsrecht—Festschrift für Gerd Pfeiffer* (Cologne, Carl Heymanns, 1988), 589–606; E. Braun, "III—Germany" in P. Behrens (ed.), *EC Competition Rules in National Courts* (Baden-Baden, Nomos, 1996) at 442.

[31] See Tesauro AG's Opinion in *Bundeskartellamt* v. *Volkswagen and VAG*, above, n. 11.

[32] Case C–128/92 *H.J. Banks* v. *British Coal Corporation* [1994] ECR I–1209.

[33] J. Stuyck, "Competition Law in the EC and in the Member States" in O. Due *et al.* (eds.), *Festschrift für Ulrich Everling—Band II*.

An objection to this particular argument is, however, that the *Banks* case underscored the difference between the EC and the ECSC Treaties. The ECSC Treaty provides for exclusive jurisdiction in the field of competition, whereas national antitrust laws are concurrently applicable under the EC Treaty.

While numerous commentators thus argue that all formal Commission exemptions pre-empt the application of conflicting national law, there are others who do not accept this broad interpretation of procedural supremacy for Community law. These commentators make a division between *types* of exemptions. In their view, some exemptions are positive Community measures in the sense of *Walt Wilhelm*, others are not. Within this strand of analysis there are considerable divergences of view on the question of *which* type of exemptions do and which do not represent positive Commission action. Accordingly, opinions vary on the appropriate dividing line between exemptions which pre-empt application of different national antitrust law and which do not.

A first line of analysis centres on the difference between *individual* and *block* exemptions. Interestingly, there are two antithetical opinions within the group of commentators who concentrate on the division between *block* and *individual*. One holds that individual exemptions do carry supremacy but block exemptions do not. In this vision, agreements benefiting from an individual exemption should be enforceable in spite of national antitrust law objections to it because the Commission, before granting the positive assessment leading to the exemption, has first concluded that a restriction of competition is implicit. Subsequently the Commission found that the positive effects of the agreement on other policy areas outweigh the arguments for prohibiting it on the basis of antitrust policy considerations. The individual positive assessment of the agreement's effects should imply that the agreement cannot be prohibited on the basis of diverging national antitrust law. Conversely, block exemptions which are granted to agreements without a significant degree of individual assessment do not constitute sufficient "positive" action in order to justify pre-emption of national antitrust law. Indeed in the case of block exemptions no positive action is considered to be taken at all *vis-à-vis* an individual agreement. Whereas formally granted individual exemptions are therefore always based on specific positive and individual action and on the Commission's balancing of specific and Community-wide interests, this cannot be said to be the case with all agreements falling under a block-exemption regulation.[34] Support for the vision that there is a qualitative difference between exemptions granted for individual agreements and exemptions which are derived from a block exemption can be found in the Court of First Instance's case law. In *Tetra Pak* the CFI held that "it is true that regulations granting block exemption, like individual exemption decisions, apply only to agreements which, in principle, satisfy the conditions set out in Article 85(3) [now Article 81(3)]. But unlike individual exemptions,

---

[34] Thus, for instance, J. María Beneyto, "Transforming Competition Law Through Subsidiarity" in Academy of European Law (ed.), *Collected Courses of the Academy of European Law*, Vol. V, Book 1 (The Hague, Kluwer Law International, 1996), 267–319.

block exemptions are, by definition, not dependent on a case-by-case examination to establish that the conditions for exemption laid down in the Treaty are satisfied. In order to qualify for a block exemption, an agreement has *only* to satisfy the criteria laid down in the relevant block-exemption regulation. The agreement itself is not subject to any *positive assessment* with regard to the conditions set out in Article 85(3) [now Article 81(3)]".[35] While the ruling concerned the relationship between exemptions and Article 82 the cited passage seems of sufficient generality to justify extension to the present discussion.[36]

Supporters of the opposite position insist that agreements which fall within a block-exemption regulation cannot be prohibited by stricter national antitrust law. The argument is that block-exemption regulations form part of Community legislation and under the Court's general supremacy case law EC law reigns supreme over national laws. National law is therefore not valid in so far as it covers the same area as a block-exemption regulation.[37] An exception is made for those block-exemption regulations which explicitly allow for the application of stricter national law.[38] Exemptions granted by the Commission to individual agreements are, on the contrary, considered not to imply positive rule-making which would pre-empt national law. An individual exemption, in the opinion of the proponents of the view that block exemptions carry more extensive supremacy than individual exemptions, merely implies that there is no objection to it from a Community antitrust law perspective, akin to negative clearances.

Logically, of the thus proposed differentiation between the operation of supremacy for individual exemptions, on the one hand, and for block exemptions, on the other, neither is acceptable to a second category of commentators who defend the position that exemptions generally prevent conflicting national antitrust law from applying. They rebut the differentiation between the type of exemption with reference to the four conditions enshrined in Article 81(3) EC which are in their view themselves sufficient guarantee that once the Commission grants an exemption it intends to act positively, irrespective of the

---

[35] Case T–51/89 *Tetra Pak* v. *Commission* [1990] ECR II–309.

[36] See also Case 226/94 *Grand Garage Albigeois and others* v. *Garage Garage de la Gare and others* [1996] ECR I–651, discussed below, n. 45.

[37] P. Ulmer, "Die Anwendung des EWG-Kartellrechts auf 'nationale' Wettbewerbsbeschränkungen und ihre Folgewirkungen für das nationale Kartellrecht" in Studienvereinigung Kartellrecht (ed.), *Neue Entwicklungen im EWG-Kartellrecht* (Cologne, Carl Heymanns, 1976), 69–91 at 81, thus also, more recently, Stuyck, above, n. 33.

[38] See for examples of Commission block-exemption regs. which allow for the application of diverging national law; the 19th recital of Commission Reg. 1984/83 on the application of Art. 85(3) of the Treaty to categories of exclusive distribution agreements ([1983] OJ L173/5) and the 13th recital of Commission Reg. 4087/88 on the application of Art. 85(3) of the Treaty to categories of franchise agreements ([1988] OJ L359/46). Whether the group exemptions which are based on the so-called opposition procedures (i.e. notified agreements which obtain an exemption *automatically* if they fall within the terms of the group exemption regulation, unless the Commission opposes them) have the same claim to the status of "positive" action is disputed among the supporters of general supremacy for exemptions. See on this issue R. Walz, "Rethinking Walt Wilhelm, or the Supremacy of Community Competition over National Law" (1996) 21 *ELR* 449–64, at 454–5.

question whether it is in the context of an individual or more general exemption.[39] Advocate General Tesauro, for instance, argued that exempted agreements are liable to affect trade between Member States because they in principle fall within Article 81(1) EC. Exemptions granted to these agreements in his view "cannot but prevent the national authorities from ignoring the positive assessment put on them by the Community authorities. Otherwise, not only would a given agreement be treated differently depending on the law of each Member State, thus detracting from the uniform application of Community law, but the full effectiveness of a Community measure—which an exemption under Article 85(3) [now Article 81(3)] undoubtedly is—would also be disregarded". A differentiation between individual and block exemptions is not justified in such a perspective.[40]

A third strand of interpretation of Community antitrust law's preemptive effect posits that, instead of differentiating between individual and block exemptions, a distinction should be made concerning the motivation which was provided for granting the relevant exemption. Only those exemptions which are granted for public policy reasons are considered to pre-empt application of a national prohibition provision. Exemptions provided for other reasons would in this view not pre-empt application of stricter national law.[41]

To understand the motivation underlying this interpretation of Community law's supremacy it is necessary to recall once more that the Commission regularly provides exemptions to agreements which do not restrict competition. Proponents of limited supremacy for Commission exemptions point to the unjustified difference which is thus made between agreements which are considered to fall short of the prohibition of Article 81(1) EC and agreements which only upon further reflection are not considered to restrict competition. The former will receive a "negative clearance" and national law may take full effect with respect to them. The latter agreements which do not have a different effect from an analytical competition perspective receive an exemption, and national antitrust law may therefore not be applied in view of the "positive" Community action.

A variant of this viewpoint is presented by commentators who argue that the supremacy of exemptions over diverging national antitrust law should depend on a qualitative assessment of the reasons for which the exemption was provided. National exceptions to the validity of agreements which benefit from an exemption should be permitted in so far as the motivation for prohibiting the

---

[39] Thus e.g., J. Zekoll, "European Community Competition Law and National Competition Laws: Compatibility Problems from a German Perspective" (1991) 24 *Vanderbilt Journal of Transantional Law* 75–111 at 105. Similarly see Verstrynge, above, n. 30.

[40] *Bundeskartellamt* v. *Volkswagen AG and VAG Leasing GmbH*, above, n. 11.

[41] K. Markert, "Some Legal and Administrative Problems of the Co-Existence of Community and National Competition Law in the EEC" (1974) 11 *CMLRev* 92–104; and apparently also K. Stockmann, "EEC Competition Law and Member State Competition Laws" in B. Hawk (ed.), *Annual Proceedings of the Fordham Corporate Law Institute 1987*.

agreement on the basis of national antitrust law is not related to the reason for which the Commission issued the exemption.[42]

That interpretation is closely linked to yet another interpretation which takes as its central question the nature and the degree of interest which the two administrative levels take in the validity of an agreement.[43] Where Community law considers the prohibition of Article 81(1) EC inapplicable to an agreement, for instance because it falls within the terms of a block-exemption regulation which is further of little significance to the Community, conflicting national antitrust law should in this view take effect if there is clearly a significant interest in the relevant Member States, for instance because the centre of gravity of the infringement of national antitrust law lies in that Member State. The relevance of this viewpoint is enhanced by the gradual expansion of the Community's jurisdictional scope as a consequence of the broad interpretation of the effect on trade between Member States criterion. The numerous agreements which fall within Community jurisdiction but which are not of "Community interest" would be affected by this test. Where Community law provides automatic exemption for those types of agreements, by way of a block-exemption regulation, advocates of this view would consider that stricter national antitrust law should take effect.

Finally, there are those commentators who, in spite of the Court's reference to "positive action" in *Walt Wilhelm*, argue that exemptions—in whatever form—do not preclude application of diverging national law. Effectively they re-establish the double-barrier test which is identified with a system of concurrent jurisdiction. A specific agreement or practice, according to supporters of the genuine double-barrier theory, must be lawful under both sets of laws in order to be valid. The basis lies in the perception that a normative conflict cannot occur between Community and Member State antitrust laws because they pursue different objectives.[44] Although such a perception lay at the basis of the Court's decision in *Walt Wilhelm* it seems that the reference which the Court makes to the full effectiveness of measures implementing Community law that should be guaranteed, in combination with the allusion to "positive" measures, is incompatible with a view that Commission exemptions do not affect the

[42] D. Wolf, "Zum Verhältnis von europäischem und deutschem Wettbewerbsrecht" (1994) 5 *EuZW* 233–8; Zekoll, above, n. 39, and, with additional qualifications, J. Temple Lang, "European Community Constitutional Law and the Enforcement of Community Antitrust Law" in B. Hawk (ed.), *Annual Proceedings of the Fordham Corporate Law Institute 1993* (New York, Transnational Juris Publications, 1994), 525–695 at 561.

[43] Stockmann, above, n. 41, and E. Niederleithinger, "Das Verhältnis nationaler und europäischer Kontrolle von Zusammenschlüssen" (1990) 25 *WuW* 721–30.

[44] See the extensive discussion of the normative and theoretical underpinning of the double barrier theory in C. Jung, *Subsidiarität im Recht der Wettbewerbsbeschränkungen*, at 87–96. Supporters of the genuine double-barrier theory rely on the precedent in US antitrust law development in which the interstate trade clause, akin to that of the European Community, was interpreted broadly to include at a certain point even purely local cartels. The Supreme Court decided that both federal and state law should be applicable (*Standard Oil Co. of Kentucky* v. *State of Tennessee* 217 US 413 (1910). Consequently, the strictest law applies in the USA, though federal antitrust law enforcement is dominant.

degree to which differing national laws may be applied. However, the Court's recent judgments on the nature of exemptions may qualify this conclusion. The Court ruled that block-exemption regulations merely provide the conditions under which Article 81(1) EC is inapplicable to an agreement even though the agreement's terms are such that it would otherwise be caught by that prohibition. Exemptions thus specify the conditions under which certain agreements are lawful having regard to *the competition rules of the Treaty*. They are concerned only with the content of agreements which parties may lawfully conclude having regard to the rules of the Treaty prohibiting restrictions affecting normal competition within the common market.[45] In view of the Court's continued reference to the diverging objectives of Community and national antitrust laws,[46] this qualification of exemptions suggests that stricter national antitrust law may be applied to agreements which benefit from a Community exemption. Nevertheless, it should be acknowledged that the *Walt Wilhelm* judgment does not mention that Community and national interests need to be weighed in order to determine whether an agreement which is exempted from the Community antitrust prohibition may be prohibited on the basis of national antitrust law. If it is accepted that the Court referred to exemptions when it ruled in *Walt Wilhelm* that the procedural supremacy of EC antitrust law extends to certain positive measures, then it must likewise be excepted that positive or "public policy" exemptions trump the application of stricter national antitrust law. Agreements which are exempted from the prohibition on restricting competition in view of their, on balance, positive effects on other Community policy areas may not therefore be prohibited on the basis of national antitrust law.

4.1.3. Commentary

The discussion of the operation of Community antitrust law's procedural supremacy over national antitrust laws illustrates that the concurrent applicability of Community and national antitrust laws remains problematic. In particular the effect of Community antitrust law exemptions on the application of stricter national antitrust law is still unclear. There are two reasons. The first is that not all exemptions can be considered positive measures in the sense of *Walt Wilhelm*. In reality exemptions which are granted to agreements which do not on balance restrict competition are similar to negative clearances. There is no justified reason for treating this type of exemption differently from negative clearances. On the basis of the principles formulated in *Walt Wilhelm* there can therefore be no simple rule that all exemptions are positive measures, the full effect of which may not be impaired on the basis of national law. Secondly, under the current broad jurisdictional scope of Article 81 EC there are agreements which are prohibited and then exempted, for instance on the basis of block-exemptions regulations, which

---

[45] *Grand Garage Albigeois and others* v. *Garage de la Gare*, above, n. 36 (emphases added).
[46] For example in "*Spanish Banks*", above, n. 17.

are not of "Community interest". In particular because the Court of Justice considers that block-exemption regulations *merely* provide the conditions under which Article 81(1) EC is *inapplicable* to an agreement even though the terms of the agreement are such that it would otherwise be caught by that prohibition, the "positive" nature of block-exemption regulations is clearly limited. It is in this respect difficult to envisage how the Community could be considered to have taken positive measures with respect to agreements which are not of Community interest, also because the Commission does not generally accept jurisdiction with respect to these agreements. It would seem unjustified to pre-empt application of national antitrust law on the basis of the "positive" action taken by the Community to agreements which fall within the substantive scope of a block-exemption regulation but which are not of Community interest.

In practice the operation of the procedural supremacy rule is complicated further by the fact that only formal Commission decisions "at the culmination of procedures" can claim supremacy over the application of national antitrust law.[47] Formal Commission decisions are very scarce. In the absence of an exemption, national antitrust law may take effect, although the institutions which apply these national laws should avoid taking decisions which may conflict with EC law.[48] Therefore these national institutions are constrained to consider the exemption question under Community law. Although this problem has its origin in the concurrent jurisdiction for national and Community antitrust laws it is more a procedural and institutional problem of the current system. It will therefore be addressed in Chapter 6 which addresses aspects of decentralised application of antitrust law. Suffice it to note here that the operation of the supremacy rule in the interrelationship between Community and national antitrust laws remains unclear. The final section of this chapter (4.3.3.) provides suggestions about how the remaining questions on the interrelationship between EC and Member State laws can be answered EC antitrust law can be answered.

4.2 MERGERS

The Community Merger Control Regulation, adopted in 1989, constituted the most prominent innovation in the Community's antitrust law system since its inception in 1958.[49] In part the Regulation formed a genuine addition to the existing system, in part it codified the Commission's merger control practice which had gradually emerged on the basis of Articles 81 and 82 EC.[50]

---

[47] *Procureur de la republique* v. *Giry and Guérlain*, above, n. 24.

[48] *Delimitis* v. *Henninger Bräu*, above, n. 1.

[49] Council Reg. 4064/89 of 21 December 1989 on the control of concentrations between undertakings; [1989] OJ L395/1 (corrected version in [1990] OJ L257/13).

[50] Arts. 81 and 82 EC enabled the Commission to control, *ex post* and to a limited extent, merger processes in the Community on the basis of Case 6/72 *Europemballage and Continental Can* v. *Commission* [1973] ECR 215 and Cases 142 & 156/84 *BAT and Reynolds* v. *Commission* [1987] ECR 4487.

Consequently, the legal basis for adoption of the Merger Control Regulation was shared between Article 83 EC (ex Article 87), which provides specific legislative competences for the Council in the antitrust law area, and Article 308 EC (ex Article 235).[51] Its basis in the latter provision enabled significant deviations from the system which is in vigour for Articles 81 and 82 EC to be adopted in the merger control regime. Because the Merger Control Regulation is based on extensive debates and negotiations on the basis of Community law as it stood by the end of the 1980s, an examination of the Regulation may well contrast with the interrelationship between traditional Community antitrust law and national antitrust law. Like the previous section this section successively reviews the jurisdictional scope and the interrelationship between Community and Member State merger control law followed by a commentary on the findings.

4.2.1 The Scope for the EC Merger Regulation

In the context of the Merger Regulation the effect on trade between Member States was abandoned as the principal criterion for establishing Community jurisdiction. Reflecting that the internal market had been formally established, the Merger Regulation did not refer to cross-border trade. Rather, the Regulation is applicable only to those transactions which are considered of significant relevance to the operation of the internal market. Thus Article 1(1) of the Regulation provides that it shall apply to all concentrations with a "Community dimension". The second paragraph specifies that for the purposes of the Merger Regulation a concentration has a Community dimension where the aggregate worldwide turnover of the companies involved exceeds five billion ECU whilst the turnover realised within the Community by each of at least two of them is more than 250 million ECU. Despite the obvious difficulties in calculating the relevant turnover figures, the scope for the Merger Regulation is determined in a fairly objective manner.[52] Originally there was one single exception to this general definition of Community interest. If all undertakings concerned achieved more than two-thirds of their respective aggregate Community-wide turnovers within one and the same state the envisaged merger would not have a Community dimension.

The thresholds in the original Merger Regulation of 1989 were high.[53] This

---

[51] See extensively on the legal base for the Merger Control Reg. and a discussion of the extent to which it might be an *ultra vires* act of the Council in view of the existing Treaty provisions, J. Venit, "The 'Merger' Control Regulation: Europe Comes of Age . . . Or Caliban's Dinner" (1990) 27 *CMLRev* 7–50, esp. at 11–18.

[52] Art. 5 of the Reg. defines the way in which turnover is to be calculated. The pertinent process was further clarified in the Commission's Notice on calculation of turnover under Council Reg. 4064/89 of 21 December 1989 on the control of concentrations between undertakings; [1994] OJ C385/21.

[53] E. Schwarz, "Politics as Usual: The History of European Community Merger Control" [1993] *Yale Journal of International Law* 607–62. See also P. Broberg, *The European Commission's Jurisdiction to Scrutinise Mergers* (The Hague, Kluwer Law International, 1998), 1–18.

was acknowledged at the time of the adoption of the Regulation. The third paragraph of Article 1 declared that the thresholds would be reviewed before the end of the fourth year following the adoption of the Regulation. Due to a number of circumstances the review did not take place in 1993 as scheduled. Yet, continued Commission insistence on the need to lower the thresholds ultimately led to a revision of the notion of Community dimension. In 1997 the Council adopted a regulation which amended the original 1989 regime.[54] The revision of the jurisdictional scope for the Merger Regulation was a central element in the Amendment Regulation. The "Community dimension" criterion was amended. While a Community dimension continues to depend on turnover thresholds, the system was adapted in order to allow for a somewhat more subtle recognition of Community and Member State interests in a given merger.

After the 1997 amendment a merger is considered to have a Community dimension if it fulfils either of two conditions. First, if the turnover of the merging companies is more than the turnover thresholds, i.e. five billion ECU world-wide (together) and 250 million ECU Community-wide (each), unless each achieves at least two-thirds of its turnover within one and the same Member State. Secondly, and alternatively, a merger has a Community dimension if:

> "(a) the combined aggregate world-wide turnover of all the undertakings concerned is more than ECU 2500 million and the aggregate Community-wide turnover of each of at least two of the undertakings concerned is more than ECU 100 million;
> (b) in each of at least three Member States, the combined aggregate turnover of all the undertakings concerned is more than ECU 100 million; and
> (c) in each of at least three Member States included for the purpose of point (b), the aggregate turnover of each of at least two of the undertakings concerned is more than ECU 25 million;
> unless each of the undertakings concerned achieves more than two-thirds of its aggregate Community-wide turnover within one and the same Member State."[55]

4.2.2. Interrelationship between EC and Member State Merger Control

The second way in which the terms of the Merger Regulation deviate significantly from the traditional antitrust law regime is by the mutually exclusive jurisdictions which it establishes for the Community and Member States. Where

---

[54] Council Reg. 1310/97 of 30 June 1997 amending Reg. 4064/89 on the control of concentrations between undertakings [1997] OJ L180/1 (corrected version in [1998] OJ L40/17).

[55] Art. 1(1)(a) and (b) of Council Reg. 1310/97, above, n. 54. The Reg. provides that the Commission shall report before 1 July 2000 to the Council on the operation of the revised thresholds and criteria. Following that report the Council may on a proposal from the Commission, acting by qualified majority, revise the thresholds and the criteria mention in the new para. 1(3) of the Merger Reg.

the Regulation applies, Member State laws do not apply. In contrast to the (mitigated) double-barrier theory which governs the relationship between Community and national antitrust laws in the area of Articles 81 and 82 EC, the merger regime establishes a single barrier system. Under the Merger Regulation this has become known as the "one-stop-shop" principle.[56] The one-stop-shop is further guaranteed by the exclusive competence of the Commission to apply the Regulation.[57] However, four exceptions to the rigid division of jurisdiction were inserted into the Merger Regulation in order to avoid all mergers between undertakings which achieve the pertinent thresholds automatically falling into the Community's exclusive competentence.

The first deviation from the principle that exclusive jurisdiction is conferred on the basis of a single turnover thresholds test is enshrined in the concept of a Community dimension itself. Where a concentration involves undertakings which achieve two-thirds of their turnover in one and the same Member State, it does not have a Community dimension irrespective of the magnitude of the worldwide turnovers concerned. This provision reflects the fact that such a concentration is likely to have more significant effects on competition within the Member State concerned than for the Community as a whole.

A second qualification to the straightforwardness of the turnover thresholds defined in Article 1 of the Regulation relates to the possibility that the Community Merger Regulation is applied to mergers which are not of a Community dimension. While the Regulation generally applies only to concentrations as defined in Article 3 of the Regulation, Article 22(3) provides an exception to that rule. It stipulates that a Member State may request the Commission to investigate a merger involving undertakings which remain below the turnover thresholds required to have a Community dimension. The Commission's investigations may lead to the conclusion that the merger thus referred to it creates or strengthens a dominant position as a result of which effective competition would be significantly impeded within the territory of the Member State concerned. If the Commission considers this to be the case it may prohibit the merger along the general lines of the Merger Regulation in so far as the concentration affects trade between Member States. The Commission's action in this respect is however limited to those measures which are strictly necessary to maintain or restore effective competition within the territory of the relevant Member State.[58]

The reverse of referral to the Community of mergers without a Community dimension is also enshrined in the Regulation. It forms the third exception to the

[56] Art. 21(2) of the Reg. The Council could do so because the Reg. was partly based on Art. 83 EC (ex Art. 87). Art. 83(2)(e) EC provides that the Council has the power to determine the relationship between national laws and Community antitrust law. It made use of this competence for the first, and so far only, time in relation to the Merger Control Reg. The adoption of the one-stop-shop procedure is seen as an important element in vital support of business for the adoption of the Community Merger Control Reg. in 1989. See Schwarz, above, n. 53.

[57] Art. 21(1) of the Reg.

[58] Art. 22(3) (4) and (5) of the Reg.

exclusive Community control of mergers with a Community dimension. The Commission may refer a notified merger to the competent authorities of a Member State. Within three weeks of the date of receipt of the copy of the notification, sent by the Commission to the Member State, a Member State may inform the Commission that the relevant concentration threatens to create or to strengthen a dominant position as a result of which effective competition will be significantly impeded on a market within that Member State which presents all the characteristics of a distinct market *or* that it affects competition on such a market which does not constitute a substantial part of the common market.[59] Before the revision of the Merger Regulation it was not sufficient for a Member State authority to demonstrate that competition was *affected* on the distinct market within that state not constituting a substantial part of the common market. Member States had to demonstrate in their requests for referral that the concentration would threaten to create or strengthen a dominant position. In view of the increased scope for the Community Merger Regulation the criteria for referral of jurisdiction from the Commission to national authorities were relaxed.[60]

If such a referral is made the Member State authority will examine the compatibility of the merger in relation to that State's national competition law. This does not imply that a merger investigation or the ensuing decision once it is referred takes on a purely national character. The Commission does not delegate power to investigate the entire case but limits the referral to those aspects that affect competition in that Member State. Article 9(8) of the Regulation further orders that the Member State, when applying its national merger law in line with the procedure provided in that Article, may take only the measures strictly necessary for safeguarding or restoring effective competition on the market concerned. Moreover, the Commission having received a request from a Member State authority to refer the merger is free to retain jurisdiction itself.

The possibility of referring cases of a Community dimension to a Member State was included in the Merger Regulation because Member States foresaw that mergers could occur which would significantly impede competition at a domestic level while it would be considered insignificant within the context of the Commission examination of the effects on competition at the Community level. Until recently the Commission was hesitant to refer merger cases to national authorities. The origin of Commission resistance to referring cases to national authorities was seen to derive from the general feeling that the terms of the Merger Regulation, particularly the thresholds for establishing a Community dimension, ensure that all mergers which fall within the provisions are necessarily of Community importance. Control by the Commission was therefore considered *a priori* appropriate. As has been said the criteria were

---

[59] Art. 9 of the Merger Reg. as amended by Art. 8 of Council Reg. 1310/97.
[60] See the 10th and 11th recitals to the amendment Reg., above, n. 81. On the effects of the changes, see S. Hirsbrunner, "Referral of Mergers in E.C. Merger Control" (1999) 20 *ECLR* 372–8.

relaxed when the scope of the Merger Regulation was expanded. Since the revision the Commission has referred more cases to national authorities.[61]

Finally, the one-stop-shop system is subject to Article 21(3) of the Merger Regulation. That provision grants Member States the power to take appropriate measures to protect legitimate interests other than those taken into consideration by the Merger Regulation itself. While public security, plurality of the media and prudential rules, relating to financial or fiscal issues, are mentioned explicitly, other national interests may also be considered legitimate for the purposes of Article 21 of the Regulation. A Member State which wants to invoke those legitimate interests must notify the Commission. The Commission examines the claim's compatibility with the general principles and other provisions of Community law. If the Commission considers the interest legitimate and compatible with Community law it will notify the Member State concerned, which may then take the intended measures.

In spite of the clear-cut and rigid thresholds test establishing Community jurisdiction in merger cases various exceptions to the allocation of Community jurisdiction therefore exist under the Merger Regulation. The resulting flexibility allows for application of national merger laws to mergers in appropriate circumstances. Moreover, in exceptional cases and upon the request of the Member State involved the Commission may apply Community law to mergers which do not reach the Community dimension thresholds. Thus, the definition of the scope for Community jurisdiction and the design of the interrelationship of EC and national merger control laws enable the balancing of interests of the Community with respect to the common market and of Member States with respect to their individual economic policies. The Merger Regulation, adopted in 1989 and amended in 1997, thus reflects the concerns which led to the introduction of the subsidiarity principle into the EC Treaty.

4.2.3. Commentary

Commission application of the substantive provisions of the Merger Regulation is generally regarded positively. Commentators praise the way in which the assessment of compatibility of mergers with the common market has typically been limited to considerations directly related to the level of competition on markets. Save for a few notable exceptions the Commission has pursued a Community merger control policy motivated solely by "pure competition policy" objectives.[62] Whereas the political compromise underlying the acceptance of a Community competence for merger control therefore resulted in a transparent and consistent policy in terms of substance, the same cannot be said with

---

[61] See, more extensively, Hirsbrunner, above, n. 60.

[62] See only M. Baron, "Die neuen Bestimmungen der Europäischen Fusionskontrolle" (1997) 47 *WuW* 579–91, at 579, who argues that the generally acknowledged success of Community merger control ensured that minor changes to the original Reg. sufficed in the context of the 1997 revision.

respect to the allocation of jurisdiction to the Community and the Member States respectively.

The general division of jurisdiction based on a narrowly constructed "Community dimension" and, even more clearly, the various exceptions to the allocation of jurisdiction enshrined in the Regulation reflect the painstaking process which enabled adoption of the Community Merger Control Regulation. The system by which jurisdiction is allocated in the Merger Regulation, particularly before the 1997 amendments, was susceptible to extensive criticism.

Two forms of criticism are prominent with respect to the Regulation's reliance on the turnover thresholds for establishing Community jurisdiction. One is that the thresholds are set at too high and, arbitrarily chosen, a level. The other is that turnover thresholds as such constitute an inadequate criterion for asserting Community jurisdiction. To start with the former, it is almost unanimously observed that the 1989 turnover thresholds were set at such an altitude as to encompass only mergers between corporate giants. Both the 5,000 million ECU aggregate worldwide turnover and the 250 million ECU to be accomplished by each are considered to exclude a significant number of smaller concentrations which are nonetheless of relevance to the functioning of the Internal Market. The origin of the inflated turnover thresholds is commonly sought in the delicate political process which led to adoption of the Regulation.[63] The objections concern the level of the separate thresholds as well as the way in which they interrelate. The requirement that the merging companies have to generate, together, at least 5,000 million ECU implies that concentrations between very large undertakings may still fall outside the reach of Community Merger Control law. The original turnover thresholds resulted in non-applicability of the Community merger regulation to a merger in the publishing industry which created the largest company of its kind in the Community.[64] Similarly, the second threshold, 250 million ECU turnover by each of at least two of the undertakings involved within the Community, was considered inappropriate as the Merger Regulation's version of *de minimis*. A number of large-scale merger operations significantly affecting the conditions for competition in the common market can be identified which did not fall within the terms of the Regulation because one of the companies did not reach the necessary level.[65] Finally, even the two-thirds rule, under which national authorities retain competence to deal with mergers with a Community dimension which are considered to have effect mainly on the national market is opposed. While acknowledging that they can have predominant effects on the national market concerned it is unacceptable to critics of the

---

[63] See e.g. Schwartz, above, n. 53, and S. Bulmer, "Institutions and Policy Change: The Case of Merger Control" (1994) 72 *Public Administration* 423–44.

[64] The merger between Reed and Elsevier, which further created the second largest publishing company in the world. See M. Broberg, "The Geographic Allocation of Turnover under the Merger Regulation" (1997) 18 *ECLR* 103–9.

[65] See the cases referred to in R. Kassamali, "From Fiction to Fallacy: Reviewing the E.C. Merger Regulation's Community-Dimension Thresholds in the Light of Economics and Experience in Merger Control" (1996) 21 *ELR/CC* 89–114, at 101–2.

two-thirds rule that these concentrations which are clearly of relevance to the the operation of the common market fall outside the Community's reach and are decided by authorities at the national level.[66]

The second line of criticism pertains to the inadequacy of turnover thresholds as the basis for Community claims to jurisdiction. Since the objective of the Commission's merger control exercise is to examine whether a given concentration is compatible with the common market the jurisdictional thresholds should in the view of critics also be based on the possible effects on the common market. An undertaking's turnover does not provide an adequate indication of the potential significance of the undertaking on the relevant market. Accordingly, mergers have been identified which, although qualifying as concentrations with a Community dimension were incapable of affecting trade between Member States in any significant manner.[67] A market share test has been put forward as an alternative. Such a test would be more appropriate because, contrary to absolute turnover figures, market shares do provide insight into the potential effects of a merger on market power and, thus, on prices.[68]

The amendments to the Regulation's jurisdictional criteria answered the criticism only partly. As demonstrated they establish additional criteria on the basis of which mergers have a Community dimension. In effect the thresholds for Community dimension are reduced, which is in line with the criticims that the thresholds for establishing a Community dimension were originally set at too high a level. However, the additional criteria are based on alternative turnover thresholds and therefore do not remedy the noted problem of turnover thresholds as the basis for establishing jurisdiction in merger cases.

As noted above, in addition to the revised scope for Community jurisdiction which the Merger Regulation introduced, the Regulation's other innovation was the mutual exclusivity of Community and national merger control jurisdiction. In the area of mergers the usual parallel applicability of Community and national competition laws was abandoned. The Commission is exclusively competent to consider concentrations with a Community dimension. Consequently, "procedural" supremacy which governs the relationship between Community and Member State antitrust law in the area of Articles 81 and 82 EC was replaced by a form of "normative supremacy".[69] This has permitted the introduction of single merger control, the "one-stop-shop". The one-stop-shop is commonly celebrated as a welcome innovation creating clarity for business and competition authorities alike.

In order to remedy unwarranted remedy in the allocation of exclusive jurisdiction the Merger Regulation provides for referrals from Community to

---

[66] T. Lampert, *Die Anwendbarkeit der EG-Fusionskontrollverordnung im Verhältnis zum Fusionskontrollrecht der Mitgliedstaaten* (Cologne, Carl Heymanns, 1995), 173–6.

[67] S. O'Keeffe, "Merger Regulation Thresholds: An Analysis of the Community-dimension Thresholds in Regulation 4064/89" (1994) 15 *ECLR* 21–31.

[68] Extensively, Kassamani, above, n. 65, at 99ff.

[69] Walz, above, n. 38.

national jurisdiction and vice versa. The process of mutual referral has not always operated satisfactory.[70] In the early years of the Merger Regulation's operation national authorities, notably that of Germany, have seen the Commission turn down many of their requests to refer mergers which in their opinion significantly impeded effective competition on the German market. The Commission reluctance was probably mainly due to its perception of the thresholds for Community dimension as being so high that if a merger falls within that narrow Community jurisdiction it should be examined by the Commission on the basis of Community law and not by the competent authorities on the basis of national law.[71] Whatever the force of this argument it is evident that some of the national authorities have at times considered the Commission disappointingly reluctant to refer appropriate mergers.[72] However, this has changed since the review of the Merger Regulation by the Council in 1997. In the period in which the review took place the Commission referred various cases where the centre of gravity of a merger's effect lay in one of the Member States. Since then the system of mutual referral seems to have operated smoothly, although clearly referrals remain an exception and as a general rule mergers with a Community dimension are dealt with by the Commission.[73]

To conclude, the restricted scope for Community antitrust law in the Merger Control Regulation and the mutual exclusivity of EC and Member State jurisdictions—in combination with the possibility of referral where appropriate—operates in a satisfactory manner. Contrary to the "mitigated double-barrier" system under Articles 81 and 82 EC the interrelationship is clearly defined. Moreover, the system allows for weighing the respective interests of the Community and Member States with respect to a particular merger. Both the possibility of referring cases to Member States, or conversely to the Community, and the possibility of protecting Member States' legitimate interests unrelated to competition form improvements to the current system of procedural supremacy of EC antitrust law under Articles 81 and 82 EC.

4.3   THE MODERNISATION OF COMMUNITY ANTITRUST LAW JURISDICTION

The Commission's antitrust law modernisation project focuses on decentralised implementation of Community antitrust law. Therefore the debate is largely

---

[70] D. Goyder, "The Role of National Competition Law—Working Paper II" in C.-D. Ehlermann and L. Laudati, *Robert Schuman Centre Annual on European Competition Law 1996* (Dordrecht, Martinus Nijhoff).

[71] Explicitly, Commission of the European Communities, *Twenty-Third Annual Report on Competition Policy* (Brussels, 1993), 7ff.

[72] Moreover, it has been argued that the Commission's discretion in deciding whether or not to refer a case to a national authority ex Art. 9(1) of the Reg. depends on the market in which the effects of a merger take place. Particularly, if the merger's relevant market does not form a substantial part of the common market, the Commission appears constrained to refer the case the relevant national authority: Lampert, above, n. 101, 109–24 at 117–19.

[73] Hirsbrunner, above, n. 60.

confined to the administrative aspects of the Community–Member State relationship. While the co-operation of the Commission and national institutions in the enforcement of Community antitrust law is an important practical issue in the context of decentralisation of EC antitrust law and decentralised application of Community law is itself an important element in the modernisation of Community antitrust law, any modernisation plan should address the consitutionally unclear issue of the interrelationship between Community and Member State antitrust laws.[74] The examination here starts from the observation that two completely divergent sets of jurisdictional rules govern the respective areas of Community antitrust law. Within "traditional" antitrust law, that is Articles 81 and 82 EC, Community and national law apply concurrently to all agreements which may affect trade between Member States. In so far as jurisdiction overlaps, national antitrust law may be applied only if it does not conflict with EC antitrust law, the latter having "procedural supremacy". Conversely, merger control law is based on mutually exclusive applicable antitrust laws. The scope for Community jurisdiction is confined to those mergers which have a "Community dimension". Agreements which have a Community dimension are examined exclusively by the EC Commission. Application of national law to that type of agreements is pre-empted, save for the Commission granting an exception as defined in the EC Merger Regulation where specific national interests arise.

The magnitude of the ensuing divergence is evident in view of the fact that Articles 81 and 82 EC are interpreted in such a manner as to exclude only those cases which are of purely local significance whereas, conversely, more than 80 per cent of cross-border mergers do not fall within the scope of the Community Merger Control Regulation.[75] While the divergence within Community antitrust law raises objections in its own right,[76] the issue which is central to this chapter is whether there are grounds for reviewing the current system of allocation of jurisdiction. As with to the rest of this study, the problem is approached with reference to general developments in Community law and politics.

---

[74] Admittedly, these two issues cannot be studied in isolation from each other. The Commission plans on modernisation set out in the White Paper have important consequences for the interrelationship between EC and Member State antitrust laws. In this book the discussion of the White Paper and its implications for the EC–Member State divide is concentrated below in Ch. 6, which focuses on decentralised enforcement of Community antitrust law.

[75] That is before the 1997 amendment Reg. See Commission of the European Communities, *Twenty-Third Annual Report on Competition Policy*, at 37. It should also be mentioned that the Bundeskartellamt estimates that more than 25% of the merger cases decided by the Commission are not of Community interest. Baron, above, n. 62, at 581–2.

[76] The differences between Art. 81 and the Merger Control Reg., e.g., led to unjustified distinctions between co-operative joint ventures which fell within Art. 81 and concentrative joint ventures which were scrutinised under the Merger Control Reg. The 1997 revision resolved this problem. See G. Zonnekeyn, "The Treatment of Joint Ventures Under the Amended Merger Regulation" (1998) 19 *ECLR* 414–21.

4.3.1. Background

It is argued throughout this book that formal establishment of the Internal Market in 1992 and adoption of the Treaty on European Union marked—and generated—qualitative changes in the nature of European integration in general and in that of European antitrust law in particular. Before returning to the specific relationship between Community and Member State antitrust laws relevant aspects of these developments are first recalled.

Simply put, the TEU increased the "breadth" of Community competences by introducing new fields of Community policies while reducing their "depth" by re-emphasising the limited character of the economic integration sought in the context of the European Union.[77] Within the EC Treaty Article 5 (ex Article 3B) forms the clearest illustration of this process. The Article contains a threefold emphasis on the limited nature of Community powers. First, with respect to the question of what the Community's powers consist it holds that the "Community shall act within the limits of the powers conferred upon it by this Treaty and of the objectives assigned to it therein". This reflects the principle of attributed powers which governs both the existence and the extent of Community powers. The Community does not have autonomous legislative powers itself and its powers are in principle limited to what has been conferred on it.[78] Secondly, the Article defines the Community's version of the principle of subsidiarity: "[i]n areas which do not fall within its exclusive competence, the Community shall take action, in accordance with the principle of subsidiarity, only if and in so far as the objectives of the proposed action cannot be sufficiently achieved by the Member States and can therefore, by reasons of the scale or effects of the proposed action, be better achieved by the Community". It was this version of the TEU's explicit expression of the limited and functional nature of the Community's powers, which acquired highest degree of prominence, both politically and academically. Finally, Article 5 EC formulates the principle of proportionality: "[a]ny action by the Community shall not go beyond what is necessary to achieve the objectives of this Treaty".

The renewed emphasis on the limits of Community competences also arose in the Community's judicial sphere.[79] In recent years the Court of Justice appears to have embarked on a closer inspection of the Community–Member State juris-

---

[77] R. Dehousse, "Community Competences: Are there Limits to Growth?" in R. Dehousse (ed.), *Europe after Maastricht, An Ever Closer Union?* (Munich, Beck, 1994), 103–25 at 106: "one cannot help but conclude that the aim of the Treaty drafters was not only to make Community intervention possible beyond the sphere of economic integration, but also to ensure that such intervention will not exceed certain limits". See also A. Dashwood, "The Limits of European Community Powers" (1996) 21 *ELR* 113–28.

[78] Dashwood, above, n. 77.

[79] Leaving aside the reactions to the TEU at the national level, as, e.g., the Brunner judgment of the *Bundesverfassungsgericht*, which were discussed in Ch. 2.

dictonal divide.[80] In this respect the restrictive reading of the Treaty's provision on free movement of goods, Article 28 (ex Article 30) EC, in *Keck* constitutes the most noted but certainly not the only example of the way in which the Community–Member State jurisdictional divide is interpreted in such a way as to allow for wider national competences.[81] The common thrust of these judgments is that Member States are granted the competence to regulate in so far as that regulation does not pose threats to conditions of equal competition on the internal market. What they have in common is emphasis on market access. Where access is guaranteed, EC law does not conflict with regulation if measures apply equally in law and fact.[82]

Both the introduction of Article 5 EC and the recent case law of the Court of Justice thus reflect concern for the appropriate balance between the requirement of a "level playing field" on the common market on the one hand and the remaining need for social regulation at the Member State level on the other. These developments underscore that the need for compromises between market integration objectives and national autonomy continues or is perhaps reinforced by the formal establishment of the common market.

As has been seen, various traditional constitutional principles, which guide the relationship between the Community and the Member States, are questioned in the new context. An example of this development may be found in one of the pillars on which the Community–Member States relationship is based, and indeed one of the fundamental elements of the Community constitutional order, the supremacy of Community law over national law. As demonstrated earlier in this book (Chapter 2), the Court of Justice grounds the supremacy of Community law over national law in the functional requirements of the Community and, in particular, those of the common market. The original basis for Community law was clearly limited, both normatively and in scope, to the functional requirements of the common market. As a consequence it was clear from the outset that the Community's principle of functionally enumerated powers was essential to retaining Community law's supremacy claim.

---

[80] T. Friedbacher, "Motive Unmasked: The European Court of Justice, Free Movement of Goods, and the Search for Legitimacy" (1996) 2 *ELJ* 226–50 and U. Everling, "Will Europe Slip on Bananas? The Bananas Judgment of the Court of Justice and National Courts" (1996) 33 *CMLRev* 401–37.

[81] Cases C–267 & 268/91 *Keck & Mithouard* [1993] ECR I–6097. See S. Weatherill, "After *Keck*: Some Thoughts on how to Clarify the Clarification" (1996) 33 *CMLRev* 885–906. See also Cases C–2/91 *Meng* [1993] ECR I–5751, C–245/91 *Ohra* [1993] ECR I–5851, and C–185/91 *Reiff* [1993] ECR I–5801 and the discussion in N. Reich, "The 'November Revolution' of the European Court of Justice: *Keck*, *Meng* and *Audi* revisited" (1994) 31 *CMLRev* 459–92.

[82] The emphasis in interpreting the motivation for *Keck* and following cases has turned away from interpreting the notion of "selling arrangements", which takes a prominent place in the *Keck* formula, to alternative interpretations: G. Tesauro, "The Community's Internal Market in the Light of the Recent Case-law of the Court of Justice" (1995) 15 *YEL* 1–16; S. Weatherill, "Recent Case Law Concerning the Free Movement of Goods: Mapping the Frontiers of Market Deregulation" (1999) 36 *CMLRev* 51–85; and J. Weiler, "The Constitution of the Common Market Place: Text and Context in the Evolution of the Free Movement of Goods" in P. Craig and G. de Búrca, *The Evolution of EU Law* (Oxford, Oxford University Press, 1999), 349–76.

However, the Community's development rendered it difficult to perceive the limits of Community action. In the course of the market integration process it became more and more evident that the degree of integration that was required was larger than what was originally realised. There was practically no end to the growth of Community competence on the basis of the requirement of the common market. This process was ultimately recognised at the Community level by the Court of Justice when it replaced in its description of the Community legal order the element "albeit within limited fields" by "ever wider fields".[83]

If the growth of Community competences can be considered to have expanded the breadth of Community law's supremacy over national laws another jurisprudential development may be considered to have "deepened" the scope for supremacy. It gradually became clear that the logic of Community law supremacy, which was based on the need for uniformity and consequently on the necessity to preclude infringements of that uniformity on the basis of national laws, compelled a reading of Community supremacy extending to national constitutional laws.[84] Accordingly, even basic human rights constitutionally granted by the Member States are subordinate to Community law.

These two expansions of EC law's supremacy rendered its limited nature largely theoretical. As a result, the question was raised whether the pursuit of a uniform structure of Community law was so important that even national constitutional choices must be set aside.[85] The immensely increased scope of EC law and policy and its ensuing pre-eminence were further questioned in other ways. While acknowledging the merits of EC law in the Internal Market project and in overcoming "the "state of nature" in international economic relations', its side-effects—leading to restructuring "national societies according to the logic of market integration"—were challenged.[86]

Following the formal achievement of the Internal Market attempts have been made to rationalise the Community's claim to supremacy. Two instruments are dominant in this process. One harks back to the original basis for Community law's supremacy as defined in *Costa* v. *ENEL*. In this approach the limited scope for Community law and, thus, for its pre-eminence over national laws is underscored. Elements of such a solution to the supremacy problem can be retraced in the Court of Justice case law following 1992, most prominently in *Keck*. The alternative stance derives from a reconsideration of the degree of uniformity that is required for the proper functioning of the common market. Since the present normative underpinning of EC law supremacy is based on the needs of the

---

[83] *Opinion 1/91 (European Economic Area)* [1991] ECR I–6084.

[84] Case 11/70 *Internationale Handelsgesellschaft* v. *Einfuhr- und Vorratstelle für Getreide und Futtermittel* [1970] ECR 1125.

[85] S. Weatherill, *Law and Integration in the European Union* (Oxford, OUP, 1995), 105. See also J. Weiler, "The Community System: The Dual Character of Supranationalism" (1981) 1 *YEL* 257–306, at 303.

[86] C. Joerges, "European Economic Law, the Nation-State and the Maastricht Treaty" in R. Dehousse (ed.), *Europe After Maastricht—An Ever Closer Union?* On the value of the supremacy doctrine—particularly in light of the enhanced scope for majority voting in Council.

common market the question may become whether total uniformity is required for its successful operation or whether a more limited interpretation of supremacy may suffice. In essence, what is required for the operation of the common market is compatibility of the national legal order with that of the Community. Supremacy of EC law over national law does not have to go beyond ensuring the compatibility of the various legal orders.[87]

Although the concepts are related and arguably lead to the same result, confining the impact of EC law's supremacy on the autonomy of national legal order, there is a difference. The first reduces the scope for Community law and thus the area within which conflicts can arise. The second reviews the nature of the conflicts and in that light suggests new solutions. The latter variant which for instance questions the degree of uniformity required on the common market has taken up a central position in the analyses of the Community legal order after the TEU. The TEU and subsequent events signal that, at least in principle, uniformity as the basic characteristic of EC law has been departed from.[88] Since it is clear that the Community does not aspire to total political harmonisation, structures will have to be found which provide the (economic) uniformity required by the common market while maintaining space for political diversity at the national level.[89] Traditional Community constitutional arrangements like pre-emption, exclusive powers, harmonisation and supremacy are ill-adapted to providing the required margins for diversity.[90] Therefore alternative concepts are sought which aim to ensure that regulatory requirements of the central—the Community—as well as the decentral level—the Member States—may be taken into account in parallel.[91] In the environment which the TEU created the requirements of the Community's internal market, typically uniformity and regulation at the supranational level, need to be reconciled with national policy concerns which might value diversity and a degree of policy autonomy. Ideally, the relationship between the Community and its Member States is characterised by a mutual search for compatible law and policy decisions.[92]

---

[87] Joerges, above, n. 86.

[88] In this sense see T. Koopmans, "Het post-Maastrichtse Europa" (1996) 71 *NJB* 305–15.

[89] See J. Weiler, "The Transformation of Europe" (1991) 100 *The Yale Law Journal* 2403–83, at 2416ff. and S. Weatherill, "Beyond Preemption? Shared Competence and Constitutional Change in the European Community" in D. O"Keeffe and P. Twomey (eds.), *Legal Issues of the Maastricht Treaty* (London, Wiley Chancery Law, 1994), 13–33. Reich underscores that, the wider the Community's competence the less exclusive its jurisdiction: N. Reich, "Competition Between Legal Orders: A New Paradigm of EC Law?" (1992) 29 *CMLRev* 861–96.

[90] Weatherill, above, n. 89; Community action no longer clearly pre-empts national competence. Nor can it in an increasingly heterogenous Community. Pre-emption renders it hard for Member States to apply their own sometimes better norms to fields where the Community has acted. While preemption and supremacy form part of the acquis communautaire, the "impression of their systematic conceptual stringency is deceptive". See also C. Joerges, "Rationalization Processes in Contract Law and the Law of Product Safety: Observations on the Impact of European Integration on Private Law". EUI Working Paper Law No. 94/5 (Florence, EUI, 1994) at 24.

[91] For example, J. Shaw, "European Legal Studies in Crisis? Towards a New Dynamic" (1996) 16 *Oxford Journal for Legal Studies* 231–53 and C. Joerges, above, n. 86.

[92] Joerges, above, n. 86 and Weatherill, above, n. 89.

In the search for more refined constitutional principles which might permit recognition and accomodation of diversity within the common market without irretrievably compromising and fragmenting the integrity of the legal order, attention has turned to mechanisms which place the different national legal systems within an overall Community framework.[93] Consequently, solutions are increasingly found in sharing considerations and policy-making power. If increased application of national law could be accomodated within the Community law framework, the Treaty's "fidelity clause", formulated in Article 10 EC (ex Article 5) may play an even more important role in the future than it does already. It might then perform a function in bridging the gap between EC and Member State policies by stressing the Community context in which national policy operates.[94]

In short, the questions of the relationship between Community antitrust law and national law and of the appropriate scope of EC antitrust law are inherently linked. The concept of supremacy, for example, cannot be expressed as an absolute rule whereby the Community or federal law trumps Member State law, but instead it should be considered as a principle whereby each law is supreme within *its sphere of competence*. This renders crucial the question of defining the spheres of competence and in particular the concomitant institutional question of which court will have the final decision on the definitions of spheres.[95]

The observation that limited powers are important for retaining Community antitrust law's supremacy claim reveals the main objection to the present arrangement under Articles 81 and 82 EC, where there is no perceptible limit to its application. The current situation is untenable because Community antitrust law remains largely unenforced for lack of Community interest. As has been demonstrated, the effect is that there are difficulties in applying national antitrust law because of the potential supremacy of application of EC antitrust law. At the same time, however, Community antitrust law is not applied because only the Commission is competent to apply Article 81 EC as a whole but is not capable of answering the need for formal decisions generated by the large scope for Article 81(1) EC. Therefore neither Community nor national antitrust law can be applied properly.

Conversely, the jurisdictional divide within the more recently adopted Merger Regulation which provides for a reduced scope for Community law answers a number of the objections to the pre-emptive effect which application of the Merger Regulation has on national antitrust laws.

---

[93] Weatherill, above, n. 89, at 32.

[94] *Ibid*. Art. 10 EC also directs Member State authorities to co-operate with each other: see Case 272/80 *Biologische Produkten* [1981] ECR 3277. Art. 10 therefore blurs the rigid competence division between the Community and Member States.

[95] See Weiler, above, n. 89, at 2414. The Italian resistence to EC law supremacy, for instance, was given up under explicit reference to the partial character of the transfer of powers "on the basis of a precise criterion of division of jurisdiction": *Frontini* [1974] 2 CMLR 372 at 385. The rationale is echoed in the jurisprudence and constitutional amendments of most other Member States: Weiler, above, n. 85, 303–4.

Next to the effects of general developments in Community law the relationship between Community and Member State antitrust laws is affected by the evolving objectives of Community antitrust law. EC antitrust policy is now mainly pursued with a view to ensuring that competition on the common market remains in a healthy state—even though it is recognised that it continues to be a natural objective of Community antitrust policy to ensure that cross-border trade *remains* undistorted.[96] Thus, the objectives of Community antitrust law are now very similar to the typical concerns of national antitrust policies. The sharp distinction which was originally drawn between the objectives of Community antitrust law, prohibiting impediments to cross-border trade, and those of the Member States, "objectives peculiar to it", is no longer warranted. First, the primary Community antitrust law objectives are similar to those of most national systems: allocative efficiency and protecting competition. Secondly, the majority of Member State antitrust laws are now based on the EC rules. They typically aim to ensure consistency with EC antitrust law practice. Therefore the division of jurisdiction in antitrust law cannot continue to be based on the distinction between the objectives of Community and national antitrust laws.[97]

Recognition that to a large extent the same objectives are pursued on the basis of Community and Member State antitrust laws questions the pertinence of the current relationship between Community and national antitrust laws. The modernisation of Community antitrust law should therefore reconsider both the scope for Community antitrust law and the interrelationship with national antitrust laws while recognising that the objectives pursued by the national and the Community antitrust laws are largely the same.

4.3.2 The Scope for EC Antitrust Law

It was demonstrated above that the broad interpretation of the "effect on trade between Member States" criterion rendered that criterion "functionless" as a demarcation of the limits of Community antitrust law jurisdiction.[98] In part the Court's expansive interpretation of the scope for Community antitrust law

---

[96] This is clearly acknowledged by the Commission which considers that the "aim of competition policy, through its impact on the basic structures of the European economy, is to ensure that markets acquire or maintain the flexibility they need to allow scope for initiative and innovation and to allow an *effective and dynamic allocation of society's resources*. . . . In the final analysis, like all other Community policies, competition policy aims to enhance the economic prosperity of the European Union and the well-being of all its people": Commission of the European Communities, *Twenty-Fifth Annual Report on Competition Policy*, 17.

[97] See the "*Spanish Banks*" case above, n. 17, which repeats the formula of the judgment in *Walt Wilhelm*, above, n. 16, dating back to 1968.

[98] C. Joerges, "The Market Without the State? States Without a Market?", *EUI Working Paper Law No. 96/2* (Florence, EUI, 1996), 13. Similarly, N. Reich, "Die Bedeutung der Binnenmarktkonzeption für die Anwendung der EWG-Wettbewerbsregeln" in J. Baur *et al.* (eds.), *Festschrift für Ernst Steindorff* (Berlin, De Gruyter, 1990), 1065–84, and Klaue, above, n. 30.

results from logical processes induced by the gradual integration of the European markets. Altered economic realities within the common market contributed to the increasing number of intra-Community transactions and thus the notion of effect on trade between Member States is more easily fulfilled.[99] In addition, the nature and intensity of cross-border trade generally changed under influence of reductions in barriers to trade on a global level resulting from worldwide liberalisations in combination with the emergence of new technologies. Growth of Community jurisdiction can be considered a natural consequence of the intensified cross-border trade. A higher number of cases with relevance for the Community is, to an extent, an automatic result of the common market project itself. However, independently of the changing economic environment the reach of Community antitrust law has been expanded consistently by the Court's—and Commission's—interpretation of the inter-state trade criterion in the light of the requirements of market integration. Conversely, it must also be acknowledged that the jurisdictional scope for EC antitrust law was reduced at some instances. The Court's judgment that the effect on trade between Member States must be appreciable is one. The Commission's "*de minimis*" notice is another.[100]

How may the constitutional developments surrounding the formal establishment of the internal market and the adoption of the TEU, described above, affect the current scope of EC antitrust law? Here the discussion is limited to the significance of the Treaty amendments and the "November revolution" in this respect.

First, of the three principles formulated in Article 5 EC only that which refers to the principle of enumerated powers forms a potential challenge to the existing jurisdictional divide in antitrust law. The other two principles of Article 5 EC, those of subsidiarity and proportionality, do not relate to the allocation of competences but rather to the exercise of those competences at the Community level.[101] With respect to the principle of attributed powers it is evident that it is incorporated in both areas of antitrust law. Articles 81 and 82 EC provide Community jurisdiction with respect to antitrust law infringements which

---

[99] Thus DG Competition's Director General; A. Schaub, "Binnenmarkt, Währungsunion, Erweiterung—Fragen an die Europäische Wettbewerbspolitik", *XVII Internationales Forum EG-Kartellrecht* organised by the Studienvereinigung Kartellrecht (Brussels, May 1997). Cf. the early recognition of this process in J. Faull, "Effect on Trade Between Member States and Community–Member State Jurisdiction" in B. Hawk (ed.), *Annual Proceedings of the Fordham Corporate Law Institute 1989* (New York, Transnational Juris, 1990), 485–508.

[100] See the revised Commission Notice on agreements of minor importance which do not fall within the meaning of Article 85(1) of the EC Treaty [1997] OJ C372/13.

[101] See the Treaty of Amsterdam Protocol on the application of the principles of subsidiarity and proportionality, Art. 2: "[t]he application of the principles of subsidiarity and proportionality shall respect the general provisions and the objectives of the Treaty, particularly as regards the maintaining in full of the *acquis communautaire* and the institutional balance; it shall not affect the principles developed by the Court of Justice regarding the relationship between national and Community law". Cf. N. Bernard, "The Future of European Economic Law in the Light of the Principle of Subsidiarity" (1996) 33 *CMLRev* 633–66. In so far as they are relevant to the present study they are therefore further discussed in Ch. 5.

affect trade between Member States. The Community's jurisdiction in the area of merger control is provided by the Merger Control Regulation for mergers with a Community dimension. Article 5 EC cannot be considered to have direct consequences for the current division of antitrust law jurisdiction between the Community and the Member States.

Secondly, the question should be addressed whether the division of jurisdiction has been altered on the basis of Court of Justice case law reflecting the *Keck* concerns. Shifts in the jurisprudence underlying the application of Article 28 EC (ex Article 30) are likely to have effect in the antitrust law area in view of the very close connection between the rules on free movement and those on competition.[102] Moreover, one of the underlying motivations of the *Keck* ruling was the perception that economic agents abused the Community free movement rules for challenging all restrictions on economic freedom in force in the Member States. From a practical viewpoint this practice led to a flood of preliminary references to the Court of Justice. The second problem it created, which was more a problem of principle, was the deregulatory effect of the broad interpretation of the prohibition to restrict trade on regulatory systems in force in the Member States. In *Keck* the Court underscored that the use of Article 28 EC should not be considered a general measure of deregulation.

Arguably, Community antitrust law faces similar questions. The original extensive interpretation of the prohibition formulated in Article 81(1) EC led to a gestation problem at the Commission and Court of Justice offices. Parties increasingly relied on Article 81 EC for annulling agreements which were lawfully concluded under national contract law. The wide scope of Community antitrust law's supremacy over national laws is potentially capable of casting aside national private law systems on the basis of the supremacy of EC antitrust law over national law. As explained above, the procedural supremacy of Community antitrust law is based on the need to ensure uniform application of Community law and on the need to avoid the binding force of measures implementing Community antitrust law differing from one Member State to another.[103] This ruling seems to imply that agreements which benefit from an exemption to the antitrust rules may not be prohibited on the basis of national law, be it national antitrust law or other forms of national (private) law. Otherwise the binding force of the exemption granted to the agreement would differ from one state to another.[104]

However, the court limited the deregulatory effect of EC antitrust law's supremacy over national law—so-called "diagonal conflicts" between EC and national law (see below)—when it ruled that agreements which benefit from EC antitrust law exemptions can still be unenforceable on the basis of national

---

[102] P. Kapteyn and P. VerLoren van Themaat, Introduction to the Law of the European Communities (ed. L. W. Gormley, Deventer, Kluwer, 1998), 836 ff.

[103] *Walt Wilhelm*, above, n. 16.

[104] In this sense see J. Schwarze, "Vorrang des Gemeinschaftsrechts und deutsches Kartell- und Wettbewerbsrecht" (1996) 51 *JZ* 57–64.

contract law. The Court underscored that Community antitrust law exemptions do not lay down mandatory provisions directly affecting the validity or content of contractual provisions nor do they oblige the contracting parties to adapt the content of their agreement to block-exemption regulations.[105]

Moreover, the Court reduced the scope for supremacy of EC antitrust law over national antitrust law by interpreting Article 81(1) EC on the basis of an economic rule of reason in *Delimitis*. As a consequence a large number of agreement fall outside Article 81(1) and therefore national antitrust law can be applied to them. In this sense the Court's judgment in *Delimitis* can be considered to be to Community antitrust law what *Keck* is to the Community rules on free movement. Though less dramatic as a jurisprudential turn-around than *Keck*, *Delimitis* did substantially reduce the scope of the prohibition defined in Article 81(1) of the Treaty. In view of the fact that national antitrust law may be applied to agreements which fall outside Article 81(1) EC, the effect of the judgment is to transfer jurisdiction to national antitrust laws.

Yet neither the limitation of EC antitrust law's supremacy over national private law nor the stricter interpretation of what constitutes a restriction of competition in the sense of Article 81(1) EC addresses the question how the inter-state trade effect criterion can be adapted to broader general developments in Community law. It is suggested here that the notion of "Community interest" forms a useful conceptual basis for establishing Community jurisdiction in the context of the formally established Internal Market.[106] The concept is clearly linked to that of Community dimension which forms the basis for Community jurisdiction under the Merger Regulation. Likewise Community interest is central in the attempts to enhance decentralised enforcement of Community antitrust law before national courts. Community interest is also the yardstick which is employed in the discussion on enhanced co-operation between the Commission and national antitrust authorities in the enforcement of Community antitrust law. Moreover, the Community interest can be related to the subsidiarity principle. Where there is no Community interest in certain antitrust behaviour it should be left to the national law system to regulate that conduct.[107]

It is therefore submitted that the criterion of effect on trade between Member States in Articles 81 and 82 EC could be replaced by a criterion which establishes Community jurisdiction on the basis of the interest which the Community takes in the potential infringement of antitrust law. Support for such a shift can be based on the observation that many antitrust law cases currently fall within the scope of Articles 81 and 82 EC even though they are not of Community interest. Within certain limits the Commission may refuse to deal with complaints con-

---

[105] Case C–41/96 *VAG-Händlerbeirat* v. *SYD-Consult* [1997] ECR I–3123 at para. 16.

[106] B. Rodger and S. Wylie, "Taking the Community Interest Line: Decentralisation and Subsidiarity in Competition Law Enforcement" (1997) 18 *ECLR* 485–91.

[107] See, more extensively, R. Wesseling, "Subsidiarity in E.C. Antitrust Law: Setting the Right Agenda" (1997) 22 *ELR* 35–54.

cerning such cases.[108] Decentralisation on this basis is however not feasible within the current legal context in which the Commission has the monopoly in applying the crucial exemption provision. The suggestion to decentralise the application of Article 81(3) EC which is central to the Commission's modernisation plans as set out in the White Paper raises objections of a different nature.[109] Chapter 6 will address these issues at greater length. Suffice it to note here that retaining the broad jurisdictional and solving the practical problems on the basis of enhanced decentralisation does not form an answer to the constitutional objections to the current division of jurisdiction between the Community and Member States.

Advocate General Trabucchi, in his opinion in the Belgian Wallpaper case argued that a unified multinational market, within which there are no longer any national frontiers impeding the movement of goods, required that the criterion "affecting trade between Member States":

> must assume a significance to match the new situation which has come into being; . . . The concept of the effect on the patterns of trade outside the country would, accordingly, be replaced by one based not merely on the local importance of the restriction of competition but on its importance for the Community, . . . The situation should, therefore, be clarified by a criterion to the effect that the Community interest which the prohibition of restrictive agreements is designed to further is not simply one of preventing the partitioning of the territory of the Community into separate national markets but *now*, *principally*, of keeping competition in a healthy state in terms of the common market.
>
> This purpose implies that the prohibition is concerned with agreements which may result in a restriction of competition *such as to be significant at Community level*, this being understood as referring not to state frontiers or geographic areas but to the effect of the agreement on the products to which it relates, viewed not from the purely national standpoints but from a wider standpoint which takes the unity of the Community economy into account.[110]

His conclusion (of 1975!) concurs with the main thesis of this chapter; the principal objectives of Community antitrust law have changed, the focus on trade between Member States in the competition analysis has been departed from and nearly all Member States have adopted antitrust laws—based on that of the Community—of their own. Effect on trade between Member States should no longer be the central criterion for Community jurisdiction but the interest which the Community takes in the competition process is what matters.

It is debatable how the criterion of "Community interest" should be defined. Two concepts could serve as the basis of a revised interpretation of the effect on inter-state trade criterion. The first is a qualitative one, along the lines suggested by Trabucchi AG in in *Papiers Peints*. The contents of the concept of

---

[108] Case T–24/90 *Automec* v. *Commission* ("*Automec II*") [1992] ECR II–2223 and Case C–119/97P *UFEX* [1999] ECR I–1341.

[109] See above Ch. 1 and below Ch. 6.

[110] Conclusion of the AG in *Papier Peints*, above, n. 22, at 1522–4, emphases added.

"Community interest" could then reflect the Commission's notion of Community interest, which it applies when deciding whether it should handle antitrust law complaints. In this respect it may be noted that the case law of the Court of Justice on the rejection of complaints for lack of "Community interest" already sets out some of the limits for the interpretation of this criterion.[111] "Community interest" has hitherto largely been defined on the basis of the economic, legal and political relevance of the cases. In addition, in the process of decentralisation it has emerged that the existence of "Community interest" depends on the overall effect of the agreement or practice concerned on competition, the nature of the infringement and the effectiveness of the protection that can be provided by non-EC institutions. The Court has also ruled that the Community may not on the basis of the notion of Community interest exclude in principle from its purview certain situations which come under the task entrusted to it by the Treaty.[112] Within these margins the effect on trade between Member States criterion could be replaced by that of Community interest.

The alternative would be to apply quantitative thresholds for the applicability of EC antitrust law, after the example of the Merger Regulation. Under the Merger Regulation a Community dimension exists "where the proposed operation is of a certain economic size".[113] Experience with the application of the Merger Regulation demonstrates that the major advantages of using turnover thresholds are their clarity and the possibility of effectively establishing mutual exclusivity in the division of jurisdiction between the Community and Member States. Mutually exclusive jurisdictions, as embodied in the Merger Regulation, generated the "one-stop-shop" procedure, popular with business and desirable for reasons of administrative efficiency. The rigidity in the division of jurisdiction between the Community and Member States, implicit in the application of quantitative criteria, is alleviated under the Merger Regulation by provisions on mutual reference between national and EC jurisdictions. The drawbacks to basing the Community solely on a transaction's economic size expressed in turnover figures is that mergers in markets which are characterised by relatively low rates of turnover are less likely to fulfil the quantitative criteria of Community dimension, while they may very well be of genuine Community interest.[114] Moreover, and probably more importantly, there are objections to basing jurisdiction on turnover thresholds in the context of Articles 81 and 82 EC which are primarily concerned with business behaviour over a longer period of time. During such a period the turnover figures are likely to vary, which could create jurisdictional problems. In contrast, control of mergers is based on assessment of structure at one single moment, that of realisation of the concentration, which renders it easier to apply turnover thresholds.

---

[111] See *UFEX*, above, n. 108.

[112] *Ibid*. See on this issue the White Paper on Modernisation at para. 119.

[113] Case T–9/93 *Air France* v. *Commission* [1994] ECR II–121 at para. 102.

[114] E.g. because of the high market shares which the companies involved have. See, extensively, Broberg, above, n. 64.

Finally, the question may be posed *how* the jurisdictional criterion for Community antitrust law can be revised. There are two alternatives. First, in accordance with Article 83(2)(e) EC the Council could adopt, on the basis of a proposal from the Commission, a regulation or directive which determines the relationship between Community and national antitrust law. A regulation could delineate the scope of EC antitrust law in such a way as to reserve for EC jurisdiction only those cases which are of relevance to the single market. In the remaining area national antitrust laws would apply.

Absent Community legislation a different way of revising the inter-state-trade effect criterion is perceivable. A revised interpretation of the jurisdictional criterion may be established in the practical application of the antitrust rules. For the inter-state-trade effect notion in EC antitrust law is a flexible instrument of legal policy. Accordingly, it can evolve as an expression of the Community interest as that interest moves from market-building to regulating and ordering a market economy.[115] The Commission is free within the jurisprudential margins set out by the case law of the Court of Justice to interpret the jurisdictional scope of EC antitrust law. Moreover, the unorthodox jurisdictional criteria in the Merger Regulation reveal that the division of jurisdiction within the European Community is not *per se* to be interpreted in the way in which it has been interpreted hitherto. Thus, it is possible for the Court of Justice to rule that the "effect on trade between Member States" has become obsolete as a criterion for establishing Community jurisdiction and that the scope of EC antitrust law should now be defined on the basis of Community interest. As reform on the basis of legislation, the new jurisdictional standard could be based on quantitative or qualitative criteria. The fact that concurrent jurisdiction of national antitrust laws would persist is a relative disadvantage of the jurisprudential option.

4.3.3. The Relationship between Community Antitrust Law and National Law

While the revised scope for Community antitrust law on the basis of a turn to "Community interest" as the jurisdictional criterion would automatically reduce the area in which conflicts may arise between national and Community antitrust law, it would not avoid the problem altogether. Community antitrust law and national antitrust law would still apply in parallel, at least in so far as the antitrust laws of the Member States do not limit jurisdiction to cases without Community interest.[116]

How could conflicts between Community and Member State antitrust laws be solved? As "Community interest" has been adopted as the jurisdictional

---

[115] Faull, above, n. 99.
[116] Above, n.15.

criterion, so the revised interrelationship could be based on formal legislation—a regulation on the basis of Article 83 EC—or in the absence of legislation the interrelationship could be based on a clear restriction of EC law's procedural supremacy to those cases where there are genuine conflicts between EC and Member State antitrust laws.

The simplest solution would be to have the Council determine the interrelationship between Community and national antitrust laws on the basis of a regulation. Like the Merger Regulation the interrelationship could be based on mutual exclusivity of jurisdiction, enabling the one-stop-shop mechanism.[117] Where there is Community interest, only Community antitrust law applies. If there is no Community interest, Member State laws may apply.

Like the Merger Regulation the regulation determining the mutual exclusivity of EC and Member State laws in the area of Articles 81 and 82 EC could combine the system of mutually exclusive jurisdictions with the possibility of referrals, either because the centre of gravity of an infringement is located in a particular Member State or because a Member State desires to protect its legitimate national interests (which could be defined in the Regulation). As demonstrated above, referral to a Member State does not imply that such a case with a Community dimension would take on a purely national character. The Community level remains in charge and only those aspects of the agreements which affect competition in the Member State concerned are dealt with under national law by a national authority. In applying its national law the national authority may take only those measures which are strictly necessary to safeguard the interests which it intends to protect. National law must moreover be applied in a manner which is compatible with the general principles and other provisions of Community law. Such a system could stimulate Member States to accept Community jurisdiction in cases which are of Community interest. If the Member States notice that their interests are considered at the Community level they will sooner be inclined to accept the superior problem-solving capacity of the Community level in cases which have a genuine Community dimension. Moreover, combined assessment of the interests of the supranational and the national level in one instance will advance one-stop-shopping, which operates satisfactorily in the area of merger control.

A consequence of the proposal to restrict jurisdiction for Community antitrust law to agreements or behaviour with a Community dimension would be the expansion of jurisdiction for Member States' antitrust laws. Two potential problems may arise. The first concerns the danger for additional compliance costs where several states claim jurisdiction. Undertakings would have to adapt their agreements and behaviour to the laws of all Member States which establish jurisdiction. Although this is certainly a potential problem its relevance

---

[117] See the arguments in favour of exclusive jurisdiction for the Community (within the current context of jurisdiction on the basis of the effect on inter-state trade criterion) in Tesauro AG's Opinion in *Bundeskartellamt* v. *VAG and Volkswagen*, above, n. 11.

should not be overestimated. First the criterion of "Community interest"—similar to the notion of Community dimension under the Merger Regulation—would normally be fulfilled where more than two Member States claim jurisdiction. Moreover it should be acknowledged that undertakings face the same problem in the current system. Undertakings already have to comply with Community antitrust law and the antitrust laws of several Member State because of the incomplete system of Community antitrust law supremacy over national antitrust laws.

The second potential objection to a greater role for Community antitrust law stems from the fear of diversity among Member States antitrust laws—which is considered incompatible with the concept of an internal market. Yet, there are three reasons why the fear of diversity is not warranted. First, the cases which after the suggested revision will be decided on the basis of national law will by definition have no profound impact on the functioning of the internal market. If they are of Community interest they will fall within Community jurisdiction. Secondly, the degree of diversity between Member State antitrust law is small and decreasing. The majority of the Member State antitrust law systems is based on the Community system. Even Member States which have antitrust laws on a different basis have recently approximated their laws to that of the Community.[118] This process of spontaneous harmonisation reduces significantly the potential for diversity in the application of national antitrust laws. The most recently adopted national antitrust laws go even further and compel the judiciary to interpret the national antitrust laws, based on the European model, in accordance with the decisions of the Commission and the case law of the Court of Justice.[119] Thirdly, the margins within which diversity will operate are further limited in view of the duties of sincere co-operation. Article 10 EC most explicitly bridges the gap between Member States and the Community by stressing the Community context in which national law occurs.[120] The remaining degree of diversity appears compatible with the concept of the internal market and the principles formulated in the TEU. The EC Treaty recognises explicitly the limits of European integration. A small degree of diversity in national market regimes would be contrary to the principles of the EC only if total uniformity and harmonisation were the goal of European integration. However, the thrust of Articles 2 and 3 of the EC Treaty is different.[121] There is no need for complete uniformity in national antitrust legislation.[122] Moreover,

---

[118] Notably, the UK and Germany.

[119] For instance the Dutch, Italian and UK antitrust laws.

[120] Weatherill, above, n. 89. Cf. the ECJ case law: Cases C–14/83 *Von Colson* [1984] ECR 189; C–106/89 *Marleasing* [1990] ECR I–4135; and Case C–2/88 Imm. *J.J. Zwartveld and Others* [1990] ECR I–3365.

[121] Weatherill, above, n. 85, at 152. See also H. Ullrich, "Harmonisation within the European Union" (1996) 17 *ECLR* 178–84.

[122] M. Dreher, "Gemeinsamer Europäischer Markt—einheitliche Wettbewerbsordnung?" in *Umbruch der Wettbewerbsordnung in Europa—Referate des XXVIII. FIW-Symposions*, 1–22. See also Ullrich, above, n. 121.

it would go against the belief in competition as an investigative process to exclude divergent insights into the operation of antitrust policy, specifically in so far as the cases concerned are not of Community interest. A "race to the bottom" is unlikely to occur with respect to the enforcement of national competition law regimes.[123]

In the absence of the proposed regulation defining the interrelationship between Community and Member State antitrust laws, the interrelationship would need to be refined within the current system of procedural supremacy. In view of the constitutional developments discussed above, the search should be for enhanced compatibility of the Community and national legal norms. In other words the principle governing the relationship between Community antitrust law and national law should aim to balance the interest which the Community has in enforcing the antitrust rules with the interest which one or more Member States may have in upholding their specific norm in a given case.[124]

Arguably, the root of such a concept of supremacy is already present in the Court of Justice's case law in the area of antitrust law, more specifically in the case law on "diagonal conflicts" between EC and national law. Contrary to "vertical conflicts"—that is conflicts between EC antitrust law and national antitrust law—"diagonal conflicts" is a term used to indicate conflicts between, for instance, Community antitrust law and national laws of a different nature, e.g. general contract law.[125] Interestingly, the Court of Justice does not resolve diagonal conflicts on the basis of the procedural supremacy rule laid down in *Walt Wilhelm*. The Court acknowledges that the supremacy of EC antitrust law does not go so far as to deregulate the national private law systems in the case of concurrent applicability of diverging EC antitrust law and national private law norms. When the Court was asked whether agreements benefiting from a Community antitrust law exemption can still be held contrary to national private law it ruled that this was indeed the case. The Court underscored that Community antitrust law exemptions do not lay down mandatory provisions directly affecting the validity or content of contractual provisions nor do they oblige the contracting parties to adapt the content of their agreement to block-exemption regulations.[126]

While this ruling primarily limits the deregulatory effect of Community antitrust law on national private law, it also reopens the question of Community

---

[123] R. van den Bergh, "Economic Criteria for Applying the Subsidiarity Principle in the European Community: The Case of Competition Policy" (1996) *International Review of Law and Economics* 363.

[124] Weatherill, above, n. 89, and Joerges, above, n. 98.

[125] Joerges, above, n. 98. See also C. Schmid, "Vertical and Diagonal Conflicts in the Europeanisation Process—Preliminary Thoughts on a Methodological Reconstruction of the Interface between European and National Law on a Conflict of Laws Basis" in C. Joerges and O. Gerstenberg, *Private Governance, Democratic Constitutionalism and Supranationalism* (Luxembourg, Office for Official Publications of EC, 1998), 185–90.

[126] *VAG-Händlerbeirat* v. *SYD-Consult*, above, n. 105, at ara. 16.

law's procedural supremacy over national antitrust law. For the judgment implies that agreements benefiting from Community antitrust law exemptions can still be invalid on the basis of national private law. The private law systems of the Member States have not been harmonised, at least not completely. The enforceability of agreements, including those which benefit from positive measures taken by the Commission, therefore depends on the diverging legal systems of the Member States. The uniformity on which EC law's supremacy is based is therefore largely a fiction. Moreover, the nature of EC law's procedural supremacy over national law is challenged by the following considerations.

If it is accepted that agreements which are exempted on the basis of Community antitrust law *may* be prohibited on the basis of national private law but that they *may not* be prohibited on the basis of national competition law, the question becomes what is competition law and what is not? This question can be answered only by an examination of the norms protected and objectives pursued by EC antitrust law and national law provisions respectively. The *VAG-Händlerbeirat* case reveals how delicate this exercise can be. At issue was the parallel application of the German *Gesetz gegen den unlauteren Wettbewerb* (the Unfair Competition Act) and Community antitrust law. It is important to note that the German Act against Unfair Competition is not the main "anti-cartel" act. That is the Competition Act (the *Gesetz gegen Wettbewerbsbeschränkungen*). When the question arose whether agreements which benefit from an EC exemption can nevertheless be invalid—or rather unenforceable *vis-à-vis* third parties—on the basis of the German Unfair Competition Act, the Court ruled that this is indeed possible. Apparently the ECJ did not consider the norm enshrined in the Unfair Competition Act to be a norm of national competition law. For if that had been the case the outcome would have been different. As illustrated above, agreements which restrict competition and therefore fall within Article 81(1) EC but which are exempted on the basis of Community antitrust law may not be prohibited on the basis of stricter national *antitrust* law.[127] If the exempted agreements were not enforceable on the basis of national law because the provisions were incompatible with the German Competition Act, then the German Act could not be applied in view of the distortion of the uniform effect of the exemption provided on the basis of EC law.

What the judgment demonstrates is that the respective interests which the Community antitrust law norm and the national law norm aim to protect must be interpreted in order to determine whether a conflict occurs at all. Only "vertical" conflicts, where the norms which are protected have the same policy background ("functional equivalents"),[128] are considered to constitute conflicts in which Community procedural supremacy takes effect. Where the conflict is between EC antitrust law and national private law the Court does not consider

---

[127] At least that is the dominant vision, see discussion above.
[128] See Schmid, above, n. 125, referring to K. Zweigert and H. Kötz, *An Introduction to Comparative Law* (Oxford, Clarendon Press, 1998).

the applicable norms to collide. Therefore the principle of supremacy can be applied only after an examination of whether the conflict between EC and national law is based on diverging principles with respect to the same subject matter. This test reveals that the current case law of the Court of Justice on the operation of the principle of procedural supremacy—in case of "diagonal conflicts"—endorses the reading of procedural supremacy put forward by those commentators who argue that the respective interests which Community and national antitrust laws aim to protect must be identified and then weighed off against each other.[129]

This could form the basis of an interpretation of procedural supremacy, not as a principle which in practice pre-empts the application of diverging national antitrust law but as a principle which aims to ensure that the interests which the Community and the Member States have in protecting the principles which are enshrined in their antitrust laws are optimally preserved. Thus Community and national antitrust laws could truly be applied concurrently. For example, agreements falling within the terms of a block-exemption regulation which are of little significance to the Community might, notwithstanding the absence of objections to its validity under Community antitrust law, be required to comply with the stricter antitrust laws of a Member State if there is clearly a significant interest in that Member State, for instance because the centre of gravity of the operation of the agreement lies in that Member State.[130] Arguably such an interpretation of procedural supremacy in case of concurrent applicability of divergent laws fits well into the current and future constitutional framework of the Community.[131]

CONCLUSION

While the current interpretation of the trade between Member States criterion is still based on the requirements of the intial period of Community antitrust law, the Commission's most comprehensive programme of modernising the application of Articles 81 and 82 EC does not address the issue.[132] The most notable practical consequence of the broad interpretation of the jurisdictional criterion is the overburden which it generates on the Community institutions. The Commission's modernisation programme attempts to reduce that problem administratively by supporting decentralised enforcement of *Community* antitrust law with respect to cases which are not of Community interest. It should be acknowledged that there are indeed clear practical advantages to enforcement of one body of antitrust law throughout the Community

---

[129] See above discussion, notably Stockmann n. 41.

[130] *Ibid.*

[131] See Joerges, above, n. 98; Weatherill, above, n. 89; and Schmid, above, n. 125 and the general discussion in Ch. 2.

[132] See further on the implicatons of the White Paper for the relationship between EC and Member State antitrust laws, below, Ch. 6, para. 6.4.2.

for infringement of whatever magnitude. In particular it would facilitate companies' compliance programmes and it may, if major improvements to co-operation between the Commission and national antitrust authorites come about, produce the "one-stop-shop", either at the Commission or at the national authority in whose territory the centre of gravity lies. Extensive reliance on Community law will also guarantee a high degree of uniformity within the common market.[133] However, the present architecture, contrary to the ideal situation just sketched, contains numerous serious obstacles to effective and efficient decentralised enforcement of Community antitrust law.[134]

In addition there are considerations from a constitutional point of view which suggest that decentralised enforcement of Community law is not necessarily the appropriate solution for the existing overload problem. From a constitutional perspective, review of the EC antitrust law system, in particular of its jurisdictional scope, appears timely. The realisation of the Single Market and, most notably, the coming into force of the TEU affect the relationship between Community and national law. They underscore that the Community operates in a multi-layered legal structure with an increasingly intricate division and sharing of powers between the layers.[135] The search should be for a division of jurisdiction which ensures and facilitates the cohabitation of Community and Member State laws by enhancing the compatibility of the various sets of legal norms. Casting aside national (antitrust) laws is not compatible with continued respect for national laws and institutions within the framework of the TEU.[136]

In antitrust law only cases of genuine Community importance are likely significantly to distort competition in the internal market. At present, this is indeed recognised by the Commission in its practice of not dealing with EC antitrust complaints which are not of Community importance and the decentralisation plans that have seen the light so far. However, contrary to the current situation, cases which are not of Community interest should be left to national authorities to be decided under their respective national laws. This can be achieved only through review of the scope of EC antitrust law. In practical terms, EC antitrust law jurisdiction would no longer be based on an effect on inter-trade but on

---

[133] Athough it should be noted that a degree of diversity is implicit in the Commission modernisation plans too. The block-exemption reg. for vertical agreements provides for the possibility that Member States' authorities withdraw the benefit of the exemption reg. for agreements with specific adverse effects on national markets and it is commonly accepted that decentralisation of enforcement of Art. 81(3) EC, envisaged in the White Paper on Modernisation, creates the danger of diverging application of that provision by national courts and national competition authorities.

[134] As has been said, the discussion of the White Paper and its implications is concentrated as much as possible in Ch. 6.

[135] It is in this context that the Commission itself considers that only an in-depth reform of the Community's jurisdiction can respond to the excess of work at the CFI. See *Agence Europe*, 26 April 1999.

[136] Note that the Commission has actively promoted adoption of national antitrust laws in the Member States. It continues to do so in the preparation for accession of the Visegrad countries to the Community. See, e.g., Commission of the European Community, *White Paper on the Preparation of the Associated Countries of Central and Eastern Europe for Integration into the Internal Market of the Union.* COM(95)163 final, Brussels, 10 May 1995.

Community interest. The practical interpretation of the Community interest concept is best based on the "qualitative" notion of Community interest, emerging from the Commission's practice towards antitrust complaints without Community interest.

5

Institutional Issues at the Central Level

AFAMOUS COMPETITION policy axiom holds that "structure determines conduct". Markets with few competitors tend to be characterised by a low degree of competition, markets with many active companies are likely to see more competitive conduct. The postulate can be extended to administrative frameworks. The institutional structure determines enforcement conduct and substantive interpretations of the rules and determination of priorities in enforcement action depend on the structure and operation of the institutions responsible. The operation of the institutions, in turn, is largely dependent on the procedural rules which guide their action. Substantive, procedural and institutional aspects of a policy system are therefore strongly interrelated. Changes in one of those fields bear consequences for the other limbs of the system.[1]

The Commission's institutional characteristics as well as the EC antitrust law's procedural rules have had a fundamental impact on the operation of the Community's antitrust policy system as well as on the interpretation of the substantive rules.[2] The intended reform of EC antitrust law, set out in the Commission White Paper on Modernisation,[3] focuses on one procedural aspect: Regulation 17. The Commission hopes that withdrawing the notification system together with decentralising the application of Article 81(1) EC brings the Community's institutional and procedural system, devised in the early 1960s, up to date. While decentralised enforcement and withdrawal of the authorisation are clearly important issues with institutional and procedural consequences these aspects of modernisation are not addressed in this chapter. Chapter 6, which is entirely devoted to decentralised enforcement, deals with those aspects of the institutional framework. What remains for this chapter is a discussion of the institutional system within which Community antitrust law operates and the way in which this is affected by the gradual transformation of EC antitrust law and the fundamental changes brought by establishment of the internal market

---

[1] S. Wilks and L. McGowan, "Disarming the Commission: The Debate over a European Cartel Office" (1995) 32 *JCMS* 259–73 at 260–2; S. Wilks, "The Metamorphosis of European Competition Policy" in F. Snyder (ed.), *European Law in Context—Volume I* (Aldershot, Dartmouth, 1992), 270–93; S. Bulmer, "Institutions and Policy Change in the European Communities: The Case of Merger Control" (1994) 72 *Public Administration* 423–44 at 424–7; G. Bruce Doern and S. Wilks, *Comparative Competition Policy. National Institutions in a Global Market* (Oxford, Clarendon Press, 1996), esp. 1–6.

[2] L. Laudati, "The European Commission as Regulator: The Uncertain Pursuit of the Competitive Market" in G. Majone, *Regulating Europe* (London, Routledge, 1996), 229–61 at 263.

[3] "White Paper on Modernisation of the Rules Implementing Arts. 81 and 82 of the E.C. Treaty" [1999] OJ C132/1.

and the Treaty on European Union (TEU). At present the Community institutions are responsible for legislation and policy-making on the one hand and antitrust law enforcement on the other. In antitrust law these two duties are closely entwined. Much of what can be considered antitrust policy-making is actually determined and developed by enforcement action. The discussion of the modernisation of EC antitrust policy's institutional framework shall therefore focus on enforcement of antitrust policy.

Following a short discussion of the institutions responsible for antitrust legislation and policy-making (5.1), the remainder of the chapter focuses on institutional and procedural features of EC antitrust law enforcement (5.2—5.5). First, the main institutional features of the present enforcement framework are set out (5.2). A review of the main criticism towards existing insitutional and procedural processes forms the basis of a discussion of two dominant concerns (5.3). The next section discusses an alternative institutional framework which is typically proposed in order to alleviate the perceived problems, the proposal to establish an independent European cartel agency (5.4). In accordance with the rest of this book the final paragraph (5.5) reviews the modernisation of EC antitrust law's institutional framework with reference to the general developments in Community law following the TEU and 1992.

5.1 EC ANTITRUST LEGISLATION

The Council, as the Community's general legislator, is the competent institution for making substantive antitrust law. Apart from adopting the Community's Merger Control Regulation in 1989 the Council has however refrained from adopting substantive antitrust legislation. Instead it delegated to the Commission the power to adopt block-exemption regulations which declare Article 81(1) EC inapplicable to certain categories of agreements and concerted practices.[4] The block-exemption regulations adopted by the Commission on this basis form the most significant body of generic policy measures in the antitrust law area. The capacity to issue block exemption-regulations enables the Commission to conduct antitrust policy complementary to the policy which it pursues by antitrust law enforcement in individual cases.

The main policy line which can be detected in the Commission's antitrust policy on the basis of block-exemption regulations is the promotion of co-operation between small- and medium-sized enterprises (SMEs). The Commission favours co-operation between SMEs, primarily on the basis of the "*de minimis*" notice but also by specific provisions in block-exemption regulations protecting the interest of SMEs.[5]

---

[4] Council Reg. 19/65 of 2 March 1965 on the application of Art. 81(3) of the Treaty to certain categories of agreements and concerted practices (exclusive dealing agreements) as amended by Council Reg. 1215/1999 of 10 June 1999, [1999] OJ L148/1.

[5] See above, Ch. 3.

While the general direction of Community antitrust policy on the basis of block-exemption regulations is therefore set by the Commission various other institutions influence this quasi-legislative process. In addition to the Council which delegates confined areas of its legislative power to the Commission, the European Parliament and the Economic and Social Committee ("ECOSOC") bring forward their views on draft block-exemption regulations. Despite the delegation of the legislative power by the Council to the Commission, Member States also influence the direction of Community antitrust policy through their role in the Advisory Committee on Restrictive Practices and Dominant Positions ("Advisory Committee") which is consulted on Commission policy initiatives.

Political control of Commission antitrust policy implicit in its enforcement action in individual cases is less well-established. Although the Advisory Committee is consulted on draft decisions in individual cases its opinion remains confidential.[6] Otherwise political control is limited to the European Parliament's and ECOSOC's opinion on the Commission's annual reports on competition policy.[7]

The Commission's modernisation plans leave the institutional structure largely untouched, although an increased role for the Advisory Committee is foreseen in the White Paper.[8]

5.2 ENFORCEMENT PROCEDURE

The main task for the Community antitrust body is therefore to implement its policy by enforcing the existing antitrust laws. This enforcement process is central to this chapter's discussion of the institutional and procedural framework for antitrust policy at the Community level. However, such a general review of the institutional and procedural in "antitrust cases" is problematic in view of the fact that there are huge differences between the sorts of cases.[9] The nature of procedures in merger cases, for example, diverges considerably from those in cartel cases which is itself again different from the abuse of dominant position cases. Even within the category of Article 81 ("anti-cartel") cases there are differences between a genuine cartel investigation on the one hand and review of a

---

[6] The situation is different with respect to the Opinion of the Advisory Committee on Concentrations where publication may be recommended and carried out by the Commission; Art. 19 of the Merger Reg.

[7] See, more extensively, V. Rose (ed.), *Bellamy and Child—Common Market Law of Competition* (London, Sweet & Maxwell, 1993), 5–6.

[8] Moreover, the procedural framework for individual antitrust cases was modernised over recent years, see Commission Reg. 2842/98 on the hearing of parties in certain procedures under Arts. 81 and 82 of the EC Treaty ([1998] OJ) L354/18, Commission Notice on the internal rules of procedure for processing resuests for access to the file ([1997] OJ C23/3) Guidelines on the method of setting fines imposed pursuant to Art. 15(2) of Reg. 17 ([1998] OJ C9/3), and the Commission Notice on the non-imposition or reduction of fines in cartel cases ([1996] OJ C207/4). See also below.

[9] *Cf.* n. 7 of the General Introduction to this book.

notified distribution agreement on the other. Moreover, not only the character of the potential antitrust law infringement and the pertinent procedures vary, the size of cases diverge as well. The institutional and procedural structure with respect to multi-jurisdictional mergers in a global sector of the economy is likely to differ from what is involved in a national abuse of dominant position case. There are therefore inherent limits to a general discussion of the pertinent procedural and institutional framework for Community antitrust law enforcement at the Community level. Taking into account these objections to generalisation it is nevertheless possible to examine the current system in light of the changed context in which EC antitrust law is applied.[10]

The procedural and institutional model which is used in this chapter is based on Article 81 EC cases. In the area of Article 81 EC four procedural phases can be identified: observation, investigation, prosecution and decision. The first phase is that in which the Commission obtains knowledge of behaviour or agreements which potentially restrict competition within the internal market. While there are three typical ways in which this may occur, notification to the Commission's Directorate-General for competition matters by the parties to the agreement is the most common in the current system.[11] Alternatively, DG Competition is alerted by complaints, often lodged by competitors of the companies involved, or by investigations into specific sectors of the economy on its own initiative.

In case the initial information thus obtained gives rise to the suspicion that an infringement of Community antitrust law occurs or has occurred, procedures enter into the second stage, that of investigation. Regulation 17 grants broad powers to the Commission to obtain the information it considers essential. In addition to its competence to request information from undertakings the Commission has the power to carry out the investigations it considers necessary to fulfil its duties in ensuring compliance with Community antitrust law.[12] On the basis of this information DG Competition—or rather the case handler ("*rapporteur*")—forms a tentative opinion on the question whether the conduct constitutes a breach of Community antitrust law. If the answer is negative and there are no grounds for continuing the proceedings on the basis of the facts known the *rapporteur* will terminate the investigation. The file will then be closed either officially by way of a negative clearance decision or—much more common—informally on the basis of a comfort letter.[13]

---

[10] Moreover, in general terms all antitrust cases consist of three stages; i.e. obtaining information, hearing views of interested parties and taking a decision. See L. Ortiz Blanco, *European Community Competition Procedure* (Oxford, Clarendon Press, 1996), 37. See also the remarks in the Introduction.

[11] While this may change with respect to Art. 81 EC on the basis of the Commission's White Paper, a duty to notify mergers will remain.

[12] See Arts. 11 and 14 of Reg. 17 and Arts. 11 of the Merger Reg. for parallel provisions with respect to merger cases.

[13] In merger procedures the first phase always ends with a formal decision.

If, conversely, an infringement of Community antitrust law is suspected the procedure goes to the next phase, that of prosecution. The initiation of that phase is heralded by the formulation of a "statement of objections" issued by the Commission and sent to the companies concerned.[14] The statement of objections forms the basis for the further procedure. The companies concerned may reply in writing to the allegations made. Subsequently, they may defend their views during an oral hearing at the offices of DG Competition.[15] On the basis of the information which is then available DG Competition decides whether or not the statement of objections was merited and whether to proceed to a prohibition decision.

If it concludes that an infringement of Community antitrust law occurs the Commission will proceed to the next phase and come to a formal decision requiring termination of any infringements—or, in the case of mergers, prohibiting the merger. DG Competition drafts a decision. It consults the Advisory Committee. On the basis of the conclusion reached by the Advisory Committee DG Competition contemplates whether it is useful to review its draft. DG Competition also consults the Commission's Legal Service. Upon approval from that institution it submits the draft decision with the opinion of the Advisory Committee attached to the Commissioner responsible for competition matters. The Commissioner may change the draft decision. When the Commissioner agrees with it, the draft decision is submitted to the College of Commissioners which may again alter the contents of the draft decision.[16]

It is evident that the Commission has strong autonomous powers in the area of antitrust law enforcement. All stages of the procedure take place within the Commission and its bureaucracy. During the procedures the Commission has complete discretion to decide whether or not to proceed to a final decision. The Commission's autonomy is conditional only on hearing the parties to the alleged anti-competitive agreements and the Advisory Committee. Thus, the Commission is master of the procedure from the outset to its finalisation. Reflecting the four stages of Community antitrust law procedure, the Commission is seen to act as police, investigator, prosecutor and judge.[17]

The pertinence of this institutional and procedural design is increasingly questioned, particularly after the adoption of the Merger Control Regulation with its high political profile.[18] The criticism is directed at the institutional

---

[14] Though it is formally a Commission document, a Statement of Objections may be drawn up by the Director-General of DG Competition. *Cf.* Case 43 & 63/82 *VBVB and VBBB* v. *Commission* [1984] ECR 19.

[15] See Commission Reg. 2842/98 on the hearing of parties in certain procedures under Arts. 81 and 82 of the EC Treaty [1998] OJ L354/18.

[16] Ortiz Blanco, above, n. 10, at 37.

[17] I. van Bael, "The Antitrust Settlement Practice of the Commission" (1986) 23 *CMLRev* 61–90.

[18] S. Wilks, "Options for Reform of European Competition Policy" in A. van Mourik (ed.), *Developments in European Competition Policy* (Maastricht, EIPA, 1996), 153–76, and J. Steenbergen, "Decision-making in Competition Cases: The Investigator, the Prosecutor and the Judge" in L. Gormley (ed.), *Current and Future Perspectives on EC Competition Law* (The Hague, Kluwer Law International, 1997), 101–8.

design as well as at the procedures. The common denominator to the criticism, the amalgamation of separate stages of a legal proces in one institution, suggests that the problem relates to the current lack of procedural, substantive and institutional transparency in EC antitrust law procedures. The absence of transparency in turn hinders accountability.[19] The next section examines the current system on the basis of the criticism to which it has been subject.

5.3 EVALUATION OF THE PRESENT SYSTEM

There are two principal strands of critique of the existing institutional and procedural regime. One has a dominant legal character. It concerns the fairness of the current antitrust law procedures in which the same institution is responsible for prosecution and decision-making. The other is more policy-related. It pertains to the lack of transparency with respect to decision-making within the College of Commissioners. A legal judgement and a political judgment are allegedly fused in the decision-making structure. For a good understanding of the problematic aspects of the current institutional framework these two lines of critique need to be separated. The first type of criticism relates to the undesirable combination of functions within DG Competition, the second to a similar problem but there the combination of functions resides within the College of Commissioners.

The main concern with respect to the combination of functions within DG Competition is the procedural fairness of antitrust law procedures. Commentators perceive antitrust law enforcement procedures as contentious procedures and expect them to follow essential principles of procedural fairness. Present procedures are considered not to live up to the standards of natural justice particularly in view of the Commission's dominant position throughout all stages of the procedure.

The principal sense of injustice is seen to lie in the fact that the same persons who suspect anti-competitive conduct substantiate their concern in a statement of objections and subsequently decide whether their earlier objections were justified. The margins of discretion for the individual case handler in deciding whether a restriction of competition occurs are very broad. The scope for discretion is enlarged because there are no formal standards to restrict the discretion of DG Competition officials in their assessment. As a consequence the nature, and even the quality, of the analysis of the effects on competition are seen to vary considerably.[20]

Another problem of procedural fairness arises in the prosecution phase. Companies which have been accused of infringements of Community antitrust law in the statement of objections can respond to the charges in two ways. The

---

[19] D. Neven et al., *Merger in Daylight—The Economics and Politics of European Merger Control* (London, CEPR, 1993). See further below.
[20] Laudati, above, n. 2, at 238.

first is responding to the statement of objections in writing. The second is orally, at the hearing which takes place within DG Competition. In order to allow them to prepare their defence companies have access to the Commission's files. The problem of procedural fairness resides in the fact that the prosecuting institution, DG Competition, itself determines to which documents a company will get access for preparing its defence. Although it is no longer the case handler itself but the independent Hearing Officer which decides these matters, the procedure is considered unfair by those commentators who perceive the procedure as contentious.[21]

The problem of procedural fairness arises in the last stage of the procedure too. If the dispute has not been settled after the oral hearing, the case handler drafts a decision. Although that draft is read and commented on by other persons in different institutions, it is this draft which forms the basis for the report and (draft) decision submitted to the College of Commissioners. The last decides exclusively on the basis of that report and will not hear the other party or parties to the proceedings. Indeed most antitrust cses are decided by the college of commissioners on the basis of the so-called written procedure, by which a draft decision is automatically accepted upon circulation to the various *cabinets* of the commissioners unless an objection is made by one of them. Again, in procedings of a contentious nature this institutional feature of Community antitrust procedure has been criticised.[22] While the European Community Courts have repeatedly scrutinised—and endorsed—the institutional framework in which antitrust law is enforced,[23] commentators continue to challenge the system.

The question of the requirements of natural justice in the existing procedures needs to be addressed when Community antitrust law is modernised. Indeed the combination of powers within the Commission offices is now held against the requirements of Article 6 of the European Convention on Human Rights (ECHR). That Article provides that "in the determination of his civil rights and obligations or of any criminal charge against him, everyone is entitled to a fair and public hearing within a reasonable time by an independent and impartial tribunal established by law". It is uncertain whether Article 6 ECHR applies to Community antitrust law proceedings, but it is generally acknowledged that the process of antitrust law enforcement includes determination of civil rights and obligations.[24] This view is consistent with the direct effect which the antitrust

---

[21] Unease with the current system increased dramatically in the aftermath of the *Italian Flat Glass* case (Joined Cases T–68 & 77–78/89 *Società Italiano Vetro and others* v. *Commission* [1992] ECR II–1403) in which it was revealed that officials in DG Competition had deleted exculpating passages before sending the file to the parties concerned.

[22] I. van Bael, "Transparency of E.C. Commission Proceedings" in P.-J. Slot and A. McDonnell, *Procedure and Enforcement in E.C. and U.S. Competition Law* (London, Sweet & Maxwell, 1993), 192–6.

[23] See e.g. Case T–11/89 *Shell* v. *Commission* [1992] ECR II–757 and Cases 100–103/80 *Musique Diffusion Française* v. *Commission* ("*Pioneer*") [1983] ECR 1825.

[24] See, e.g., W. Wils, "La comptabilité des procédures communautaires en matière de concurrence avec la Convention européenne des droits de l'homme" (1996) 32 *CDE* 329–54 and D. Waelbroeck and D. Fosselard, "Should the Decision Making Power in EC Antitrust Procedures

law provisions have. For directly effective Treaty provisions impose obligations on individuals but are also intended to confer rights upon them. The Commission, itself the prosecutor in antitrust law procedures, cannot be considered an independent and impartial tribunal. If Article 6 applies the question is therefore whether the European Courts fulfil the criteria set out in the Convention. Hitherto the question whether the degree of review of Commission decisions exercised by the Court of First Instance lives up to the standards of Article 6 has remained unanswered. The ECHR has not yet decided whether the Court's restriction to a marginal review of complex economical or technical issues in combination with an examination of manifest error of appraisal or misuse of powers attains the standards of natural justice of Article 6 ECHR.[25]

The Community's Court of First Instance provided a partial answer to the question whether the Article 6 principles apply when it ruled that antitrust law enforcement procedures are guided by the principle of "equality of arms".[26] Reference to the principle was made in the context of matters relating to the opportunity for parties to antitrust law proceedings to have access to the Commission files. The meaning of the Court's reference to the principle and the scope of its consequences remain uncertain.[27] Yet, it appears that the applicability of the principle of the "equality of arms" in Community antitrust law implies that the current system will not stand. There cannot be equality between DG Competition and private parties in procedures which are conducted by DG Competition itself. It is unthinkable that arms are considered equal where one of the parties is competent to make the decision on the outcome of a battle. The Court's *Soda Ash* judgment may therefore have profound consequences for the future of the institutional framework within which Community antitrust law is enforced.

The second major institutional objection to Community antitrust law procedures identified above pertains to a different aspect of the combination of functions within the EC Commission. It relates to the final phase of the antitrust policy enforcement process in which the College of Commissioners takes a decision. To understand the critique it is necessary to recall the dual nature of Community antitrust law decision-making. First, the impact of an agreement, practice or merger on competition is examined. If competition is significantly reduced by the agreement or merger it is in principle prohibited by EC antitrust law. The Commission may then consider whether the restraints on competition

be Left to an Independent Judge?" (1994) 14 *YEL* 111–50. More tentatively, C.-D. Ehlermann, "Decision Making at the Centre—Working Paper II" in C.-D. Ehlermann and L. Laudati (eds.), *Robert Schuman Centre Annual on European Competition Law* (The Hague, Kluwer Law International, 1997), 29–44.

[25] The literature is not unanimous. See the opposing views in K. Lenaerts and J. Vanhamme, "Procedural Rights of Private Parties in the Community Administrative Process" (1997) 34 *CMLRev* 531–69 at 556 and Waelbroeck and Fosselard, above, n. 24, respectively.

[26] Case T–36/91 *ICI* v. *Commission* ("*Soda Ash*") [1995] ECR II–1847.

[27] See C.-D. Ehlermann and B.-J. Drijber, "Legal Protection of Enterprises: Administrative Procedure, in Particular Access to Files and Confidentiality" (1996) 17 *ECLR* 375–83.

are outweighed by positive effects (on other Community policies). If the Commission considers this to be the case it may exempt the agreement from the prohibition. Simply put, Community antitrust law procedures first assess the effects on competition. Where the effects are negative an additional assessment follows which allows for other policy considerations.[28]

In Community antitrust law procedures, the separation between these two analytically divergent decisions cannot be identified. Since the deliberations during meetings of the College of Commissioners are secret, options chosen in the decision-making process cannot be clearly related to policy choices and consequently political decisions cannot be attributed to the Commission. The published version of the Commission's antitrust decisions does not always provide an adequate distinction between the separate types of judgment. Published versions of Commission decisions in Article 81 EC cases do distinguish between the two steps by which it is (first) established whether a restriction of competition occurs and then (secondly) whether an exemption may be granted but the wording of the reasoning in the decisions together with the wide margins of discretion which are implicit in the application of the antitrust law provisions can conceal the "real" motives underlying certain judgments. To take a practical example, there is clear suspicion that the exemption granted by the Commission to a joint venture between Volkswagen and Ford for development of a "multi-purpose vehicle" was partly based on employment and cohesion policy considerations. In its decision the Commission ruled out those motives and argued along "pure" competition lines. Yet, from a "pure" competition point of view it was very doubtful whether the joint venture between two of the biggest car manufacturers was really indispensable to the arrival of a competitor to the then dominant firm on the multi-purpose vehicle market. Similarly, the Commission's holding that the combination of VW and Ford technology was required to further technical progress is doubtful. The potential for reasoning which aims to justify, *ex post*, a decision already made is exacerbated under the Merger Control Regulation where there is no divergence between the two distinctive tests, like in Article 81(1) and (3) EC.[29] Hence the fusion both *qua* institution and *qua* moment of two distinct tests generates decisions based on

---

[28] While the analytical divide between the two steps is most clearly apparent in Art. 81 EC cases, which feature an explicit exemption provision, assessment of mergers entails a similar two-tier assessment. Appraisal of mergers is exclusively based on their "compatibility" with the common market. The appropriate test is limited to the question whether a dominant position will be created or extended as a result of which effective competition will be significantly impeded (Art. 2(3) of the Merger Reg.). Nevertheless, the elements which may be taken into account in the application of this criterion allow for considering other Community policies. In particular since assessment of the compatibility with the common market takes place within the general framework of the the achievement of the fundamental objectives referred to in Art. 2 EC including the strengthening of economic and social cohesion and protecting the environment (recital 13 to the Merger Reg.).

[29] See V. Korah, "Tetra Pak II—Lack of Reasoning in Court's Judgment" (1997) 18 *ECLR* 98–103 and "Future Competition Law" in L. Laudati and C.-D. Ehlermann (eds.), *Robert Schuman Centre Annual on European Competition Law 1997* (Oxford, Hart, 1998). In the same vein, G Amato, *Antitrust and the Bounds of Power* (Oxford, Hart, 1997).

untransparent reasoning. The resulting margins for political horse-trading within the Commission have been noted repeatedly.[30] It may therefore be concluded that the belief that the Commission would ensure the minimisation of political interference with the enforcement of competition law has proven wrong.[31]

Akin to the first objection to Community antitrust law procedures, the conflation of the legal and political decision is more acute than it used to be due to recent developments. In particular, the introduction of the Community Merger Control Regulation has enhanced the significance of the untransparent institutional and procedural framework in which the Community antitrust rules are applied. In contrast to restrictive clauses, for example in distribution agreements, or abuses of dominant position, regulation of mergers enjoys a high political profile.[32] Moreover, the text of the Merger Regulation limits the Commission's assessment explicitly to a merger's compatibility with the common market. The pure competition criteria should in theory render the second political stage of antitrust law decisions obsolete. However, in light of Article 2(1)(b) and Recital 13 of the Merger Regulation it remains disputed whether the Merger Regulation does indeed adhere to pure competition criteria. Whatever the outcome of that controversy, it is evident that the Merger Regulation enhanced the desire to be able to distinguish between the enforcement of legal norms and the pursuit of alternative policy objectives.[33] The aspirations to European economic and political union enshrined in the Treaty on European Union also enhanced the political relevance of Community antitrust law enforcement.

5.4 INDEPENDENT AGENCY

Various options for reform of the procedural and institutional system enhancing the fairness and transparency of Community antitrust law enforcement have been proposed. The proposals vary from moderate changes within the existing legal context to radical insitutional reform which would require new legislation.

The first category encompasses the idea of separating functions within DG Competition by appointing separate officials for the investigative phase and the phase in which the the draft decision is drawn up.[34] Likewise, further expansion of the role and independence of the Hearing Officer forms a moderate improve-

---

[30] An inside observer of Commission practice noted that "internal deals on competition policy were always being made": G. Ross, *Jacques Delors and European Integration* (Oxford, Polity Press, 1995), 131.

[31] Laudati, above, n. 2, at 239.

[32] E. Schwartz, "Politics As Usual: The History of European Community Merger Control" (1993) 18 *Yale Journal of International Law* 607–62; Bulmer, above, n. 1; and W. Kartte, "Zur institutionellen Absicherung der EG-Fusionskontrolle" (1993) 44 *Jahrbuch für die Ordnung von Wirtschaft und Gesellschaft* (ORDO) 405–13.

[33] D. Wolf, "Panel Discussion" in Laudati and Ehlermann (eds.), n. 24, 9.

[34] Ehlermann, above, n. 24, at 32.

ment within the existing framework which is sometimes promoted.[35] While these measures could be relatively easily taken, they would not appear to solve the fundamental objections to the system. Prosecution and judgment power would remain in the same hands, just as the legal and political judgments would continue to be made by one institution.

More radical proposals in which the Commission would have to dispose of one of its current functions have therefore been made. In those alternatives the Commission would either retain its prosecuting function and discard the adjudicative role or it would remain responsible for judgments but would rid itself of its role as prosecutor.[36]

One variant of the more radical reform options is particularly persistent and requires more extensive discussion in the context of a discussion of the modernisation of Community antitrust policy. It is the proposal to relocate the enforcement of Community antitrust law from the Commission to an independent EC antitrust agency.

The original proposals for an independent European Cartel Office date far back, but following the broadening of Community competences to include industrial policy in the Single European Act and the general attention for the enhanced political elements of Community powers under the Treaty on European Union the issue was recently revitalised.[37] The debate on the merits of an independent European antitrust law enforcement agency acquired practical significance when the German delegation to the 1996 Intergovernmental Conference proposed the establishment of such an institution.[38] The debate on modernisation of the institutional framework consequently focuses on the merits of establishing an independent European Cartel Office.

Though broad support for an independent antitrust agency exists, the debate is somewhat confused because the proponents of an independent agency tend to vary in their preference for the degree of independence and for the phase in which this independent body is to enter the procedure.[39] The divergence stems from the different objectives which the various supporters of an independent agency pursue. On the one hand there are those who merely want to enhance procedural and institutional transparency. The ambition is not necessarily to *exclude* or *abandon* politics as an element in the assessment of the compatibility

---

[35] As is promoted by the House of Lords, above, n. 24. But see the further reflections on this topic in M. van der Woude, "Hearing Officers and EC Antitrust Procedures; the Art of Making Subjective Procedures More Objective" (1996) 33 *CMLRev* 531–46 at 544–6.

[36] Waelbroeck and Fosselard, above, n. 24.

[37] The proposal to establish an independent competition office (in Luxembourg) was already discussed in the negotiations which led to the EEC Treaty. See, for instance, B. Seliger, "Ein unabhängiges Kartellamt für Europa—ordnungs- und wettbewerbspolitischen Aspekte" (1997) 47 *WuW* 874–81.

[38] Although it is in essence a German desire there is now support for an independent agency in other Member States as well: C.-D. Ehlermann, "Reflections on a European Cartel Office" (1995) 32 *CMLRev* 471–86; *Financial Times*, "Italy Seeks Separate EU Antitrust Body", 8 May 1996, 3; and *Frankfurter Allgemeine Zeitung*, "Das Europäische Kartellamt findet immer mehr Befürworter", 9.

[39] Wilks and McGowan, above, n. 1, and Wilks, above, n. 18.

of a potentially anti-competitive agreement with the common market but rather to reveal the motivation for the ultimate decision. As demonstrated above, present antitrust law enforcement practice does not reveal what the assessment of the effects on competition was with respect to individual agreements or mergers. The published version of the Commission decision does provide a passage on the effects on competition. The wording and reasoning of that decision, however, at the same time justify the final judgment. This is considered to constitute an architectural flaw which precludes transparency.[40] It should be clear to what extent antitrust policy enforcement decisions are based on economic concerns associated with a reduction of the level of competition and to what extent agreements are endorsed on the basis of a non-competition—or "political"—motivation. On the other hand, there are those who seek an adjustment of substantive antitrust law. In their view, establishment of a "single purpose" antitrust agency would rule out political interference with antitrust law enforcement. The supporters of this type of independent antitrust agency are inspired by the German system of antitrust law enforcement.[41] In Germany competition law is primarily enforced by a federal agency, the Bundeskartellamt, which operates independently of the German government. Thus, the debate on the *separation* of the two types of assessments in the decision-making process has become equated with the related but analytically separate question of the desirability of an *independent* competition agency. Still the debate generally focuses on the second model, particularly since the German government proposed the establishment of an European antitrust agency following the Bundeskartellamt model.[42]

When examining the merits of an indepedent European Cartel Office on the basis of the Bundeskartellamt model it is essential to start by setting out the main institutional features of the Bundeskartellamt within the German system in which the law is central to the maintenance of undistorted competition.[43] It is primarily the task of the Bundeskartellamt to uphold and promote competition on the basis of the main competition statute.[44] While it is formally and administratively part of the Ministry of Economic Affairs it operates independently of it both in specific cases and in its case selection.[45] All decisions taken

---

[40] Neven et al., above, n. 19, at 224.

[41] See, e.g., P. Bartodziej, *Reform der EG-Wettbewerbsaufsicht und Gemeinschafsrecht*, at 18–38.

[42] See *ibid.* Alternatives have been proposed for the area of merger control: D. Goyder, "The Implementation of the EC Merger Regulation—New Wine in Old Bottles" (1992) 45 *Current Legal Problems* 117–43 and Neven *et al.*, above, n. 25.

[43] R. Sturm, "The German Cartel Office in a Hostile Environment" in G. Bruce Doern and S. Wilks, *Comparative Competition Policy* (Oxford, Clarendon Press, 1996), 185–224 at 201–10.

[44] The *Gesetz gegen Wettbewerbsbeschränkungen* (GWB). Other institutions which play a role are the Federal Economics Ministry, the courts, the *Monopolkommission* and cartel authorities of the *Länder*: Sturm, above, n. 43.

[45] It remains disputed whether the Economics Ministry may direct the Bundeskartellamt in individual cases. See the discussion in P. Baake and O. Oerschau, "The Law and Policy of Competition in Germany", in G. Majone, *Regulating Europe* (London, Routledge, 1996), 131–56 at 152–3. The Bundeskartellamt is subdivided into ten divisions which are responsible for investigation as well as final decision-making: K. Markert, "Die Rolle des Bundeskartellamtes bei der Durchsetzung des

by the Bundeskartellamt are subject to review by the German courts on the application of the parties concerned. At first instance, the Kammergericht (Court of Appeals) in Berlin, a civil court, reviews the merits, facts included, of the decision. Further appeal from its decision is then open on points of law to the Bundesgerichtshof (Federal Supreme Court).

The Bundeskartellamt is typically presented as an appropriate prototype for a European Cartel Office which would be responsible for testing the effects on competition. In particular an independent European Cartel Office would be responsible only for assessing whether agreements, behaviour or mergers led to a restriction of competition. It would thus be responsible for the application of Articles 81(1) and 82 EC and the Merger Regulation. The transfer would be limited to enforcement action in relation to these provisions and all regulatory competences would continue to be exercised by the Commission. Moreover, most proponents of an independent antitrust agency in this form make the independent agency's judgement subject to a political exception, akin to the German *Ministererlaubnis*.[46] The Commission would also retain its responsibility for enforcing the Treaty's competition rules towards Member States and public undertakings.

It is submitted however that the Bundeskartellamt model does not form an adequate model for EC antitrust law enforcement in the context of the Treaty on European Union, for two reasons. First, there are fundamental disparities in the economic, social and political context between Germany and the European Community. Secondly, the merits of a Bundeskartellamt-type institution themselves are questionnable.

To start with the former line of argument, the Bundeskartellamt administers the observance of competition law on the basis of a nationally shared esteem for economic freedom and competition.[47] German insistence on the desirability of an independent agency, which would be responsible for applying the Merger Regulation and Articles 81 and 82 EC should be understood from this perspective.[48]

Wettbewerbsrechts in der Bundesrepublik Deutschland" in B. Blaurock (ed.), *Institutionen und Grundfragen des Wettbewerbsrecht* (Frankfurt, Metzner, 1988). It will be noted that there is even less of a division of powers in this procedural arrangement than there is under present Community antitrust law procedures.

[46] Typically, the Commission is considered to be the appropriate institution to overrule, in exceptional circumstances, the independent agency's judgement on pure competition criteria. However, alternatives have been suggested, e.g. the Council, or even other institutions: Seliger, above, n. 37. See also Ehlermann, above, n. 24, at 38. There are also commentators who would exclude the political exception ("*Ministererlaubnis*") within the Community system: T. Janicki and B. Molitor, "Wettbewerbssicherung durch Schaffung eines europäischen Kartellamtes" (1995) 75 *Wirtschaftsdienst* 75–7.

[47] Sturm, above, n. 43, at 196–201.

[48] This is, e.g., evident from a statement on the matter by Wolgang Kartte, a former President of the Bundeskartellamt. In critical cases, he says, "the prohibition for a merger that would culminate in a dominant market position, is not decided by DG Competition, but by all 17 Commissioners. Thus, the politicization of European meger control has been guaranteed": W. Kartte, "Die Politisierung der Europäischen Fusionskontrolle ist Programmiert", *Die Welt*, 31 December 1990; cited in the translation by Wilks and McGowan, above, n. 1, at 265.

It is sometimes argued that the EC antitrust law operates within an economic constitution which comprises similar values. In this view the EC Treaty forms the Community's economic constitution which guarantees freedom of competition as a constitutional value.[49] Accordingly, an independent agency which protects this value of the economic constitution would form a logical element in the Community antitrust law system. However, it is evident that the EC Treaty does not constitute an economic constitution which guarantees the prominence of free competition. Under Community law freedom of competition may be made subject to regulation. Conflicts between competition policy and other Community policies are solved on the basis of political deliberation rather than on a hierarchy of norms.[50] Neither the Treaty itself nor the case law of the Court of Justice posits free competition as a value or objective superior to other values and objectives. What is true for the Community as a whole is in this respect also true for EC antitrust policy. The Community's commitment to undistorted competition has been qualified on numerous occasions by the Commission and the Court of Justice.[51]

Germany's legalised concept of competition law varies from that of the Community because in the EC enforcement of antitrust law has evident political features. Merger control in particular is suffused with deals. This was clearly recognised by ex-commissioner Van Miert who argued that competition policy is not neutral but "politics". Consequently, Germany's institutional framework is an inappropriate model for the European Community. Rather than concealing the policy choices behind a legal justification of decisions, economic and political arguments should be seen to play a role in EC antitrust law enforcement.[52]

This leads to the second objection to adopting the Bundeskartellamt model, which stems from the qualifications which can be made in respect of the alleged independence of the Bundeskartellamt itself. Despite its formal independence, the Bundeskartellamt is not free from political pressures. Its autonomous power is considered to be "limited and marginal".[53] For example, the Federal Minister of Economic Affairs may prohibit investigations which divisions of the Bundeskartellamt intend to launch into potential anti-competitive behaviour.[54]

---

[49] See, e.g., M. Streit and W. Mussler, "The Economic Constitution of the European Community: From 'Rome' to 'Maastricht' " (1995) 1 *ELJ* 5–30.

[50] See, for instance, Case C–280/93 *Germany* v. *Council* (*"Bananas"*) [1994] ECR I–4973 and *Opinion 1/91 European Economic Area* [1991] ECR I–6079.

[51] See Case 17/93 *Matra Hachette* v. *Commission* [1994] ECR II–595 (Art. 81(3)) and Case T–12/93 *Vittel* v. *Commission* [1995] ECR II–1247 (mergers). This is implicit in the Community concept of workable competition as adopted by the ECJ in Case 26/76 *Metro* v. *Commission* (*"Metro I"*) [1977] ECR 1875. See further ch.3.

[52] See, for instance, B. Bishop and S. Bishop, "Reforming Competition Policy: Bundeskartellamt—Model or Muddle?" (1996) 17 *ECLR* 207–9; Wilks and McGowan, above, n. 1; and A. Dashwood (ed.), *Reviewing Maastricht—Issues for the IGC 1996* (London, Sweet & Maxwell, 1996), 54ff.

[53] A. Riley, "The European Cartel Office: A Guardian Without Weapons?" (1997) 18 *ECLR* 3–16.

[54] Thus, Baake and Perschau, above, n. 45, 153.

Further, the Minister has the right to override a Bundeskartellamt veto against a merger. The *Ministererlaubnis* then replaces the consent of the Bundeskartellamt and the merger may take place.[55] Although this competence is rarely used the influence of the mere potentiality is considered to compromise the autonomy of the Bundeskartellamt. The numerous sectoral exceptions to the general competition rules further qualify the German model's commitment to pure competition criteria.[56] Finally, and most fundamentally, there is room for the Bundeskartellamt to take into account criteria other than those which might indicate whether or not competition is reduced. The informal character of administrative procedures especially the exchange of views prior to a merger deal provide opportunities for the exercise of political discretion.[57] In recognition of these elements of the German system the idea that politics can be completely excluded from a major field of economic regulation has been labelled "as offensive as . . . absurd".[58]

In addition to these two principal reasons for rejecting the Bundeskartellamt model for the European Community, a number of practical and legal objections to the establishment of an independent European cartel agency should be mentioned. First, in the context of the European Community the process of establishing a new institution be it an agency or a different institution, is very complicated. Experience with the establishment of new bodies and institutions suggests that the establishment of an independent cartel agency would be a complicated, protracted and, most importantly, a highly politicised process. Once established the European cartel office could still suffer from the political interference to which the Commission is currently subject. There is no *a priori* reason to believe that a single-purpose agency would be exempt from political interference by Member States.[59] A second practical problem which the establishment of a separate cartel agency might create is the co-ordination of separate strands to competition policy. Enforcement of the Treaty's antitrust rules is by its very nature narrowly linked to competition policy towards state aids, public monopolies and anti-dumping. Creation of a separate enforcement body for the antitrust rules would isolate the assessment of those cases from broader competition policy concerns.[60] Moreover, if it were to operate as a genuine

---

[55] Art. 24(3) of the *Gesetz gegen Wettbewerbsbeschränkungen*. The procedures are highly transparent; public attention is guaranteed when a minister makes use of his power to set aside the Bundeskartellamt's negative assessment of the effects on competition: McGowan and Wilks, above, n. 1, at 269.

[56] Seliger, above, n. 37.

[57] S. Wilks and L. McGowan, "Discretion in European Merger Control: The German Regime in Context" (1995) 2 *Journal of European Public Policy* 41–67, at 56. The ambiguous nature of the micro-economic tests implied in the assessment of the effects on competition heighten the level of discretion. Thus, increased employment through mergers has been identified as a factor of which the Bundeskartellamt takes account in merger assessments: Riley, above, n. 53, at 9.

[58] Wilks and McGowan, above, n. 57.

[59] Dashwood (ed.), above, n. 52, at 59ff.

[60] Schaub, "Decision Making at the Centre—Working Paper V" in Laudati and Ehlermann (eds.), above, n. 24, 79–87. Similarly, Riley, above, n. 53, at 5, and Ehlermann, above, n. 38.

indenpendent regulatory agency with real decision-making powers a Treaty amemendment would be required before a cartel office could be established.[61]

5.5 THE MODERNISATION OF THE INSTITUTIONAL FRAMEWORK

The fact that the Bundeskartellamt model does not fit well into the Community antitrust law system does not imply that the existing institutional structure should remain untouched. On the contrary, the institutional framework in which Community antitrust law is applied needs to be revised in order to alleviate the objections to the current system set out in the third section of this chapter.

Part I of this study described how the nature of Community antitrust law developed as the internal market was gradually established. In 1957 when the Rome Treaty was signed and in 1962 when the first regulation for the implementation of Articles 81 and 82 EC was adopted the perception of Community antitrust law was intimately linked to its role in promoting market integration. Agreements which were likely to enhance competition at the expense of free intra-Community trade were declared incompatible with the integration objective. Under certain conditions an exemption would be granted to agreements which hindered trade between Member States but which were beneficial to the Community for other reasons. The enforcement of these basic rules of the EEC Treaty was allocated to the Community's supranational institutions, the Commission and the Court of Justice. The Commission obtained the exclusive power to exempt an agreement from the prohibition on hindering trade between Member States. Given that the prohibition in Article 81(1) EC was interpreted so explicitly with respect to the needs of integration towards the common market, it was evident that the Commission as the supranational body most involved with the administration of the common market was best capable of judging whether an exemption should be provided.[62] For the same reason Regulation 17 introduced an administrative scheme in which all agreements which potentially hindered inter-state trade were to be notified to the Commission in order for them to be liable for exemption. In the original setting there were no logical alternatives to the Commission as the institution responsible for enforcing the Treaty's antitrust rules.

However, three subsequent developments altered the character of Community antitrust law. The changes which they generated affect the institutional framework. The first is the direct effect which the Court of Justice ascribed to the Treaty's antitrust law provisions. The second is the altered function of

---

[61] Case 9/56 *Meroni* v. *High Authority* [1958] ECR 9.

[62] The fact that application of the exemption provision in Art. 81(3) of the Treaty entails a comprehensive weighing of Community interest continues to be the reason for the Commission exemption monopoly. See the considerations in Case 234/89 *Delimitis* [1991] ECR I–978 (particularly Van Gerven AG's Opinion).

Community antitrust law. The third is the gradual adoption of national antitrust law systems in the Community's Member States.

The EEC Treaty was adopted as an international treaty. Generally international treaties do not themselves create rights which individuals of the states which are party to that agreement can invoke in legal proceedings. Arguably, the framers of the Treaty did not foresee that the Court of Justice would rule that the EEC Treaty created a new legal order which granted directly effective rights to individuals of the Member States. When the Court ruled that the Treaty's antitrust rules have direct effect it added a third category of Community antitrust law enforcers (national courts) to the two foreseen in the Treaty and Regulation 17 (the Commission and national antitrust authorities). The logic of the original institutional framework was thus invalidated. The Community antitrust law system was no longer an exclusively supranational affair. Individuals turned out to have certain rights which national courts had to protect. Since national courts are acting as Community courts of general jurisdiction when they apply the Treaty's directly effective antitrust law provisions there are no legal limits to their autonomy in interpreting those provisions.[63] Private parties may seek to uphold their private rights before national courts. In the interpretation of Community antitrust law national courts may make preliminary references to the Court of Justice. As a consequence the influence of the Court of Justice on Community antitrust policy grew. Its judicial interpretation of the scope of the rights and prohibitions laid down in Articles 81(1) and 82 EC replaced the Commission's administrative practice as constituents of Community antitrust law jurisprudence and case law. While previously it was not of much practical relevance whether the Commission provided negative clearance or an exemption for a particular notified agreement because either way the Commission had to provide a decision in order for the agreement to be valid, this changed fundamentally when national courts started taking decisions on the compatibility of an agreement with the Treaty's antitrust rules.[64] Although the Commission remained responsible for the implementation and general orientation of Community antitrust policy, in particular through its exclusive competence to exempt agreements from the prohibition laid down in Article 81(1) EC, the nature of antitrust law was no longer exclusively administrative. For the Commission cannot deprive, for example by way of a broad interpretation of the scope of the prohibitions defined in Articles 81 and 82 EC, individuals of directly effective rights which they hold under the Treaty itself. Ultimately, it is the Court of Justice which has the competence to interpret the the scope of the rights which undertakings have under Articles 81(1) and 82 EC. Generally, (national) courts are appropriate institutions for applying the antitrust Articles which grant individuals directly effective rights.

---

[63] Case T–51/89 *Tetra Pak* v. *Commission* [1990] ECR II–309, at para. 42. Except for the limits set out in Case C–234/89 *Delimitis*, above, n. 62.

[64] Case 127/73 *BRT* v. *SABAM* [1974] ECR 51, at para. 17.

If this first development can therefore be described as judicialisation of the original administrative procedure, the second factor which changed the nature of Community antitrust law was its transformation as the Internal Market was gradually established. As described at length in previous parts of this book, the traditional function of Community antitrust law (promoting integration) evolved into a more political one. In particular through its exemption practice, the Commission pursued broad economic policy objectives on the basis of enforcement of Community antitrust law. "It can therefore be said that the European Commission conducts a real *policy* and does not limit its role to the mere enforcement of legal rules as a prosecution authority would do, with decisions whether to prosecute or not given violations. This "competition policy" can then be influenced by the general economic policy (including industrial policy) which the European Commission is conducting in the framework of the EEC Treaty".[65] Thus, enforcement of Community antitrust law acquired high political salience. The advent of a Community merger control competence further enhanced the political elements in the antitrust law system. While the Commission, as the Community supranational administration primarily responsible for furthering the integration objective, was the pertinent institution to apply the Community's antitrust rules when their main function was to promote integration, this is much less evidently the case when the antitrust rules play a broader economic policy role. The tacit shift within Community antitrust law from negative to positive integration created a rarely expressed legitimacy gap, since the basis for EC antitrust policy continues to rest in its role in promoting market integration. One feature of the often-noted democratic deficit of the Community is the unaccountability of the Commission with respect to the policy it conducts on the basis of enforcement of the antitrust rules. Control of Commission practice is limited to the judicial control exercised by the Court of Justice. In view of the limited degree of legal control provided by the Court in combination with the clear political tenets of current Commission practice this appears inadequate.

The growing number of national antitrust authorities is the third development which affected the institutional structure in which Community antitrust law is applied. In the period in which the EEC Treaty and Regulation 17 were adopted there was no significant number of specialised antitrust agencies. Germany apart, the Member States lacked expertise and interest in antitrust law. Partly under influence of the growing relevance of Community antitrust law the situation changed. Most Member States adopted national antitrust laws or they significantly modified existing laws. In this process various Member States established specialised antitrust agencies or courts. Naturally, these new institutions look for ways to increase their influence on the process of European antitrust law deci-

---

[65] J.-F. Verstrynge, "Current Antitrust Policy Issues in the EEC: Some Reflections on the Second Generation of Competition Policy" in B. Hawk (ed.), *Annual Proceedings of the Fordham Corporate Law Institute 1985: Antitrust and Trade Policies in International Trade* (New York, Matthew Bender, 1986), 673–98 at 676–7.

sion-making, especially since the scope of Community antitrust law is so broad as to encompass many cases which are mainly of national relevance. In the existing institutional framework the Member States' authorities do not have a vital role in the decision-making process. Their role is limited to providing the Commission with their common opinion in the Advisory Committees on restrictive practices and mergers respectively (see further below).

The crititique of elements of the existing institutional framework should arguably be perceived with reference to these three developments. The first line of criticism, which reads that the Commission's administrative procedures are inappropriate for the determination of civil rights and obligations, finds its origin in the doctrine of direct effect. DG Competition and the European Commission as a whole lack the guarantees of independence and impartiality that can be expected from a tribunal which interprets the scope of private rights. The Court of First Instance judgment that Community antitrust law proceedings should guarantee "equality of arms", as well as the argument made in the literature that Community antitrust law procedures should, in accordance with Article 6 ECHR, provide for a fair and public hearing within a reasonable time by an independent and impartial tribunal, should be understood in that light. Current efforts to increase the transparency of procedures within DG Competition and to enhance the independence of the Hearing Officer are unlikely to bring the Community system in line with those requirements.[66] The second line of criticism concerns the lack of transparency within the current institutitional design. Since the Commission is exclusively responsible for all phases of the application of EC antitrust law the legal and political elements in antitrust law enforcement are blurred. The College of Commissioners combines the responsibility to assess whether an agreement causes a reduction of competition with the competence to judge—when it considers that a reduction of competition is generated—whether there are political reasons for deciding that the agreement is nevertheless compatible with the common market. It was demonstrated above that the fact that decisions reached in the different stages—(i) is competition reduced? and (ii) are there alternative policy reasons for tolerating the reduction of competition?—can not be retraced was seen to generate a lack of transparency.[67] That, in turn, reduces the Commission's accountability for the political choices it makes.

On the basis of these observations it is submitted that reform of EC antitrust law's institutional structure should be based on a separation of responsibility for the two stages in procedures.[68] The institution responsible for the first stage

---

[66] In this sense see also M. Levitt, "Commission Hearings and the Role of the Hearing Officer: Suggestions for Reform" (1998) 19 *ECLR* 404–8.

[67] Wilks and McGowan, above, n. 1, and Neven *et al*. above, n. 19.

[68] The Court of First Instance endorsed a perception of Community antitrust law enforcement being based on two stages explicitly in the context of Art. 81. It ruled that "[a]pplication of Article 85 [now Art. 81] involves two stages: a finding that Article 85(1) [now Art. 81] has been infringed followed, where appropriate, by exemption from that prohibition if the agreement, decision or concerted practice in question satisfies the conditions laid down in Article 85(3)": *Tetra Pak v. Commission*, above, n. 63, at para. 25.

examines whether the agreement, decision or concerted practice (or merger) at hand entails a reduction of competition. Only if competition is considered to be reduced will the case proceed to the next stage in which considerations of competition policy are weighed against other policy concerns. A political body should be responsible for the deliberation and decision in this second stage.

The institution responsible for the assessment of whether a particular agreement, decision or concerted practice infringes Community antitrust law should be an independent institution, ideally a court.[69] It would have competence to apply the Treaty's antitrust law provisions which have direct effect, possibly complemented by the power to assert the effects of mergers on competition. Such an adjustment would be appropriate in view of the nature of the directly effective antitrust law provisions as expounded by the Court of Justice. EC antitrust law confers individual rights and obligations. While generally in Europe private law rights are guaranteed by courts this is not yet the case for those rights stemming from EC antitrust law. While this structure may have been justified in the initial period of Community antitrust law in view of the comprehensive and combined nature of the assessment of the effect on trade between Member States which was assigned to the EC Commission, this is no longer so since the Court of Justice has ruled that the antitrust provisions confer private rights on individuals. In view of the extensive case law on the interpretation of those directly effective provisions it seems no longer warranted that the Commission should be responsible for taking decisions which affect those individual rights and obligations.[70]

Recent Court of Justice judgments which have reduced the scope of the prohibition formulated in Article 81(1) of the Treaty should in this respect be considered encouraging.[71] By limiting the need for exemption decisions—which in the present system can only be provided by the Commission—these judgments extend the potential for comprehensive judicial enforcement of Community antitrust law.[72] The system, thus adjusted, would still allow for both public and private enforcement action. The Commission's Directorate General for compe-

---

[69] A specialised chamber of the existing CFI could be an option. An alternative which has been proposed at several instances would be the creation of regional courts specialised in EC antitrust law. See, e.g., A. Riley, "More Radicalism, Please: The Notice on Cooperation Between National Courts and the Commission in Applying Articles 85 and 86 of the EEC Treaty" (1994) 15 *ECLR* 91–6. The fact that the creation of regional courts would increase the number of decision-making institutions will by itself enhance transparency and decentralised enforcement of Community antitrust law: E. Fox, "Decision Making at the Centre—Panel Discussion" in Ehlermann and Laudati, above, n. 24, 15.

[70] See the considerations in A. Fels, "Decision Making at the Centre—Working Paper III" in Ehlermann and Laudati (eds.), above, n. 24, 45–69 at 52.

[71] *Delimitis* v. *Henninger Bräu*, above, n. 62. See also the discussion in Ch. 3.

[72] To argue for increased judicial enforcement does not necessarily imply denial of the discretionary elements in the first phase of antitrust law decision-making. It is acknowledged that competition law is not "neutral", in the sense that economic law is never value-free. *Cf.* R. Whish and B. Sufrin, "Article 85 and the Rule of Reason" (1987) 7 *YEL* 1–38. Nevertheless courts are not incapable of employing the discretion: R. Pitofsky, "The Political Content of Antitrust" (1979) 127 *University of Pennsylvania Law Review* 1051–75.

tition matters could act as public prosecutor,[73] which would take special care of those interests which are likely to be under-represented in private enforcement action.[74] This could also form a way of solving a practical objection to the proposed system, namely that it will normally be impossible for private parties to obtain and present the relevant facts in complicated cases like major cartels and mergers.

Only where the tribunal concludes that competition is likely to be reduced or significantly impeded as a consequence of the agreement at issue will the procedure move into a second stage. In that stage it will have to be determined whether the anti-competitive agreement or merger should nevertheless be allowed because of its beneficial effects on policy areas other than that of competition. In this second phase it will therefore be determined whether there are political reasons for granting an exemption to the prohibition on reducing competition. Naturally, the institution which would be responsible for making the political judgement in the second phase should not be an "independent" agency. On the contrary, it should be a politically accountable body. The College of Commissioners might be an appropriate institution for this phase.[75] Since the Commission is at present responsible for the entire process through which antitrust law cases go it would of course imply that the institutional design for the second stage would basically remain the same. Nevertheless, the perceived transparency deficit would not occur in the new context. The lack of transparency in the current system springs from the absence of a division between the examination of the effects on competition and their compatibility with the Community's antitrust rules on the one hand, and the possibility of exempting agreements on the basis of other policy goals on the other. The structure here proposed contains a clear demarcation of the two stages, with the judiciary being responsible for the first test and the Commission for the political discretion implicit in the exemption decision.

While procedural transparency would therefore be ensured by the clear separation the problem that the Commission's political exemption practice remains uncontrolled would endure. This problem is related to the general democracy deficit of European Community governance. The uneven development of European integration, in which the continuing increase in political power at the executive European level is not matched by a similar relocation of control (majoritarian or other), is at the heart of the Community's weakness in this

---

[73] It would have a function similar to that of the US Federal Trade Commission. Settlements reached between the FTC and parties subject to an investigation need to be confirmed by a judge in the US system. See the remarks in "Panel Discussion—The Role of the Judge" in Ehlermann and Laudati (eds.), above, n. 24, 318. It would enhance transparency and accountability.

[74] D. Neven *et al.*, above, n. 19, at 11. Like those of shareholders of the companies concerned, consumers and employees.

[75] As the Community's supranational institution: Ehlermann, above, n. 48. Alternatively, the Council, with its clear political character and the accountability of its members to national parliaments, has been put forward as forming the appropriate institution. See the discussion in Bartodziej, above, n. 54. Cf. the slightly divergent model proposed in Sir Gordon Borrie, "Time for a Euro-MMC", *Financial Times*, 11 November 1991, 11.

respect. The European Parliament lacks legitimacy as the controlling body because it cannot be said to represent the European people. This is so mainly because in absence of a European *demos* there is no European-wide polity.[76] While this situation may change and a genuine European polity may emerge in due time to enhance the Parliament's legitimacy, it is not at all clear whether such a development would be desirable in view of the *sui generis* nature of the Community which is unlikely to develop into either a unitary state or a fully-fledged federation. The objections to the present system, with its democracy deficit, as well as the objections to the apparently simplest solution, expansion of the European Parliament's controlling powers, are well-known. As a consequence alternatives to majoritarian control which better reflect the specific character of European Community regulation have been developed.[77] The surge of independent agencies has been referred to above but it was concluded that such agencies would not provide the pertinent framework for taking the political decision in the second phase of antitrust law enforcement. The various committees which are active within Community decision-making procedures ("comitology") form an alternative to majoritarian control of the Commission's antitrust and merger decisions in the second phase.

The term "comitology" denotes a set of co-operative decision-making procedures typically involving Member States' representatives and experts which were devised in the course of the Community's development in order to control the delegation of the Council's powers to the Commission.[78] In particular it forms a counterweight to a concentration of uncontrolled power in the Commission in those policy areas in which centralised Community decision-making is required. Comitology procedures enable forms of joint decisions by the supranational and central Commission on the one hand and the inter-governmental bodies and dispersed Member States on the other. Moreover, it reduces the tension which exists between the Community's need for uniform rules guiding the internal market on the one hand and the continued Member State responsibility for the implementation of Community as well as their national policies on the other.[79] Comitology therefore strikes a balance between

---

[76] See the much more elaborate considerations in J. Weiler *et al.*, "European Democracy and Its Critique" (1995) 18 *West European Politics* 4 and I. Kielmansegg, "Integration und Demokratie" in M. Jachtenfuchs and B. Kohler-Koch (eds.), *Europäische Integration* (Opladen, 1996), 42–72.

[77] J. Weiler, "The State 'über alles'. Demos, Telos and the German Maastricht Decision" (1995) 1 *ELJ* 219–58 and Joerges, above, n. 72. See also R. Dehousse, "Constitutional Reform in the European Community. Are there Alternatives to the Majority Avenue?" (1995) 18 *West European Politics* 118–36.

[78] G. Majone, *Regulating Europe* (London, Routledge, 1996), 73. The comitology procedures can be seen to embody two distinct power-struggles: on the one hand that between the Commission and Council for the power to make implementing rules; and, on the other, that between Council and the European Parliament for the power to supervise the Commission: G. Edwards and D. Spence, *The European Commission* (Harlow, Longman, 1995), 121.

[79] The fact that Member States remain the main implementors of Community law and policy is the result of principled (i.e. subsidiarity) and practical (lack of manpower and expertise within the Commission) considerations. R Dehousse: "Regulation by Networks in the European Community: The Role of European Agencies" (1997) 4 *European Journal of Public Policy* 246–61.

the efficiency and effectiveness of central Commission decision-making and the need to ensure Member States' interests in that process.[80]

The relevance of the committee system was enhanced as a consequence of the new approach to legislation and harmonisation enhsrined in the Single European Act. The natural consequence of the preference for relatively broad framework directives was that the implementation process took on new significance. In anticipation of the expected increase in supervising duties the Member States added a third indent to Article 202 (ex Article 145) EC which provided that the Council would confer on the Commission powers for the implementation of the rules which the Council lays down. In spite of this provision, however, the power to implement Council legislation was not left to the Commission alone. In its original Comitology Decision the Council preserved significant powers to itself.[81] The amended decision of 1999 did not reduce the relative power of the Member States in the committees.[82]

The committees are chaired by a Commission official. The Commission submits the draft decision to the Committee and it determines the agenda.[83] The different comitology procedures vary most notably with respect to the degree of autonomy that the Commission enjoys in decision-making. In order of increasing Commission autonomy the three codified types of committee procedures are: (1) the regulatory committee procedure; (2) the management committee procedure; and (3) the advisory committee procedure.[84] Under the regulatory committee procedure the Commission can adopt a measure only when the relevant committee has adopted a favourable decision on the draft.[85] The second procedure, in which the management committee is involved, has the longest history and is typically employed within the day-to-day implementation of the decisions in the realm of the Common Agricultural Policy. If the management committee adopts by qualified majority an unfavourable opinion on a draft measure submitted by the Commission the decision-making power is referred back to the Council. In case that happens two variants exist within the management committee procedure. Under the first the Commission's draft decision may yet be adopted and it will enter into force immediately. Only if the Council itself rejects the Commission's decision by a qualified majority vote will the Commission's decision be annulled. The alternative is stricter. The Commission's decision is deferred and the Council has up to three months in which to reverse it,

---

[80] Edwards and Spence, above, n. 78, at 121–2.

[81] Council Decision 87/373/EEC of 13 July 1987 laying down the procedures for the exercise of implementing powers conferred on the Commission [1987] OJ L197/33). See C. Joerges and J. Neyer, "From Intergovernmental Bargaining to Deliberative Political Processes: The Constitutionalisation of Comitology" (1997) 3 *ELJ* 273–99.

[82] The new revised decision of 28 June 1999 was published in [1999] OJ L184/23.

[83] See generally, Edwards and Spence, above, n. 78, at 121–45.

[84] *Ibid.*

[85] There are two versions of the regulatory committee procedure. Under the first the Commission may adopt a measure with immediate effect as soon as the committee has adopted a favourable opinion on the basis of a qualified majority vote. Under the second procedure the Council can block the proposal by a simple majority. *Ibid.*, at 128.

again on the basis of a qualified majority vote. The third form of comitology, the advisory committee procedure, represents the highest degree of autonomy for the Commission. While the Commission does have to take careful account of the advisory committee's opinion it is in practice free to adopt its own draft in spite of objections of whatever magnitude from the advisory committee. There is no possibility for a referral to the Council.[86]

Perceiving the increased use of comitology procedures after the Single European Act as an outcome of power-conflicts between the Community and Member States is one way of looking at it, but a more positive approach to the phenomenon is also possible. The strength of the comitology concept lies in the co-operation between the various actors which are implied in regulatory decision-making because of their interest and/or expertise under co-ordination by the Commission. The thus established supranational networks permit extensive deliberation between experts and interested parties, like representatives of national ministries or agencies, which guide the Commission in its decision-making process. In a way this process of common decision-making at the supranational level is the Community's alternative to both the majoritarian control—which is problematic at the European level because of the problems associated with the European Parliaments legitimacy—and the independent agency model—which is problematic in those policy areas where conflicts between diverging policy values need to be solved on the basis of political processes.[87] Given the political nature of the second stage of antitrust policy decisions and the need to ensure the interests of Member States as well as the concerns of industry, consumers and employees, this specific form of supranational decision-making through the committees may provide an adequate alternative to the current system.

Comitology is of course not alien to Community antitrust law procedures because the existing institutional framework already features the Advisory Committee. Formally the Advisory Committee on Restrictive Practices and Monopolies can perhaps not be considered part of comitology since it cannot be said that the Commission is the delegee of rules which the Council has laid down with respect to the implementation of Articles 81 and 82 EC. But the Advisory Committee on Concentrations does fit into the general scheme, since, under the Merger Regulation, the powers for its implementation conferred on the Commission do constitute rules laid down by the Council.

It should be noted that there are more differences between the procedures of the two types of advisory committees active in the area of antitrust law. This reflects that the Advisory Committee on Concentrations was established after

---

[86] This procedure emphasises that resort to comitology, associated with increased control of Commission regulatory discretion, does not necessarily curb the Commission's powers. Typically the Commission consults parties. It presides over the debates and it may steer them as well as participate in them. Ultimately, it remains free to choose which ideas and proposals to back. It retains the power to take decisions: Majone, above, n. 78, at 73.

[87] See specifically on these issues Joerges and Neyer, above, n. 81.

the Council's 1987 Comitology Decision. There are two notable differences. First, contrary to the Advisory Committee on Restrictive Practices and Monopolies, the Advisory Committee on Concentrations may recommend publication of its opinion—which the Commission may act upon. However, the draft decision on which the opinion is based is not made public, which reduces the practical relevance of this small step toward transparency. Secondly, the Merger Regulation stipulates that the Commission shall take "the utmost account" of the opinion delivered by the Concentration Committee and it shall even inform the Committee of the manner in which its opinion has been taken into account. The Commission does not have similar duties under Regulation 17 with respect to the opinion delivered by the Advisory Committee on Restrictive Practices and Monopolies.

At first sight the advisory committee appears particularly fitting in the context of antitrust policy decision-making. It may again be repeated that Community antitrust law was initially perceived as the primary tool for preventing undertakings from hindering intra-Community trade. The allocation of primary implementing powers to the Commission was sensible in this perspective, and for policy areas most directly linked to internal market integration recourse to the advisory committee is considered to be the appropriate procedure.[88]

Yet it has been argued throughout this book that the nature of EC antitrust law changed and that the integration objective is no longer the exclusive or even the primary concern of antitrust law enforcement action. While the Commission holds a natural central position in the process through which the normative political decision is made at Community level it may be wondered whether the Community's central authority should be exclusively competent to make the political judgement. The problems perceived in relation to the Commission's political accountability reinforce that doubt.

It has been demonstrated, conversely, that forms of comitology can facilitate mediation between the various concerns of interested parties at the national as well as the supranational level.[89] In that light it may be queried whether the existing institutional design for the second stage of Community antitrust law enforcement might not be strengthened by having recourse to a type of committee procedure, different from the existing one, in which the political interests of the Member States are better represented in the decision-making process.[90] Though *ex post* political accountability of the Commission's antitrust policy would not increase the direct voice and influence which Member States would have on the exemptions based on non-competition policy objectives would ensure that the Commission takes the "utmost account" of the views of the Committee's members.

The alternative to the present advisory committee system, in which the Commission may be seen to hold too much uncontrollable power, would be

---

[88] Edwards and Spence, above, n. 78, at 124.
[89] Joerges and Neyer, above, n. 81 at the text following n. 22.
[90] Cf. the reference to competition policy comitology in Wilks, above, n. 18, at 171.

the management committee procedure. The management committee procedure originated in the context of the Common Agricultural Policy, a policy area as closely linked to the operation of the common market as antitrust policy. The management committees have proven to be particularly apt for policy areas which see day-to-day implementing decisions, which is also the case in antitrust policy enforcement.[91] The value of the management committee procedure is that it leaves the Commission a high degree of autonomy, in contrast to the regulatory committee, while at the same time it provides the opportunity for Member States and third parties with an interest to intervene where there are profound and widely shared objections to a proposed measure. Thus, a balance could be struck between competition policy concerns which are derived from the requirements of the internal market and further economic policy consideration of a general nature.[92] Constitutionally and institutionally, the Commission is responsible for the former area of policy. The Member States remain competent to pursue their specific economic policy interests. Thus, replacing the advisory committee procedure by the management committee procedure in the second stage of antitrust law decision-making would be in line with the specific character of European governance which features decisions and decision-making processes which can no longer be attributed to any singular body or level of government. The role of third parties could be further enhanced by introducing (in addition) alternative committee procedures which do not form part of the narrow concept of comitology which is restricted to the balance between the Commission and Member States. The Commission has set up many committees of interest groups and experts.[93] The mixture of expertise and representation of interests is reflected in the composition of these advisory committees. Undertakings, employees and consumers as well as scientific experts may sit in these committees. The mandate of such an advisory committee is restricted to informing the Commission of the views of these interest groups on issues arising from the operation of the Internal Market and in particular on draft decisions of the Commission. Such committees provide invaluable expertise to the Commission in policy areas in which the Commission, if only for its lack of manpower, does not have the required knowledge or resources to obtain the knowledge. Opinions expounded in these advisory committees by interest groups can give the Commission a first-hand impression of the views of interested parties. Though they are precluded from voting, all actors may present their views which will be transmitted to the Commission, and in certain circumstances also to the relevant committee. Although this type of advisory committee does exist in an informal form, wider use of the potential to hear direct views of interest groups would strengthen the decision-making process. Instead of the assumptions of consumer interest which now dominate the Commission's own deliberations on whether, for example, an exemption is in the interest of

---

[91] Edwards and Spence, above, n. 78, at 127.
[92] Joerges and Neyer, above, n. 81, at the text accompanying n. 54.
[93] See Edwards and Spence, above, n. 78, at 133.

consumers, direct consultation would enhance the legitimacy of those assumptions. Similarly, the potential for workers and consumers to ventilate their opinions in a formalised procedure could strengthen merger control decisions. An essential element in a system in which the management committee procedure (representing the Community–Member State balance) and an "advisory committee" procedure (in which interest groups could state their views) would consist of the widest possible publication of the relevant reports.[94]

Such a system would implement the principle of subsidiarity in the application of EC antitrust law. A spin-off advantage of a stronger committee network underpinning the Community's antitrust policy decisions would consist of the positive effects which regulatory networks usually generate. They provide the opportunity for extensive exchange of experts' views and thus allow for a degree of cross-fertilisation.[95] Moreover, with respect to antitrust law enforcement the intensified co-operation could promote further co-operation between national antitrust authorities *inter se* and between the Commission and national antitrust authorities which is widely held to be desirable.[96]

To be sure, several objections can be made to the arguments in favour of a management committee procedure replacing the advisory committee procedure in the area of antitrust law enforcement. It may for instance be submitted that the Merger Regulation was adopted as recently as 1989 and that in its context the advisory committee was nevertheless unanimously considered appropriate by the Council. If even the Member States represented in the Council accept that the Commission's merger policy is best guided by the advisory committee procedure it seems exaggerated to promote a procedure by which Council influence would be enhanced. However, counter-arguments to such a rejection of the idea of enlarging the scope of deliberative supranationalism in the area of antitrust policy can be found. In relation to the Merger Regulation it should first be remembered that it could only be adopted by the Council because it included extremely high jurisdictional thresholds. Thus, Member States ensured their national interests in a different manner.[97] Secondly, the Merger Regulation, which was adopted in 1989, that is at the height of the internal market programme, was directly linked to completion of the internal market. Like traditional Community antitrust law, Articles 81 and 82 EC, at the outset merger control was considered a functional competence allocated to the Commission in view of the requirements of the Internal Market.[98] Thirdly, the Merger Regulation appeared to adopt a pure competition test for the assessment of a merger's compatibility with the common market. In that perspective it was logical not to institutionalise direct influence from Member States and interest groups. In the meantime the case law of the Court of First Instance has revealed

---

[94]   Joerges and Neyer, above, n. 81, at the text preceding n. 82.
[95]   Dehousse, above, n. 97 and Majone, above, n. 78, at 273.
[96]   See for instance the Commission White Paper on Modernisation, above, n. 3.
[97]   Bulmer, above, n. 1, at 434. See also Edwards and Spence, above, n. 78, at 126.
[98]   Majone, above, n. 78, at 74–5.

that other than pure competition considerations can play a role in the assessment.[99] That reveals the political character of Community merger control policy which might be reflected in the institutional framework.

Another objection that could be made to enhancing Member State influence by increasing their role in the committee procedure is that the proposed change would imply a step back from the level of integration achieved. Less autonomy for the Commission implies reduced supranational decision-making and more Member State influence. It may be argued that such a step would be contrary to the aspiration of an ever closer union among the Member States. However, as discussed in Chapter 2, the trend discernible in the TEU is towards an increased role for Member States in European policy-making, the most noted manifestation being the introduction of the subsidiarity principle. This can take the form of decentralised policy-making at Member State level, but it can also be implemented by an enhanced role for Member States in decision-making processes at the Community level.

Still, practical problems would remain to be solved. In particular there is the problem of timing with respect to enforcement of private rights before courts in combination with the potential for exemption by the administration on public policy grounds. While the magnitude of that problem is not to be underestimated it may be noted that the present system suffers from the same problem. Various procedural devices limiting the potential for conflicting decisions which have been developed in the existing context could be further developed within the alternative system proposed.[100]

The value of the model proposed would lie in its contribution to solving the two most widely acknowledged institutional problems in the existing framework, that is, the problem of natural justice inherent in an administrative body's responsibility for prosecution and decision-making in increasingly adversarial proceedings, as well as the objection to the lack of transparency implicit in the amalgamation of two separate assessments in one institution, the College of Commissioners. The grounds for decisions presently muddled in intransparent procedures within one "administrative" institution would be clearly allocated to appropriate bodies. In line with Article 6 ECHR a judicial body would take up the responsibility for the "determination of civil rights and obligations or of any criminal charge".

The enhanced role for Member State authorities in the management committee procedure would remedy another fundamental flaw of the present system. The decision to declare a Treaty prohibition inapplicable to an agreement or to approve of a merger in view of extra-competition policy benefits is a political decision. In the present context there is no clear reason why the European Commission, an unaccountable administrative institution, should be exclusively competent to take those decisions. In view of the general Community

---

[99] See *Vittel* v. *Commission*, above, n. 51.
[100] See *Delimitis* v. *Henninger Bräu*, above, n. 62.

developments it is unlikely and perhaps undesirable that political accountability will be established at the Community level by enhanced majoritarian control. An enhanced role for Member State authorities in the second stage of antitrust law enforcement action could introduce an alternative way of controlling the Commission's political discretion.

As argued in the introduction to Part II there are obvious links between the institutional issues discussed in this chapter and the topics of the other chapters in this part. First, the limits to Community law's territorial jurisdiction need to be determined in order to make it possible for Member States to agree on the non-competition policy objectives which may be taken into account in the second phase of procedures. It is likely that this will be easier when it concerns problems of genuine European or supranational interest. Experience with the Merger Regulation appears to confirm that consensus on the application of Community antitrust law can be reached as long as the issues are commonly perceived as truly European and can therefore be solved only at the Community level. The contours of EC competition policy should be based on integration and maintenance of workable competition. Secondly, the management committee procedure strikes a balance between the requirements of the common market on the one hand and those of social and other specific national policies on the other. Thus, the institutional structure enables a new concept of the division of powers and competences to take shape. Rather than the conflictual model in which supremacy of EC law over national law was established the concept moves toward compatibility of EC and Member State laws, discussed in Chapter 4. Finally, increased transparency in EC antitrust law enforcement is also a prerequisite for effective co-operation between the various institutions implied in its enforcement, an issue discussed in Chapter 6.[101]

CONCLUSION

There are three different types of objections to the current procedural and institutional framework within which EC antitrust law is enforced. First, the combination of prosecution functions with adjudicatory functions within one and the same body seems irreconcilable with the ruling by the Court of First Instance that the principle of natural justice and procedural fairness implies that the principle of equality of arms should be respected in antitrust law cases. Secondly, the combined assessment by the College of Commissioners of the legal and of the political aspects is challenged. The case law of the European Courts illustrates that a full examination of the effects on competition is required in the context

---

[101] The EC Commission acknowledges that the essential prerequisite for decentralisation, in whatever form, is increased transparency with respect to Community antitrust law objectives and procedures: Commission of the European Community, *Twenty-First Annual Report on Competition Policy* (Brussels, 1991), paras. 66–8.

of Article 81(1). The possibility of declaring Article 81(1) inapplicable pursuant to Article 81(3) is a public policy exemption. Thirdly, the institutional system is affected by the gradual establishment of national antitrust authorities in all Member States. While the main role of these authorities is to enforce Community (and their national) antitrust law at a decentralised level, they also represent Member States' interests in Community antitrust law decision-making at the central level by way of their representation in the advisory committees. The Advisory Committee on Restrictive Practices and Monopolies, which is active in the areas of Articles 81 and 82 EC, plays an unclear role in antitrust law enforcement at the Community level. The growing importance of national representation in the decision-making process at Community level is only reflected in the enhanced prominence of the Advisory Committee on Concentrations, which was established along with the Community Merger Control Regulation. The opinions of the latter advisory committee may be published, the Commission is explicitly charged with taking careful account of the opinion delivered by the committee and it has a duty to inform the committee of the way in which its opinion has been taken into account. While the Commission's broad autonomous powers are somewhat controlled by the new role for the Advisory Committee regarding mergers the transparency of the decision-making is still limited.

Since ex-Commissioner Van Miert conceded that the institutional famework needed to be reformed, it appeared that the institutional reforms would form an important element in the Commission's plans to modernise the implementation of Community antitrust policy.[102] Yet the modernisation does not encompass the institutional structure at the Community level. Nevertheless this chapter argues that the procedural and institutional framework requires reform in view of general developments in EC law. In light of those developments this chapter has argued that the hitherto dominant proposal for the necessary reforms, establishing an independent European Cartel Office, does not constitute an adequate solution to the existing institutional and procedural problems. Events which followed formal achievement of the common market objective and the adoption of the Treaty on European Union confirm that the EC Treaty does not establish an economic constitution with a hierarchical superiority of free competition over other policy concerns. Alternatives to independence should therefore be sought to alleviate the tensions arising out of the current institutional pattern.

This chapter has suggested that the solution may be found in a separation of the judicial and political aspects of Community antitrust law. The Treaty provides directly effective rights which can be protected by national courts. In so far as these individual rights are concerned it seems appropriate to confer the competence to protect them on the judiciary. The Commission may still pursue antitrust policy in the public or Community interest on the basis of law enforce-

---

[102] Wilks and McGowan, above, n. 1, at 271ff.

ment, but instead of prosecuting and judging at the same time, the latter task should be allocated to an independent tribunal. Only thus can "equality of arms" and a decision by an impartial tribunal be guaranteed in the process of the determination of civil rights. A second institutional level should accomodate the potential for exempting certain agreements from the legal prohibition on restricting competition in view of its positive effects on alternative Community policies. Though the Commission could certainly maintain its central position in this process, the constitutional framework provided by the Treaty on European Union suggests that there should be room for the representation of third party interests. The existing management committee procedure seems to provide an adequate framework through which the weight of Member States' views may be elevated. Intensified participation of Member States in political decision-making at the Community level is the proper way to enhance the legitimacy of political decisions at the Community level within the framework of the Treaty on European Union.

6

Institutional Issues at the Decentral Level

INTRODUCTION

THE FOURTH and final issue addressed in this second part of the book is the co-operation between Community and Member State institutions in the enforcement of Community antitrust law. Co-operation between the Commission and national institutions which are empowered to enforce Articles 81 and 82 EC facilitates decentralised enforcement of EC antitrust law. A combination of factors turned decentralised enforcement of EC antitrust law into the most prominent element in the Commission modernisation plans. First, the European Courts handed down two judgments which underscored the potential for decentralised enforcement of Articles 81 and 82. The Court of Justice's judgment in *Delimitis* provided guidelines on the ways in which national court can enforce EC antitrust law in co-operation with the Commission.[1] Shortly after that judgment the Court of First Instance ruled in *Automec II* that complainants do not have an unqualified right to Commission action if they file a complaint. The Commission may set priorities in its enforcement action and accordingly it can decide, under conditions which the Court of First Instance defined, not to initiate proceedings with respect to alleged infringements of the antitrust provisions if they are of minor Community importance.[2]

Subsequently, the Commission issued two notices, the first on decentralised enforcement of Community antitrust law by national courts, the second on decentralised enforcement of Community antitrust law by national antitrust authorities.[3] Both notices clarify that Commission enforcement action should focus on cases which have particular Community interest. Simple cases which are of no particular economic, legal or political importance may be "decentralised" to national authorities.

---

[1] Case C–234/89 *Delimitis* v. *Henninger Bräu* [1991] ECR I–935.

[2] Case T–24/90 *Automec* v. *Commission* (*No. 2*) [1992] ECR II–2223. See now also Case C–119/97P *UFEX* [1999] ECR I–1341, discussed below.

[3] Commission Notice on co-operation between the Commission and national courts [1993] OJ C39/6 (hereafter "National courts Notice") and Commission Notice on co-operation between national competition authorities and the Commission [1997] OJ C313/3 (hereafter "National Authorities Notice").

Yet the clarification of Commisson priorities on the one hand and of the potential for decentralised enforcement of EC antitrust law on the other which the notices provided did not lead to enhanced decentralised enforcement. The Commission considers that the efforts to decentralise were unsuccessful because of the current legislative framework within which Articles 81 and 82 EC are applied. It considers that the rules implementing the Treaty's antitrust law provisions are no longer pertinent in the altered context within which Community antitrust law is enforced. In this light it based its most far-reaching proposals for modernising Community antitrust law, the White Paper on Modernisation of the Rules Implementing Articles 81 and 82 of the EC Treaty (the "White Paper"), on reform of the procedural framework, mainly Regulation 17/62.

This chapter reviews the decentralisation of EC antitrust law enforcement as the principal element of modernisation. Again the Commission plans are held up to comparison with the implications of the formal establishment of the internal market and the constitutional context provided by the TEU. Throughout this book formal establishment of the internal market was perceived as an illustration of the fact that the objectives of Community antitrust law moved away from the exclusive focus on promoting integration. The enforcement of EC antitrust law provisions is now primarily directed to achieving various economic and social policy objectives. Concurrently, and under the influence of Community antitrust law, most Member States have adopted antitrust laws of their own.

While the Commission now acknowledges the changed context within which Community antitrust law is applied,[4] and reference is made to these changes in the White Paper, it fails to make an explicit link between those changes and its proposals for reform. Instead the Commission plans are primarily based on the administrative capacity of the Commission on the one hand and the need for decisions and judgments on the basis of the current interpretation of Articles 81 and 82 on the other. Conversely, this chapter aims to approach the issue of co-operation between the Commission and national instituons on the basis of an examination of the implications of the transformation of EC antitrust law to which the Commission refers in the White Paper.

First the current framework in which decentralised enforcement takes place is set out. Then the Commission's initial efforts to decentralise part of its case load on the basis of the Notices are discussed (6.2). This leads to the White Paper and a discussion of the modernisation of EC antitrust law on the basis of decentralisation (6.3). These modernisation plans are then reviewed in the light of the constitutional framework provided by the TEU (6.4).

---

[4] *Cf.* R. Wesseling, "Subsidiarity in E.C. Antitrust Law: Setting the Right Agenda" (1997) 22 *ELRev.* 35–54.

6.1 CURRENT FRAMEWORK

Decentralised enforcement of Community antitrust law takes two forms. Articles 81(1) and 82 EC can be applied by national courts as well as by national antitrust authorities. While the principles which guide the way in which these institutions enforce EC antitrust law are very similar, there are notable divergencies with respect to the procedures. The differences are partly due to the difference in the legal basis for action of the respective institutions. National antitrust authorities find their competence to apply Community antitrust law in Articles 83 and 84 EC and Regulation 17. Courts apply Articles 81 and 82 EC on the basis of the direct effect of these provisions. This section presents the way in which national courts and national antitrust authorities enforce Community antitrust law.

6.1.1 National Courts

Since Articles 81 and 82 EC have direct effect, national courts may apply those provisions directly.[5] At present national courts may not provide exemptions on the basis of Article 81(3) EC. The competence to issue exemptions is reserved to the EC Commission. Nevertheless national courts can, and must, uphold the rights which parties derive from exemptions once granted to an agreement.[6] For agreements which fall within the terms of a block-exemption regulation this results from the general direct applicability and entirely binding nature of regulations pursuant to Article 249 EC (ex Article 189).[7] While there is no explicit ruling that the same is true for individual exemptions, it is reasonable to assume, as the Commission does, that national courts should adhere to the operative part of an individual exemption decision. This view also follows implicitly from the *Delimitis* judgment in which the Court of Justice underscored the need to avoid contradictory decisions by the Commission and national courts on the basis of EC antitrust law.[8] The Court advised national courts to stay proceedings if an agreement at issue in their view potentially qualifies for an exemption. *A fortiori* a national court should not deviate from an exemption which has

---

[5] Direct effect has been expressly granted to Art. 81(1) in Case 127/73 *BRT* v. *SABAM* [1974] ECR 51, to Art. 81(2) in Case 48/72 *Brasserie de Haecht* v. *Wilkin (No 2)* [1973] ECR 77, and to Art. 82 in *BRT* v. *SABAM* (above) and Case 155/73 *Sacchi* [1974] ECR 409.

[6] National courts are not bound by unofficial Commission decisions: Case C–31/80 *L'Oréal* v. *De Nieuwe AMCK* [1980] ECR 3775, paras 22–3 and Case 99/79 *Lancôme* v. *Etos* [1980] ECR 2511, at para. 11.

[7] See, with respect to EC antitrust law; Case 63/75 *Fonderies Roubaix-Wattrelos* v. *Fonderies Roux* [1976] ECR 111 at 118.

[8] It is questionnable whether the Commission has a similar duty with respect to previous judgments by national courts on the applicability of Art. 81(1) EC. See the "Irish Ice Cream" case discussed in M. Rowe, "Ice Cream: The Saga Continues" (1998) 19 *ECLR* 479–81.

already been issued by the Commission.[9] Where the Commission has issued an exemption for an agreement, national courts are therefore capable of delivering a judgment on the EC antitrust issues involved in a case. But even if there is no decision, courts can decide on the applicability of Article 81 EC in some situations.[10]

The difficulty in applying Article 81 EC at the national level is due to the contradiction which is implicit in the Article's wording and structure. On the one hand Article 81(2) EC declares that all agreements which fall within the scope of Article 81(1) EC are "automatically" void. On the other hand Article 81(3) EC provides that the provisions of Article 81(1) EC may be declared inapplicable under a number of conditions. There is obvious friction between the "automatic" nullity of agreements and the possibility of a discretionary exemption being granted to an agreement.[11] There is one way to conceal this friction and that is by deciding in one instance whether the agreement falls within Article 81(1) EC—and would therefore be void automatically—or whether the agreement qualifies for exemption. The time lag between the automatic nullity and the recovering of the agreement's validity on the basis of the exemption is thus not noticeable. The notification system enshrined in Regulation 17 is based on such a system. Exemptions can be granted only to agreements which have been notified. The exemption can take effect only from the date of notification. The fiction thus created is that the questions whether it falls within Article 81(1) EC and whether the agreement qualifies for an exemption are answered at the same time, i.e. at the time of notification.

In the case of decentralised enforcement of Article 81 EC the friction cannot be concealed. National courts may apply only Article 81(1) EC—not Article 81(3). If a national court finds than an agreement falls within Article 81(1) EC the assessment terminates there. A national court cannot conceal the split between the automatic nullity and the possibility of obtaining an exemption. Where a national court therefore judges that an agreement falls within Article 81(1) EC it should stay procedings in order to examine whether an exemption may be provided.[12]

---

[9] See National Courts Notice, above, n. 3 and *Delimitis*, above, n. 1.

[10] With respect to the direct applicability of Art. 82 EC there is no difficulty at all because national courts may judge that an abuse of dominant position occurrs irrespective of possible future Commission action with respect to the same behaviour—although national courts must of course avoid the possibility of contradictory decisions on the basis of the principles set out in *Delimitis*.

[11] This ambivalence forms one part of the "double legal compromise" which Lagrange AG identified with respect to Reg. 17 and Art. 81 EC. That is the compromise between "the doctrine of '*l'exception legale*', which is the only one wholly compatible with the principle of automatic nullity contained in Article 85(2), and the doctrine of 'constitutive effect' which as in German law, should logically be accompanied by a power given to the cartel authorities to 'declare ineffective' . . . agreements contrary to the law—which involve a concept very different from automatic nullity". See Lagrange AG's Opinion in Case 13/61 *De Geus* v. *Bosch* [1962] ECR 45, at 69.

[12] The situation is different with respect to "old" agreements (agreements which existed before the Rome Treaty came into force) which have subsequently been notified to the Commission. They enjoy provisional validity under Art. 81 unless and until the Commission has decided otherwise. National courts should therefore treat "old" agreements as valid under EC antitrust law: *Lancôme* v. *Etos*, above, n. 6 and Case C–1/70 *Rochas* v. *Bitsch* [1970] ECR 515.

While this certainly creates problems in a number of cases, national courts can still reach a final judgment in some of these situations. The reason is that not all agreements are exemptable on the basis of Article 81(3) EC. Most notably, to be exemptable an agreement must typically have been notified to the Commission. National courts which find that an agreement which was not notified to the Commission fulfils the conditions of Article 81(1) EC may declare that agreement void on the basis of Article 81(2) EC. As has been seen, a national court can also apply block-exemption regulations. Courts can therefore reach final judgments with respect to agreements which fall within the terms of such regulations. Only in the situations in which none of these conditions applies will national courts meet an obstacle to rendering a final judgment in the case before it. While a national court may then adopt interim measures or stay proceedings while awaiting a Commission decision on the exemption question it cannot deliver a final judgment.

The above depiction of the competence of national courts to apply EC antitrust law sets out the formal legal situation. In practice there are margins, developed by the Court of Justice, within which national courts are capable of rendering final judgments. The Court of Justice has ruled that national courts may under certain circumstances deviate from the formal division of competences. Accordingly, national courts may declare a duly notified agreement void if it falls within Article 81(1) of the Treaty and it is patently obvious that that agreement will not qualify for a Commission exemption on the basis of Article 81(3).[13] Under such a procedure the Court does not actually apply Article 81(3) EC. It simply rules out the Commission providing an exemption for the agreement. The reverse, however, is not allowed. A national court may not speculate in a positive manner on the possibility that the Commission will grant an exemption to an agreement which it considers to fall within Article 81(1) EC. The public policy element in exemptions to the antitrust law prohibition prevents national courts from issuing pseudo-exemptions. Similarly, national courts cannot extend the scope of a block-exemption regulation.[14]

6.1.2 National Antitrust Authorities

Contrary to the situation for national courts, which apply the antitrust rules on the basis of their direct effect, national antitrust authorities derive their competence to apply Community antitrust law from specific provisions in the Treaty. Article 85(2) EC provides that the Commission may authorise Member States to take measures needed to remedy antitrust law infringements. Further, on the basis of Article 83 EC the Council adopted Regulation 17. Article 9(3) of that Regulation provides that authorities of the Member States are competent to apply Articles 81(1) and 82 EC provided that Commission has not initiated

---

[13] *Delimitis* v. *Henninger Bräu*, above, n. 1, at para. 50.
[14] *Delimitis* v. *Henninger Bräu*, above, n. 1, at para. 55.

proceedings.[15] Like national courts, national authorities are not competent to provide exemptions on the basis of Article 81(3) EC. Article 9(1) of Regulation 17 grants sole power to the Commission to issue exemptions.

Before Member State authorities are able to make proper use of their capacity to apply Articles 81(1) and 82 EC implementing legislation has to be adopted at the national level.[16] The Commission successfully promotes adoption of appropriate implementing laws by the Member States.[17] So far eight Member States have adopted the required legislation.[18] The remaining states may be considered committed to doing the same. Article 10 EC is regularly referred to as the basis for the duty of Member States to enable national antitrust authorities to enforce Community competition law effectively. A basis for this duty can also be found in the Court of Justice ruling that national arrangements taken as a whole must be sufficiently effective to enable national authorities to apply EC law correctly and effectively.[19]

If the required national implementing legislation is adopted national antitrust authorities, like national courts, do not experience prohibitive difficulties in the application of Articles 81(1) and 82 EC. They can prohibit an agreement or type of behaviour when they consider it to fall within the terms of those prohibitions. The difficulties which arise as a consequence of national antitrust authorities' inability to provide exemptions are reduced in the same practical manner as with respect to national courts. Agreements which have not been notified to the Commission cannot qualify for an exemption. National antitrust authorities may also consider the block-exemption regulations in force and conclude that

---

[15] For those fields of the economy for which there are no implementing measures equivalent to Reg. 17, national authorities derive their competence to apply Community antitrust law (including Art. 81(3)) from Art. 84 EC. A number of airline alliances were examined by the Commission and national authorities in parallel within the framework of Arts. 84 and 85 EC. See Commission of the European Community, *Twenty-Sixth Annual Report on Competition Policy—1996*, 323–7 and on the treatment by the Commission: [1998] OJ C239/5 and C239/10.

[16] But see J. Temple Lang, "Community Antitrust Law: Compliance and Enforcement" (1981) 18 *CMLRev* 335–62 who argues that national legislation is not required. The viability of Temple Lang's position ultimately depends on the judgment of the respective national courts. In the UK the lack of national implementing legislation obstructed decentralised enforcement by the national authority: C. Kerse, "Enforcing Community Competition Policy under Articles 88 and 89 of the E.C. Treaty—New Powers for U.K. Competition Authorities" (1997) 18 *ECLR* 17–23. The new UK Competition Act 1998 does not provide for the possibility of decentralised enforcement of EC antitrust law by national authorities. Similarly, the competent German court (Berlin Kammergericht) denied Bundeskartellamt competence to apply Community antitrust law provisions in the absence of an explicit authorisation provision in the relevant German law: the *"Landegebühren"* Decision of 4 November 1988, reported in WuW/Entscheidungssammlung OLG 4291. The decision induced reforms in German competition laws in the fifth amendment of the *Gesetz gegen Wettbewerbsbeschränkungen ("5. GWB-Novelle")*. The GWB now confers explicitly on the Bundeskartellamt the right to employ the instruments of national antitrust law when applying EC antitrust law.

[17] See Commission of the European Community, *Twenty-Sixth Annual Report on Competition Policy—1996*, at 26.

[18] See J. Temple Lang, "General Report" at 1998 FIDE Congress: *Application of Community Competition Law on Enterprises by National Courts and National Authorities.*

[19] Case C–8/88 *Germany* v. *Commission* [1990] ECR I–2321.

an agreement which falls within the Article 81(1) prohibition profits from such a regulation.

It is more difficult, however, to circumvent the problems arising from the Commission's exemption monopoly in proceedings before national authorities than it is with respect to national court procedures. This derives from the divergencies in the respective forms of concurrent jurisdiction. Contrary to national courts, which remain competent to apply the antitrust provisions if the Commission initiates proceedings *vis-à-vis* the same agreement, the competence of national authorities ends whenever the Commission initiates proceedings with respect to the same case.[20] Staying procedures until the Commission has taken a decision is therefore not a viable route for national antitrust authorities. The Commission has to initiate procedures in the sense of Article 9(3) of Regulation 17 in order to be able to take a decision on the exemptability of the agreements at issue. At that point the national antitrust authorities lose their competence to apply Community antitrust law. The procedural design set out by the Court in *Delimitis* for national courts to deal with cases in which an agreement may be exemptable is therefore of little relevance to national antitrust authorities which intend to apply EC antitrust law.

The fact that the Commission can terminate antitrust action by national antitrust authorities on the basis of EC law is one explanation for the observation that national authorities have seldom applied EC antitrust law.[21] The lack of guarantees for national authorities that they will be able to bring a case to an end emerged most clearly on one of the few occasions on which a national antitrust authority intended to prohibit an agreement on the basis of Article 81(1) EC. Before the (German) national authority was able to take a final decision declaring the agreement under scrutiny incompatible with Article 81(1) EC the parties notified the agreement to the Commission which initiated proceedings. These proceedings led to a Commission exemption for the agreement.[22]

The inability to provide an exemption where required and the danger that they will lose competence upon a Commission decision to initiate procedures in the same case has discouraged national antitrust authorities from applying Community antitrust law. Further, there is still a significant number of the Member States antitrust authorities which do not hold the required implementing powers.

As a consequence, national antitrust authorities tend to rely on their national antitrust laws under which no danger exists that the Commission will take on

---

[20] Art. 9(3) of Reg. 17. The Commission is considered to initiate a procedure through an "authoritative act" demonstrating its intentions to take a decision under Arts. 81 and 82 EC: *Brasserie de Haecht* v. *Wilkin-Janssens*, above, n. 5.

[21] See U. Zinsmeister, E. Rikkers and T. Jones, "The Application of Articles 85 and 86 of the E.C. Treaty by National Competition Authorities" (1999) 20 *ECLR* 275–9 and A. Klimisch and B. Krueger, "Decentralised Application of EC Competition Law Current Practice and Future Prospects" (1999) 24 *ELRev* 463–82.

[22] Decision of the Commission regarding the request for exemption of the Volkswagen/Ford joint-venture for multi-purpose vehicles in Portugal; [1993] OJ L20/14.

the case after substantial efforts on the part of the national authorities. By operating on the basis of national law they also circumvent the problem with respect to exemptions. The Commission's broad interpretation of the scope of Article 81(1) of the Treaty commands exemption decisions in a high proportion of cases. Since national authorities cannot provide exemptions their procedures on the basis of Article 81 EC often end in the exemption-monopoly deadlock.

Despite the possibility that Community antitrust law may be applied before national courts and authorities, the EC Commission is therefore the sole institution which actively enforces Articles 81 and 82 EC within the current legislative framework.

6.2 THE FIRST ATTEMPT TO DECENTRALISE: THE COMMISSION NOTICES

The previous section sketched the legal background against which the Commission issued two notices on decentralised enforcement of the Community antitrust rules. The first is the Notice on co-operation between national courts and the Commission in applying Articles 81 and 82 of the Treaty, issued in 1993. The second is a similar notice focused on co-operation with national competition authorities which was adopted in 1997.[23] The notices sketch the circumstances under which national authorities are practical alternatives to the Commission as enforcement agencies. The Commission hoped that the Notices would raise the awareness of European companies that national institutions may apply Community antitrust law. Increased awareness might then boost the number of cased decided on the basis of EC antitrust law. Thus the effectiveness of the Treaty's antitrust rules would be enhanced. Moreover, increased decentralised enforcement would enable the Commission to establish priorities among antitrust cases. Cases with insufficient "Community interest" would be dealt with at the national level. The Commission's broad interpretation of the Treaty's antitrust law prohibitions generates a scope for Community antitrust law which is so vast as to render it impossible for the Commission to take decisions in even a fraction of the cases. As a consequence and in combination with other procedural features, such as the duty to notify and the burdensome process required for taking formal decisions, a backlog of cases persists within the Commission's offices.

6.2.1. The National Courts Notice

In addition to sketching the way in which national courts can apply Community antitrust law and expressing the Commission's intention of establishing enforcement priorities, the National Courts Notice had two aims. It communicated the Commission's vision of the type of remedies which should be available before national courts and it sketched the forms of co-operation which the

---

[23] Above, n. 3.

Commission envisaged between itself and national courts which apply Community antitrust law.

To start with the first element, the notice reiterates the divergent ways in which the Commission and national courts exercise their powers. The Commission operates within the framework of Regulation 17, whereas national courts enforce Community antitrust law in private disputes in the context of their national procedural law. Citing the *Rewe* judgment, the National Courts Notice states that in spite of the fact that private parties can rely upon EC law directly before their national courts it was not the intention of the drafters of the Treaty to create new remedies in those courts to ensure the observance of Community law. Nevertheless, in order for Community law to be effective, individuals and companies bringing cases on the basis of that law must have access to all procedural remedies provided for by national law on the same conditions as would apply if a comparable breach of national law were involved. "Consequently, it is the right of parties subject to Community law that national courts should take *provisional measures*, that an effective end should be brought, by *injunction*, to the infringement of Community competition rules of which they are victims, and that *compensation* should be awarded for the damage suffered as a result of infringements, where such remedies are available in proceedings relation to similar national law".[24] The availability of these remedies should in the Commission's view ensure the effectiveness of national courts when dealing with EC antitrust law issues. Indeed the section on remedies led the Commission to argue that there are significant advantages for undertakings in national procedures, in particular the possibilities to have compensation for damages awarded, to obtain interim relief, to combine claims on the basis of Community law with claims under national law and to have the legal costs awarded in case of success.[25]

The other main theme of the National Courts Notice concerned the patterns of co-operation which the Commission conceived between itself and national courts. The notice recalled the guiding principles which the Court pronounced in *Zwartveld*. The Commission has a duty of sincere co-operation *vis-à-vis* judicial authorities of the Member States which are responsible for ensuring that Community law is applied and respected in the national legal system.[26] The Notice then restated the Commission's intention to work towards closer co-operation with national courts in order to guarantee the strict, effective and

---

[24] National Courts Notice, above, n. 3, at para. 11 (emphases added). This can now be considered a conservative standpoint on the nature of the remedies available before national courts. See Case C–231/89 R v. *Secretary of State for Transport, ex parte Factortame (No. 1)* [1990] ECR I–2433 where the ECJ ruled that procedural restrictions on the availability of particular remedies must be disapplied if this is required to ensure the full effect of Community law and Case C–271/91 *Marshall v. Southampton and South West Hampshire Area Health Authority (Teaching)* [1993] ECR I–4367 where it was decided that restrictions on the amount of compensation provided for under national law may not be applied where this leads to depriving parties of compensation and an effective remedy.

[25] National Courts Notice, above, n. 3, at para. 16.

[26] Case C–2/88 Imm. *Zwartveld* [1990] ECR I–3365, at para. 18.

consistent application of Community antitrust law—while allowing the Commission time to pay more attention to its administrative priorities. To this end the Commission summed up the ways in which it can provide information to national courts upon their request and within the limits of national procedural law. In addition to overviews of the general corpus of Court of Justice case law, Commission decisions and secondary legislation, like block-exemption regulations, the Commission may provide specific information relevant to the case before the national court. It may inform the national court on procedural matters, for instance on whether the Commission has already taken a decision with respect to the agreement at issue or intends to do so. If the Commission is handling the case it may indicate how much time is likely to be required before a final decision will be reached. Secondly, the Commission suggested that it would advise on points of law. In what may be considered an informal preliminary reference type of process, the Commission held itself available for consultation on its practice with respect to the interpretation of the effect on trade between Member States criterion and with respect to the appreciability of a given restriction of competition. Thirdly, and finally, the Commission stated that national courts may request information from the Commission regarding factual data in so far as the required information is already at the disposal of the Commission and the Commission is permitted to communicate the data in view of, in particular, the rules on confidentiality.

In essence the National Courts Notice therefore repeated and clarified the pattern of co-operation between national courts and the Commission as it was defined by the Court of Justice in *Delimitis*. A national court which is uncertain whether a particular agreement will obtain an exemption from the antitrust law prohibition may stay procedings while awaiting a Commission decision with respect to the same subject matter. The notice aimed to further the effectiveness of co-operation by providing for less time-consuming and less formal ways of obtaining the Commission's view on a particular matter.

6.2.2. The National Authorities Notice

Many of the issues which were considered with respect to the Commission's Notice on co-operation with national courts in applying Articles 81 and 82 recur under the co-operation procedures between the Commission and national antitrust authorities. This could be expected since most of the problems which face national institutions in the enforcement of Community antitrust law can be retraced to the structure of Article 81 EC. Nonetheless, there are substantial procedural differences between the two forms of co-operation.

In the Commission's view national antitrust authorities, like the Commission—but contrary to national courts, apply the Community antitrust rules primarily for general public interest purposes. The framework within which they perform this task under Regulation 17 was set out in the previous section. The National Authorities Notice started from the assumption that duplication of checks on compliance with the Community competition rules should be avoided as far as possible and that Articles 81 and 82 EC should therefore be applied by a single authority. Where appropriate cases could still be handled on a joint basis by two national authorities but "one-stop-shop" procedures are preferred in view of the advantages which they generate for European business.[27] A particular advantage of national antitrust authorities is that they can provide a one-stop-shop even for those cases which are based partly on national law and partly on EC law. In such cases the Commission considers it preferable that national authorities apply their national law in combination with Community law, instead of referring the EC law elements to the Commission. The guidelines set out in the National Authorities Notice should prevent inconsistent or conflicting decisions being taken by the various competent authorities. In contrast to the National Courts Notice which provided guidelines for national courts which deal with cases that might at the same time be subject to Commission investigations the National Authorities Notice aimed to prevent parallel procedures.

The Commission acknowledges that the potential for decentralised enforcement by national antitrust authorities is essentially limited to restrictions of competition which in view of their effect on trade between Member States are prohibited by Community antitrust law but which nevertheless essentially concern the territory of one Member State. Thus, the criteria which the Commission takes into account in allocating cases between itself and Member States' authorities relate primarily to the effects and to the nature of the restriction of competition. Irrespective of the territorial spread of the effects, the Commission announced that it will continue to take on cases which display particular Community interest from an economic and legal point of view.

The Commission differentiated in the envisaged forms of co-operation between cases which are based on complaints and those which arise from notification combined with a request for negative clearance or exemption. It stated that complaints which do not demonstrate sufficient Community interest would be rejected. The Commission acknowledged that it may reject complaints only under a number of conditions defined by the Court of First Instance.[28] The Commission announced that it intended to reject complaints in cases which fulfil these criteria and to refer them to the national authority of the Member State in which the centre of gravity is located. When thus referring a case, the Commission would place the relevant documents in its possession at the national authority's disposal. Crucially, however, the national authorities are not entitled to use those documents as evidence in their own proceedings in so far as that evidence concerns unpublished information contained in replies to Commission requests for information or information obtained in the context of

---

[27] National Authorities Notice, above, n. 3, at para. 4.
[28] These criteria were subsequently refined by the ECJ in *UFEX*, above, n. 2. See also below.

Commission inspections carried on the basis of its powers stemming from Regulation 17.[29] With respect to notifications which typically consist of a request for negative clearance or alternatively exemption from the antitrust law prohibitions there is no room for decentralised enforcement or co-operation with national antitrust authorities. The Commission's exclusive competence to provide exemptions confers on the applicant for an exemption the right to obtain from the Commission a decision on the substance of his request.[30] In situations where national authorities handle antitrust law cases on the basis of EC law on their own initiative the same pattern of co-operation applies as between the Commission and national courts. The Commission announced itself available to provide information on points of law, procedure and fact which it also provides to national courts.

An innovative element in the National Authorities Notice is the special treatment of "dilatory" notifications. The Commission acknowledges the right of firms which notify their agreements to the Commission with a view to obtaining an exemption to a decision on the substance of their requests. However, if the Commission were to take the view that such notification is chiefly aimed at suspending procedures initiated by national authorities on the basis of Community or national antitrust law it would consider itself justified in not examining the notification as a matter of priority—in spite of its exclusive competence to provide the exemption and the consequent duty to provide a reasoned decision. The Commission examines the matter on a preliminary basis in order to come to a provisional opinion on the likelihood of an exemption being granted. If it were to conclude that an exemption was highly unlikely the Commission would communicate this to the relevant national authority and the notifying party. At the same time it would revoke the immunity from fines which the parties ensure for themselves by notifying the agreement on the basis of Article 15(5) of Regulation 17. The Commission advises that the national antitrust authority may then proceed towards a prohibition decision on the basis of Community or national antitrust law in spite of the formal application for exemption being still pending. If, conversely, the national authority upon further investigation does not agree with the Commission's provisional conclusion that the agreement does not qualify for exemption it should contact the Commission. The Commission may then decide whether or not to take the case out of the hands of the national authority. It committed itself to do so only in "quite exceptional circumstances".

---

[29] This fundamental impediment to swift co-operation and referral of cases from the Commission to national antitrust authorities stems from the ECJ's judgment in the "*Spanish Banks*" case: Case C–67/91 *Dirección General de Defensa de la Competencia* v. *Asociación Española de Banca Privada and others* [1992] ECR I–4785. But see with respect to national courts Case T–30/90 *SEP* v. *Commission* [1991] ECR II–1497, upheld on appeal in Case C–36/92 P *SEP* [1994] ECR I–1914.

[30] Case C–282/95 P *Guérin Automobiles* [1997] ECR I–1503 and Joined Cases T–213/95 and T–18/96 *SCK and FNK* v. *Commission* [1997] ECR II–1739.

The Notices thus revealed that there is more room for genuine interaction and dialogue in the co-operation between national antitrust authorities and the Commission than there is in co-operation between the Commission and national courts. This may be considered an advantage of decentralised enforcement before those authorities. Disadvantages arise from the relatively narrow margins for information-sharing between the Commission and national authorities and the automatic termination of the competence of national antitrust authorities to apply Community antitrust law when the Commission initiates proceedings with respect to the same subject matter.

6.2.3. Effects of the Notices

The Notices attracted much academic attention and thus fulfilled at least one of the Commission objectives.[31] The Commission's intention of enhancing the effectiveness of Community antitrust law was generally appreciated. In particular the efforts to reduce the backlog of cases were endorsed. But overall scepticism prevailed in view of the systematic obstacles to effective enforcement of Article 81 EC by institutions other than the Commission. Three central aspects of the decentralisation notices (enhancing the effectiveness of EC antitrust law, decentralisation of cases without sufficient Community interest and promoting co-operation between the Commission and national authorities) were subject to criticism.

Decentralisation of EC antitrust law enforcement is founded on the belief that national authorities provide an adequate alternative to the Commission as administrators. This belief is not unanimously shared and annotations of the notices have stressed a series of problems which are likely to occur more or less frequently when Community antitrust law is enforced at the national level. With respect to national courts the focus has been on the problems which individuals may encounter when they bring their EC antitrust law case before a local court. The first hurdle which has been identified is that of jurisdiction. In view of the cross-border aspect of the case which is itself a precondition for the applicability of EC antitrust law problems of jurisdiction are likely to arise. The Commission considers that the Brussels Convention on jurisdiction and enforcement of judgments in civil and commercial matters applies to Community competition law but that opinion remains contested.[32] If the Convention does not apply, parties which intend to bring a case before a national court will have to consider carefully where to bring it. It is therefore not

---

[31] See the bibliography annexed to the Bundeskartellamt's "*Arbeitsunterlage für die Sitzung des Arbeitskreises Kartellrecht*", available from the Bundeskartellamt's website; http://www.bundeskartellamt.de/

[32] Brussels Convention of 27 September 1968 [1978] OJ L304/77. See National Courts Notice, above, n. 3, at para. 44. Contrary, V. Power, "Competition Law in the EU: Should there be a Convention?" (1995) 16 *ECLR* 75–7.

at all clear that, in comparison with lodging a complaint at the Commission, the implementation level "closer to the citizen" is advantageous to private plaintiffs.

Once the first obstacle to bringing a case before the court is overcome the next problem with respect to private actions on the basis of EC antitrust law arises. It is related to obtaining the necessary factual evidence. Evidence in antitrust law cases is typically based on internal business documents the unavailability of which may well be prohibitive to the bringing of an action before a national court. In contrast to the Commission which has broad powers under Regulation 17 to request information from undertakings and which may have recourse to involuntary investigations private parties do not have discovery powers under Community law. The magnitude of the problem is again significantly expanded in view of the necessarily cross-border nature of the agreement and therefore of the evidence.

Thirdly, a potential problem arises with respect to the remedies available before national courts. Commentators argue that it is questionable whether all remedies which the Commission considers to be available before national courts can indeed be obtained in private antitrust actions. In particular, it is not evident that compensation for damages and interim relief can be secured before courts in all the Member States.

Finally, if the first three hurdles have been taken and a judgment is handed down by a national court the problem of enforceability arises. Again the transnational character of Community antitrust law creates a problem at the national level. Somewhat like the considerations with respect to the jurisdiction question, applicability of the Brussels Convention would provide some relief.

Most commentators were not convinced that undertakings would rationally opt for bringing a private case under these uncertain and often unfavourable conditions where they might also have recourse to the administrative procedure of the Commission. The advantage alluded to by the Commission in the National Courts Notice, that a plaintiff's costs may be awarded by a national court whereas this is impossible with respect to Commission procedures, is generally not considered to provide a decisive incentive to undertakings to bring a case before a court. An important reason is that the relative advantage of lodging a complaint with the Commission is that it is practically costless. In response to the problems foreseen for companies in bringing private suits it should be noted however that the problem of remedies is perhaps overestimated in view of the case law of the Court of Justice. As a matter of EC law effective enforcement remedies should be available before Member State courts.[33] In the same way the

---

[33] See, for instance, the discussion of the UK situation in B. Rodger and A. MacCulloch, "Community Competition Law Enforcement—Deregulation and Re-Regulation: The Commission, National Authorities and Private Enforcement" (1998) 4 *CJEL* 579–612 at pp. 597–600. Temple Lang has consistently argued that these remedies must be available before national courts on the basis of their duties under Community law, irrespective of national procedural laws. See, e.g., J. Temple Lang, "The Duties of National Courts under Community Constitutional Law" (1997) 22 *ELR* 3–18 and "The Duties of National Authorities under Community Constitutional Law" (1998) 23 *ELR* 109–31.

problems concerning the collection of the necessary evidence may be alleviated by the Community judiciary. The Court of First Instance's *Postbank* judgment reduced the burden on private parties producing evidence by ruling that companies which receive information from the Commission may disclose that information in national court procedures.[34]

Another concern in relation to the Commission notices is that of the uniform application of EC law. A degree of diversity on the basis of the diverging procedural law will remain in spite of the minimum degree of remedies which should be available under EC law.[35] In national procedures standards of proof differ and remedies will also differ among courts in the various Member States. Although a degree of diversity does not necessarily impede uniform application of Community antitrust law to such an extent as to be incompatible with the idea of a common market, the danger for forum shopping is apparent. Such a process may reduce the effectiveness of Community antitrust law.[36]

The second strand of criticism pertains to the concept of decentralisation itself. As explained above the Commission's move towards enhanced national implementation of Community antitrust law is founded on a division between cases which fall within the scope of Community antitrust law and which are of "Community interest", on the one hand, and those which fall within the scope of Community antitrust law but are not of sufficient concern to the Community to justify action, on the other. Community interest in the Commission's view exists where cases have particular political, economic or legal significance to the Community. The Commission further considers that there is insufficient Community interest when plaintiffs are able to secure adequate protection of their rights before national courts or authorities. Though objections have been raised to both criteria, particularly to their ambiguous and discretionary character, commentators have focused on the question of what constitutes "adequate" protection. They have pointed to the difficulties which arise in the interpretation of what constitutes "adequate" protection and the way in which the Commission will assess whether individual rights are indeed adequately protected.[37]

Some of the doubts were however dispelled by the clarifications which the Court provided in the numerous judgments on the rejection of complaints, initiated in the aftermath of the National Courts Notice.[38] In particular, the Court ruled on the

---

[34] Case T–353/94 *Postbank* v. *Commission* [1996] ECR II–1141.

[35] The Court's recent *Van Schijndel* judgment, for instance, demonstrates that at least one element of competition law procedures before national courts will continue to differ. The duty for national judges to raise points of Community law on their own initiative depends on national procedural law. Only where it is the court's normal role to raise issues of law which have not been submitted by parties to the procedure is the national court held to do so: Joined Cases C–430 & 431/93 *Van Schijndel* [1995] ECR I–4705.

[36] Rodger and MacCulloch, above, n. 33, at 600.

[37] B. Rodger, "Decentralisation and National Competition Authorities: Comparison with the Conflicts/Tensions under the Merger Regulation" (1994) 15 *ECLR* 251–4 and S. Weatherill, "Annotation of Case C–415/93 *Bosman*" (1996) 33 *CMLRev* 991–1033 at 1025.

[38] In addition to the cases mentioned below, see Case C–19/93 *Rendo* [1995] ECR I–3319; Case T–114/92 *BEMIM* [1995] ECR II–147; Case T–5/93 *Tremblay I* [1995] ECR II–185; Case T–224/95

specific duties of the Commission in these procedures. The Commission's test cannot be limited to a formal reference test. The Commission must examine whether adequate protection for individual rights is guaranteed in proceedings before national authorities.[39] Moreover, in setting priorities the Commission may not exclude in principle dealing with cases on the basis of the observation that the complainant is capable of bringing an action before national courts or authorities. Within its competence under EC antitrust law the Commission is required to assess how serious the alleged interferences with competition are and how persistent their consequences are. "That obligation means in particular that it must take into account the duration and extent of the infringements complained of and their effect on the competition situation in the Community".[40] The Commission must exercise a certain degree of care and diligence in its examination. In this process the Commission has to take into account the specific aspects of the case by examining carefully the facts and points of law brought to its notice by the complainant in order to decide whether they disclose conduct liable to distort competition in the internal market and affect trade between Member States.[41] A complainant has to have the opportunity to communicate its views to the Commission and he is entitled to a final decision in which the Commission sets out its reasons for not considering the complaint. Such a decision may be challenged before the Court under Article 230 EC (ex Article 173).

In view of the above it may be observed that the Commission's decentralisation project and the ensuing rejections of complaints appears, contrary to its objective, to have significantly increased the workload of the Community institutions. There is now an abundance of case law on the rejection of complaints on the basis of a lack of Community interest. Inevitably these cases in which the Commission is a party increase the Commission's workload. The overburden on the European Courts is also enhanced. While the number of cases will probably reduce after the initial period, it is unclear for how long the rejection of complaint types of cases will continue to absorb the considerable administrative and judical resources of the Community.[42] The issue of "Community interest" is certainly not settled at present.[43]

Tremblay II [1997] ECR II–2218; Case T–186/94 *Guérin* [1995] ECR II–1756; Case C–282/95P *Guérin* [1997] ECR I–1531; Case T–110/95 *IECC* [1998] ECR II–3605.

[39] *Tremblay I*, above, n. 38 (upheld on appeal: Case C–91/95 P *Tremblay* [1996] ECR I–5547). When relying on the argument that the Commission has to initiate proceedings because a national court will not be able adequately to protect its rights, a complainant has the burden of proof: Case T–575/93 *Koelman* v. *Commission* [1996] ECR II–1 and Case C–59/96P *Koelman* [1997] ECR I–4430.

[40] *UFEX*, above, n. 2.

[41] *Koelman* v. *Commission*, above, n. 39 and, in connection with state-aids, Case C–367/95 P, *Sytraval and Banks France* v. *Commission* [1998] ECR I–1719.

[42] In this sense see also the Economic and Social Committee's reaction to the notices. The Committee concludes that the (national authorities) Notice will be "inadequate and unconvincing" and that it is "to be hoped that the speed of the procedure will improve rather than worsen"; *Opinion of the Economic and Social Committee on the "XXVth report on competition policy (1995)"* [1997] OJ C75/22.

[43] See for instance the pending case Case T–26/99 *Garage Trabisco* v. *Commission* [1999] OJ C100/21.

Thirdly, and finally, the merits of decentralisation as depicted by the Commission in the Notices have been challenged. Commentators suggest that decentralisation will not lead to a reduction of the Commission's workload in view of its crucial role in the co-operation procedures. Moreover, the complexity of the co-operation procedures is considered to exacerbate that problem by creating more legal problems than the notices have solved. Further the fundamental objection to effective decentralisation in the current situation is not confronted in the notices. As long as (part of) the assessment of the effects on competition is made under Article 81(3) EC, national institutions require the competence to apply that paragraph in order to be able to reach judgment in the majority of the cases. Either the Commission's monopoly on the application of Article 81(3) EC would have to be withdrawn or the Commission would have to interpret Article 81(1) EC in such a manner as to enable national institutions to make the assessment of the overall effects on competition under that provision. While the first option is impossible in the context of a notice, the Commission also refrained from pursuing the alternative option, which implies that the hurdles to enforcement of Article 81 EC by an institution other than the Commission were kept in place.

6.3 MORE RADICAL REFORM: THE WHITE PAPER ON MODERNISATION

By issuing the White Paper on the Modernisation of the Rules Implementing Articles 81 and 82 EC the Commission acknowledged that the Notices did not lead to enhanced decentralised enforcement.[44] The Notices did not solve the problems which they were aimed to solve. The overburden on the Commission and the resulting backlog of cases at the Commission persists. These problems are central to the Commission White Paper.

The White Paper's title, which suggests that the Commission intends to undertake a general and comprehensive review of its antitrust policy, is arguably somewhat misleading. The White Paper goes further than the Notices because it envisages modification of (secondary) legislation, mainly Regulation 17, but the objectives behind the reform continue to be limited to reforming the administration of the current system. Thus, the "modernisation" does not go to the heart of the Community antitrust law system. While the Introduction to and Chapter I of the White Paper sketch the significant divergencies in the environment in which Community antitrust law was applied in the early 1960s, in which it is applied today and in which it will be applied after the envisaged enlargement of the Community, the remainder of the White Paper does not address the consequences of these changes. Instead the proposals aim to ensure a balance between the effectiveness of the supervision over compliance with the Treaty's antitrust provisions on the one hand and simplification of control on the other.[45]

---

[44] Explicitly, White Paper, para. 39.
[45] *Ibid.*, para. 41, reflecting Art. 83(2)(a) and (b) EC.

The Commission therefore bases its vision on the future framework within which EC antitrust law (and national antitrust laws) will be applied on administrative problems generated by its current interpretation of Articles 81 and 82 EC. But the administration of EC antitrust law cannot be studied in isolation from the substantive and constitutional aspects. Because the Commission intends to limit the scope of the revision to the administrative part of the system, it fails to acknowledge that the modernisation of EC antitrust law enforcement should clarify the substantive objectives of EC antitrust law, the institutional framework at the Community level and the interrelationship between EC and Member State antitrust laws in the altered context which the Commission sketches in the first part of the White Paper. Moreover, the White Paper disregards the substantive and constitutional implications of the proposals put forward.

In view of this critique, this section sketches the contents of the White Paper. The next section addresses constitutional issues of decentralised implementation of EC antitrust law.

As has been said the White Paper's Introduction illustrates the need for reform by underscoring that Community antitrust policy is now conducted "in a world which is very different to that known by the authors of the basic texts" on which the current policy is based.[46] Chapter I of the White Paper then depicts the development of Community antitrust law from its inception. Regulation 17 is the central element in the presentation. The Commission explains that the original objectives behind the enforcement regulation (gaining knowledge of business conduct, providing legal certainty to businesses and ensuring the uniform application of Article 81(3) EC) required a central authorisation system in which the Commission was exclusively competent to provide exemptions to the prohibition on entering into restrictive agreements. Crucially, the Commission argues that the formulation in Article 81(3) EC, that Article 81(1) EC "may be declared inapplicable", is a compromise which leaves room for a system in which exemptions are provided on the basis of authorisation by an administrative body as well as a system in which Article 81(3) EC is directly applicable and in which exemptions are therefore not required.[47] The White Paper continues with a discussion of the way in which the authorisation system, established by Regulation 17, led to mass requests for exemption. The Commission tried to deal with the mass problem by reducing the need for individual notification (the criterion of appreciable effect, notices as guidelines and block-exemption regulations) and by speeding up the administration of individual notifications by closing files on the basis of comfort letters. The Commission also mentions its efforts to encourage decentralised enforcement as a means of reducing the effects of the mass notification problem. This leads to the Commission's interim conclusion which reads as follows:

---

[46] *Ibid.*, para. 4.
[47] *Ibid.*, paras. 12–13. See further below, para. 4.4.

The Commission has therefore managed to stem the flood of notifications, but at the cost of focusing less on the most serious restrictions of competition which, generally, are never notified. In addition, the Commission is not able to close all of the cases which it handles by a formal decision, to the detriment of undertakings' legal certainty. It is clear from the foregoing that the measures taken have reached their limits and that more radical reforms must be considered. The need is all the more pressing as the closer integration of national markets aggravates the effects of restrictions of competition, compelling the Commission to take stronger measures against the most harmful restrictive practices. In a Union with over 20 Member States, it will no longer be possible to retain a centralised prior authorisation system in Brussels, involving the individual assessment of thousands of cases. Such a system would be cumbersome, inefficient and impose excessive burdens on economic operators.[48]

Chapter II of the White Paper turns to the direction of the reforms. First it defines the objectives of modernisation as balancing the need to ensure effective supervision with the need to simplify administration. With respect to the former the Commission continues to stress the potential of decentralised enforcement of Community antitrust law, provided that the obstacles to effective decentralised enforcement are removed. Concerning the simplification of administration the Commission argues that a notification duty is no longer required. The Commission is rather brief in its reasoning for this turn. It contends that it is inconceivable that, in an enlarged European Union, undertakings should have to notify and the Commission would have to examine thousands of restrictive practices.[49] Lastly, the Commission argues, "the current division between paragraph 1 and paragraph 3 in implementing Article 81 is artificial and runs counter to the integral nature of Article 81, which requires economic analysis of the overall impact of restrictive practices".[50]

The second part of Chapter II discusses five options which the Commission has identified as potential reform measures. Four of the options are based on improvements of the authorisation system, the fifth option consists of abolishing the authorisation system and switching to a system in which Article 81(3) EC would be applied directly by national courts and authorities.

Two of the reform options which would improve the authorisation system are limited reforms of the notification system enshrined in Regultion 17. The first option identified by the Commission is broadening the scope of Article 4(2) of Regulation 17. This form of modernisation was employed by the Commission in the context of the vertical restraints reform. Article 4(2) of Regulation 17 now covers all vertical restraints. In the context of the White Paper the Commission refutes wider use of this option because it would maintain the Commission's monopoly on applying Article 81(3) EC and would therefore not permit decentralised enforcement. The second option limited to

---

[48] *Ibid.*, para. 40.

[49] It is noteworthy that the White Paper (at para. 25) states that the Commission was faced with 37,450 cases in 1967. Why this *was* conceivable in 1967 but is not conceivable today is not explained.

[50] *Ibid.*, para. 49.

procedural aspects is general procedural simplification. This option too is rebutted in view of the fact that it would not reduce the number of notifications and that it would not enable more decentralised enforcement.

The two alternative options for reform within an authorisation system which the Commission presents are decentralising the application of Article 81(3) EC and revising the Commission interpretation of Article 81(1) EC. These options would go beyond mere reforms of the procedural framework since they have clear substantive and institutional implications. With respect to the first option, the Commission suggests that there are two ways in which the application of Article 81(3) EC, which is now a Commission monopoly, could be shared with national antitrust authorities. One is by allocating the power to provide exemptions to the appropriate national competition authority cases on the basis of a centre of gravity test. The other is by allocating the exemption cases to the national competition authorities on the basis of turnover thresholds. National antitrust authorities would be empowered to issue exemptions for those agreements between companies which have their effects mainly in the relevant Member State and for those agreements (or parties thereto) which do not reach certain thresholds, respectively. In essence this option forms an extension of the system envisaged in the National Authorities Notice, with the amendment that national antitrust authorities would be able to apply Article 81(3) themselves under the guidance of the Commission. The Commission concludes that neither alternative within this third option for reform forms a viable improvement, mainly because there is a danger of the re-nationalisation of antitrust policy and because the Commission fears challenges to the uniform application of EC antitrust law.

The fourth and final alternative for improving the authorisation system which the Commission presents is that of the revised interpretation of Article 81 EC. Since this book has argued that such a revision would indeed be an adequate way of "modernising" the Community's antitrust system, it is worth citing the Commission's considerations with respect to this option in full:

> One option that is sometimes put forward is to change the interpretation of Article 81 so as to include analysis of the harmful and beneficial effects of an agreement in the assessment under Article 81(1). Application of the exemption provided for in Article 81(3) would then be restricted to those cases in which the need to ensure consistency between competition policy and other Community policies took precedence over the results of the competition analysis. *It would in a way mean interpreting Article 81(1) as incorporating a "rule of reason".* Such a system would ease the notification constraints imposed on undertakings, since they would not be required to notify agreements in order to obtain negative clearance.
>
> The Commission has already adopted this approach to a limited extent and has carried out an assessment of the pro- and anti-competitive aspects of some restrictive practices under Article 81(1). *This approach has been endorsed by the Court of Justice.* However, the structure of Article 81 is such as to prevent greater use being made of this approach: *if more systematic use were made under Article 81(1) of an analysis of the pro- and anti-competitive aspects of a restrictive agreement, Article*

81(3) would be cast aside, whereas any such change could be made only through revision of the Treaty. It would at the very least be paradoxical to cast aside Article 81(3) when that provision in fact contains all the elements of a "rule of reason". It would moreover be dangerous if modernisation of the competition rules were to be based on developments in decision-making practice, subject to such developments being upheld by the Community Courts. Any such approach would mean that modernisation was contingent upon the cases submitted to the Commission and could take many years. Lastly, this option would run the risk of diverting Article 81(3) from its purpose, which is to provide a legal framework for the economic assessment of restrictive practices and not to allow application of the competition rules to be set aside because of political considerations.[51]

It is clear from the cited passage that the Commission does not consider that improvement of the authorisation system would form a viable way of modernising the implementation of Articles 81 and 82 EC. It is therefore unsurprising that the fifth option for reform, that is abolishing the authorisation system and switching to a directly applicable legal exception system, is endorsed by the White Paper. Within such a system Article 81 EC would become "a unitary norm comprising a rule establishing the principle of prohibition, unless certain conditions are met".[52] The Commission considers that direct applicability of the exemption provision is now possible because national courts and national antitrust authorities should be able to understand the conditions under which exemptions are granted to agreements on the basis of the 40 years of Commission practice and case law of the European Courts. The Commission underscores that it will also be much easier for national courts and national antitrust authorities to enforce Community antitrust law at the decentral level in view of the block-exemption regulation for vertical restraints.

Chapter III of the White Paper sketches how the new system, in which the notification and authorisation system would be abolished and in which Article 81(3) EC would be applied by national authorities and courts, would operate in practice. The Commission envisages that some aspects of the authorisation system will be retained in order to provide legal certainty to businesses where required, e.g in the case of joint ventures. Further the Commission envisages that it will provide guidance in specific cases which raise antitrust policy issues which are new. In this context the Commission intends to adopt "positive decisions" in exceptional cases on grounds of general interest. In the Commission's view "these positive decisions would confine themselves to a finding that an agreement is compatible with Article 81 as a whole, whether because it falls outside Article 81(1), or because it satisfies the tests of Article 81(3). They would be of a declaratory nature, and would have the same legal effect as

---

[51] *Ibid.*, paras. 56 and 57 (emphases added). For a review of these arguments, see above chapters 3 and 4. See also R. Wesseling, "The Commission White Paper on Modernisation of E.C. Antitrust Law: Unspoken consequences and Incomplete Treatment of Alternative Options", (1999) 20 *ECLR* 420–33

[52] *Ibid.*, para. 69.

negative clearance decisions have at present".[53] In the remainder of the White Paper the Commission sets out the way in which it will supervise the decentralised enforcement of Articles 81 and 82 EC in order to ensure consistent and uniform application of EC law. The Commission also argues that it requires additional powers in order to be able to intensify the *ex post* control which would replace the authorisation process. Finally, the White Paper addresses the issues of transition to the new system and of sectoral exceptions to the general system.[54]

6.4 MODERNISATION OF CO-OPERATION BETWEEN THE COMMISSION AND NATIONAL INSTITUTIONS

The Commission's modernisation plans give rise to various questions relating to procedural aspects of the system which remain unanswered in the White Paper. In particular principles and procedures guiding the allocation of cases to the respective national antitrust authorities remain unclear. Likewise it remains unclear how mutual recognition and trans-national enforceability of national antitrust authorities' decisions and national court judgments will be ensured.[55] Also the question remains whether the system sketched in the White Paper would not redirect the workload to the European Courts.[56] Moreover, and more relevant to this study, in spite of the reference which the White Paper makes to the systemic changes which EC antitrust policy has undergone since the 1960s, the proposals for reform are exclusively directed at solving administrative problems which the Commission faces. The modernisation of EC antitrust policy is thus reduced to a technical issue of effectiveness and simplifying administration. The policy choices which the Commission's favoured option for reform entails remain concealed.[57]

The remainder of this chapter therefore aims to reveal some of the broader implications of decentralisation of EC antitrust law, in particular the way of decentralisation put forward in the White Paper.[58]

6.4.1. Substantive Implications

First, the Commission's preference for rendering the whole of Article 81 EC directly applicable has consequences for the substantive interpretation of that Article. The current system is based on the principle that agreements which

---

[53] *Ibid.*, para. 89.

[54] See for a more detailed overview of the White Paper's content B. Rodger, "The Commission White Paper on Modernisation of the Rules Implementing Articles 85 and 86 of the EC Treaty" (1999) 24 *ELRev* 653–63.

[55] Rodger, above, n. 54.

[56] E.-J. Mestmäcker, "Versuch einer kartellpolitischen Wende in der EU" (1999) 10 *EuZW* 523–9.

[57] Thus, it forms a archetype of the general debate on the legal and political future of the Community: F. Snyder, "The Effectiveness of European Community Law: Institutions, Processes, Tools and Techniques" (1993) 56 *MLR* 19–54 at 53.

[58] The remainder of this ch. largely draws on Wesseling above, n. 51.

restrict competition may, under certain circumstances, be granted an exemption to the Community prohibition on restricting competition. These exemptions can be provided only by the EC Commission. In order to obtain exemptions for their agreements companies have to notify their agreements to the Commission.

The Commission considers that too many agreements are currently notified in order to obtain exemptions. As a consequence of the resulting overburden the Commission is not able to allocate administrative resources to the detection of potentially more serious infringements of the Treaty's antitrust rules. The solution to this problem presented in the White Paper is simple. By rendering Article 81(3) EC directly applicable both the duty to notify and the Commission monopoly on providing exemptions become obsolete.

In the Commission's view there are no objections to making this crucial shift. First, agreements which are notified tend not to be serious infringements of EC antitrust law. It is a waste of the Commission's limited administrative resources to provide exemptions to these agreements. In so far as agreements which are now notified form infringements of the Treaty's antitrust rules, these rules can in the Commission's view be enforced *ex post* by private parties which suffer from the effects of the anti-competitive agreement.

However, such a view denies the constant need which companies have for (*ex ante*) legal certainty. There is no principal reason why the Community administration should be able to limit providing legal certainty to agreements in relation to joint ventures, with respect to which the Commission acknowledges that the related investments and financial commitments require *ex ante* legal certainty.[59] Arguably, different kinds of contracts typically involve comparable financial investments and long-term policy decisions with respect to which companies require legal certainty. As long as Article 81(3) EC provides the possibility of declaring Article 81(1) inapplicable to agreements which contribute to improving the production or distribution of goods or to promoting technical or economic progress—in other words, as long as the application of Article 81(3) implies a degree of policy discretion—companies should have the possibility of obtaining an *ex ante* declaration that their agreement fulfils the requirements for exemption and that the agreement will therefore be enforceable.

This observation leads to a second substantive consequence of rendering Article 81(3) EC directly applicable; i.e. that such a revision would withdraw the possibility of obtaining an exemption to the prohibition on restricting competition in view of an agreement's positive effects on (non-competition) Community policy objectives. To understand the importance of this consequence it is necessary to recall the conclusions which Chapter 3 drew with respect to the interpretation of Article 81(1) and (3) EC.

It was shown in that chapter that the case law of the Court of Justice is clear. The application of Article 81(3) EC entails a degree of policy discretion. The

---

[59] White Paper, para. 79.

ECJ has repeatedly endorsed Commission decisions which took into account non-competition concerns when determining whether an agreement fulfilled all four preconditions of Article 81(3) EC. The Court continues to stress that the administrative discretion involved in this assessment cannot be subject to judicial control. From the outset the ECJ emphasised that, as a judicial body, it is not fit itself to assess the complex "economic" facts implied in the exercise of issuing exemptions. Instead the Commission, the Community's administration, is the body competent to balance the policy concerns at the Community level.[60]

Two conclusions can be drawn from the Court's case law with respect to Article 81(3) EC. First, Article 81(3) requires the balancing of competition policy objectives and non-competition policy objectives. Community antitrust policy is not supreme over alternative Community policies (and instruments to implement those policies) formulated in Articles 2 and 3 EC. Because these Community policies with the same constitutional status do not always provide the same answer to policy questions which arise, for example, in the application of Article 81(3) EC, the Commission, as the Community's central adminstration, is exclusively competent to make the policy choices in individual cases.

The White Paper posits that the purpose of Article 81(3) EC is to provide "a legal framework for the economic assessment of restrictive practices and not to allow application of the competition rules to be set aside because of political considerations".[61] While it is true that the competition rules may not be set aside because of political considerations, the suggestion which the cited passage creates is that application of Article 81(3) EC is a pure competition analysis. As has been seen, that is not in line with the case law of the Court of Justice from which it emerges that non-competition policy objectives may be taken into account provided that a degree of competition remains.

The practical problem arising from the fact that the Commission has to devote considerable administrative resources to examining whether agreements qualify for exemption cannot form a sufficient reason to change this fundamental element of substantive Community antitrust law. A more logical approach to the administrative overburden which the large number of requests for exemption creates is first to examine whether the number of requests for exemption can be reduced within the current procedural and substantive framework which the framers of EC Treaty have established. This book has demonstrated that there is indeed ample margin for reducing the demand for exemptions. First it was argued that the number of exemptions required would diminish considerably if the Commission were to bring its interpretation of Article 81(1) EC in line with that of the Court of Justice and the Court of First Instance. Agreements which do not on balance appreciably restrict competition should be considered compatible with Article 81(1) EC. They should not require an exemption. This

---

[60] Cases 56 and 58/64 *Consten and Grundig* v. *Commission* [1966] ECR 341. See also Case 71/74 *Frubo* [1975] ECR 563 where the Commission's margins for administrative discretion were refined, and Case T–17/93 *Matra Hachette* v. *Commission* [1994] ECR II–595.
[61] White Paper, para. 57.

would considerably reduce the demand for exemptions.[62] Secondly, measures could be taken to restrict the scope of Community antitrust rules to those cases which are of genuine Community interest. Contrary to the present situation in which all agreements of any commercial significance fall within the scope of Community law, Articles 81 and 82 EC should apply only if the effects of the restrictive practices are relevant to the operation of the common market. Restricting Community jurisdiction to cases of genuine Community-wide importance would further reduce the need for exemptions on the basis of Article 81(3) EC.[63] If the Commission were still not able to provide the required number of exemptions after these adjustments of its interpretation of Article 81 EC there would be a logical and strong case for increasing the staff of DG Competition.

6.4.2. Jurisdictional implications

Even though the White Paper on Modernisation does not address the interrelationship between Community and Member State antitrust laws (as noted above, Chapter 4) the plans which the Commission unfolds in the White Paper will have significant consequences for this relationship.[64] The root lies in the Commission's assertion that "the current division between paragraph 1 and 3 in implementing Article 81 is artificial and runs counter to the integral nature of Article 81, which requires economic analysis of the overall impact of restrictive practices".[65] Chapter 4 demonstrated that the division of Article 81 is a crucial element in the interrelationship between EC and Member State antitrust laws. Under the "procedural supremacy" rule established by the Court of Justice in *Walt Wilhelm*, national antitrust law may be applied only in so far as the application of national law does not prejudice the full and uniform application of Community law or the effects of the measures taken or to be taken to implement it.[66] The thus established supremacy of Community over national antitrust law is particularly relevant with respect to "positive though indirect measures" taken by the Community authorities. In other words, national authorities cannot on the basis of national antitrust law prohibit agreements which benefit from a Commission exemption ex Article 81(3) EC.

---

[62] See, extensively, Ch. 3.

[63] See, extensively, Ch. 4.

[64] The interrelationship between EC and national antitrust law is of course not exclusively an "issue at the decentral level", to which this ch. is devoted. However, it does make sense to concentrate the comments on the White Paper on Modernisation in this ch., in particular because it will be demonstrated below that the interrelationship between the two sets of law is directly affected by the system of decentralised enforcement of EC antitrust law which the Commission proposed in the White Paper and because this interrelationship is not addressed in the White Paper.

[65] White Paper, para. 49.

[66] Case 14/68 *Walt Wilhelm* v. *Bundeskartellamt* [1969] ECR 1.

Thus, the picture on the interrelationship of Community and national antitrust law is as follows. Where EC antitrust law is stricter, more lenient national antitrust law does not take effect. Where national antitrust law is stricter, this law can be applied if the agreement or behaviour at hand does not fall within Article 81(1) EC. However, if the Commission has provided a genuine "positive" exemption, be it in the form of a block-exemption regulation or a formal individual exemption, stricter national antitrust law cannot be applied.

There are two further relevant observations. First, because the prevailing interpretation of the jurisdictional criterion in Article 81 EC is so broad as to encompass almost all agreements of any commercial significance the scope for overlap between EC and Member State laws is broad. Secondly, the Commission provides very few formal exemptions and only formal exemptions pre-empt the application of stricter national antitrust laws.

With the current interrelationship between Community and national antitrust law in mind the consequences of the Commission assertion that the division between Article 81(1) and (3) EC is artificial and that it runs counter to the integral nature of Article 81 EC are evident. As has been seen, the White Paper proposes to discard the type of public policy exemption to which the Court of Justice referred when it stated that the procedural supremacy of Community law encompasses "positive but indirect action" by the Community authorities. The reason the Commission wants to invalidate the difference between Article 81(1) and (3) is that the purpose of Article 81(3), just like that of Article 81(1), is in the Commission's view to provide a legal framework for the economic assessment of restrictive practices and not to allow application of the competition rules to be set aside because of political considerations.[67]

Evidently, this will have an effect on the interrelationship between Community antitrust law and national antitrust law. If Article 81 EC requires only "economic analysis of the overall impact of restrictions of competition" and the "economic rule of reason" is applied under Article 81(3), as the Commission proposes, then the positive, public policy element in exemptions is eliminated. That in turn will imply that national antitrust law on the basis of which an agreement would be prohibited may be applied even if the Commission—or a national antitrust authority or national court—has judged that the agreement is valid under EC antitrust law. After all only "positive" Community exemptions preclude the application of stricter national law.

The same problem arises in connection with future individual decisions in exceptional cases. The Commission intends to limit itself to assessing whether an agreement is compatible with Article 81 EC as a whole—leaving aside the question whether this is so because the agreement does not fall within Article 81(1) or because the agreement fulfils the criteria of Article 81(3). If these decisions were to have the same legal effect as negative clearance decisions, as the Commission suggests, then this would leave open the possibility of applying

---

[67] White Paper, para. 57.

stricter national antitrust law. Negative clearance decisions do not prevent the application of national antitrust law.[68]

That result seems unsatisfactory, particularly in view of the considerations of the Court of Justice in *Walt Wilhelm*. While the uniform interpretation of EC law itself is not at stake, the guaranteed uniformity is potentially irrelevant. All agreements which are not prohibited on the basis of EC antitrust law could be prohibited on the basis of national antitrust law. This would open the way to a renationalisation of EC competition law, which the Commission fears. Since there is no exclusive jurisdiction for Community law and there is no limit to the concurrent national jurisdiction on the basis of EC law, there would not be a ceiling to this process. The White Paper does not consider these potential consequences.

In view of these observations on the potential effects of increased decentralised enforcement of Community antitrust law it is submitted that modernisation of the Community antitrust law enforcement system cannot be undertaken without considering the interrelationship between Community and Member State antitrust laws. In the context of modernising Community antitrust law it is indispensable to confront both the scope for Community antitrust law and its elationship with national (antitrust) laws. Reference is made to Chapter 4 for a review of this constitutional issue.

6.4.3. Institutional Implications

The third broader issue in the context of the White Paper is that of the future relationship between the Commission and national institutions. In this respect two elements of the White Paper are particularly relevant. One is the greater reliance which the Commission intends to place on *ex post* enforcement of Community antitrust law. In essence the envisaged shift from *ex ante* to *ex post* signifies a move from a publicly enforced competition law regime to a system which relies on private enforcement. The other element in the White Paper with constitutional consequences is the blueprint which the Commission sketches for the Community's administrative architecture in the field of antitrust policy.

It would exceed the scope of this chapter to discuss extensively the implications of the shift from private to public enforcement to which the Commission aspires. In this instance it should suffice to highlight that the choice for a privately enforced system will have substantive as well as practical implications. The substantive direction of Community antitrust law will automatically be affected by a shift from public to private enforcement.[69] The practical obstacles

---

[68] Part of this problem is evident from the Commission's attempts to qualify these "negative clearance decisions" as "positive" decisions: White Paper, § 89. The Commission's intention of adopting a reg. which spells out that agreements which are exempted by a block exemption should not be held contrary to national law reduces the effects of the noted problem.

[69] W. Collins and S. Sunshine, "Is Private Enforcement Effective Antitrust Policy?" (& discussion) and B. Hawk and J. Veltrop, "Dual Antitrust Enforcement in the United States: Positive or

to private enforcement of Community antitrust law, which the White Paper—like the National Courts Notice—does not address were already noted above (in section 6.2) in the context of the discussion of the Notice on co-operation between the Commission and national courts in the enforcement of EC antitrust law. Various commentators have pointed to the numerous practical and in-principle objections to effective enforcement of EC antitrust law before national courts within the current procedural framework. Decentralised enforcement of Community antitrust law through national courts cannot be promoted if these problems are not resolved in parallel. In particular it appears that private enforcement of antitrust law is only effective in combination with parallel public enforcement action.[70] This suggests that the shift to more *ex post* private enforcement is likely to limit—instead of further—the effectiveness of Community antitrust law. Alternatively, commentators argue that effective decentralisation requires structural innovations in the Community's judicial architecture, which the White Paper fails to address. In particular, the option of establishing Community regional courts in the Member States in order to guarantee that rights which undertakings have under Community antitrust law are observed deserves attention. With common rules of procedure and a common loyalty to the Community, local Community courts would be able to ensure the enforcement of a plaintiff's rights based on Community law in all Member States.[71]

The other element in the White Paper which directly affects the relationship between the Commission and national institutions is the structure of the network of antitrust law enforcement agencies which the Commission intends to build. As noted, the White Paper merely describes the envisaged network structure in general terms. The majority of the reactions to the White Paper have pointed to the fact that, in particular with respect to this aspect, the complex and crucial features of the system lie in the elaboration of its details.[72] With

Negative Lessons for the European Community" both in P.-J. Slot and A. McDonnel (eds.), *Procedure and Enforcement in E.C. and U.S. Competition Law* (London, Sweet & Maxwell, 1993), at 50–62 and 21–31. In its commentary (*"Sondergutachten"*) on the White Paper the German *Monopolkommission* warns the Commission that its desire for enhanced private enforcement, after the example of the USA, disregards fundamental differences between the EC and US competition law regimes. See the summary of the *Monopolkommission*'s commentary in "Auszug aus dem Sondergutachten 28 der Monopolkommission: Kartellpolitische Wende in der Europäischen Union?" (1999) 49 *WuW* 977–9.

[70] See Rodger and MacCulloch, above, n. 33, at 597ff.

[71] J. Jacqué and J. Weiler, "On the Road to the European Union, A New Judicial Architecture" (1990) 27 *CMLRev* 185; J. Weiler, "Journey to an Unknown Destination: A Retrospective and the Prospective of the European Court of Justice in the Arena of Political Integration" (1993) 31 *JCMS* 417–46, at 442; I. Forrester, "Competition Structures for the 21st Century" in B. Hawk (ed.), *Annual Proceedings of the Fordham Corporate Law Institute 1994* (New York, Kluwer, 1995), 445–503; and A. Riley, "More Radicalism, Please: The Notice on Co-operation Between National Courts and the Commission in Applying Articles 85 and 86 of the EEC Treaty" (1994) 15 *ECLR* 91–6.

[72] For instance the reactions to the White Paper by the German, the UK and the Dutch governments (available from the respective websites of the national antitrust authorities). See also Rodger, above, n. 54.

respect to decentralisation of EC antitrust law by national antitrust authorities there are four technical problems which need to be solved before the system can operate effectively. First, the allocation of cases to the respective authorities needs to be regulated. While the allocation of the competence to deal with a specific case is a more evident problem in a system in which companies have to notify their agreements in order to obtain exemptions, abolishing the authorisation system does not eliminate the problem. In particular where companies can make complaints with various national antitrust authorities, the potential for forum-shopping and for conflicts between national antitrust authorities is noteworthy. The second issue to be resolved is related. It concerns the scope of the validity of decisions taken by national antitrust authorities. A Community-wide network can only operate effectively where decisions are mutually recognised throughout all Member States. At present there are numerous obstacles to such a system of mutual recognition. Thirdly, and again relatedly, substantive consistency in the decisions by the various actors in the network needs to be ensured. In antitrust law with its complex assessment of economic facts—which are moreover not static—this is a particularly pertinent concern. Finally, the existing obstacles to the exchange of information between the participans in the network need to be overcome.

Arguably, the ineffectiveness of the National Antitrust Authorities Notice was due to the fact that the Commission did not—and in the context of a notice was not able to—address these crucial aspects of a network. Disappointingly, the White Paper—in the context of which major reforms are proposed—also refrains from working out the details of the network within which the Commission and the national antitrust authorities would operate.[73]

Because the White Paper is weak on this issue, it is impossible at this stage to discuss the Commission's plans in any detail. In broad lines, however, the structure which the Commission envisages, with greater reliance on a network of Community and Member State enforcement agencies, is in line with the general developments in EC institutional law and policy. It will be recalled that Chapter 5 argued that general developments in EC institutional law indicate that the current centralised system within which EC antitrust policy is made is outdated. The strengthening of the role of the Advisory Committee on Restrictive Practices by establishing a network of national antitrust authorities and the Commission would form a viable alternative to the present system in which the role of the Commission is over-emphasised. At the same time the network would reduce the sharp distinction which now exists between central and decentral enforcement of Community antitrust law. A reform of the administrative structure could generate a more integrated structure in which the Commission and one or more national antitrust authorities cooperate on the basis of equality. In the White Paper the Commission embraces this idea, although not

---

[73] The most comprehensive effort to resolve the obstacles to establishing a Community-wide network was made by (officials of) the *Bundeskartellamt*. See Klimisch and Krueger, above, n. 21.

wholeheartedly. The Commission wants to retain a clause similar to the current Article 9(3) of Regulation 17 on the basis of which it can take cases away from national antitrust authorities dealing with it where the Commission fears a conflict of views or where the case raises issues of Community importance. In a genuine network based on equality more subtle mechanisms could be developed to replace this dominant power of the Commission. In the absence of such mechanisms the willingness of national antitrust authorities to co-operate within the Community framework is tested.[74] Any network established at the Community level should take the national antitrust authorities seriously. Otherwise such authorities are likely to leave the system, which would be harmful to the operation of the Single Market. In answer to the minor role that is envisaged for them in the current system, national antitrust authorities have already sought forms of co-operation outside the Community system.[75] This process could be stopped if a smoothly operating network were established at the Community level. These networks could then also form the basis for increased "horizontal" co-operation, that is between Member State authorities *inter se*, both in cases of Community importance and in cases of regional significance. The big advantage from the Community point of view is that the co-operation between Member States would operate within the Community framework.[76]

CONCLUSION

Co-operation between the Commission and national institutions in the implementation of Community antitrust law and policy is essential to the effective functioning of the internal market. In order to reduce its case load and to increase the effectiveness of Community antitrust law, the Commission intends to decentralise part of Community antitrust law enforcement. Following the National Courts and National Antitrust Authorities Notices, the Commission

[74] See the hesitance with respect to this aspect of the White Paper in para. 57 of the UK government's reaction.

[75] V. Power, above, n. 32. Agreements have been concluded between Member State antitrust authorities in order to stimulate co-operation in the enforcement of national antitrust laws. The most important ones are the agreement between the French and German authorities for antitrust matters (published in (1985) 35 *WuW* 476–81) and the agreement between the French, German and the UK authorities in the merger area. These agreements generate a one-stop-shop system for international mergers outside the Community framework. Thus, national authorites can be seen to compete with the Commission for the favour of multinationals.

[76] The example of the USA where the Attorneys General of the states combine their antitrust law enforcement efforts through the National Association of Attorneys General may be indicative: B. Hawk and L Laudati, "Antitrust Federalism in the United States and Decentralisation of Competition Law Enforcement in the European Union: A Comparison" (1996) 20 *FILJ* 18–49. See also I. S. Forrester, "Modernisation of EC Competition Law" in B. Hawk (ed.), *Annual Proceedings of the Fordham Corporate Law Institute 1999* (forthcoming 2000). Moreover, experience in the USA suggests that involvement of State Attorneys General in the enforcement of federal law tends to further harmonisation of state laws: E. Fox, "Decision Making at the Centre—Working Paper IV" in C.-D. Ehlermann and L. Laudati (eds.), *Robert Schuman Centre Annual on European Competition Law 1996* (The Hague, Kluwer Law International, 1997), 71–8.

sketched its vision of the future framework within which Community antitrust law is enforced in its White Paper on the Modernisation of the Rules Implementing Articles 81 and 82 EC. Other than what the title suggests, however, the plans set out in the White Paper, if adopted, will have important repercussions on substantive and institutional aspects of the Community's antitrust law regime.

This chapter illustrated that a revision, or "modernisation", of the procedural rules cannot be undertaken in isolation. Rather, the modernisation of the relationship between the Commission and national institutions in the antitrust law field should consider the qualitative changes in Community antitrust law—flagged by the establishment of the internal market and adoption of the TEU. Recognition of those developments may well indicate that alternative options for modernisation—such as a revised (Commission) interpretation of the scope for Article 81(1) EC—should be pursued, or at least scrutinised, before a shift to a system based on *ex post* control and without an authorisation option should be made.

Thus, the conclusion of Chapter 6 is in line with the observations made throughout Part II of this study. Part II confronted topical questions in Community antitrust law on the basis of the observations made in this study's first part. Chapters 3 and 4 addressed substantive issues. Institutional and procedural issues were taken up in Chapters 5 and 6. The discussion demonstrated that all problems which were confronted are strongly interrelated. Solutions to the problems in decentralised enforcement of Community antitrust law (Chapter 6), for instance, cannot be found without considering the objectives of Community antitrust law (Chapter 3). Likewise, the division of jurisdiction between Community and Member State antitrust laws (Chapter 4) depends at least in part on the way in which Member State interests are protected in the decision-making structure at the Community level (Chapter 5).

Thus, Part II has shown that all these topical problems in Community antitrust law have their common root in the fundamentally altered character of Community antitrust law. Although the Commission refers to the changed environment in which Community antitrust law is enforced in its White Paper the implications of this transformation are not sufficiently acknowledged in the option for modernisation which it proposes in that same document. Hopefully, the consultation process which the Commisson initiated on the basis of the White Paper will provide the opportunity to consider in a comprehensive manner the implications of the transformation of Community antitrust law. On that basis only will the White Paper form the basis for genuine modernisation of European Community antitrust law.

Conclusion

THERE IS broad consensus that time is ripe to modernise aspects of the EC antitrust law system. Some commentators argue that the objectives of Community antitrust policy need to be adapted. Others focus on institutional features of the current system. They promote the establishment of an independent EC cartel office. Arguments for procedural improvements are also longstanding. Indeed the Commission modernisation plans—most notably the White Paper on Modernisation but also other recent reforms—focus on procedures.

This book has argued that there are reasons for undertaking a comprehensive review of the substantive, procedural and institutional operation of the current Community antitrust law system. The reason is that the character of EC integration—and hence EC antitrust law—changed fundamentally between 1958 and today. The original construction of the Community's antitrust law system needs to be reconsidered in the light of the alteration of the context within which EC antitrust law is applied. With the formal realisation of the internal market by 1993, Community antitrust law lost its normative underpinning, which was traditionally found in its role in promoting market integration. Current problems in EC antitrust law, which have triggered the modernisation debate, can therefore only be answered with reference to the fundamental changes in the European integration process.

Part I of this book demonstrated two things. First, it sketched the transformation of Community antitrust law. Initially focused on integration motives, antitrust law enforcement evolved into a broader Community policy which is now primarily a form of Community industrial policy directed at enhancing industrial competitiveness and—ultimately—consumer welfare. Secondly, Part I underscored the difference between the general development of European law and integration and the way in which Community antitrust policy evolved. Whereas progress in European integration policies was often dependent on a delicate and complex interplay between the supranational Community interests and the interests of the Member States (collectively and those of individual Member States), Community antitrust policy evolved almost exclusively in the supranational sphere. The direct connection which was initially perceived between Community competition policy and market integration ensured that the supranational Community institutions, the Commission and the Court of Justice, obtained broad and autonomous powers in this field. The Commission was able to realise some of its aspirations to policy competencies by expanding its antitrust law enforcement action. Thus, the Commission developed its competence to offer exemptions to the antitrust rules into a tool for conducting

Community-wide industrial policy. As the separate national markets were gradually integrated into one common market, Community antitrust policy imperceptibly moved further along those lines. Whatever the origin of Community antitrust law in the market integration project, EC antitrust law enforcement today is a highly political activity. The realisation of the internal market in 1992 symbolises this development. The legitimacy of Community antitrust law enforcement can no longer be derived (exclusively) from its role in promoting market integration. Nevertheless, Community antitrust policy's uncommon position, exclusively in the supranational administrative domain, has not been challenged. Instead, as has been seen, the envisaged modernisation of EC antitrust law is confined to a review of procedural aspects of the system, while leaving the constitutional, insitutional and substantive structure untouched. The second part of this book therefore undertook a more comprehensive review of EC antitrust law in light of the formal establishment of the internal market and the Treaty on European Union within which the EC Treaty is now set.

Chapter 1 reviewed the objectives of Community antitrust policy. By taking the application of Article 81 EC as a model, the Chapter argued that EC antitrust law is now primarily enforced with a view to protecting workable competition on markets, which should promote an efficient allocation of production factors and, thus, consumer welfare. While the integration objective of EC antitrust law will continue to play a role, especially following enlargement of the Community towards Eastern Europe, protection of competition now takes up the central position in antitrust law enforcement action. This does not imply, however, that the TEU provides for an economic constitution in which the principle of free competition overrides all other policy concerns. The Treaty and the Merger Control Regulation allow for extra-competition policy concerns to outweigh free competition.

This observation connects Chapter 3 with Chapter 5, which examined the institutional structure within which Community antitrust policy is executed. It is sometimes argued that an independent European cartel office should replace the Commission as the central enforcer of EC antitrust law. Such an independent office should ensure that non-competition policy concerns cannot play a role in the enforcement of the Treaty's competition law provisions. Primarily because the EC Treaty allows for balancing competition policy objectives with other Treaty objectives, Chapter 5 argued that there is no reason for establishing an independent European cartel office. A central, "political" body should be entrusted with making the policy considerations implicit in weighing competition policy and other Treaty objectives. Nevertheless there are pertinent objections to the existing institutional framework within which the Commission is responsible for all aspects (detection, prosecution, decision-making) of EC antitrust law enforcement at the Community level. While this may have been a logical arrangement in the early years of Community antitrust law, it is less so today. The Treaty's antitrust law provisions give individual rights which have direct effect. It was argued that an administrative body like the Commission is not the most appropriate institution for enforcing those rights. Instead, one or more courts could determine those rights. This judicial test could still be topped by a political reappraisal at the Community level, although the Commission is not necessarily the most appropriate institution to be provided with this power. It suffers from a lack of political accountability which cannot be resolved directly at the Community level, *inter alia* as a consequence of the general democratic deficit of European Community Politics. Parallel to a general tendency in the Community after the TEU, the solution may therefore be found in enhanced implication of the Member States in central decision-making. It was suggested that the Member States and other interested parties could play a more decisive role in the committee procedure.

This relates to Chapters 4 and 6 which addressed the relationship between the Community and Member States in the area of antitrust policy. Chapter 4 concluded that there is a case for abandoning the traditional broad interpretation of Community antitrust law territorial jurisdiction. Several constitutional developments suggest that the strong pre-emptive effect of EC antitrust law on national laws obstructs effective enforcement of antitrust law throughout the Community. The positive experience with the Merger Control Regulation, which was only recently adopted, indicates that limiting the scope for Community jurisdiction to cases with a Community dimension is likely to have positive effects. Limiting Community jurisdiction to what has a Community dimension is moreover in line with the Commission's intention to decentralise cases which are not of Community interest.

Decentralisation of EC antitrust law enforcement was discussed in Chapter 6. The chapter emphasised that the envisaged shift from a centralised authorisation system to a system of decentralised, *ex post* enforcement has important, and so far unacknowledged, substantive and institutional implications. Before the direct applicability of Article 81(3) EC can take effect, these questions should be addressed, together with the completion of the procedural design of the new system.

In sum, the modernisation of EC antitrust law provides an opportunity for undertaking the necessary comprehensive review of the EC antitrust law system. This book has made a number of suggestions about the direction which the ensuing reforms may take.

Bibliography

AHLBORN, C., and TURNER, V., "Expanding Success? Reform of the E.C. Merger Regulation" (1998) 19 *ECLR* 249–62

ALLEN, D., "Managing the Common Market: The Community's Competition Policy" in H. Wallace, W. Wallace and C. Webb (eds.), *The Dynamics of European Integration* (London, Pinter Publishers, 1983), 209–36

ALTER, K., and MEUNIER-AITSAHALIA, S., "Judicial Politics in the European Community, European Integration and the Pathbreaking *Cassis de Dijon* Decision" (1994) 26 *Comparative Political Studies* 535–61

AMATO, G., *Antitrust and the Bounds of Power* (Hart, Oxford, 1997)

ANDRIESSEN, F., "The Role of Anti-trust in the Face of Economic Recession; State Aids in the EEC" (1983) 4 *ECLR* 286–96

ARNULL, A., "Owning Up to Fallibility: Precedent and the Court of Justice" (1993) 30 *CMLRev.* 247–75

—— "Judging the New Europe" (1994) 19 *ELR* 3–15

—— "The European Court and Judicial Objectivity: A Reply to Professor Hartley" (1996) 112 *The Law Quarterly Review* 411–23

ART, J.-Y., and VAN LIEDEKERKE, D., "Developments in EC Competition Law in 1995— An Overview" (1996) 33 *CMLRev.* 719–75

——, and ——, "Developments in EC Competition Law in 1996—An Overview" (1997) 34 *CMLRev.* 895–956

BAAKE, P., and PERSCHAU, O., "The Law and Policy of Competition in Germany" in G. Majone, *Regulating Europe* (London, Routledge, 1996), 131–56

BADEN FULLER, C.W.F., "Price Variations—The Distillers Case and Article 85 EEC" (1979) 28 *ICLQ* 128–42

BACON, K., "State Regulation of the Market and EC Competition Rules: Articles 85 and 86 Compared" (1997) 18 *ECLR* 283–91

VAN BAEL, I., "Heretical Reflections on the Basic Dogma: Single Market Integration" (1980) 10 *Revue Suisse du droit international de la concurrence* 39–56

—— "The Antitrust Settlement Practice of the EC Commission" (1986) 23 *CMLRev.* 61–90

—— "Transparency of E.C. Commission Proceedings" in P.-J. Slot and A. McDonnell, *Procedure and Enforcement in E.C. and U.S. Competition Law* (London, Sweet & Maxwell, 1993), 192–6

—— "The Role of National Courts" (1994) 15 *ECLR* 3–7

BARENTS, R., "The Community and the Unity of the Common Market" (1990) 33 *German Yearbook of International Law* 9–36

BARON, M., "Die neuen Bestimmungen der Europäischen Fusionskontrolle" (1997) 47 *WuW* 579–91

BARTODZIEJ, P., *Reform der EG-Wettbewerbsaufsicht und Gemeinschaftsrecht* (Baden-Baden, Nomos, 1994)

BEAUMONT, P., and WEATHERILL, S., *EC Law* (London, Penguin, 1996)

BECHTOLD, R., "Die Durchsetzung europäischen Kartellrechts durch die Zivilgerichte" (1996) 160 *ZHR* 660–72

BEHRENS, P. (ed.), *EC Competition Rules in National Courts* (*I*) Part One: United Kingdom (by J. Shaw) and Italy (by A. Ligustro) (Baden-Baden, Nomos, 1992)

—— (ed.), *EC Competition Rules in National Courts* (*II*) Part Two: Benelux (by J. Noirfalisse and K. Sevinga) and Ireland (by I. Maher) (Baden-Baden, Nomos, 1994)

—— (ed.), *EC Competition Rules in National Courts* (*III*) Part Three: Germany (by E. Braun) (Baden-Baden, Nomos, 1996)

BENGOETXEA, J., *The Legal Reasoning of the European Court of Justice—Towards a European Jurisprudence* (Oxford, Clarendon Press, 1993)

BENTIL, J., "Control of the Abuse of Monopoly Power in EEC Business Law" (1975) 12 *CMLRev.* 59–75

BERCUSSON, B., "Maastricht: A Fundamental Change in European Labour Law" (1992) 23 *Industrial Relations Journal* 177–90

VAN DEN BERGH, R., "Modern Industrial Organisation versus Old-fashioned European Competition Law" (1996) 17 *ECLR* 75–87

—— "Economic Criteria for Applying the Subsidiarity Principle in the European Community: The Case of Competition Policy" (1996) *International Review of Law and Economics* 363

BERMANN, G., "The Single European Act: A New Constitution for the Community?" (1989) 27 *Columbia Journal of Transnational Law* 529–87

—— "Regulatory Decisionmaking in the European Commission" (1995) 1 *CJEL* 415–33

BERNARD, N., "The Future of European Economic Law in the Light of the Principle of Subsidiarity" (1996) 33 *CMLRev.* 633–66

BISHOP, B., and BISHOP, S., "Reforming Competition Policy: Bundeskartellamt—Model or Muddle?" (1996) 17 *ECLR* 207–9

BISHOP, M., "European or National? The Community's New Merger Regulation" in M. Bishop and J. Kay (eds.), *European Mergers & Merger Policy* (Oxford, OUP, 1993), 294–317

BLACK, O., "Per Se Rules and Rules of Reason: What Are They?" (1997) 18 *ECLR* 145–61

BORNKAMM, J., "Anwendung der Art. 85, 86 EWG-Vertrag im Zivilprozeß" in M. Henssler *et al.* (eds.), *Europäische Integration und globaler Wettbewerb* (Heidelberg, Recht und Wirtschaft, 1994), 549–62

BORK, R., *The Antitrust Paradox. A Policy at War with Itself* (New York, The Free Press, 1993)

BOURGEOIS, J., "EC Competition Law and Member State Courts" (1994) 17 *FILJ* 331–52

—— and LANGEHEINE, B., "Jurisdictional Issues: EEC Merger Regulation. Member State Laws and Articles 85–86" in B. Hawk (ed.), *Annual Proceedings of the Fordham Corporate Law Institute 1991* (Irvington-on-Hudson, Transnational Juris Publications, 1992), 583–609

BOUTERSE, R., *Competition and Integration—What Goals Count?* (The Hague, Kluwer Law International, 1995)

BRAAKMAN, A.J. (ed.), *The Application of Articles 85 and 86 of the EC Treaty by National Courts in the Member States* (Luxembourg, Office for Official Publications, 1997)

BRIGHT, C., "EU Competition Policy: Rules, Objectives and Deregulation" (1996) 16 *Oxford Journal of Legal Studies* 535–59

BRINKER, I., "Ansätze für eine EG-konforme Auslegung des nationalen Kartellrechtes" (1996) *WuW* 549–58

BRITTAN, SIR LEON, *Competition Policy and Merger Control in the Single European Market* (Cambridge, Grotius, 1991)

BROBERG, M., "The De Minimis Notice" (1995) 20 *ELR* 371–87

—— "The EC Commission's Green Paper on the Review of the Merger Regulation" (1996) 17 *ECLR* 289–94

—— "The Geographic Allocation of Turnover under the Merger Regulation" (1997) 18 *ECLR* 103–9

—— *The European Commission's Jurisdiction to Scrutinise Mergers* (The Hague, Kluwer Law International, 1998)

DE BRONETT, G.-K., "Akteneinsicht in Wettbewerbsverfahren der Europäischen Kommission" (1997) 47 *WuW* 383–93

BROWN, A., "Distinguishing between Concentrative and Cooperative Joint Ventures: Getting Any Easier?" (1996) 17 *ECLR* 240–9

BULMER, S., "Institutions and Policy Change in the European Communities: The Case of Merger Control" (1994) 72 *Public Administration* 423–44

BURCHARDT, G., and TEBBE, G., "Die Gemeinsame Aussen- und Sicherheitspolitik der Europäischen Union—Rechtliche Struktur und Politischer Prozeß" (1995) 30 *EuR* 1–20

BURNSIDE, A., "Dance of the Veils? Reform of the EC Merger Regulation" (1996) 17 *ECLR* 371–4

——, and MACKENZIE STUART, L., "Joint Venture Analysis: The Latest Chapter" (1995) 16 *ECLR* 138–46

CANENBLEY, C., "Decentralisation of Enforcement of Community Law—Working Paper IV" in C.-D. Ehlermann and L. Laudati (eds.), *Proceedings of the RSC Workshop on Competition Law: Antitrust in a 'Federal' Context* (The Hague, Kluwer Law International, 1997), 139–46

CLARCK, J., *Competition as a Dynamic Process* (Washington, DC, Brookings Institution, 1961)

COLLINS, W., and SUNSHINE, S., "Is Private Enforcement Effective Antitrust Policy?" in P.J. Slot and A. McDonnel (eds.), *Procedure and Enforcement in E.C. and U.S. Competition Law* (London, Sweet & Maxwell, 1993), 50–62

CONSTANTINESCO, V., "La structure du Traité instituant l'Union Européenne" (1993) 29 *CDE* 251–84

CRAIG, P., and DE BURCA, G., *The Evolution of EU Law* (Oxford, Oxford University Press, 1999)

CURTIN, D., "The Constitutional Structure of the Union: A Europe of Bits and Pieces" (1993) 30 *CMLRev.* 17–69

DASHWOOD, A., "The Limits of European Community Powers" (1996) 21 *ELR* 113–28

—— (ed.), *Reviewing Maastricht—Issues for the 1996 IGC* (London, Sweet & Maxwell, 1996)

—— "States in The European Union" (1998) 23 *ELR* 201–16

DAVIDOW, J., "Competition Policy, Merger Control and the European Community's 1992 Program" (1991) 29 *Columbia Journal for Transnational Law* 11–40

DEACON, D., "Vertical Restraints under EU Competition Law: New Directions" in B. Hawk (ed.), *Annual Proceedings of the Fordham Corporate Law Institute 1995* (Irvington-on-Hudson, Transnational Juris Publications, 1996), 307–24

DEHOUSSE, R., "Integration v. Regulation? On the Dynamics of Regulation in the Community" (1992) 30 *JCMS* 383–402

DEHOUSSE, R., "Community Competences: Are there Limits to Growth?" in R. Dehousse (ed.), *Europe after Maastricht: An Ever Closer Union?* (Munich, Beck, 1994), 103–25

—— (ed.), *Europe after Maastricht: An Ever Closer Union?* (Munich, Beck, 1994)

—— "Constitutional Reform in the European Community. Are there Alternatives to the Majority Avenue?" (1995) 18 *West European Politics* 118–36

—— "Regulation by Networks in the European Community: The Role of European Agencies" (1997) 4 *Journal of European Public Policy* 246–61

—— and MAJONE, G., "The Institutional Dynamics of European Integration: From the Single Act to the Maastricht Treaty" in S. Martin (ed.), *The Construction of Europe* (Dordrecht, Kluwer, 1994), 91–112

—— and J. WEILER, "The Legal Dimension" in W. Wallace (ed.), *The Dynamics of European Integration.* (London, Pinter, 1983), 242–60

—— *et al.*, "Europe after 1992—New Regulatory Strategies", *EUI Working Paper Law* 92/31 (Florence, EUI, 1992)

DEVROE, W., "Privatizations and Community Law: Neutrality versus Policy" (1997) 34 *CMLRev.* 267–306

DIERICKX, L., *Het europese besluitvormingsproces en het europese integratieproces* (Brussels, Editions de l'Université de Bruxelles, 1972)

DOCKSEY, C., and WILLIAMS, K., "The Commission and the Execution of Community Policy" in G. Edwards and D. Spence (eds.), *The European Commission* (Harlow, Longman, 1994), 117–45

DOERN, G. BRUCE, and WILKS, S., *Comparative Competition Policy. National Institutions in a Global Market* (Oxford, Clarendon Press, 1996)

DOWNES, T., and MACDOUGALL, D., "Significantly Impeding Effective Competition" (1994) 19 *ELR* 286–303

DREHER, M., "Gemeinsamer Europäischer Markt—einheitliche Wettbewerbsordnung?" in *Umbruch der Wettbebwerbsordnung in Europa—Referate des XXVIII. FIW-Symposions*

DUBOIS, J., "Les nouvelles propositions de la Commission Européenne concernant l'application du droit communautaire de la concurrence par les autorités nationales" (1995) *Revue Internationale de la Concurrence* no. 176

EDWARDS, G., and SPENCE, D. (eds.), *The European Commission* (Harlow, Longman, 1994)

EDWARD, M., and HOSKINS, D., "Article 90: Deregulation and EC Law: Reflections Arising from the XVI FIDE Conference" (1995) 32 *CMLRev.* 157–86

EHLERMANN, C.-D., "How Flexible is Community Law? An Unusual Approach to the Concept of 'Two Speeds' " (1984) 82 *Michigan Law Review* 1274–93

—— "The Internal Market Following the Single European Act" (1987) 24 *CMLRev.* 361–409

—— "The Contribution of EC Competition Policy to the Single Market" (1992) 29 *CMLRev.* 257–82

—— "Managing Monopolies: The Role of the State in Controlling Market Dominance in the European Community" (1993) 14 *ECLR* 61–9

—— "Ist die Verordnung Nr. 17 noch zeitgemäß?" (1993) 43 *WuW* 997–1001

—— "The European Administration and the Public Administration of Member States with Regard to Competition Law" (1995) 16 *ECLR* 454–60

—— "Anwendung des Gemeinschaftskartellrechts durch Behörden und Gerichte der

Mitgliedstaaten" in A. Randelzhofer, R. Scholz and D. Wilke (eds.), *Gedächtnisschrift für Eberhard Grabitz* (Munich, Beck, 1995), 45–55

—— "Reflections on a European Cartel Office" (1995) 32 *CMLRev.* 471–86

—— "The Evolution in Relations Between the EC Commission and National Antitrust Authorities" in *Antitrust fra diritto nazionale e diritto Comunitario*—Atti del II convengo di Treviso (Milan, Giuffré, 1996), 55–69

—— "Implementation of EC Competition Law by National Anti-Trust Authorities" (1996) 17 *ECLR* 20–7

—— "Increased Differentiation or Stronger Uniformity" in J. Winter *et al.* (eds.), *Reforming the Treaty on European Union—The Legal Debate* (Kluwer Law International, The Hague, 1996), 27–50

—— "Decision Making at the Centre—Working Paper II" in C.-D. Ehlermann and L. Laudati (eds.), *Robert Schuman Centre Annual on European Competition Law* (The Hague, Kluwer Law International, 1997), 29–44

—— "Cooperation between Competition Authorities within the European Union", in Atti del IV convegno di Treviso, *Antitrust fra diritto nazionale e diritto comunitario* (Milan, Giuffré, 1998)

——, and Drijber, B.-J., "Legal Protection of Enterprises: Administrative Procedure, in Particular Acces to Files and Confidentiality" (1996) 17 *ECLR* 375–83

——, and Laudati, L., "Introduction", in C.-D. Ehlermann and L. Laudati (eds.), *Robert Schuman Centre Annual on European Competition Law 1996* (The Hague, Kluwer Law International, 1997), pp. ix–xiv

——, and —— (eds.), *Proceedings of the European Competition Forum* (Chichester, John Wiley & Sons, 1997)

——, and —— (eds.), *Robert Schuman Centre Annual on European Competition Law 1996* (The Hague Kluwer Law International, 1997)

——, and —— (eds.), *Robert Schuman Centre Annual on European Competition Law 1997* (Oxford, Hart, 1998)

Eleftheriadis, P., "Begging the Constitutional Question" (1998) 36 *JCMS* 255–72

Esch, B. Van der, "E.E.C. Competition Rules: Basic Principles and Policy Aims" (1980) 7 *LIEI* II–75–85

—— "The Principles of Interpretation Applied by the Court of Justice of the European Communities and their Relevance for the Scope of the EEC Competition Rules" (1991–2) 15 *FILJ* 366–97

Esser-Wellié, M., "Die Anwendung der Artikel 85 und 86 EG-Vertrag durch national Gerichte" (1995) 45 *WuW* 457–74

Everling, U., "Die Koordinierung der Wirtschaftspolitik in der Europäischen Wirtschaftsgemeinschaft als Rechtsproblem" in U. Everling, *Das Europäische Gemeinschaftsrecht im Spannungsfeld von Politik und Wirtschaft* (Baden-Baden, Nomos, 1985), 195–235

—— *Das Europäische Gemeinschaftsrecht im Spannungsfeld von Politik und Wirtschaft: Ausgewählte Aufsätze, 1964–1984* (Baden-Baden, Nomos, 1985)

—— "The *Maastricht* Judgment of the German Federal Constitutional Court and its Significance for the Development of the European Union" (1994) 14 *YEL* 1–19

—— "Will Europe Slip on Bananas? The Bananas Judgement of the Court of Justice and National Courts" (1996) 33 *CMLRev.* 401–37

Everson, M., "Independent Agencies: Hierarchy Beaters?" (1995) 1 *ELJ* 180–204

Faull, J., "Effect on Trade Between Member States and Community-Member State

Jurisdiction" in B. Hawk (ed.), *Annual Proceedings of the Fordham Corporate Law Institute 1989* (New York, Transnational Juris, 1990), 485–508

FELS, A., "Decision Making at the Centre—Working Paper III" in C.-D. Ehlermann and L. Laudati (eds.), *Robert Schuman Centre Annual on European Competition Law 1996* (The Hague Kluwer Law International, 1997), 45–69

FENNELLY, N., "Reflections of an Irish Advocate General" (1996) 5 *Irish Journal of European Law* 5–19

FIERSTRA, M., "Europese Mededingingsregels in het perspectief van het Witboek voor de Interne Markt" (1989) 38 *Ars Aequi* 428–35

FLIGSTEIN, and MARA-DRITA, I., "How to Make a Market: Reflections on the Attempt to Create a Single Market in the European Union" (1996) 102 *American Journal of Sociology* 1–33

FORRESTER, I., "Competition Structures for the 21st Century" in B. Hawk (ed.), *Annual Proceedings of the Fordham Corporate Law Institute 1994—International Antitrust Law & Policy* (New York, Kluwer, 1995), 445–503

—— "The Current Goals of EC Competition Policy" in C.-D. Ehlermann and L. Laudati (eds.), *Robert Schuman Centre Annual on Competition Law—1997* (Oxford, Hart, 1998)

—— "Modernisation of EC Competition Law" in B. Hawk (ed.), *Annual Proceedings of the Fordham Corporate Law Institute 1999* (forthcoming 2000)

——, and NORALL, C., "The Laicization of Community Law: Self-help and the Rule of Reason: How Competition Law Is and Could Be Applied" (1984) 21 *CMLRev.* 11–51

FOX, E., "Decision Making at the Centre—Working Paper IV" in C.D. Ehlermann and L. Laudati (eds.), *Robert Schuman Centre Annual on European Competition Law 1996* (The Hague, Kluwer Law International, 1997), 71–8

——, and SULLIVAN, "Antitrust—Retrospective and Prospective: Where are We Coming From? Where are We Going To?" (1987) 62 *New York University Law Review* 936–88

FRAZER, T., "Competition Policy after 1992: The Next Step" (1990) 53 *MLR* 609–23

FRIEDBACHER, T., "Motive Unmasked: The European Court of Justice, the Free Movement of Goods, and the Search for Legitimacy" (1996) 2 *ELJ* 226–50

FRITZSCHE, V., " 'Notwendige' Wettbewerbsbeschränkungen im Spannungsfeld von Verbot und Freistellung nach Art. 85 EGV" (1996) 160 *ZGH* 31–108

GARCIA DE ENTERRIA, E., "The Extension of Jurisdiction of National Administrative Courts by Community Law: The Judgment of the Court of Justice in *Borelli* and Article 5 of the EC Treaty" (1993) 13 *YEL* 19–37

GARDNER, A., "The Velvet Revolution: Article 90 and the Triumph of the Free Market in Europe's Regulated Sectors" (1995) 16 *ECLR* 78–86

GELLHORN, E., "Climbing the Antitrust Law Staircase" (1986) 30 *The Antitrust Bulletin* 341–57

GERBER, D., "Law and the Abuse of Economic Power in Europe" (1987) 62 *Tulane Law Review* 57–107

—— "The Origins of European Competition Law in Fin-de-Siècle Austria" (1992) 36 *The American Journal of Legal History* 405–40

—— "The Transformation of European Community Competition Law?" (1994) 35 *Harvard International Law Journal* 97–147

—— "Constitutionalizing the Economy: German Neo-liberalism, Competition Law and the 'New' Europe" (1994) 42 *The American Journal of Comparative Law* 25–84

—— "European Law: Thinking about it and Teaching It" (1995) 1 *CJEL* 379–95

—— *Law and Competition in Twentieth Century Europe. Protecting Prometheus* (Oxford, Clarendon Press, 1998)

GERVEN, W. VAN, "Twelve Years EEC Competition Law (1962–1973) Revisited" (1974) 11 *CMLRev*. 38–61

—— "Bridging the Gap Between Community and National Laws: Towards a Principle of Homogeneity in the Field of Legal Remedies" (1995) 32 *CMLRev*. 679–702

—— "Bridging the Unbridgeable: Community and National Tort Laws after *Francovich* and *Brasserie*" (1996) 45 *ICLQ* 507–44

GOH, J., "Enforcing EC Competition Law in Member States" (1993) 14 *ECLR* 114–17

GONZALEZ DIAZ, F., "The Notion of Ancillary Retraints under EC Competition Law" (1996) 19 *FILJ* 951–98

GOYDER, D., "The Implementation of the EC Merger Regulation—New Wine in Old Bottles" (1992) 45 *Current Legal Problems* 117–43

—— *EC Competition Law* (Oxford, Clarendon Press, 1998)

—— "The Role of National Competition Law—Working Paper II" in C.-D. Ehlermann and L. Laudati, *Robert Schuman Centre Annual on European Competition Law 1996* (The Hague, Kluwer Law International, 1997), 263–70

GRAUPNER, F., "Commission Decision-Making on Competition Questions" (1973) 10 *CMLRev*. 291–305

GREEN, N., "Article 85 in Perspective: Stretching Jurisdiction, Narrowing the Concept of a Restriction and Plugging a Few Gaps" (1988) 9 *ECLR* 190–206

GRIFFITHS, R., "The European Integration Experience" in K. Middlemas, *Orchestrating Europe* (London, Fontana Press, 1995), 1–70

—— "Agricultural Pressure Groups and the Origins of the Common Agricultural Policy" (1995) 3 *European Review* 233–42

GROEBEN, H. VON DER, "A European Policy on Competition" [1960] *Bulletin of the European Economic Community* (No. 3)

—— *The European Community: The Formative Years. The Struggle to Establish the Common Market and the Political Union* (Brussels, European Perspectives Series, 1985)

—— *Die Europäische Gemeinschaft und die Herausforderungen unserer Zeit; Aufsätze und Reden 1967–1987* (Baden-Baden, Nomos Verlagsgesellschaft, 1987)

GROGER, T., and JANICKI, T., "Weiterentwicklung des europäischen Wettbewerbsrechts" (1992) 42 *WuW* 991–1005

GYSELEN, L., "Le juge national face aux règles de concurrence communautaires applicable aux entreprises" (1993) 1 *JTDE* 25–33

HAAS, E., *The Uniting of Europe, Political Social, and Economic Corces 1950–1957* (Stanford, Cal., Stanford University Press, 1958)

HALL, D., "Enforcement of E.C. Competition Law by National Courts" in P. Slot and A. McDonnell, *Procedure and Enforcement in E.C. and U.S. Competition Law* (London, Sweet & Maxwell, 1993), 41–9

HALLSTEIN, W., *Die europäische Gemeinschaft* (Düsseldorf, Econ Verlag, 1973)

—— *Europe in the Making* (London, George Allen & Unwin, 1976)

HARMSEN, R., "A European Union of Variable Geometry: Problems and Perspectives" (1994) 45 *Northern Ireland Legal Quarterly* 109–33

HARTLEY, T.C., "Federalism, Courts and Legal Systems; The Emerging Constitution of the European Community" (1986) 34 *AJCL* 229–47

HARTLEY, T.C., "Constitutional and Institutional Aspects of the Maastricht Agreement" (1993) 42 *ICLQ* 213–37

—— "The European Court and Judicial Objectivity and the Constitution of the European Union" (1996) 112 *The Law Quarterly Review* 95–109

HAWK, B., "System Failure: Vertical Restraints and EC Competition Law" (1995) 32 *CMLRev.* 973–89

——, and LAUDATI, L., "Antitrust Federalism in the United States and Decentralisation of Competition Law Enforcement in the European Union: A Comparison" (1996) 20 *FILJ* 18–49

——, and VELTROP, J., "Dual Antitrust Enforcement in the United States: Positive or Negative Lessons for the European Community" in P.J. Slot and A. McDonnel (eds.), *Procedure and Enforcement in E.C. and U.S. Competition Law* (London, Sweet & Maxwell, 1993), 21–31

——, and ——, "Recent Developments in U.S. Antitrust Law" in *Antitrust fra diritto nazionale e diritto Comunitario*—Atti del II convegno di Treviso (Milano, Giuffré, 1996)

HEISTERMANN, F., "Praxis der EG-Kommission und des Bundeskartellamtes zur Fusionskontrolle" in *Schwerpunkte des Kartellrechts 1993/94—Referate des Zweiundzwanzigsten FIW-Seminars 1994* (Cologne, Carl Heymanns, 1995), 51–70

HEUKELS, T., BLOKKER, N., and BRUS, M. (eds.), *The European Union after Amsterdam—A Legal Analysis* (The Hague, Kluwer Law International, 1998)

HIRSBRUNNER, S., "Referral of Mergers in E.C. Merger Control" (1999) 20 *ECLR* 372–8

HORNSBY, S., "Competition Policy in the 80s: More Policy, Less Competition" (1987) 12 *ELR* 79–101

House of Lords Select Committee on the European Communities, *Merger Control*, Session 1988/89—6th Report (London, HMSO, 1989)

—— *Enforcement of Community Competition Rules*, 1st Report, Session 1993–94 (HL Paper 7) (London, HMSO, 1993)

JACHTENFUCHS, M., "Theoretical Perspectives on European Governance" (1995) 1 *ELJ* 115–33

JACQUÉ, J., and WEILER, J., "On the Road to the European Union, A New Judicial Architecture" (1990) 27 *CMLRev.* 185–207

JANICKI, T., and MOLITOR, B., "Wettbewerbssicherung durch Schaffung eines europäischen Kartellamtes" (1995) 75 *Wirtschaftsdienst* 7577

JOERGES, C., "Contract and Status in Franchising Law" in C. Joerges (ed.), *Franchising and the Law* (Baden-Baden, Nomos, 1991), 11–66

—— "Rationalization Processes in Contract Law and the Law of Product Safety: Observations on the Impact of European Integration on Private Law", *EUI Working Paper Law No. 94/5* (Florence, EUI, 1994)

—— "European Economic Law, the Nation-State and the Maastricht Treaty" in R. Dehousse (ed.), *Europe After Maastricht—An Ever Closer Union?* (Munich, Beck, 1994)

—— "The Market Without the State? States Without a Market?", *EUI Working Paper Law* No. 96/2 (Florence, EUI, 1996)

—— "The Impact of European Integration on Private Law Reductionist Perceptions, True Conflicts and a New Constitutional Perspective" (1997) 3 *ELJ* 378–406

——, and NEYER, J., "From Intergovernmental Bargaining to Deliberative Political Processes: The Constitutionalisation of Comitology" (1997) 3 *ELJ* 273–99

JUNG, C., *Subsidiarität im Recht der Wettbewerbsbeschränkungen* (Heidelberg, C.F. Müller, 1994)

KAPTEYN, P., "Outgrowing the Treaty of Rome: From Market Integration to Policy Integration" in *Mélanges Fernand Dehousse* (Volume 2) (Paris, Fernand Nathan, 1979), 45–55

——, and VERLOREN VAN THEMAAT, P., *Introduction to the Law of the European Communities* (Deventer, Kluwer, 1999)

KARTTE, W., "Zur institutionellen Absicherung der EG-Fusionskontrolle" (1993) 44 *Jahrbuch für die Ordnung von Wirtschaft und Gesellschaft (ORDO)* 405–13

KASSAMALI, R., "From Fiction to Fallacy: Reviewing the E.C. Merger Regulation's Community-Dimension Thresholds in the Light of Economics and Experience in Merger Control" (1996) 21 *ELR/CC* 89–114

O'KEEFFE, D., "The Schengen Conventions: A Suitable Model for European Integration?" (1991) 11 *YEL* 185–220

—— "Recasting the Third Pillar" (1995) 32 *CMLRev.* 893–920

O'KEEFFE, S., "Merger Regulation Thresholds: An Analysis of the Community-dimension Thresholds in Regulation 4064/89" (1994) 15 *ECLR* 21–31

KELLEHER, G., "Antitrust Trade Regulation in the European Common Market" in *Foreign Operations of American Business Enterprises* (New York, Fordham University Press, 1962), 91–104

—— "The Common Market Antitrust Laws: The First Ten Years" (1967) 12 *The Antitrust Bulletin* 1219–52

KERBER, W., *Die Europäische Fusionskontrollpraxis und die Wettbewerbskonzeption der EG* (Bayreuth, P.C.O., 1994)

KERSE, C.S., *EC Antitrust Procedure* (London, Sweet & Maxwell, 1994)

—— "Enforcing Community Competition Policy under Articles 88 and 89 of the E.C. Treaty—New Powers for U.K. Competition Authorities" (1997) 18 *ECLR* 17–23

—— "The Complainant in Competition Cases: A Progress Report" (1997) 34 *CMLRev.* 213–65

KIELMANSEGG, I., "Integration und Demokratie" in M. Jachtenfuchs and B. Kohler-Koch (eds.), *Europäische Integration* (Opladen, 1996), 47–72

KLAUE, S., "Einige Bemerkungen über die Zukunft des Zweischrankentheorie" in J. Baur *et al.* (eds.), *Festschrift für Ernst Steindorff* (Berlin, Walter de Gruyter, 1990), 979–82

KLIMISCH, A., and KRUEGER, B., "Decentralised Application of EC Competition Law Current Practice and Future Prospects" (1999) 23 *EL Rev.* 463–82

KOENIGS, F., "Die Beeinträchtigung des Handels zwischen Mitgliedstaaten als Abgrenzungskriterium zwischen dem EWG-Kartellrecht und dem nationalen Recht der Mitgliedstaaten" in O. von Gamm *et al.*, *Strafrecht, Unternehmensrecht, Anwaltsrecht—Festschrift für Gerd Pfeiffer* (Cologne, Carl Heymanns, 1988), 569–87

KON, S., and MAXWELL, A., "Enforcement in National Courts of the E.C. and New U.K. Competition Rules: Obstacles to Effective Enforcement" (1998) 19 *ECLR* 443–54

KOOPMANS, T., "Europe and Its Lawyers in 1984" (1985) 22 *CMLRev.* 9–18

—— "The Role of Law in the Next Stage of European Integration" (1986) 35 *ICLQ* 925–31

—— "De plaats van het kartelrecht in het EG mededingingsrecht" (1987) 35 *SEW* 421–31

—— "Het post-Maastrichtse Europa" (1996) 71 *Nederlands Juristenblad* 305–15

KORAH, V., "Goodbye, Red Label; Condemnation of Dual Pricing by Distillers" (1978) 2 *ELR* 62–71

—— "Comfort Letters—Reflections on the Perfume Cases" (1981) 6 *ELR* 14–39

—— "EEC Competition Policy—Legal Form or Economic Efficiency" (1986) 39 *Current Legal Problems* 85–109

KORAH, V., "The Judgment in *Delimitis*-A Milestone Towards a Realistic Assessment of the Effects of an Agreement—or a Damp Squib?" (1993) 8 *Tulane European & Civil Law Forum* 17–51

—— "Collaborative Joint Ventures for Research and Development where Markets are Concentrated: The Competition Rules of the Common Market and the Invalidity of Contracts" (1993) 13 *YEL* 39–81

—— "Tetra Pak II—Lack of Reasoning in Court's Judgment" (1997) 18 *ECLR* 98–103

—— "Future Competition Law" in L. Laudati and C.-D. Ehlermann (eds.), *Robert Schuman Centre Annual on European Competition Law 1997* (Oxford, Hart, 1998)

——, and HORSPOOL, M., "Competition" (1992) 37 *Antitrust Bulletin* 337–85

KOVAR, R., "Marché intérieur et politique de concurrence" (1989) 15 *Droit et pratique du commerce international* 230–46

KUILWIJK, K.J., and WRIGHT, R. (eds.), *European Trade and Industry in the 21st Century—Future Directions in EC Law and Policy* (Beuningen, Nexed Editions, 1996)

KÜSTERS, H.-J., *Fondements de la Communauté Economique Européenne* (Luxembourg, Office des Publications Officielles des Communautés Européennes, 1990)

LADEUR, K.-H., "Towards a Legal Theory of Supranationality—The Viability of the Network Concept" (1997) 3 *ELJ* 33–54

LAMPERT, T., *Die Anwendbarkeit der EG-Fusionskontrollverordnung im Verhältnis zum Fusionskontrollrecht der Mitgliedstaaten* (Cologne, Carl Heymanns, 1995)

LAUDATI, L., "The European Commission as Regulator: The Uncertain Pursuit of the Competitive Market" in G. Majone, *Regulating Europe* (London, Routledge, 1996), 229–61

LAURILA, M., "The De Minimis Doctrine in EEC Competition Law: Agreements of Minor Importance" (1993) 14 *ECLR* 97–102

LAVDAS, K., and MENDRINOU, M., "Competition Policy and Institutional Politics in the European Community: State-aid Control and Small Business Promotion" (1995) 28 *European Journal of Political Research* 171–201

LENAERTS, K., "Constitutionalism and the Many Faces of Federalism" (1990) 38 *AJCL* 205–63

—— "Some Thoughts About the Interaction Between Judges and Politicians" [1992] *The University of Chicago Legal Forum* 93–133

——, and VANHAMME, J., "Procedural Rights of Private Parties in the Community Administrative Process" (1997) 34 *CMLRev.* 531–69

LENZ, C.-O., "Das Amt des Generalanwalts am Europäischen Gerichtshof" in O. Due, Lutter and J. Schwarze (eds.), *Festschrift für Ulrich Everling* (Baden-Baden, Nomos, 1995), 719–27

LEVITT, M., "Commission Hearings and the Role of the Hearing Officer: Suggestions for Reform" (1998) 19 *ECLR* 404–8

LIEBERKNECHT, O., "Das Verhältnis der EWG-Gruppenfreistellungsverordnungen zum deutschen Kartellrecht" in O. von Gamm *et al.*, *Strafrecht, Unternehmensrecht, Anwaltsrecht—Festschrift für Gerd Pfeiffer* (Köln, Carl Heymanns, 1988), 589–606

LUGARD, H.H. PAUL, "E.C. Competition Law and Arbitration: Opposing Principles?" (1998) 19 *ECLR* 295–301

LUKOFF, F., European Competition Law and Distribution in the Motor Vehicle Industry: Commission Regulation 123/85 of 12 December 1984" (1986) 23 *CMLRev.* 841–66

MAJONE, G., "Deregulation or Re-Regulation? Policymaking in the European Community Since the Single Act" *EUI Working Paper SPS No. 93/2* (Florence, EUI, 1993)

—— "The European Commission as Regulator" in G. Majone, *Regulating Europe* (London, Routledge, 1996), 61–79

—— *Regulating Europe* (London, Routledge, 1996)

MANCINI, F., "The Making of a Constitution for Europe" (1989) 26 *CMLRev.* 595–614

MANCINI, G., and KEELING, F., "Language, Culture and Politics in the Life of the European Court of Justice" (1995) 1 *CJEL* 397–413

MANZINI, P., "La rule of reason nel Diritto Comunitario della Concorrenza" (1991) 31 *Rivista di Diritto Europeo* 859–82

MARENCO, G., "The Uneasy Enforcement of Article 85 EEC as Between Community and National Levels" in B. Hawk (ed.), *Annual Proceedings of the Fordham Corporate Law Institute 1993, Antitrust in a Global Economy* (New York, Transnational Juris Publications, 1994), 605–27

MARKERT, K., "Some Legal and Administrative Problems of the Co-Existence of Community and National Competition Law in the EEC" (1974) 11 *CMLRev.* 92–104

—— "Die Rolle des Bundeskartellamtes bei der Durchsetzung des Wettbewerbsrechts in der Bundesrepublik Deutschland" in B. Blaurock (ed.), *Institutionen und Grundfragen des Wettbewerbsrecht* (Frankfurt, Metzner, 1988)

MARIA BENEYTO, J., "Transforming Competition Law Through Subsidiarity" in Academy of European Law (ed.), *Collected Courses of the Academy of European Law, Vol. V, Book 1* (The Hague, Kluwer Law International, 1996), 267–319

MARTINEZ LAGE, S., "The Role of National Law—Working Paper V" in C.-D. Ehlermann and L. Laudati (eds.), *Robert Schuman Centre Annual on Competition Law 1996* (The Hague, Kluwer Law International, 1997), 283–90

MASELIS, I., and GILLIAMS, H., "Rights of Complainants in Community Law" (1997) 22 *ELR* 103–24

MASSEY, P., "Reform of EC Competition Law—Substance, Procedure and Institutions in B. Hawk (ed.), *Annual Proceedings of the Fordham Corporate Law Institute 1996* (London, Sweet & Maxwell, 1997), 91–124

MAY, J., "Historical Analysis in Antitrust Law" (1990) 35 *New York Law School Law Review* 857–79

MAYNE, R., *The Recovery of Europe: From Devastation to Unity* (New York, Harper & Row, 1970)

McGOWAN, L., and WILKS, S., "The First Supranational Policy in the European Union: Competition Policy" (1995) 28 *European Journal of Political Research* 141–69

McKENZIE STUART, L., "Joint Venture Analysis: The Latest Chapter" (1995) 16 *ECLR* 138–49

MESTMÄCKER, E.-J., "Fusionskontrolle im Gemeinsamen Markt zwischen Wettbewerbspolitik und Industriepolitik" (1988) 23 *EuR* 349–77

—— "Versuch einer Kartellpolitischen Wende in der EU" (1999) 49 *WuW* 523–9

MEUNIER, P., "La Cour de justice des Communautés européennes et l'applicabilité directe des règles de concurrence du Traité CECA" (1996) 32 *RTDE* 243–58

MIERT, K. VAN, "The Proposal for a European Competition Agency" (1996) 2 *Competition Policy Newsletter* (No.2) 1–4

—— "The Future of Merger Control in Europe" (Fiesole, European University Institute, 26 September 1997)

MILWARD, A., *The Reconstruction of Europe, 1945–1951* (London, Methuen, 1984)

MOK, M., "The Cartel Policy of the EEC Commission 1962–1967. Analysis of the Application of Some Basic Concepts in Article 85 of the EEC Treaty" (1968) 6 *CMLRev.* 67–103

Monopolkommission, *Hauptgutachten 1988/89 "Wettbewerbspolitik vor neuen Herausforderungen"* (Baden-Baden, Nomos, 1990)

MONTAG, S., "The Case for a Radical Reform of the Infringement Procedure under Regulation 17" (1996) 17 *ECLR* 430–2

MORAVCSIK, A., "Negotiating the Single Market Act: National Interests and Conventional Statecraft in the European Community" (1991) 45 *International Organization* 19–56

MORTELMANS, K., "Community Law: More Than A Functional Area of Law, Less Than A Legal System" (1996) *LIEI* I–23–50

MOURIK, A. VAN, "Five Years of Community Merger Control" in A. van Mourik (ed.), *Developments in European Competition Policy* (Maastricht, European Institute of Public Administration, 1996), 19–52

MÜLLER-GRAF, P., "Die Freistellung vom Kartellverbot" (1992) 27 *EuR* 1–40

NEILL, SIR PATRICK, "The European Court of Justice: A Case Study of Judicial Activism" in House of Lords Select Committee, *1996 Inter-Governmental Conference Minutes of Evidence*. Session 1994–95, 18th Report. (London, HMSO, 1995)

NERI, S., and SPERL, H., *Traité instituant la Communauté Economique Européenne, Travaux préparatoires* (Luxembourg, Cour de Justice des Communités Européennes, 1960)

NEVEN, D. *et al.*, *Merger in Daylight—The Economics and Politics of European Merger Control* (London, CEPR, 1993)

NEYER, J., and WOLF, D., "Zusammenfügen was zusammengehört!" (1996) 3 *Zeitschrift für Internationale Beziehungen* 399–408

NIEDERLEITHINGER, E., "Das Verhältnis nationaler und europäischer Kontrolle von Zusammenschlüssen" (1990) 25 *WuW* 721–30

NOEL, P.-E., "Efficiency Considerations in the Assessment of Horizontal Mergers under European and U.S. Antitrust Law" (1997) 18 *ECLR* 498–519

OBERENDER, P., and OKRUCH, S., "Gegenwärtige Probleme und zukünftige Perspektiven der europäischen Wettbewerbspolitik" (1994) 44 *WuW* 507–20

OECD, *Competition Policy and Vertical Restraints: Franchising Agreements* (Paris, OECD, 1994)

ORTIZ BLANCO, L., *European Community Competition Procedure* (Oxford, Clarendon Press, 1996)

PAPPALARDO, A., "Les relations entre le droit Communautaire et les droits nationaux de la concurrence" (1995) 9 *Revue Internationale de Droit Economique* 123–60

PAULIS, E., "Decentralisation of Enforcement of Community Law—Panel Discussion" in C.-D. Ehlermann and L. Laudati (eds.), *Robert Schuman Centre Annual on European Commpetition Law 1996* (London, Kluwer Law International, 1997), 98–100

PERA, A., "Enforcement of EC Competition Rules—Need For A Reform?" in B. Hawk (ed.), *Annual Proceedings of the FCLI 1996* (London, Sweet & Maxwell, 1997), 125–48

PESCATORE, P., "Les Objectifs de la Communauté Euopéenne comme Principes d'Interprétation dans la Jurisprudence de la Court de Justice" in *Miscellanea W.J. Ganshof van der Meersch* (Tome deuxième) (Bruxelles, Émile Bruylant, 1972), 325–63

—— "Public and Private Aspects of European Community Competition Law" (1987) 10 *FILJ* 373–419

—— "Some Critical Remarks on the Single European Act" (1987) 24 *CMLRev.* 9–18

PITOFSKY, R., "The Political Content of Antitrust" (1979) 127 *University of Pennsylvania Law Review* 1051–75

POWER, V., "Competition Law in the EU: Should there be a Convention?" (1995) 16 *ECLR* 75–7

RATING, S., "Die Kommission schlägt eine neue Bagatelbekanntmachung vor" (1997) 3 *Competition Policy Newsletter* 8–10

REICH, N., "Die Bedeutung der Binnenmarktkonzeption für die Anwendung der EWG-Wettbewerbsregeln" in J. Baur *et al.* (eds.), *Festschrift für Ernst Steindorff* (Berlin, De Gruyter, 1990), 1065–84

—— "Competition Between Legal Orders: A New Paradigm of EC Law?" (1992) 29 *CMLRev.* 861–96

—— "The 'November Revolution' of the European Court of Justice: *Keck, Meng* and *Audi* Revisited" (1994) 31 *CMLRev.* 459–92

REYNOLDS, M., "The Future of Merger Control in Europe" (1998) 26 *International Business Lawyer* 100–1

RIEGER, E., "Agrarpolitik: Integration durch Gemeinschaftspolitik?" in M. Jachtenfuchs and B. Kohler-Koch (eds.), *Europäische Integration* (Opladen, Leske + Budrich, 1996), 401–28

RILEY, A., "More Radicalism, Please: The Notice on Co-operation Between National Courts and the Commission in Applying Articles 85 and 86 of the EEC Treaty" (1994) 15 *ECLR* 91–6

—— "The European Cartel Office: A Guardian Without Weapons?" (1997) 18 *ECLR* 3–16

RODGER, B., "Decentralisation and National Competition Authorities: Comparison with the Conflicts/Tensions under the Merger Regulation" (1994) 15 *ECLR* 251–4

—— "Decentralisation, the Public Interest and the 'Pursuit of Certainty' " (1995) 16 *ECLR* 395–9

——, and MACCULLOCH, A., "Community Competition Law Enforcement—Deregulation and Re-Regulation: The Commission, National Authorities and Private Enforcement" (1998) 4 *CJEL* 579–612

——, and WYLIE, S., "Taking the Community Interest Line: Decentralisation and Subsidiarity in Competition Law Enforcement" (1997) 18 *ECLR* 485–91

—— "The Commission White Paper on Modernisation of the Rules Implementing Articles 81 and 82 of the EC Treaty" (1999) 24 *EL Rev.* 553–63

ROHRARDT, K., "Grünbuch über vertikale Beschränkungen des Wettbewerbs—Diskussion Frei?" (1997) 47 *WuW* 473–85

ROSE, V. (ed.), *Bellamy and Child Common Market Law of Competition* (London, Sweet & Maxwell, 1993)

Ross, G., *Jacques Delors and European Integration* (Oxford, Polity Press, 1995)

Rowe, M., "Ice Cream: The Saga Continues" (1998) 19 *ECLR* 479–81

Samkalden, I., and Druker, I., "Legal Problems Relating to Article 86 of the Rome Treaty" (1966) 3 *CMLRev*. 158–83

Sandholtz, W., and Zysman, J., "1992: Recasting the European Bargain" (1989) 42 *World Politics* 95–128

Sauter, H., "Zusammenarbeit zwischen nationalen Wettbewerbsbehörden und der Kommission" in J. Kruse *et al*. (eds.), *Wettbewerbspolitik im Spannungsfeld nationaler und internationaler Kartellrechtsordnungen* (Baden-Baden, Nomos, 1997), 97–108

Sauter, W., "The Economic Constitution of the European Union" (1998) 4 *CJEL* 27–68

Scharpf, F., "Negative and Positive Integration in the Political Economy of European Welfare States", pp. 15–39, in G. Marks (*et al*.), *Governance in the European Union* (London, Sage, 1995)

—— "Economic Integration, Democracy and the Welfare State" (1997) 4 *Journal of European Public Policy* 18–36

Schaub, A., "Binnenmarkt, Währungsunion, Erweiterung—Fragen an die Europäische Wettbewerbspolitik", *XVII Internationales Forum EG-Kartellrecht* organised by the Studienvereinigung Kartellrecht (Brussels, May 1997)

—— "Decision Making at the Centre—Working Paper V" in C.-D. Ehlermann and L. Laudati (eds.), *Robert Schuman Centre Annual on Competition Policy 1996* (The Hague, Kluwer Law International, 1997), 79–87

Schmid, C., "Vertical and Diagonal Conflicts in the Europeanisation Process-Preliminary Thoughts on a Methodological Reconstruction of the Interface between European and National Law on a Conflict of Laws Basis" in C. Joerges and O. Gerstenberg, *Private Governance, Democratic Constitutionalism and Supranationalism* (Luxembourg, Office for Official Publications of the EC, 1998), 185–90

Schödermeier, M., and Wagner, A., "Rechtsschutz gegen Verwaltungsschreiben der EG-Kommission" (1994) 44 *WuW* 403–14

Schröter, H., "The Application of Article 85 of the EEC Treaty to Distribution Agreements—Principles and Recent Developments" in B. Hawk (ed.), *Annual Proceedings of the Fordham Corporate Law Institute 1983* (New York, Matthew Bender, 1984), 375–451

—— "Antitrust Analysis under Article 85(1) and (3)" in B. Hawk (ed.), *Annual Proceedings of the Fordham Corporate Law Institute* (Irvington-on-Hudson, Transnational Juris Publications, 1988), 645–92

—— "Zur Beurteilung vertikaler Wettbewerbsbeschränkungen nach Artikel 85 des EG-Vertrages", FIW Seminar Brussels, 24 September 1996

—— "Vertical Restrictions under Article 85 EC: Towards a Moderate Reform of Current Competition Policy" in L. Gormley (ed.), *Current and Future Perspectives on EC Competition Law* (London, Kluwer Law International, 1997), 15–30

Schwartz, E., "Politics as Usual: The History of European Community Merger Control" (1993) 18 *Yale Journal of International Law* 607–62

Schwarze, J., "Vorrang des Gemeinschaftsrechts und deutsches Kartell- und Wettbewerbsrecht" (1996) 51 *JuristenZeitung* 57–64

Seabright, P., "European Union Policy Towards Vertical Restraints: A Proposal and an Assessment", paper presented at CEPR/RSC Workshop, *Recent Developments in the Design and Implementation of Competition Policy*, held in Florence on 29/30 November 1996

SELIGER, B., "Ein unabhängiges Kartellamt für Europa—ordnungs- und wettbewerbspolitischen Aspekte" (1997) 47 *WuW* 874–81

SHARPE, T., "The Distillers Decision" (1978) 15 *CMLRev.* 447–64

—— "The Commission's Proposals on Crisis Cartels" (1980) 17 *CMLRev.* 75–90

SHAW, J., "Introduction" in J. Shaw and G. More (eds.), *New Legal Dynamics of European Union* (Oxford, Clarendon Press, 1995), 1–14

—— "Decentralization and Law Enforcement in EC Competition Law" (1995) 15 *Legal Studies* 128–68

—— "European Legal Studies in Crisis? Towards a New Dynamic?" (1996) 16 *Oxford Journal of Legal Studies* 231–53

—— "The Treaty of Amsterdam: Challenges of Flexibility and Legitimacy" (1998) 4 *ELJ* 63–86

SIMSON, W. VON, "The Concept of Competition in the European Community" in J. Schwarze and H. Schermers (eds.), *Structure and Dimensions of European Community Policy* (Baden-Baden, Nomos Verlagsgesellschaft, 1988), 139–46

SIRAGUSA, M., "The Lowering of the Thresholds: An Opportunity to Harmonise Merger Control" (1993) 14 *ECLR* 139–42

——, and SCASSELLATI-SFORZOLINI, G., "Italian and EC Competition Law: A New Relationship—Reciprocal Exclusivity and Common Principles" (1992) 29 *CMLRev.* 93–131

——, and SUBIOTTO, M., "The EEC Merger Control Regulation: The Commission's Evolving Case Law" (1991) 28 *CMLRev.* 877–99

SLAUGHTER-BURLEY, A.-M., "New Directions in Legal Research on the European Community" (1993) 31 *JCMS* 391–400

SLOT, P., "The Enforcement of EC Competition Law in Arbitral Proceedings" (1996) 23 *LIEI* 1–101–13

SLYNN, G., "EEC Competition Law From the Perspective of the Court of Justice" in B. Hawk (ed.), *Annual Proceedings of the Fordham Corporate Law Institute 1985* (New York, Matthew Bender, 1986), 383–408

SNELDERS, R., "Developments in E.C. Merger Control in 1995" (1996) 21 *ELR/CC* No. 2, 66–88

SNYDER, F., "New Directions in European Community Law" (1987) 14 *Journal of Law and Society* 167–82

—— *New Directions in European Community Law* (London, Weidenfeld & Nicholson, 1990)

—— "The Effectiveness of European Community Law: Institutions, Processes, Tools and Techniques" (1993) 56 *MLR* 19–54

—— "Soft Law and Institutional Practice in the European Community" in S. Martin (ed.), *The Construction of Europe—Essays in Honour of Emile Noel* (Dordrecht, Kluwer, 1994), 179–225

—— "EMU—Metaphor for European Union? Institutions, Rules and Types of Regulation" in R. Dehousse (ed.), *Europe After Maastricht—An Ever Closer Union?* (Munich, Beck, 1994), 63–99

—— "General Course on Constitutional Law of the European Union" in Academy of European Law (ed.), *Collected Courses of the Academy of European Law 1996, Volume VI, Book 1* (Dordrecht, Kluwer, 1997)

SOUTY, F., "La politique de la concurrence trente ans après Chicago: principaux enseigne-ments" in J. Kruse *et al.* (eds.), *Wettbewerbspolitik im Spannungsfeld nationaler und internationaler Kartellrechtsordnungen* (Baden-Baden, Nomos, 1997), 85–96

SPENCE, D., "Structure, Functions and Procedures in the Commission" in G. Edwards and D. Spence (eds.), *The European Commission*

STEENBERGEN, J., "Decision-making in Competition Cases: The Investigator, the Prosecutor and the Judge" in L. Gormley (ed.), *Current and Future Perspectives on EC Competition Law* (The Hague, Kluwer Law International, 1997), 101–8

STEIN, E., "Lawyers, Judges, and the Making of a Transnational Constitution" (1981) 75 *The American Journal of International Law* 1–27

—— "The European Community in 1983: A Less Perfect Union?" (1983) 20 *CMLRev.* 641–56

STEINDORFF, E., "Spannungen zwischen deutschem und europäischem Wettbewerbs-recht" in *Schwerpunkte des Kartellrechts 1986/87* (Cologne, Carl Heymanns, 1988), 27–54

STEVENS, D., "The "Comfort Letter": Old Problems, New Developments" (1994) 15 *ECLR* 81–8

STOCKMANN, K., "EEC Competition Law and Member State Competition Laws" in B. Hawk (ed.), *Annual Proceedings of the Fordham Corporate Law Institute 1987* (New York, Transnational Juris Publications, 1988), 265–300

STREIT, M., "Economic Order, Private Law and Public Policy: The Freiburg School of Law and Economics in Perspective" (1992) 148 *Journal of Industrial and Theoretical Economics* 675–704

——, and MUSSLER, W., "The Economic Constitution of the European Community: From 'Rome' to 'Maastricht' " (1995) 1 *ELJ* 5–30

STUBB, A., "The 1996 Intergovernmental Conference and the Management of Flexible Integration" (1997) 4 *Journal of European Public Policy* 37–55

STUCYK, J., "Competition Law in the EC and in the Member States" in O. Due *et al.* (eds.), *Festschrift für Ulrich Everling—Band II* (Baden-Baden, Nomos, 1995), 1511–27

STURM, R., "The German Cartel Office in a Hostile Environment" in G. Bruce Doern and S. Wilks, *Comparative Competition Policy* (Oxford, Clarendon Press, 1996), 185–224

TASH, A., "Remedies for European Community Law Claims in Member State Courts: Toward a European Standard" (1993) 31 *Columbia Journal for Transnational Law* 377–401

TEMPLE LANG, J., "Community Antitrust Law: Compliance and Enforcement" (1981) 18 *CMLRev.* 335–62

—— "The Core of Community Constitutional Law: Article 5 of the EC Treaty" (1990) 27 *CMLRev.* 645–81

—— "European Community Constitutional Law and the Enforcement of Community Antitrust Law" in B. Hawk (ed.), *Annual Proceedings of the Fordham Corporate Law Institute 1993* (New York, Transnational Juris Publications, 1994), 525–605

—— "The Duties of National Courts under Community Constitutional Law" (1997) 22 *ELR* 3–18

—— "The Duties of National Authorities under Community Constitutional Law" (1998) 23 *ELR* 109–31

—— "General Report", at 1998 FIDE Congress *Application of Community Competition Law on Enterprises by National Courts and National Authorities*

TESAURO, G., "The Community's Internal Market in the light of the Recent Case-law of the Court of Justice" (1995) 15 *YEL* 1–16

TINBERGEN, J., *International Economic Integration* (2nd edn., Amsterdam, Elsevier, 1965)

TORREMANS, P., and STAMATOUDI, I., "Collecting Societies: Sorry, the Community is No Longer Interested!" (1997) 22 *ELR* 352–9

TRABUCCHI, A., " 'Neues und Altes' in der Entwicklung auf dem Gebiet des Wettbewerbs in der Europäischen Gemeinschaft" in Studienvereinigung Kartellrecht eV (ed.), *Neue Entwicklungen im EWG-Kartellrecht* (Cologne, Carl Heymanns Verlag KG, 1975), 13–26

TSOUKALIS, L., *The New European Economy—The Politics and Economics of Integration* (Oxford, Oxford University Press, 1993)

ULLRICH, H., "Harmonisation within the European Union" (1996) 17 *ECLR* 178–84

ULMER, P., "Die Anwendung des EWG-Kartellrechts auf 'nationale' Wettbewerbs-beschränkungen und ihre Folgewirkungen für das nationale Kartellrecht" in Studienvereinigung Kartellrecht eV (ed.), *Neue Entwicklungen im EWG-Kartellrecht* (Cologne, Carl Heymanns, 1976), 69–91

USHER, J., "Variable Geometry or Concentric Circles: Patterns for the European Union" (1997) 46 *ICLQ* 243–73

VÄTH, A., *Die Wettbewerbskonzeption des Europäischen Gerichtshof* (Bayreuth, Verlag P.C.O., 1987)

VENIT, J., "The 'Merger' Control Regulation: Europe Comes of Age . . . Or Caliban's Dinner" (1990) 27 *CMLRev.* 7–50

—— "Economic Analysis, 'Quick Looks' and Article 85: A Way Forward?" in L. Laudati and C.-D. Ehlermann (eds.), *Robert Schuman Centre Annual on Competition Law 1997* (Oxford, Hart, 1998)

VERLOREN VAN THEMAAT, P., "Hoofdlijnen en doelstellingen van de artikelen 85–90 van het EEG-verdrag. Geschiedenis van de Verordening no. 17" in Snijders *et al.*, *Europees Kartelrecht* (Deventer, Kluwer, 1963), 41–60

—— "Some Preliminary Observations on the Intergovernmental Conferences: The Relations Between a Common Market, A Monetary Union, an Economic Union, a Political Union and Sovereignty" (1991) 28 *CMLRev.* 29–51

—— "The Dialectic Relationship between Institutional Law and Substantive Tasks in and after the Treaty of Maastricht: Some Lessons from Henry G. Schermers and from Jean Monnet" in D. Curtin and T. Heukels, *Institutional Dynamics of European Integration—Essays in Honour of Henry G. Schermers* (Martinus Nijhoff, Dordrecht, 1994), ii, 3–21

—— "Einige Betrachtungen über die Zukunft der Europäischen Union aus der Sicht eines weltoffenen Nachbarlands" in O. Due, M. Lubber, and J. Schwarze (eds.), *Festschrift für Ulrich Everling* (Baden-Baden, Nomos, 1995), 1543–60

—— "Einige Betrachtungen über die Entwicklung der Wettbewerbspolitik in Europa vor und seit dem Zustandekommen der Verordnung 17/62" in U. Everling, Narjes and Sedemund (eds.), *Europarecht, Kartellrecht, Wirtschaftsrecht. Festschrift für Arved Deringer* (Baden-Baden, Nomos Verlagsgesellschaft, 1996), 398–415

VERSTRYNGE, J.-F., "The Relationship Between National and Community Antitrust Law: An Overview after the Perfume Cases" (1981) 3 *Northwestern Journal of International Law and Business* 358–83

—— "Current Antitrust Policy Issues in the EEC: Some Reflections on the Second Generation of EEC Competition Policy" in B. Hawk (ed.), *Annual Proceedings of the Fordham Corporate Law Institute 1984: Antitrust and Trade Policies in International Trade* (New York, Transjuris, 1985), 673–98

VESTERDORFF, B., "Complaints Concerning Infringements of Competition Law Within the Context of European Community Law" (1994) 31 *CMLRev.* 77–104

WAELBROECK, D., and FOSSELARD, D., "Should the Decision Making Power in EC Antitrust Procedures be Left to an Independent Judge?" (1994) 14 *YEL* 111–50

—— "Competition, Integration and Economic Efficiency in the EEC from the Point of View of the Private Firm" in Michigan Law Review Association (ed.), *The Art of Governance. Festschrift zu Ehren von Eric Stein* (Baden-Baden, Nomos Verlagsgesellschaft, 1987), 301–8

—— "Antitrust Analysis under Article 85(1) and Article 85(3)" in B. Hawk (ed.), *Annual Proceedings of the Fordham Corporate Law Institute 1987* (New York, Matthew Bender, 1988), 693–724

WALLACE, W. *et al.* (eds.), *The Dynamics of European Integration* (London, Pinter, 1993)

WALLER, A., "Decentralization of the Enforcement Process of EC Competition Law— The Greater Role of National Courts" (1996) 27 *LIEI* I–1–34

WALZ, R., *Der Vorrang des Europäischen vor dem nationalen Kartellrecht* (Baden-Baden, Nomos Verlagsgesellschaft, 1994)

—— "Rethinking *Walt Wilhelm*, or the Supremacy of Community Competition Law over National Law" (1996) 21 *ELR* 449–64

WEATHERILL, S., "Beyond Pre-emption? Shared Competence and Constitutional Change in the European Community" in D. O'Keeffe and P. Twomey (eds.), *Legal Issues of the Maastricht Treaty* (Chichester, Wiley Chancery, 1994), 13–33

—— *Law and Integration in the European Union* (Oxford, Clarendon Press, 1995)

—— "After *Keck*: Some Thoughts on how to Clarify the Clarification" (1996) 33 *CMLRev.* 885–906

WEILER, J., "The Community System: The Dual Character of Supranationalism" (1981) 1 *YEL* 267–306

—— "The Transformation of Europe" (1991) 100 *The Yale Law Journal* 2403–83

—— "Journey to an Unknown Destination: A Retrospective and Prospective of the European Court of Justice in the Arena of Political Integration" (1993) 31 *JCMS* 417–46

—— "The State 'über alles'. Demos, Telos and the German Maastricht Decision" (1995) 1 *ELJ* 219–58

—— "European Neo-constitutionalism: In Search of Foundations for the European Constitutional Order" (1996) 44 *Political Studies* 517–33

—— "The Reformation of European Constitutionalism" (1997) 35 *JCMS* 97–131

—— *The Constitution of Europe* (Cambridge, Cambridge University Press, 1999)

—— "The Constitution of the Common Market Place: Text and Context in the Evolution of the Free Movement of Goods" in P. Craig and G. de Búrca, *The Evolution of EU Law* (Oxford, Oxford University Press, 1999), 349–76

—— *et al.*, "European Democracy and Its Critique" (1995) 18 *West European Politics* 4–32

WESSELING, R., "Subsidiarity in Community Antitrust Law; Setting the Right Agenda" (1997) 22 *ELR* 35–54

—— "The Commission Notices on Decentralisation of E.C. Antitrust Law: In for a Penny, Not for a Pound" (1997) 18 *ECLR* 94–7

—— "The Commission White Paper on Modernisation of E.C. Antitrust Law:

Unspoken Consequences and Incomplete Treatment of Alternative Options" (1999) 20 *ECLR* 420–33

WHISH, R., *Competition Law* 2nd edn. (London, Butterworths, 1993)

—— "The Enforcement of EC Competition Law in the Domestic Courts of Member States" (1994) 3 *EBLR* 3–9

—— "The Enforcement of EC Competition Law in the Domestic Courts of Member States" (1994) 15 *ECLR* 60–7

——, and SUFRIN, B., "Article 85 and the Rule of Reason" (1987) 7 *YEL* 1–38

WILKS, S., "The Metamorphosis of European Competition Law" in F. Snyder (ed.), *European Community Law* (Aldershot, Dartmouth, 1993), i, 270–93

—— "Options for Reform in European Competition Policy" in A. van Mourik (ed.), *Developments in European Competition Policy* (Maastricht, EIPA, 1996), 153–76

——, and MCGOWAN, L., "Discretion in European Merger Control; The German Regime in Context" (1995) 2 *Journal of European Public Policy* 41–67

——, and ——, "Disarming the Commission: The Debate over a European Cartel Office" (1995) 32 *JCMS* 259–73

——, and ——, "Competition Policy in the European Union—Creating a Federal Agency?", pp. 225–67, in G. Bruce Doern and S. Wilks (eds.), *Comparative Competition Policy—National Institutions in a Global Market*

WILS, W., "La comptabilité des procédures communautaires en matière de concurrence avec la Convention européenne des droits de l'homme" (1996) 32 *CDE* 329–54

WOLF, D., "Zusammenwirken von EG-Kommission und Bundeskartellamt" in *Schwerpunkte des Kartellrechts 1991/92*

—— "Zum Verhältnis von europäischem und deutschem Wettbewerbsrecht" (1994) 5 *EuZW* 233–8

WOUDE, M. VAN DER, "Hearing Officers and EC Antitrust Procedures; the Art of Making Subjective Procedures More Objective" (1996) 33 *CMLRev.* 531–46

ZEKOLL, J., "European Community Competition Law and National Competition Laws: Compatibility Problems from a German Perspective" (1991) 24 *Vanderbilt Journal of Transantional Law* 75–111

ZINSMEISTER, U., "Die Anwendung der Artikel 85 und 86 EG-Vertrag durch die national Behörden" (1997) 47 *WuW* 5–15

—— Rikkers, E., and Jones, T., "The Application of Articles 81 and 82 of the E.C. Treaty by National Competition Authorities" (1999) 20 *ECLR* 275–9

ZONNEKEYN, G., "The Treatment of Joint Ventures Under the Amended Merger Regulation" (1998) 19 *ECLR* 414–21

ZULEEG, M., "Der Rang des europäischen im Verhältnis zum nationalen Wettbewerbsrecht" (1990) 25 *EuR* 123–34

Index